FINCHES

and soft-billed birds

By HENRY BATES and
ROBERT BUSENBARK

Distributed in the U.S.A. by T.F.H. Publications, Inc., 211 West Sylvania Avenue, P.O. Box 27, Neptune City, N.J. 07753; in England by T.F.H. (Gt. Britain) Ltd., 13 Nutley Lane, Reigate, Surrey; in Canada to the book store and library trade by Clarke, Irwin & Company, Clarwin House, 791 St. Clair Avenue West, Toronto 10, Ontario; in Canada to the pet trade by Rolf C. Hagen Ltd., 3225 Sartelon Street, Montreal 382, Quebec; in Southeast Asia by Y.W. Ong, 9 Lorong 36 Geylang, Singapore 14; in Australia and the south Pacific by Pet Imports Pty. Ltd., P.O. Box 149, Brookvale 2100, N.S.W., Australia. Published by T.F.H. Publications, Inc. Ltd., The British Crown Colony of Hong Kong.

ISBN 0-87666-421-4

Photography LOUISE VAN DER MEID

TABLE OF CONTENTS

Flamingos, though not falling in the softbilled bird category, are nevertheless kept by a surprising number of aviculturists because they are very interesting as well as showy. Owned by Jerome Buteyn.

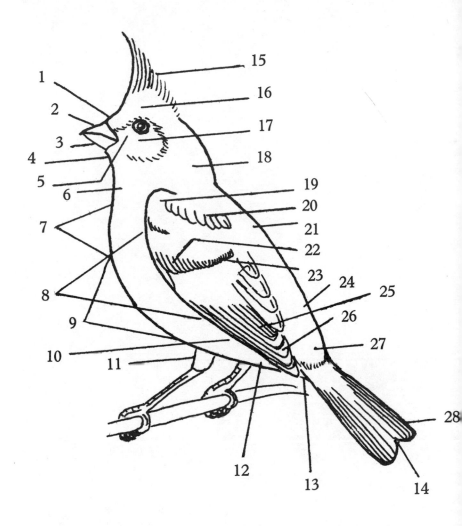

Diagrams of the most important bird parts used in descriptions in the text. In Hummingbirds, the throat area is called the gorget if iridescence is present.
1 Forehead; 2 Upper Mandible; 3 Lower Mandible; 4 Chin; 5 Lores; 6 Throat; 7 Chest; 8 Side; 9 Abdomen; 10 Flank; 11 Upper leg or Tibia; 12 Ventral area; 13 Undertail coverts; 14 Central tail feathers; 15 Crest; 16 Crown; 17 Cheek; 18 Nape; 19 Bend of wing; 20 Scapulars; 21 Back; 22 Primary Coverts; 23 Secondary Coverts; 24 Rump; 25 Secondary Flights; 26 Primary Flights; 27 Upper Tail Coverts; 28 Tail.

Jerome Buteyn and Hank Bates administer to an exotic African Crowned Crane injured in shipment.

PREFACE

FINCHES AND SOFTBILLED BIRDS is meant as a companion volume to PARROTS AND RELATED BIRDS to complete a trilogy on the three most important families in aviculture. This book is really two volumes in one with its coverage of both the finch and softbilled fields. Each of these two groups could form a book in itself with the amount of material presented in this volume.

The writers have attempted to span two huge phases of aviculture in this one volume. All extraneous material has, of necessity, been eliminated, but pertinent facts and regularly available birds have been given detailed reporting. Even those very rare birds which sometimes occur in aviculture have been covered.

Finches and softbilled birds are engrossing subjects which are now receiving proper avicultural attention. The problems of needed care of both of these diversified fields are given more than adequate coverage in this book.

Even so, there are other methods of feeding which completely fill the needs of the birds. Some of these alternatives are discussed. The writers have no intention of setting up hard and fast rules about bird care, but they would like to pass on to other fanciers those procedures which have been successful with them.

ACKNOWLEDGMENTS

People who write books about pets basically wish to contribute something to their hobby. People who help have the same desire. The writers wish to acknowledge those who have contributed to this book.

Carl Papp of Lynwood, California, and William Lasky of Malibu, California, opened their aviaries to the writers and Mrs. Van der Meid for many of the pictures in this book. Without their birds, the total number of illustrations would have dwindled considerably.

Jack Throp, Curator of the Jerome Buteyn Foreign Bird Farm in San Luis Rey, California, contributed several experiences and basic knowledge about cranes and flamingos. Mr. Throp and Mr. Buteyn, ever friendly, have frequently been of immense help to the writers over the past several years and have never failed to give needed advice concerning any of the bird problems which have arisen. Several of the rarest birds pictured in this book are from Mr. Buteyn's fine collection.

While the writers were in Europe not long ago, they found a magnificent collection of birds housed in perfect surroundings at the Louise Hall in Dierenpark Wassenaar in Holland. Despite the many difficulties in photographing the birds from outside their enclosures and through the wire mesh, some of the photographs which were reproduceable have been included in this volume. The writers gratefully acknowledge the permission to publish these pictures.

R. Glenn McIsaac of Wilmington, California, one day walked into the Palos Verdes Bird Farm with an absurd looking home made cage of very lengthy proportions. He announced that he would like to photograph some birds in flight. Four of the many examples of Mr. McIsaac's contrived genius at high speed photography appear in this book. The photograph of the Pintail Whydahs especially represents a very high degree of camera artistry that has seldom been excelled in bird pictures.

Louise Van der Meid's patience and camera skill show in most of the pictures in this book. Avicultural photography is an extremely difficult and time consuming task, but the pictures in this book prove that the end result is worth the effort.

All of the birds pictured in this book, unless otherwise designated, were photographed at the Palos Verdes Bird Farm in Walteria, California.

A few of the birds illustrated in this volume were painted in water colors or drawn in pen and ink by Henry J. Bates.

Two tasks of no small magnitude included the typing of the manuscript by Marie Moore and subsequent proofreading and corrections by Alfred R. Bates. These two tasks required countless hours of their time, and the writers are greatly indebted for their services.

HENRY J. BATES
ROBERT L. BUSENBARK
Walteria, California.

SECTION I

CHAPTER 1

Introduction to the Finch and Softbill Families

The importance of a hobby or avocation has been established by doctors, psychiatrists, teachers, and many other authorities who seek to upgrade the status of mankind's emotional welfare and enjoyment of living in the frenzied pace of today's nervous atomic age. Relaxation with a hobby tends to balance a perspective which becomes frayed from overwork and mental stress. At no time in history has there been such an abundance of avocational "safety valves," nor has there ever been such a need for hobbies. Certainly one of the most satisfying and pleasant of all hobbies is the vast field of aviculture: *the keeping of birds in captivity*.

The term *aviculture* embraces all types of birds which can be maintained in good health and long life in cages or aviaries. The many devotees of aviculture have included men and women from all fields who have used their talents in developing proper diets and techniques of maintenance to such a degree that birds in captivity usually live greater life spans and remain in better condition than they would if they were in their natural wild state. Their adverse weather elements are removed; their food requirements are provided; and spacious aviaries give them all the freedom and exercise necessary.

In aviculture man attempts to imitate the native requirements of birds so that they may be adequately and properly housed in satisfactory artificial habitats. In so doing, man becomes not the master but the servant. If he takes any living thing from its native habitat, he also takes upon himself the responsibility of caring for that living thing. Therefore, the happiest of aviculturists is not the person who desires to "master" nature. Instead he is the person who has the desire to serve and to make his charges healthy and happy in artificial environments. The proof of his labors is the willingness of birds to respond and show their happiness by their robust health and willingness to procreate and to nurture their nestlings—to bring forth their own kind into these artificial surroundings. The desire to procreate, elusive in many birds, proves the aviculturist's triumph over the many other obstacles brought into being by aviculture's artificial environments and artificial selection of dietary requirements. The master aviculturist is always the most efficient of servants.

Aviculturists accept the responsibilities of caring for their birds, and the birds respond with every possible talent in their engaging personalities. Some sing; some become tame; others develop amusing idiosyncracies; many rear offspring; and all give us a close relationship with nature's beauty and variety. Therefore, when we use the harsh sounding word *captivity*, we really mean the more gentle and cooperative term *domesticity*.

This book, covering the richly diversified families of finches and softbills, is meant as a companion volume to **Parrots and Related Birds** to give as much coverage as possible to the three most important phases of aviculture. Like the parrot family, finches and softbills run the full gamut of color combinations, shapes, sizes, and personality variations.

Finches are mainly dependent upon seeds as the major source of foods; but many prefer and even require some fruit and insects in their diet, especially if they are to be successful at rearing young. Finches are sometimes called *hardbills* because of their diet of seeds.

Although there is a considerable range in size, most finches are rather small and seldom exceed six inches in length. The more prevalent and popular African Waxbills average about three inches in length. Few become finger tame, but a collection of finches shows variable color patterns and personalities which evoke undeniable charm. Furthermore, there are greater numbers of congenial and companionable varieties of finches than found among parrotlike and softbilled birds.

A group of colorful and popular finches. From left, Red-eared Waxbills hiding behind a male Australian Fire or Blood Finch followed by male Strawberry, Society, Chestnut Breasted, and Masked Grassfinch. Owned by Palos Verdes Bird Farm.

Netting birds. This Diamond Dove with wings still outstretched shows proper way for catching bird in a net. Always follow the bird with the net. Never catch it head on or injury and broken neck may result.

Technically all have individual songs, but only a few can be called melodious. Many hardly reach beyond a call note or a squeaky little twitter. The writers prefer to think of a collection of finches as a little native orchestra in which those with melodious songs, such as Strawberries, Stars, European Goldfinches, or Green Singing Finches, are the soloists accompanied by the rest of the collection.

Many finches readily breed in captivity. Some do well in mixed collections whereas others prefer remaining by themselves. Some, though popular favorites, ignore all nesting possibilities. Certain finches should not be mixed with others because of aggressiveness and greater size. All these points will be expanded upon and detailed in appropriate sections of this volume.

Two great advantages of finches over softbilled birds are simplicity of diet and, generally speaking, lower prices. Furthermore, they do well in smaller aviaries. Many are kept as cage birds, but they fare much better in aviaries.

Softbills are available in a far greater range of sizes, shapes, and varieties than finches. Many, though excellent avicultural subjects, are exceedingly

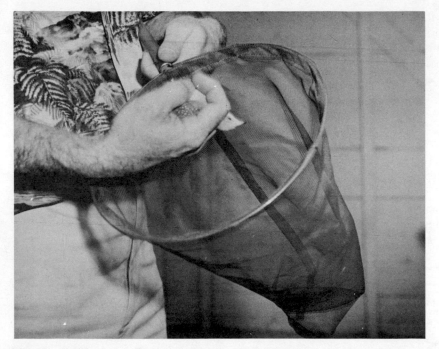

Removing bird from net. To get proper grip, use hardly any pressure; but be sure the wings are covered and the head is resting between two fingers.

rare and little known in captivity. Those which are known are generally very highly regarded by bird fanciers. Many become very tame pets in cage or aviary. Some talk, many have incredibly melodious songs, and some are good breeders. Each species has its particular outstanding characteristic responsible for its being included among avicultural favorites. Personality differences are also exceptionally diversified. Some especially seem to have been endowed with unbelievable beauty which is even more breathtaking than the most beautiful parrots. Nature seems to have gone the limit in designing birds, and many of the most outstanding beauties are among the softbilled group.

Softbills usually cost more than most popular finches and require more varied diets, but recent dietary developments have removed many of the complications in feeding. Also, because of greater interest in the past few years, increased importations have brought proportionate prices down considerably. Air shipments have greatly reduced time en route and have landed the birds in far superior condition than ever before.

Many people are bringing their gardens to life by the addition of an aviary stocked with flashy and personable softbilled birds. In fact, many softbill aviaries become beautiful gardens in themselves. Most softbills thrive best in planted aviaries. They do not destroy plants, and, almost without exception, the plants thrive because the birds quickly consume any insect infestations.

Softbills are so called because they live mainly on soft foods, such as fruits and insects, instead of seeds. Some softbills eat a few seeds, but most do not require them.

Newcomers are usually introduced to aviculture through Zebra Finches, Java Rice Birds, Pekin Nightingales, or Japanese Tumblers. From these introductions, the budding aviculturist discovers a new enchantment open to him.

An absorbing and gratifying enchantment it is; and, by following suggestions and routines outlined in this book, the enthusiasm will never dim. Study and observation never cease to be entertaining and fascinating diversions from the pressures of a fast-paced, modern-day life.

The writers must add a word of caution here. For best results, the novice

A rather firm hold at back of skull and jawbone but without pressure helps to keep powerful beaks out of reach of fingers while attending to birds. This Himalayan Barbet has one of the most powerful beaks to be found on softbills.

bird fancier must curb his natural acquisitive tendencies for the sake of his birds as well as for his own well-being. Novice aviculturists are prone to assume more responsibilities than can successfully be handled because of their discovery of the tremendous fascination found in so many birds. New fanciers soon tire of a hobby if the belabored efforts in care and maintenance exceed the pleasure and relaxation. Acquire birds only in a direct ratio to time which can be spent upon their care and enjoyment if this pleasant avocation is to remain a hobby. It is wise to use every labor saving device possible and to simplify diets, provided they still remain complete. In this way, the pleasure can be extended to include larger collections with a minimum of upkeep.

PLUMAGE ECLIPSE

One of the interesting changes which occurs in many birds in both finch and softbill families is a plumage eclipse. During the breeding seasons, some male birds blossom out into fantastic changes of plumage which are designed to attract mates. Personalities change into attitudes of frequent displays, often pompous and sometimes aggressive. During these periods the birds are said to be *in color*.

Whydahs, for example, grow long tail feathers and change their sparrow-like drabness into richly contrasting shades of blacks, whites, and browns, adding, in some cases, flashes of yellows and reds to give added attractions. Weavers and Strawberry Finches change colors completely.

In the softbill family, the most notable changes occur in Honeycreepers, Birds of Paradise, Bower Birds, and the magnificent Quetzal. Vividness and brilliance of color, as well as graceful or bizarre feather extensions, mark some of these variations.

When the birds are in their *out of color* phase, which is normally from four to six months, they usually assume a very ordinary personality and a drab appearance usually very much like the all-year appearance of females of the species.

Because of the *in color* and *out of color* phases, prices frequently vary considerably. *In color* birds are more expensive, and often one must buy some of these changeable species while they are in color to be certain of the sex.

SONGBIRDS

Some finches and many softbills pour out cheerful songs providing the bird fancier and all who happen to be in hearing range with unique and melodious songs. These wild songs, unlike the cultured and laborious song of canaries, show exceptional variety and lovely silvery tones. In the softbill family, some of the more outstanding musicians are Solitaires and Thrushes. Though better known as songbirds, Pekin Nightingales and most Bulbuls, which really have pleasant songs, cannot compare with the aforementioned families.

Many of these birds are kept as household pets in cages. The proper equipment and cages will be described later in this chapter, and diet will be explained in the next chapter.

TALKING PETS

In addition to talents for singing, some birds in the softbill classes are renowned for their talking ability. The most famous and most talented are the Greater India Hill Mynah and the large Javan Mynah. Crows, Ravens, and certain Magpies also fall into this category. There are other lesser known birds which also will learn to talk.

Frequent repetition is the most important factor in teaching a bird to talk. Your pet shop has a variety of phonograph records for Parrakeets and Mynah Birds which will simplify the process.

The Troupial is best known for a remarkable whistling talent. It is frequently called the Bugle Bird because of its long range talent for mimicry in which it has learned to whistle certain bugle calls in their entirety.

TAME HOUSEHOLD PETS

The majority of these birds are kept as individual pets so that they might provide some sort of entertainment as well as flattering performances to extoll the talents of their owners.

Nearly all of these birds, which do well in cages, were handfed as babies

Nearly any bird can be tamed if it is hand reared, even the traditionally timid quail. This very tame Valley Quail is just coming into adult plumage. It was handfed from the day after hatching by the authors, and it always retained an imperturbable calmness and genuine affection for humans. Photographed at Palos Verdes Bird Farm.

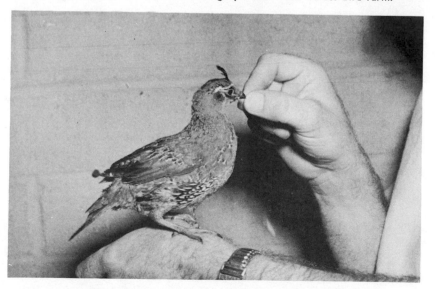

and show an unusual tameness. There are a number of exceptions, and these will be pointed out in the coverage of the different species.

One of the most notable exceptions is the very calm and beguiling songster, the Clarino. This very plain looking creature with the large trusting eyes has a disarming poise in captivity. He looks at his owner with a fixed stare and quietly begins a serenade of incomparable beauty which seems designed only for those humans who will hover near enough to appreciate each silvery note.

Birds which are handfed as youngsters invariably become very tame. Not only do they appreciate the food, but the frequent handling during the process also removes any natural or instinctive fear which has not yet developed during this early period in their lives. This fact holds true even for such birds as Quails which are usually reputed to be the wildest of all birds. Though they do not require handfeeding, Quails must be taught to eat when they are newly hatched and the close association during this period produces the same tame results.

The diet for handfeeding youngsters is given in the next chapter. The process is difficult and time consuming and is usually an effort to save abandoned nestlings. Fortunately, handfed birds usually help to wean themselves before the normal time-span, and this self help results in a great saving of time and effort for the bird lover.

Clipping wings in immature Java Rice Bird. If for taming, clip one wing. If for reducing aggressiveness, clip both wings to provide a slowdown.

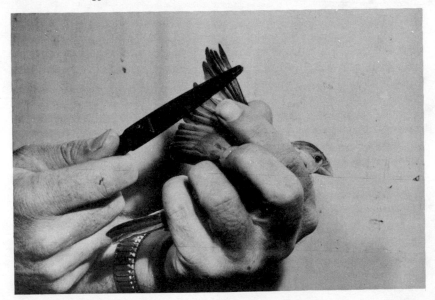

Taming birds to become household pets if they have not been handfed is a goal not too often accomplished. For softbilled birds, the procedure is easier because the trainer does not require much more than patience. The process is a longer one because it merely involves the gaining of the bird's confidence through the repeated offering of preferred items in the diet such as mealworms and bits of fruit. If the birds to be trained are immature, the process of learning is much faster. The writers have never felt it wise to clip wings on softbilled birds due to the softness of the feathers and because the regrowth process is particularly difficult.

For finches, the technique is quite different. For the main part, the process follows the same pattern as used in taming Parrakeets and Cockatiels. The wing should be clipped, and the bird should be young. It must be isolated from other birds, and the training should be a concentrated effort rather than a prolonged one. The clipped feathers should be only the primary flights, and the outer edges of the primary coverts should be used as a guide in the pattern of clipping. If flights are clipped shorter than the outer edges of the primary coverts, the end result may be split shafts which may eventually lead to ingrown feathers.

The gaining of confidence is not quite so simple as in the talented Budgerigar and Cockatiel, and a more gentle perseverance is required. The bird will need a crutch or, perhaps more suitably stated, a helping hand. This helping hand should never be a grasping hand because fear is always more easily entrenched by such a practice. When the flightless bird attempts to fly, it should be retrieved in a casual and gentle manner with outstretched fingers on an outspread hand. In this manner the fingers become perches for the bird, and a gentle lifting from underneath the bird will quickly prompt the bird to perch on the finger. For some time the bird will not grasp the significance of the offering and will go off in all directions, but perseverance will calm all fears in a reasonably short period. Continued attention after this initial training period will insure and entrench the calmness of a finger tamed bird.

CAGES

The type of bird will determine the type of cage required for your household pet. Your local pet shop can show you a large variety of cages suitable for nearly any size and type of bird. The larger cage is always better. A long lasting chrome, stainless steel, or electroplated finish is much more satisfactory than a painted finish.

If your pet bird is a small finch, be sure to stipulate that you require finch spacing. Small Waxbills often can fly through the bars of many cages sold for Parrakeets and Canaries. Mynah birds and other softbilled birds are more easily maintained if their cages have a grill above the floor of the cage to separate the droppings from the general area of the bird's activity.

Six pairs of congenial finches can easily rear families in this large uncluttered flight cage.

A large flight cage for finches. This cage is on rollers so that it can easily be moved and is therefore excellent for patio or birdroom. Photographed at Palos Verdes Bird Farm.

A popular carrying cage for one or two small birds. Close wire spacing prevents escape of even the smallest finch. For birds which panic easily, the cage should be covered on all sides to prevent injury.

A small collection of finches can easily and happily be housed in a standard flight cage which is at least double the size of a standard canary cage.

The standard canary cage is suitable for a pair of finches or two congenial but unrelated species. Many very small finches can fly through widespread bars of some cages.

NOMENCLATURE

A tremendous amount of effort has been spent in trying to list all birds in order of relationships and to record correct scientific names. As this particular project in writing this book progressed, it became all too apparent that the object of science has undergone continual and disputed changes over the years. The original idea was that each bird was to have just one proper scientific name despite the fact that it may have any number of popular or colloquial names.

Because scientists are often interested in very technical differences and similarities, it is a natural conclusion that many names will be held in dispute. The aviculturist is far more interested in the birds themselves than in controversial ornithological nomenclature.

Wherever possible, the writers, trying very hard and hoping to be correct, have followed Peters' *Checklist of Birds of the World*. This monumental work, which is still being carried on by the staff of Cambridge University after Dr. Peters' death, is recognized as the most correct authority the world over. Still there are many minor errors and it will undoubtedly have more revisions from time to time.

The writers, leaning towards the avicultural side, must remain impartial in these controversies. Wherever possible, the current controversial scientific names will be given whether they are one, two, or three in number. It is not a matter of "letting the chips fall where they may" nearly so much as it is a humble regard for the work of the many dedicated ornithologists in the world today.

Ornithologically speaking, we aviculturists are all wrong in calling, as we do, the great number of seed eating birds *finches*. The *true finches* are only a small group of birds in the avicultural sense. At that, they are not a truly popular group. However, since this is a book designed for aviculturists rather than taxonomic ornithologists, the writers group those birds which are mainly seed eaters into the broad term **FINCHES** and separate those insectivorous birds into the category of **SOFTBILLS.**

In scientific nomenclature, the first italicized name is the generic name which is always capitalized; the second is the species name; and the third is a subspecies name. In the text a third or subspecies name is often given singularly in italics to cut down needless wordage. In all cases, these are designated as subspecies in the hope that the reader will understand that the nearest preceding full scientific name will indicate the generic and species names.

The broader divisions, such as Families, Subfamilies, and Orders are not given. The chapter headings will help to serve as distinctive divisions.

Not all birds in these classifications are listed in this book. Many are not available in aviculture, and others prove to be too difficult to serve in a domestic state.

In measuring the birds, the writers have measured from the top of the head to the tip of the tail rather than from the tip of the beak to the tip of the tail.

CHAPTER 2

Diet

FINCHES

The diet of finches is best if it remains very simple in order to be certain that it will be consistently followed. Basically, it consists of finch mix, health grit, greens, a dietary supplement, an insectile mix and cuttlebone. Some birds require some modifications such as the addition of extra niger, extra canary seed, fruit, mealworms, and spray millet. Some of the larger finches can use Parrakeet mix instead of finch mix. Those birds which require these extras will be mentioned under their respective headings.

SEED MIXES

Finch mix consists of four parts small Australian millet, two parts plain canary, one part white proso millet, and one-half part oat groats. No red millet is used. Most pet shops carry a good finch mix. Some include niger and other seeds in their mixture, but the writers prefer to feed this ration in a separate dish. Canary song or treat food has all these extra seeds, several of which help to give glossier plumage.

Webby seed is not necessarily old or stale. A tiny seed moth becomes very active during hot months. Little caterpillars hatch in seed and spin webs before going into pupal cocoons, after which they emerge as moths. The warmer the weather, the more activity from the moths and caterpillars. In most cases, the birds derive additional animal protein from these caterpillars and do not object to the webby seed.

Seeds, to be nourishing, must be alive. To check the value of your seed mixes, plant a little now and then or sprout some in a shallow covering of water to determine percentages of live seed. If you are in doubt about the value of your present seed mix, compare it with another in this same manner.

DIETARY SUPPLEMENTS

The dietary supplement can be one or more of several selections. Liquid vitamins for birds are now available in a form which can be added to drinking water without the quick evaporation characteristic of vitamins prepared for human consumption. These vitamins prepared for birds show no appreciable evaporation until after forty-eight hours, whereas those prepared for human consumption have, upon exposure to air, lost their value within a surprisingly short time. Moreover, those prepared for pets are cheaper than those prepared for humans and have even greater efficiency.

There are several powdered or ground food supplements on the market which the bird fancier may prefer over liquid vitamins. Most of these, unlike liquid vitamins, also contain certain trace minerals which are very necessary in a bird's diet.

Charles Hudson tends birds in a pet shop from pull out feed bins placed conveniently below the cages.

CUTTLEBONE

Cuttlebone provides necessary lime and should be available at all times either crushed and added to health grit or attached to the side of the aviary in a convenient location. The soft side of the cuttlebone must be accessible to the birds.

GREENS

Green food is extremely important for finches and should be fed every day. Either commercially dehydrated greens specifically prepared for birds or freshly picked greens should be fed. Since greens are a further very rich source of vitamins and minerals, it is important that the proper selection should be made.

Dark green leaves are far superior to pale yellowish-green leaves such as found inside a head of lettuce. Celery tops and head lettuce are rather weak in food value. Among the best greens are carrot tops, dandelion, water cress, spinach, and most lawn clippings. Anything coming from a market should be washed and dried before feeding because of the possibility of dangerous residue from insecticides.

An excellent source of greens and one which the birds thoroughly enjoy is home grown heads of ripening millet. White Proso Millet is fast growing and easily cultivated.

Fresh greens do not, as many people believe, cause diarrhea. If offered unwisely and inconsistently, greenfood can cause loose droppings because the birds gorge themselves at every opportunity when the feeding of green-food is inconsistent and occasional. If started sparingly and fed every day, the birds will never overeat.

Dehydrated greens for birds are available in most pet shops. Besides being wonderfully convenient, they usually have additional vitamin and mineral supplements and cannot cause loose droppings. Some birds refuse to be tempted by dehydrated greens. In such instances, the writers add some of the pellets of greens to the seed mix and some of the seed mix to the dish containing the greens. Gradually the reluctant ones come around.

GRIT

Health grit or gravel serves two purposes. It acts as a grinding agent for the seed in the bird's crop because of its base of crushed granite, and, if it is a true health grit, furnishes several necessary minerals including salt, iron oxide, calcium, lime, phosphorus, and also a trace of charcoal. Too much charcoal is harmful because it inhibits the assimilation of several vitamins even though it sweetens the digestive system.

LIVE FOODS

Many birds relish some live food each day and require it during the breeding season. In the United States, the most prevalent live food source is mealworms, which many pet shops carry. Mealworms are 90% protein and furnish excellent food values, but they should not be overfed. Most finches should be limited to two or three mealworms per day, but this amount can at least be doubled during the breeding season. Even small finches can manage the large worms because they pulverize the skin and consume only the milky insides.

Trying to apportion them properly in a community aviary is impossible because there are certain individuals, like Cuban Melodious Finches and Button Quail, that quickly consume three to four times their own ration. Any bird showing indifference or indecision is out of luck with these birds around. Over indulgence in mealworms brings about an overweight condition which is quite dangerous. In trying to fly, those extremely overweight birds fall to the ground and stagger. Loss of balance is particularly noticeable. In cases such as this, total withdrawal of all mealworms and the addition of extra fresh greens will help to regain the normal balance.

Mealworms can easily be raised at home. Kept in a tall metal can so they cannot climb out, mealworms live simply and frugally on red bran with a slice of raw potato or apple for moisture. The total life span at an average temperature is six months. First comes the larva or mealworm, next the pupa, and finally the beetle which lives in the same medium as the worm and which does not fly. The six months' cycle can be speeded up by increasing the temperature or slowed down by lowering the temperature.

White worms (*Enchytrae*) cultures are sometimes available and are an excellent live food source for birds as well as for tropical fish. These worms thrive in moist peat and will congregate under a layer of mashed potatoes or bread soaked in milk for easy collection. Because they reproduce rapidly under these conditions, they can become a self-perpetuating source of live food.

Since many finches are highly insectivorous, the fancier may draw from other live foods used for softbills.

OTHER USEFUL FOODS

Spray millet is an excellent treat for finches, and the writers consider it a necessity for many Australian finches. Finches attack stalks of spray millet with surprising vigor and never seem to tire of them.

Fruit is also much relished by many finches. The writers offer oranges and red apples whenever available but never get into the habit of feeding just one or the other. They especially avoid overfeeding orange because of the high acid content.

A small dish of peanut butter is available in all finch aviaries at all times. Many birds pay no attention to it, but those who do derive much food value from this highly nutritious food.

Mockingbird food or softbill meal is also served in a small dish for those who benefit from insectivorous foods. Again, many finches ignore this fare; but many will take to it quite readily and frequently arouse the interest of other birds as well.

Hard boiled eggs are beneficial for some breeding finches. For the proper procedure check with the routine for preparation under **SOFTBILL DIETS.**

Neither finches nor softbills can be regarded as quick to accept new foods. Most foods should be fed in separate dishes for greater efficiency and less waste, but many of the unfamiliar additions in the beginning will be accepted more readily if they are mixed with already familiar foods.

The writers have constantly faced the problem of enticing the acceptance of new foods because of the steady importations of finches and softbills. The simplest solution is to house new importations with a few older birds already accustomed to the different types of foods. The new birds usually follow the example of acclimated birds in the proper selection of the new foods.

Hank Bates prepares food for softbills while pet mynah Sahib searches for samples. Nectar food, peanut butter, fruit, pound cake, and liquid vitamins are among the daily preparations.

SOFTBILLS

The large family of softbilled birds requires several variations in diet, and often the number of dietetic methods exceeds the number of softbill fanciers. Because of the difficulties of complicated diets, many of which fail to include some obscure but integral nutritional necessities which eventually cause troubles, the number of softbill fanciers has been limited. However, those fanciers, the true fanciers, who remained loyal to their birds whether as a hobby or as a business, regarded the dietary problems as challenges, and the proper solution brought avian exuberance, unbelievable song, and robust health to their birds.

The basic softbill diet comprises insectivorous food, fruit, live food, peanut butter, and certain variations which are required by some species of birds. These variations include nectar food for some, increased carnivore rations for others, and even some seeds for a few other members. All those birds needing these variations will be covered under the various families.

Today's softbill diet is a far more simple procedure than the ponderous diets of a few years ago. Because of the new simplicity in caring for softbills, the number of softbilled bird fanciers has increased tremendously.

The writers prefer a simple diet which is easily fed and which is a highly nutritious basic fare for most softbilled birds. Though some fanciers will

White worms (*Enchytrae*) as mentioned for finches are excellent. Nearly any insect available is very much relished. *Aphis* are often available and the gardener is glad to be rid of them.

Fruitflies (*Drosophila*) are an excellent source of live food for many finches and small softbills, especially nectar feeders. A fruitfly culture is as simple as it is beneficial. Any ordinary metal can from one gallon to five gallons in size is satisfactory. Overripe fruits, parings, or rinds are placed in the can to attract the little gnats. If the food supply is replenished frequently, the fruitflies reproduce quickly to provide a steady supply of live foods for the birds. A cover made of quarter inch mesh will prevent the birds from getting into the spoiling food. The birds like to huddle near the mesh to capture all venturesome fruitflies. With Sunbirds and Hummingbirds, fruitflies are a necessity.

The mealworm dish gains the center of attention of all softbilled birds at this feeding station which is serviceable from the safety aisle. Eagerly awaiting the mealworm ration are a Spotted Breasted Oriole, an Indian Black Bulbul, and a Japanese Tumbler. Photographed at Palos Verdes Bird Farm.

A simple method for attracting hordes of small butterflies and possibly other insects is to place lantana plants in close proximity to aviaries. Many of these insects will get inside, and the birds will quickly capture them.

A night light, useful in other ways also, will attract night flying insects. A twenty-five watt bulb will give enough light to allow the birds to capture the insects.

Gentles are maggots and are widely used as a source of live food in Europe, but not often in the United States. In England there are commercial suppliers of gentles. There are many different opinions regarding both mealworms and gentles. Some experts prefer mealworms to gentles, and many give preference to gentles. Perhaps it would be wiser to follow the same precautions as given for mealworms in not overfeeding. However, gentles need not be so strictly limited as must mealworms.

At first thought, the production of maggots and the attraction of flies to one's home is quite a revolting prospect. If decaying and odorous meat is used to attract the flies and to raise the maggots, they must be cleaned by putting them in bran for a day before feeding them to the birds.

A much more pleasant and comparatively odorless production method for maggots is through the use of bran which is soaked in water. The container is then placed in the sun. After about three days or so, the gentles can be "harvested" regularly with no additional period of cleaning.

Many softbills like earthworms, and many will eat baby mice. Some of the larger birds will even eat grown mice.

The raw meat which the writers prefer to use is the horsemeat available at nearly all pet shops. Horsemeat has less fat than ground beef; but, since it has more of an acid content, it is fed carefully. Indeed, in nearly all additional foods surrounding the basic diet, it is important not to lose sight of safe proportions. Lean ground beef is also quite satisfactory.

PEANUT BUTTER

Peanut butter is kept in a small jar for all softbills because it is very nourishing and has beneficial and easily digested oils which help plumage. The birds may not take to it at first, but they quickly learn to like it.

NECTAR FOOD

Certain types of birds, as mentioned before, require nectar. Nearly all softbills and even some finches gladly accept nectar and show obvious benefit from its inclusion in the diet. The writers offer it as a matter of course and let those birds who prefer it gain the initial advantages. Most other birds quickly follow the leader's example and gain similar benefits. Even such unlikely birds as Toucans, Barbets, and Woodpeckers take to the nectar food.

There are several recipes for nectar foods, and many individual fanciers will extol the various advantages of each. Various birds will also show preferences and individual benefits from the myriad mixtures. Nectar feeding extends into the advanced stages of bird keeping, and techniques of feeding are always controversial. The writers can only report their own successful methods and suggest that the reader concoct his own variations which may be necessary from the standpoint of varying climates and available supplies.

Prejudicial preferences also extend to the species preferred by the fancier. Some birds ignore mixtures in which beef extracts are included.

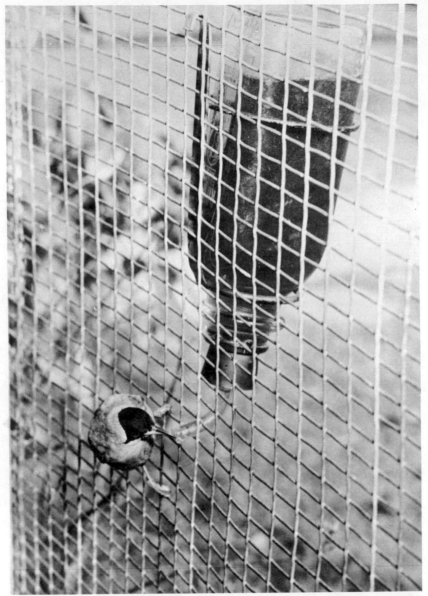

A Black Capped Sugarbird demonstrates the use of a gravity type water feeder. In this picture, the feeder contains liquid nectar food. The vacuum at the top of the bottle prevents the liquid from dripping out of the tube. As the liquid is extracted by birds, a bubble of air goes up the tube. Used as a waterer, this device is satisfactory for canaries, finches, softbills, budgies, and all birds whose beaks are small enough to make use of the glass tube. Water given in this way remains cleaner and has no chance for pollution from foreign articles such as seed hulls usually scattered in open water dishes. Photographed at aviaries of Carl Papp.

Hummingbirds, because of their requirements for extremely high carbohydrates, live on a restricted diet but insist on small amounts of beef extract in the basic nectar food. Some Sugarbirds ignore nectar foods which contain high animal protein factors because these requisites are supplied in other readily accepted forms. Bird fanciers must resort to experiments to determine proper percentages.

The basic and probably the most beneficial all-around nectar food consists of honey, beef extract, water and liquid vitamins. These proportions consist of five parts water, one part honey, liquid vitamins, and, for Hummingbirds, Sunbirds, or equally insectivorous species, one bouillon cube per quart added for the beef extract. A week's supply at a time is mixed and stored in the refrigerator. For Sugarbirds and the average softbill, the bouillon cube is omitted because of other softbill fare which is usually accepted in proper proportions. Some fanciers add milk to the nectar. If the birds will accept it, the writers offer instead dry soya powder on the side. This helps to avoid souring. If they refuse the soya powder, two parts canned milk are added to the nectar when it is served.

Hummingbirds eat only the nectar and an average of fifteen fruitflies per day. Other basic nectar feeders are Sunbirds, Honeycreepers, Flower Peckers, Bananaquits, Honey Eaters, and Zosterops; but they should also be given standard softbill diets. Tanagers, Manakins, and Chloropsis should also have nectar.

There is a commercial nectar concentrate available from England which the writers have used to very great advantage. This concentrate requires no milk or any other additive and is wonderfully convenient as well as dietetically efficient.

Other frequently used nectar concoctions are as follows: honey, canned milk, and baby food; corn syrup, honey, beef extract, liquid vitamins, liquid protein, raw egg yolk, and skim milk; and the simplest of all, though it is not sufficient for the true nectar feeders, white corn syrup, milk, and water. All three of these mixtures must, of course, be diluted with water. The nectar may be served in hummingbird feeders or in containers with small openings. If served in large dishes, some birds may accidentally try to bathe in it. Also, if the aviary contains a mixed collection, both of the first named feeding containers should be used if the smaller species such as Sunbirds are not to be crowded away by the larger birds.

MOCKINGBIRD FOOD

The manufacturers of Mynah Bird pellets also offer the same formula in a meal form, and there are several other brands of mockingbird food distributed by pet shops. Some of these are too oily to be completely safe for all softbills; therefore, many bird fanciers mix two or more brands together until the desired consistency is achieved. Advanced fanciers will formulate their own preferences as to various mixtures and few, if any, will follow the same procedures. Most, of course, add finely grated carrot or apple to add moisture as well as additional food value. The moisture added in this manner must be just enough to give a damp crumbly texture. Soggy or saturated textures should be avoided.

There are a few fanciers who feed certain dry dog foods which come in small pellet form. The writers at one time used dog food until the Mynah Bird pellets were perfected. Now, however, the advent of Mynah pellets erases the necessity for many additions which the dog food required. Only in those areas in which Mynah pellets are not yet available should dog food be suggested for the average fancier. Some fanciers with large collections will complain that Mynah pellets are expensive compared to the dog food pellets. The complaint is true, but the saving in labor and in cost for extra foods will still justify the use of the Mynah pellets. A successful alternative diet is given below.

ALTERNATE SOFTBILL DIET

The writers include at this point an alternate diet as administered to a large and diversified collection of softbills by Jack Throp, Curator of the Jerome Buteyn Bird Ranch in San Luis Rey, California.

The collection includes Quetzals, Trogons, Touracos, Cocks of the Rock, and many varieties of toucans, jays, thrushes, tanagers, solitaires, barbets, starlings, and hornbills. The diet outlined by Mr. Throp is used for all these birds, and the different dietary requirements of individuals allows considerable room for natural selection.

Boiled brown rice, raisins (or grapes in season), diced bananas, diced apples, and other soft fruits as they come into season are all mixed together along with a "trace mineral" compound and fed in one dish. Small dog food pellets are placed in another dish.

Live food requirements are fulfilled by furnishing maggots and fruit flies. Mealworms are not used.

This simplified diet is a low cost, mass-produced diet for a very large collection. While it would not be suitable for all softbills, it certainly is satisfactory for a great number of diversified birds. Proof of its efficiency shows in several rather difficult breedings of softbilled birds. The most recent successful breeding on this diet was of Troupials which rarely breed in captivity.

Several of the birds pictured in this book are from Mr. Buteyn's bird collection, and the excellent condition of these birds is adequate proof that a simple domesticated diet can still be nutritionally all-inclusive. Those birds which are more insectivorous will naturally select a higher proportion of dog food pellets, and those who naturally live on fruits will have plenty to satisfy their natural requirements.

OPTIONAL DIETARY ADDITIONS

Most softbilled birds pay little attention to greenfood, but the writers

38

prefer to offer fresh supplies every day for those who might take to it. In most instances, those softbilled birds which require seeds in their diet are the ones which will accept greens. Possibly the reason that few softbills owned by the writers ever accept greenfood is that their diet is quite satisfactory and nutritionally complete. Also, in planted aviaries, greenfood can be selected at any time.

Many fanciers believe in feeding milk to all their softbilled birds. Some families of birds, mostly nectar feeders, require milk in one form or other. The writers feel that fresh milk often poses harsh digestive problems. If milk must be used, the writers prefer to dilute canned evaporated milk if the birds refuse dry soya powder.

Ant eggs and dried flies have long been considered useful in feeding softbills. For all practical purposes, the writers feel there is little to be gained by the addition of these foods. Ant eggs are excellent if they are alive and fresh, but they are rarely available in this form to the bird fancier. Some softbill fanciers soak dried ant eggs in hot milk or water before feeding them to the birds. The value is questionable, and dried ant eggs are expensive. The writers therefore do not use them.

If the value of dried ant eggs is questionable, *the value of dried flies is not.* They really are quite useless from the standpoint of nutrition. The dried shells of flies undoubtedly contain some minerals, but modern dietary improvements have eliminated the need for dried flies. Admittedly, most commercial mockingbird foods still include dried flies in their formulation because many people will not use a mockingbird food unless it does contain dried flies. This is just one instance which shows that public demand is often in a rut, and changes gain favor slowly. Birds also are sometimes in a rut and will not accept a mockingbird food unless dried flies are included.

Hard boiled eggs provide a good source of nutrition, but the amounts should be limited. Delicate softbills usually accept eggs so readily that they frequently become a necessity, but the writers use eggs only when absolutely necessary. For many softbills, eggs are superfluous and their inclusion is just one more complication in the diet.

Even though Jays, Magpies, and many similar birds like nothing better than robbing nests of eggs, fresh eggs are nevertheless not easily digested. The writers boil eggs for twenty minutes to increase digestibility for softbills or for breeding finches. If the birds show good judgment in selecting both white and yolk, the egg is cut in half. If the birds ignore either the white or the yolk, the egg is grated so that the selection will include both parts of the egg.

For delicate birds, hard boiled grated egg is a springboard towards acceptance of other dietary ingredients. Mockingbird food or Mynah meal is included, sparingly at first, in the grated egg ration. Slowly, the meal is increased until the holdouts will accept the meal without the egg.

Hard boiled eggs spoil quickly in hot weather and can become deadly poisonous in a short time because of botulism. It is important, therefore, that egg rations should be fed frequently in small portions rather than in a full day's supply at one time. Any eggs prepared in advance should be stored in a refrigerator.

Cheese, freshly grated, along with certain ground nuts, such as pecans, are added to mockingbird foods by some fanciers.

Pound or sponge cake is nearly indispensable for small nectar feeders and is a highly relished, though optional, food for tanagers and Pekin Nightingales. Pound cake is easily fed and can be stored in a refrigerator for a considerable length of time. Some fanciers soak the pound cake in nectar food.

Some fanciers prefer baby cereals mixed with milk or nectar base as an alternative to pound cake. Though highly nourishing and undoubtedly of benefit, the writers seldom use these cereals because they require a little more time for preparation as well as a watchful eye to be sure they are removed before they become inedible and require replacement with a fresh supply. Baby cereals prove fattening to some birds.

HOUSEHOLD PET DIETS

The diets of household pets usually should be the simplest of all diets but should still be all-inclusive. Since most household pets spend a major part of their time in cages, fattening foods should be limited. The birds should be given as much exercise as possible. If the wings are not clipped for the training process, the birds should be given time for flying about a room whenever possible. If the bird is a member of the softbill family, it should naturally be exercised in a room which can easily be cleaned and which will suffer no damage from the copious droppings. Exercise is most important to help maintain proper body tone.

If the household pet is a finch, the diet will remain the standard finch mix with greenfood, health grit, cuttlebone, and a dietary supplement. Spray millet is a very acceptable treat food. If the bird is one of the more insectivorous finches, mealworms should be limited to one or two per day depending upon the nature and extent of its activity. If an insectile mixture is given, it should be a Mynah meal rather than an oily mockingbird food. Cardinals, Grosbeaks, and Hawfinches should be given Mynah pellets and more fruit than offered to most finches.

For softbills kept as pets, the diet will depend largely upon the bird. Clarinos and Pekin Nightingales should be restricted to about two mealworms per day plus an unlimited supply of Mynah pellets and a variety of fruits such as apple, orange, and soaked raisins. Troupials and Thrushes can have about four mealworms and a very little raw meat each day in addition to the other items mentioned above. Mynahs can fare very well on Mynah pellets

40

alone but will remain more tame if some fruit is offered from the fingers each day.

Household pet diets offer a considerable amount of leeway in their successful administration, but the above factors should be given prime consideration.

HANDFEEDING

The task of handfeeding baby birds is a very difficult and time consuming job. Many who undertake the task fail because they are unable to devote enough time necessary for the frequent feedings. It is much wiser to feed smaller amounts every three hours than to stuff the nestlings every five or six hours. Small finches are nearly impossible to feed because of their minute size, but they have been successfully reared by hand by some of the most devoted aviculturists.

The diet varies with the species to be handfed. If the birds are finches ranging in size from Zebras to Java Rice Birds, the diet is simple. The basis is a mixed cereal baby food fortified with liquid vitamins and varying amounts of Mynah meal and canary nestling food depending upon the natural insectivorous nature of the species. The percentage of Mynah meal is very small at first but may be gradually increased up to one-third of the total mixture for insectivorous finches as growth progresses. Enough water must be added to permit easy feeding through a small eydropper. Later, with a normal growth period, the birds eagerly accept thicker mixtures from the end of a toothpick. At this stage the droppings assume a more normal and less watery consistency.

Handfed babies are usually weaned earlier than they would be if the natural parents were feeding them. As soon as they accept seeds, they must also be given health grit.

Softbilled birds require different diets, but they are much easier to feed because they are usually larger and basically more intelligent. Variations must occur depending upon the natural ratio of fruits to insects. The writers start with canned applesauce to which is added liquid vitamins and Mynah meal. If the birds are naturally highly insectivorous, more Mynah meal is added along with gelatin. These are the purest and most digestible elements obtainable. The addition of eggs and raw meat invite digestive problems.

As the weaning period approaches, small mealworms or those which have just shed their skins are offered along with Mynah pellets. The birds soon accept these foods and will begin to seek them without being prodded. Small diced fruits follow these two items and in a very short while, the handfeeding may cease.

In all instances, successful handfeeding also results in delightfully tame pets whether the species is a rescued baby Sparrow, Mockingbird, or an exotic imported species.

SUMMARY

In all instances of diet, the writers prefer to suggest the simpler diets provided, of course, they fulfill all the necessary requirements. Diets which are easily prepared and which adequately furnish all the requirements are far more likely to be consistently followed than the complicated and time consuming variations extolled by some books and many fanciers. The complicated diets require more time than the average fancier can devote, and he becomes shackled with so many chores that he cannot fully enjoy any leisurely "bird watching." When this point has been reached, much of the original purposeful relaxation and diversions of the hobby have vanished. Also, complicated diets are usually more expensive in the long run than the simplified diets.

Naturally, with simplified diets, some of the more highly diversified and delicate species must be bypassed unless the bird fancier specializes in certain families. There are, however, many strikingly beautiful and personable species of birds which fare extremely well on the simple diets outlined by the writers. For those bird fanciers who do not wish to be in any way limited to species which thrive on the standard and simplified diet, the writers wish to offer every possible encouragement. These are the people who continue to add much knowledge to aviculture by their acceptance of the challenge of discovering obscure and as yet unknown requisites in the diet of many wonderful birds which are not yet successfully established in avicultural domesticity.

The proper diet of finches and softbills is the most important factor in any bird's welfare. If given reasonable attention, most illnesses and deficiency conditions can be avoided merely by careful administration of the correct diets.

CHAPTER 3

Importation and Acclimation

Nearly all of aviculture's softbilled birds and a great majority of its finches are imported from various countries of the world. Many are hand-reared nestlings cared for by natives. Others are trapped wild birds, and many are reared by bird breeders in other countries.

Birds can be shipped by air freight from opposite points of the world and arrive in excellent condition if they are given proper care en route and if the exporters send them in roomy shipping crates with adequate food and instructions for necessary care during the journey.

Fast air deliveries from foreign ports land birds in better shape than ever before with fewer losses and shorter necessary acclimation periods, all of which result in lower prices for nearly all birds.

Before air shipments were possible, long ocean voyages took a heavy toll in losses and skyrocketed costs with handling charges for care and feeding. Adverse weather conditions frequently added to the losses, and the close confinement often resulted in considerable plumage damage. The acclimation periods invariably were much longer than are necessary today.

Today's bird fancier can enjoy many species of birds which were formerly impossible because of improved transportation, acclimation, and more efficient developments in diet.

Seasons of availability are highly diversified. Fortunately, not all varieties become available at once, and there is always something different at those pet shops which specialize in birds.

European birds become available in November, and the period of availability is usually very short. Indian finches and mynahs are available during most of the summer months, but most of the lovely softbilled varieties become available later in summer and in early fall. African birds are imported during spring, summer, and early fall. Japanese birds are mostly available the year around. South American birds usually appear in the spring, but importations are often erratic—sometimes early, frequently late. South American export compounds seem to show less stability and more numerous

Importations of different varieties of quarrelsome softbilled birds arrive in better conditions if they are shipped in sectioned crates allowing one bird for each compartment. Though far more expensive from a freight standpoint, losses are greatly reduced; and humane factors are highly commendable. Photographed at Palos Verdes Bird Farm.

changes in ownership than occur in most countries. During some years there may not be any of the popular favorites available from South America.

Laws, also, are constantly changing to affect shipping conditions. Australian finches are usually very reliably exported to points all over the world beginning in November and ending in January or February. In 1961 an Australian ban prevented the exportation of all wildlife for commercial purposes. Whether or not the ban is to be lifted will be decided at a later date. Oriental birds are usually available from Hong Kong at most seasons, though some of the species are seasonal.

The countries of origin listed above are the principal sources of exotic birds for world-wide aviculture. A few other countries sometimes figure importantly as sources for aviculture with some very lovely species, but internal political strife, total prohibitive laws, or absence of exporters prevents any consistency of availability.

Many wonderful birds are available in Cuba, when political conditions are stable enough to risk attempting imports.

The Philippine Islands and many South Pacific islands have many beautiful softbilled birds and several varieties of finches, but exporters do not usually remain in business long enough to establish worldwide recognition for their birds.

PROTECTIVE AND PROHIBITIVE LAWS

The United States protects nearly all of the native birds and will allow no exportation of the protected species except under certain very stringent conditions. With very few exceptions, American aviculturists are not permitted to maintain native birds in a state of captivity.

Mexico at present prohibits the exportation of nearly all its native birds, but some shipments do get through anyway.

Many countries of the world control exportation of their native wildlife. Controls are usually enacted to prevent the disappearance of many desirable and beneficial species. In these cases the controls are necessary and admirable. Everyone should help prevent the extinction of birds the world over. Some countries control the importation of wildlife and prevent many undesirable species from entering areas where they might become nuisances.

Unfortunately most controls have both beneficial and detrimental aspects. None of the present wildlife regulatory laws in the United States are precisely black and white. The vast gray areas of inconsistencies have clouded the original intentions of the lawmakers and leave the way open for questionable interpretations and various elaborations. Clearly obvious is the lack of well-informed advisers or the presence of pressure groups surrounding those lawmakers who have constructed the unwieldy bulk of legal red tape surrounding importations or exportations of livestock even though the intention to be fair cannot be questioned. People who are in the business of importing birds never quite know what to expect when a shipment arrives. All incoming livestock shipments must be inspected by a Federal appointee and sometimes a state official as well. Because of the lack of precise delineations of just which birds are admissible, four inspectors may have four different interpretations of the statutes. The confusion is a constant headache for livestock importers.

In many instances, some prohibited species are passed and some admissible species are prevented entry. European Bullfinches, very highly regarded aviculturally, are not permitted entry. However, some ports of entry pass them without question. Confusing? Yes, but there are dozens of examples far more confusing.

A few years ago the writers, while on a holiday in Mexico, stopped at the border to inquire of customs authorities which varieties of birds they might bring back with them. For a period of two hours they were shuttled from office to office in a vain attempt to compile a list. The final result came from one official who suggested they bring back anything they like except psittacine birds and then he would say whether or not they were permissible.

All these unclear statutes naturally result in many controversies between importers and the Federal examiners. It is understandably embarrassing to the examiners when an importer can prove a bird's admissibility after the

45

examiner has denied its entry. Also, some importers have been known to deliberately import certain birds which are illegal. It takes only a few such instances to bring into effect further restrictive rules.

PROBLEMS OF IMPORTATION

Another area of disagreement concerns customs duty. All cage and aviary birds imported into the United States have a customs duty levied against them. The law was originally designed to protect commercial producers (bird breeders), but the majority of imported finches and softbills are not commercially raised in the United States. If they were, there would be no need to import them. Importers have tried to lift this discriminatory duty, but the law is no longer being used to protect breeders. Instead it is now another means of obtaining revenue.

The airline carriers frequently are a source of many problems for bird importers. A heavy surcharge on bird shipments is ostensibly levied to cover the cost of additional care en route. In many cases, the extra care or attention is never given. In many others the wrong care is given despite very clear and concise instructions printed on tags affixed to the cage by exporters.

Another constant worry of the importers regarding the extra care is whether or not the birds are kept indoors and out of drafts during stopovers. Frequently they are left out in cold and drafty loading docks or open warehouses. The resulting chill can be very dangerous and often fatal.

In most instances, the only attention necessary is the addition of fresh water during the journey; but frequently water is not given on a regular basis. The writers will never forget a disheartening experience on a shipment of delicate Sunbirds from India. The exporter carefully labelled each compartment of a large shipping crate with the instructions that all food necessary for the journey had been provided in clearly visible receptacles but that fresh water would be necessary each day en route.

Disregarding these explicit instructions someone along the way poured generous amounts of canary mix, an impossible food for these fragile little nectar feeders, all over the food and even in the nectar containers. The hapless little Sunbirds all had starved to death before their arrival.

All the above instances are written to show some of the difficulties in becoming an importer of livestock. There are many other difficulties, but the writers wish to emphasize that no person should enter into the importation of birds lightheartedly or haphazardly without considerable study and preparation. Above all, the prime concern should always be for the birds themselves.

PROPER ACCLIMATION

The essence of successful bird importation is the time factor. The successful importer must expedite in every possible manner the release of his consignment of birds from the airport and must rush the birds to acclimation

Paradise Whydahs in an acclimation flight show the effect of a long overseas flight. The frayed tails will not satisfactorily be repaired until the next season in color. The best stage to import male Paradise Whydahs is while they are in partial color before the long tails grow out. Some of these birds are in this ideal shipping stage.

cages or aviaries. The separation of more robust and aggressive birds who might crowd weaker birds away from badly needed food and fresh water must be immediate. Weak and listless birds must be hospitalized. Recuperation is, fortunately, very rapid if proper facilities are provided. These prime requisites are important for finches but are even more so for softbills.

In preparing for acclimation, the writers use a simple and effective procedure. Southern California's mild climate makes outdoor acclimation possible and even advisable the year around. Acclimating birds in other climates should follow the same procedure except the aviaries should have the protection of indoor temperature controls. Proper ventilation should be given and overcrowding should be avoided. Failure on these points can quickly destroy the entire flock with infectious enteritis.

Before the newly imported birds are turned into the aviary, open food dishes are placed at several levels. Open water dishes contain proportionate amounts of Aureomycin for birds. Since birds liberated from shipping boxes are always thirsty and eager for a bath, they receive a helpful dose of Aureomycin to aid in preventing illnesses. Even though the birds bathe in the water containing the Aureomycin, there will be no problem.

47

Acclimation aviaries should be prepared before newly imported birds are released. In this picture, Hank Bates adds precautionary aureomycin tablets to water to safeguard against illness of birds after a long flight in close confinement. Large open feed dishes are placed near heat lamp so that birds out of condition can maintain proper temperature and be attracted to food at all times during crucial forty-eight hour period.

Those finches which show a need for hospitalization are put into cages with the addition of one of the sulfamethazine products for birds in addition to the Aureomycin. The two antibiotics offer a greater area of effectiveness and a greater chance for recovery.

Softbills need a quick energy diet booster more than any antibiotic, if they arrive in poor condition. Frequently they need to be tempted with a wide variety of foods. Nectar food is especially beneficial.

Hospital cages and acclimation aviaries require heat. The writers try to maintain a temperature of 80°F. in hospital cages. In acclimation aviaries, high wattage electric light bulbs are distributed at different levels in the aviary and are left burning both day and night. The most important one is over a food dish on the floor. Birds not feeling well after the long journey huddle near the heat of the bulb and are encouraged to eat. Many newly arrived birds eat at frequent intervals all through the day and night and quickly regain their full strength. Those individuals which may require

Hank Bates adds B-complex vitamins to the drinking water to stimulate appetite of birds in improvised hospital cage for newly imported, out of condition European Goldfinches.

Newly imported birds which arrive in poor condition must be separated from more aggressive companions and given special care. Open feed dishes, medicated drinking water, and heat bring them back into prime condition within a very short period.

Robert Busenbark opens a carton containing European Goldfinches and prods them into their spacious acclimation flight at Palos Verdes Bird Farm.

European Goldfinches flying from shipping crates into acclimation aviary.

hospitalization, but were not detected at the beginning, are easily spotted huddling under the light.

Within three days, the heat may, in most instances, be removed from acclimation aviaries. Over a period of the following two weeks, those birds which are most active and robust and are obviously in perfect condition should be gradually removed to other aviaries. Most finches have completed acclimation within two weeks, but many softbills may require up to ninety days to repair feathers damaged on their journey and to change over to their new domesticated diet.

Unquestionably, the simplest method of acclimating new birds for dealer or fancier is to have some birds which are fully settled in their environment and which will lead the newcomers onto domesticated dietary substances. This procedure, which the writers always follow, eliminates the period of doubtful acceptance which in many cases could result in starvation or the unbalanced status of the acceptance of just one or two items in the diet. For instance, nearly all softbills readily accept mealworms and raw meat, but these elements do not constitute a balanced diet. The feeding of these elements alone, which starts in desperation, ends up as a frequently unbreakable habit much to the detriment of the birds. It is important that newly imported birds be dietetically acclimated from the beginning.

In almost all cases, newly imported birds head for a bath upon being liberated from confining shipping crates. This European Goldfinch is ready for a second dip.

Removing broken stubs of tail feathers so new ones will grow quickly. Extracted feathers are replaced in six weeks, but natural regrowth through the moult may take six months.

Since the period of acclimation is very important for any imported bird, it naturally follows that your birds should be purchased from a reliable importer or from a pet shop supplied by a reliable and experienced importer. Many people enter the complicated and difficult field of importing birds and stay just long enough to damage the reputations of the entire industry. Their capital investment is quickly depleted, and they realize they can far more easily earn a living in some other field. However, before their departure they leave a shambling scar on all those people who diligently seek to upgrade this fascinating industry. Price cutting and selling birds of poor quality quickly enter into the downward spiral of the failing enterprises. *No matter how low the price may seem, no dying bird is a bargain.* It is much better for the bird fancier to pay a little more from a reliable source, where birds are given proper care, than to gamble with a questionable supplier.

CHAPTER 4

Aviaries, Equipment, and Breeding

An aviary provides the most ideal environment for birds in aviculture, and it is therefore important that the bird fancier adhere to certain basic precepts in its design.

Beyond these certain requirements, the bird fancier may run the full gamut in adaptations.

BASIC REQUISITES

Two of the basic requirements are a wired flight and a protected shelter. The open-air, wired-in flight can be any size preferred by the aviculturist. The bigger it is, the better it is for the birds. Limitations in size must in some part be dictated by the number and sociability of the birds. This requisite is also true for the shelter but is primarily contingent upon the climate. In moderate Southern California climates, the flights and shelters need not be separated; but, in cold climates, each should be separate constructions with a controllable accessibility. Normally this accessibility is accomplished by a small easily controlled doorway.

If the object is to breed birds, the fancier is wiser to divide space into separate flights rather than to release a large number of birds into one over-sized aviary. Some birds are gregarious and tend to mind everyone's business except their own. Others are overly aggressive during their courtship and nesting periods. The interference on all counts tends to diminish the number of successfully reared offspring.

CONSTRUCTION MATERIALS

The framework of the flight may be of galvanized metal pipe or lumber.

Galvanized metal pipe, available at builders' supply firms or plumbing shops, is more expensive than lumber, but maintenance costs are greatly reduced if not altogether removed. Lumber is highly satisfactory and is the most widely used material. For most aviaries of moderate size, 2×2 inch lumber is the ideal framework size. 2×4 inch lumber and, in some instances where greater support is needed, the 2×6 inch or 4×4 inch size is necessary.

In some cold climates, certain aviary birds prefer to roost in nestboxes rather than large enclosed shelters. With such birds, roosting shelters such as these are ideal.

Access from enclosed birdroom to outside flight in Carl Papp's aviary is accomplished through this small entrance. The shelf is a door controlled by a handle outside the aviary. It lifts up to shut birds inside during bad weather. The window is covered by small mesh to prevent birds from flying into the glass.

An attractive aviary in Carl Papp's garden houses finches and delicate softbills. The enclosed birdroom has an inside flight for protection against bad weather and for all feeding arrangements. The rest of the birdroom is given over to individual cages and storage for supplies. A constantly dripping water spout insures fresh water at all times, and the water basin is easily serviced from outside the aviary by a cubicle extension just to the left of the birdroom. Nectar bottle is attached to the mesh above the water basin. The densely planted aviary lends charm and beauty as well as diverse nesting sites. Shy birds find plenty of secluded retreats from overly aggressive companions in Mr. Papp's highly diversified collection.

These variations are contingent upon the size of the aviaries. The writers use these greater strengths only for really large flights. Finches and softbills do not chew everything in sight as do parrots, so wooden frameworks and flights will probably remain the most popular of aviary building materials for the birds discussed in this book.

There are two types of highly successful wire mesh used for aviary construction. These are hexagonally shaped aviary netting with a diameter of half an inch and welded wire fabric both of which are galvanized and long lasting in nearly any climate.

Aviary netting is the least expensive and most widely available of the two. *Be certain that the diameter is not more than half an inch.* One disadvantage is that it must be stretched over the framework to prevent unsightly sagging which usually occurs after a time. This stretching can be a considerable chore, and the writers have given up aviary netting in most instances in favor of the far more easily applied welded wire fabric.

Welded wire fabric is available in two forms suitable for finches or soft-bills: one-half by one inch and one-half by one-half inch in a smaller gauge. Any form larger than this size is not recommended.

Though more costly than aviary netting, welded wire fabric outclasses aviary netting in many ways. It has a neat and trim appearance and saves time in applying. Also, it lasts much longer because of its sturdier nature. Due to its strength, the half by one inch welded wire fabric needs no framework for reasonably large flight cages or small aviaries.

C-clips or *pig rings* are useful in connecting the wire mesh if the framework does not fit the average limits of the widths of the wire dimensions. If the mesh is aviary netting, the connecting links must be closer and more tautly stretched than for welded wire fabric.

PROTECTION AGAINST PREDATORS

There are many nocturnal nuisances which are severely detrimental to aviary birds. The variety of predatory animals depends upon the natural habitat, but the house cat is perhaps the most prevalent and most universal of all. Cats have the disarming habit of stalking the tops of aviaries at night

William Lasky's aviaries have simplicity and trimness in design. The wooden framework and shelters are coated with a finish to enhance the grain of the wood and to blend with a rustic canyon environment. Finches and softbills live amicably in the dense underbrush in these aviaries. Branches and a large clump of weed stalk provide cover and nesting sites for many varieties of birds. Button and Harlequin Quails especially like the thicket. Running water and growing shrubs add beauty to the central flight at the far end which contains bulbuls, cardinals, thrushes, tanagers, orioles, and large finches.

For a collection of toucans and toucanettes, Jerome Buteyn added a tall flight extending twice the height of most of his aviaries to give ample flying space for these awkward flyers and to enclose a growing tree. This picture is taken at roof level overlooking the sheltered portion of the aviaries. Metal pipes give a slim and graceful framework with minimal maintenance.

seemingly with the realization that they can see even though the birds cannot. With this advantage and resultant panic of most birds, the cat can easily exact a toll which most bird fanciers consider disastrous. The writers confess an extreme fondness for cats, but only if their predatory natures are held in check. The domesticated cat should be prevented from reverting to its natural instincts wherever possible. Anyone who feels any affection for his cat will curb such nocturnal depredations.

Unfortunately, far too many people fail to set good examples and show an utter disregard for all interests which do not suit themselves. Such failures to accept basic responsibilities fall upon cat owners far more than upon the cats. The writers have frequently been forced to devise foils for such predators.

An excellent, though not particularly attractive, foil against these nocturnal predators is wartime camouflage netting, which is still often available. Fishermen's netting also serves as a deterrent if properly used. The writers have effectively used both materials in repelling even the most persistent cats. Either material is stretched over the tops of aviaries with tentlike instability formed by palings at various intervals. Cats and other predators desire sound footing, and this arrangement does not afford this possibility because the covering is carefully battened down to prevent any entry beneath the covering. This arrangement does not deter marauders from the sides of aviaries, but these depradations seem far less bothersome and less frequent than prowlers roaming the tops of aviaries.

Small outdoor flight of aviary for rare and delicate finches and small softbills has self watering device and nectar feeder serviceable from outside the aviary. Cleverly designed by aviculturist Carl Papp.

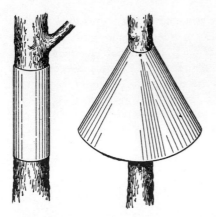

In large planted aviaries, mice and even rats can become severe problems. A good deterrent is to place feeding stations atop posts and to use sheet metal guards such as these to prevent access to foods. Used in gardens, these devices also deter cats from wild bird feeding stations.

There are several other predators which cannot be controlled by this adaptation. Snakes and mice effect entries from the ground. Both of these dangerous pests can be deterred by an eighteen inch strip of corrugated metal surrounding the entire aviary. Care must be taken, of course, to prevent this surrounding block from offering loopholes from beneath or a foothold to climb the blockade. The writers recently found a four foot King Snake casually and easily squeezing through the one-half by one inch welded wire fabric. This snake somehow climbed a five foot barricade of corrugated metal. Despite the beneficial aspects of the King Snake in disposing of harmful rodents and frightening Rattlesnakes, the writers are cognizant of the fact that snakes of even the most reputable character are extremely dangerous to all birds. Eggs and nestlings form delectable fare for such reptiles, and the writers showed perhaps even more panic than did the birds. Fortunately, most such predators are deterred by eighteen inch barriers extending above the ground and a concrete foundation reaching eighteen inches below the ground.

Very few aviaries for softbills, and none for finches should have mesh which exceeds half inch dimensions. Those which exceed such dimensions do admit vermin ranging from sparrows to mice, but the inhabitants are usually large enough and carnivorous enough to be of the opinion that such intruders are fair game and that they form a desirable addition to the diet. Many large softbills are excellent mousers. The Roadrunner is the only bird of its size, to the knowledge of the writers, which is an efficient snake eradicator. Therefore, the writers prefer to take every precaution against such intruders.

AVIARY VARIATIONS

There are many types of aviaries designed for both finches and softbills. The deciding factors are available space, type of birds, climate, and wind direction. All birds should be protected from wind. The prevailing wind is not the sole determining factor in wind direction. During storms, the wind is usually much stronger and rages from different directions than normal. Of course, in most areas where the weather is often cold, the shelter is an entirely closed area which permits the bird fancier to close passageways to flights during storms. In balmy Southern California and many other parts of the world, enclosed shelters are not customary and in these aviaries, sudden storms become problems. If planted, the aviaries afford adequate protection because the birds will seek shelter in suitable foliage.

There are very few ready made aviaries available in the world today because of the individual factors mentioned above. Each aviary is unique and must be designed with a sharp eye to fill every requirement as well as to meet every necessary precaution. However, every garden is a perfect setting for an aviary, and most bird fanciers are able to find additional space as the collection grows even if it means sacrificing a Petunia here or there. Most patios provide excellent aviary locations. Those with inside picture windows provide the most enjoyable sites because the birds can be enjoyed from indoors as well as outdoors. Modern ranch type houses with huge overhanging eaves are ideal for a small decorative aviary.

Aviaries for softbills and most finches are much more enjoyable if they are planted. Finch and softbilled fanciers definitely have the advantage in this area as compared to fanciers of parrotlike birds which love to chew and destroy anything and everything within their reach. Those fanciers with an eye for beauty have landscaped their aviaries to give admirable settings and backgrounds to enhance the beauty of their birds. The birds usually show their appreciation for these more naturalized surroundings by more frequent songs and by more frequent nestings.

The writers particularly despise those untidy and haphazardly designed aviaries which do not even satisfactorily house backyard chickens. The beauty and charm of the birds in aviculture deserve attractive or at least pleasantly neat environments. Concrete floors are tidy and neat and are easily maintained, but, unless potted plants are added, there is not much chance of giving a landscaped background.

There are a tremendous number of versatile and hardy plants which are ideal for aviaries. Some add beauty as well as serviceability by offering perching areas and, in some cases, by producing small fruits which the birds enjoy. Others attract insects to provide additional live food in the diet.

Perhaps the ideal in aviaries is the so-called *wilderness aviary* which nowadays is very expensive to construct. The wilderness aviary should be a huge enclosure around naturalized plantings. It should simulate as close as possible a wild environment for the birds and should never be overcrowded or subjected to constant human interference. Even the most reticent of birds are most likely to go to nest and successfully rear young in wilderness aviaries.

A conservatory aviary is an excellent and beautiful environment for those softbills which do not destroy foliage. Humidity must be kept low for most softbills. Those which especially require high humidity are mentioned under family coverage.

Another very attractive but expensive aviary is the *conservatory aviary* which is usually found in colder climates and is used for the more delicate and rare tropical exotics. Lush tropical plants help to make conservatory aviaries palaces of beauty enlivened by the obvious happiness of the different birds housed within.

AVIARY PLANTS

A lavish variety of plants, shrubs, and trees are suitable for planted aviaries. The aviculturist should select those plants which are sturdy and easily grown in the average garden. Each climate has certain restrictions and adaptations, and the aviary imposes a few further restrictions. The writers do not care to use in aviaries stickery Junipers or thorny plants such as Flowering Quince, Roses, and many types of Palms. They would exclude the *Pyracantha* because of the sharp thorns if it did not offer the fine perching areas and excellent berries which furnish excellent fare to many birds. Naturally all poisonous plants, such as Oleander and Castor Bean, should be excluded.

Olive trees add height and a wonderful resilience to bouncy perching birds. Though the foliage is not particularly attractive, the olive tree is hardy and has strong leaves which most birds cannot destroy. The Bottle Bushes are equally hardy in most climates. They also have uninteresting but abundant foliage and resilient branches. They do not offer many perching areas, but they add a bright touch of color and an exotic flair when they blossom. Among some of the shrubs ideal for aviaries are *Pittosporums* in several varieties; Japanese, Texas, and all other Privets; species of *Euonymous*;

Softbilled birds and some finches do not destroy vegetation, and so a small collection can be housed in a beautifully landscaped setting as in this prize winning window display at Palos Verdes Pet Shop in Hermosa Beach, California.

Another nest in the interior of Carl Papp's aviary shows an ornamental as well as useful nestbox. Under the honeysuckle is a carefully prepared open nest built within a wire framework. This nest was built by a Pekin Nightingale.

Forsythia; *Cotoneasters*; California Holly, and one of the really ideal specimens, the Tulip tree or deciduous Magnolia (*Magnolia rustica rubra*). The Australia Fire Ball Bush is an excellent specimen plant growing to an average of eight feet in height. Honeysuckle is an adaptable and hardy vine which affords many secluded nesting sites. Bamboos, in many varieties, afford equally secluded nesting sites, and some are very attractive. Others are too large for most planted aviaries. The Silk Tree or Mimosa is excellent for planted aviaries if it is maintained within reasonable bounds. It is pretty, but it can grow through the roof if not kept in check.

Hawaiian Tree Ferns, Egyptian Paper Reeds, Gingers, Bird of Paradise plants, Aralias, Philodendrons, Bananas, and several of the smaller thornless palms add tropical atmospheres but should not be included with very many large birds because many such birds will either break tender foliage or blot it with the harshness of damaging droppings. For small exotics, these plants are ideal.

In most cases, the aviculturist with a flair for gardening can combine these two pursuits into the most spectacular of all results. Most of his limitations depend upon the extent of the offerings of bird dealers and plant nurseries. Additional accents can be provided by small pools, lawn patches, fancy bird baths and feeders, stepping-stones or picturesque paths, and any other idea which the talented mind may devise.

AVIARY EQUIPMENT

Equipment in aviaries should be sufficient enough to fulfill the requirements of the birds but should not detract from the general attractiveness of the aviary. Those aviculturists with a flair for beauty fortunately have in their local pet shops a fine selection of bird baths and feeders which may serve as attractive accents in their planted aviaries. Pet shops also offer many feeders and waterers which are strictly utilitarian in purpose.

Feeding station for this aviary designed by Carl Papp is in the enclosed bird room so that birds show no hesitation about entering and so that feeding arrangements do not mar naturalized appearance of outside flight. *Pyracantha* berries are greatly enjoyed by many birds.

Feeders must allow for the different types of birds and types of foods which must be offered. Local pet shops which specialize in birds will undoubtedly be able to offer a selection of feeders to meet every requirement. Watering devices also follow many suitable patterns, many of which are admirably designed to include supplementary vitamins. Hummingbird feeders show several attractive and utilitarian variations for nectarine birds.

Each family of birds and many individual species will require some of these variations and modifications in feeders, waterers, and nectar receptacles. The bird fancier must exercise his own initiative in these selections, and these determinations must be based upon individual requirements. For finches, the average aviary should contain a seed feeder, waterer, bath dish, health grit dish, a container for insectile mixture, another for canary song food, and a dish for the dietary supplement. Other containers should be selected as needed. For softbills, the writers have often used sunflower seed hoppers to store Mynah pellets in the average aviary. Other receptacles should suit the needs of the foods being offered.

Perches should fit the feet of the birds and should be of varying thicknesses. Many of the long toenail problems arise from incorrect perches. Softbills clean their beaks frequently and always do so on their perches. Therefore, the perches should be cleaned often. The writers prefer to use both dowels and natural branches for perches. The branches must be frequently replaced, but dowels are easily cleaned.

Several inexpensive bird baths are now available in your pet shop. Many of these are attractive and ideal for aviaries. Recirculating water pumps, also comparatively inexpensive, transform bird baths into fountains; but the birds must learn not to fear the running water before they will take advantage of most fountains.

Closeup of self-watering set-up showing constantly fresh water supply dripping from small pipe. Overflow drains into gravel filled pit below. Cover lifts up for easy accessibility at cleaning time. This set-up was designed by Carl Papp.

Wherever possible, the writers prefer to service aviaries from outside and to avoid entry. This procedure saves time and also saves some discomposure on the part of the birds. All outside feeding is done from safety aisles which are enlargements of the standard safety door.

A safety door should be a part of every aviary to prevent escapes. For multi-flighted aviaries, the safety aisle also precludes the necessity of entering each aviary to reach the last one. A safety door is nothing more than a vestibule-like area between two doors. If a bird should fly out of the aviary door, it can easily be retrieved from the intervening area.

Equipment for breeding aviaries involves the addition of nesting facilities. There are several types of finch nests available at pet shops and bird stores. Finches use several types of nests. The most standard is a small box with the average dimensions of $5\frac{1}{2}$ inches high by 4 or 5 inches square.

In cleaning water receptacles, a sponge helps to remove dangerous scum and algae.

Wild bird feeders and hummingbird feeders are extremely useful in aviaries as well. Most pet shops have a good selection.

A small entrance hole is nearly 1½ inches in diameter and a perch should extend outwards at least 1½ inches from just below the entrance hole. One variation is to have the top half of the front cut away instead of having an entrance hole.

Frequently available now are woven wicker nests which are very popular with finch fanciers. Some birds stuff these nests so full of material that the low entry causes babies to fall out of the nest prematurely. Those prodigious nest builders do better with the standard finch box.

Some finches prefer canary nests as a basis and usually carefully weave material over the top to enclose all but the entrance. The writers always offer a variety of nests and sites so that the birds may select their own preferences.

Dried grasses are usually the basis for most nests, and the lining ordinarily consists of commercial nesting hair or fine feathers. The dried grasses are usually hung in a large hammock enclosed by ordinary chicken wire which is like aviary netting except in much larger mesh. Some finches often find this an ideal nesting site and will enter from the sides to construct a pleasant compartment. If enough finches choose this hammock as a site, it frequently becomes an apartment house for finches. Unfortunately, other finches may follow its intended purpose and deplete the hammock of materials for their nests in other areas.

Wild bird feeders such as these are ideal in an aviary for seed or mynah pellets.

Some finches show no qualms at stealing nesting material from other nests. The bird fancier should always have more than ample material on hand.

To prevent bullying of certain birds, the aviculturist may wisely resort to additional feeding stations. Bullies should be removed from aviaries to maintain harmony, but sometimes the bullying culprits cannot be determined before considerable damage has been done. Extra feeding stations usually eliminate starvation of weaker or extremely peaceful birds.

In cold climates some form of heat should be offered, and in any climate a night light should always be present. The night light can be a twenty-five watt bulb placed near food supplies. Any bird disturbed during the night will automatically gravitate towards the light. Most ill birds will seek the warmth of the light and will usually benefit from having foods at close range. This arrangement allows the bird fancier to spot any bird not feeling well and to give immediate care. Without the light any bird needing care would usually huddle in an obscure corner and may easily escape the attention of the bird fancier.

This deluxe and attractive feeder has a holder on the side for greenfood.

These two attractive and ornate feeders, though designed to feed wild birds, are readily adaptable to aviary use. The one on the left is best for seed, and the one on the right has a central area for mynah pellets and side areas for impaling apple and orange halves.

Charles Hudson adding seeds to a pull out tray in this practical aviary which can be serviced from outside.

Four types of finch nests. (1) Standard canary nest with pad and behind it nesting hair. (2) Standard finch box. (3) Woven reed finch nest with clips to hook it on cage. (4) Yorkshire Canary nest suitable for miniature doves.

This small garden aviary designed and built by Carl Papp embodies all the principles of efficient planning to meet requirements for finches and delicate softbills. The safety door prevents escapes. The inside shelter has fitted panels on the front to protect the birds at night or in bad weather. During the day the panels are removed, but no draft can enter. The planted outside flight is accessible by a sliding window which can be closed from outside the flight when the birds are to be enclosed in the shelter. The glass is frosted to show it as a barrier, thereby preventing headlong crashes against the pane. An opaque panel could be used in its place, but the frosted glass admits light when the protective panels on the front of the aviary are in place.

The interior of Mr. Papp's planted aviary offers an abundance of nesting sites of every description. One style of nest preferred by some finches is this bank of dried grasses held in place by a grate. This grass apartment can house many nests.

This indoor aviary for finches has a hamper for dried grasses used for nest building such as the carefully constructed nest in the upper right hand corner of the picture. Photographed at Carl Papp's aviaries.

This large nest hammock is inhabited by several pairs of birds. Grass is packed in large wire mesh and suspended from the ceiling. The nests are lined with feathers and commercial nesting material. Photographed in Carl Papp's aviaries.

A variety of nests for finches is helpful. The grass enclosed in large wire mesh is used as a nesting site for several pairs or as a holder for dried grasses used for other nests.

Several finches nest readily in coconut shells provided a suitable entrance is prepared. Whatever is used to hold the shell in place, such as this wire and netting, should be safe from toenail entanglements.

The most effective heating arrangement for cold climates is cable heating. Electric cables which mildly exude warmth can be placed strategically throughout enclosed shelters. It is natural to assume that any aviary which requires heat will also have a fully enclosed shelter. These cables are obtainable from most electric shops, and they should always be thermostatically controlled.

There are many other appropriate methods of furnishing heat in cold climates, but none are quite so efficient or free from maintenance as cable heating. Of course, during severe storms, the power supply may fail. Even the most carefree of heating systems are not without problems. Oil and gas heaters may have to be used in some areas, but the resultant fumes may present additional hazards which must be carefully watched.

CHAPTER 5

Diseases and Ailments

The task of clearing up diseases and ailments is very difficult and time consuming. Most softbills, once they become ill, fail rapidly and only occasionally recover once they lose their stamina. Unfortunately many birds show no interest in their recovery and will fight all efforts made in their behalf. Birds of the parrot family are far more easily treated. The majority of ailments and disabilities occur as results of inadequate or unbalanced diets and improper housing. Attention to these details can remove most of the dangers of these unnecessary problems.

Another common problem with softbilled birds is a quiet and slow aggressiveness which is not easy to detect. One may be quite sure of the efficiency of the diet and take pride in the fact that everything is progressing nicely until suddenly a bird shows alarming signs of debility. If not removed at once, many of the more aggressive softbills will form a teamwork strategy to destroy the individual. Not often recognizable, the subtle schemes of many and aggressive softbills in chasing nearly equally aggressive softbills from food supplies are slow to take effect. However, once the victim is suitably weakened, the clever schemers are swift to take action and to destroy the individual in an all-out attack.

Birds may fall prey to many ailments and diseases. Fortunately, finches and softbills usually seem less prone to as many disorders as parrotlike birds, but many disorders do arise. The bird fancier must always be alert to the *first* signs of danger, for then the patient has a greater chance for recovery. The loss of stamina and the will to live occur remarkably fast. If not caught in the early stages, most illnesses become fatal.

The recognition of danger signals is not at all difficult for the experienced fancier, but the novice frequently does not become cognizant of the symptoms until it is too late. Any undue listlessness and lack of sheen on the plumage give cause for immediate examination Often the eyes lack luster and the feathers look puffy. In many cases, loose droppings are present. In most cases, the bird will be losing weight very rapidly.

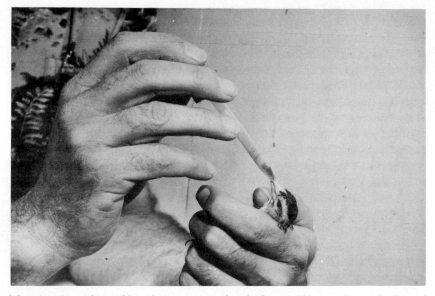

Administering a drop of liquid vitamins to a female Orange Weaver. Forced feeding of liquids must be done one drop at a time.

FIRST AID

The most important, and often the only necessary, requirement for a sick bird is to give it adequate first aid. Many birds show a miraculous recuperation if first aid is given in time. First aid gives every bird a fighting chance to recover. *Heat, appetizers, generous and easily accessible food supplies, and a precautionary antibiotic to help prevent secondary infections are the main components of first aid.*

Because of a very high metabolic rate, nearly all birds have an average body temperature of 104° F. The application of heat averaging 80° F. helps immensely in giving any sick bird a chance to recover. Heat may be applied in any commercial hospital cage or in a home-devised alternative. Hospital cages are not often available on the market, but every bird fancier can set up his own device to meet emergencies. Hospital cages should be covered on three sides and the top. Heat may be applied by adding a twenty-five watt bulb either inside or closely hanging outside the cage. This light must be burning day and night. The brightness of the light does not deter the patient from sleeping, but it does give access to much needed food supplies at any time of the day or night and frequent feedings are the most positive factors for recovery.

Any sick bird usually follows a rapid downward spiral of loss in stamina which quickly results in death. Because of the lack of heat, most sick birds

78

show a lack of interest in food. This refusal to eat results in a lower temperature and less stamina as well as a loss of interest in living.

The writers usually place a very wide dietary selection in easily accessible containers. Perches are either removed or placed strategically close to food supplies. Fortunately, the bird market now offers liquid appetizers to add to the drinking water. These are invaluable in boosting the very necessary interest in food. Liquid vitamins, also added to drinking water, help to maintain stamina and to restore health. For both softbills and finches, nectar food is invaluable in restoring quick energy and needed food values in their purest and most easily digestible forms.

If one treatment fails to show a response, another should be tried immediately.

USEFUL MEDICATIONS

Bird fanciers should always have on hand a number of medications to meet all emergencies. These remedies have a wide range of efficiency and are obtainable at nearly all stores specializing in birds. A few must be obtained from drug stores.

Antibiotic bird remedies are available from pet shops. The two most useful are Aureomycin pills and sulfamethazine in liquid solution. These two remedies may be used together. They constitute the most effective safeguard against secondary infections as well as quelling those infections already encountered. The sulfamethazine remedies are usually designed to be administered full strength. The size of the bird and average intake is usually in a correct ratio of natural thirst. Aureomycin pills are added to this remedy in direct proportion to size. Instructions are usually given on the package. Achromycin has proved its efficiency many times, but it is not yet commercially available without a prescription.

Antibiotics are often over-used because these remedies are usually the first to be recommended. Though extremely valuable, over-use often causes many problems. Too much antibiotics kills desirable and helpful bacteria as well as detrimental bacteria. Bird fanciers should select those antibiotics especially prepared for birds and should follow instructions carefully.

Liquid appetizers are not yet well distributed, but they often provide the deciding factor by giving many birds the will to live. The writers find them invaluable. The basic components are Vitamins B_1 and B_{12}.

Yellow oxide of mercury (ophthalmic style) in a 2% strength helps most eye conditions and even assists in opening clogged sinuses in some cases. This is a particularly useful medication and every bird fancier should have it on hand for use when needed.

Both hydrogen peroxide in household strength and iron sulfate (popularly called *Monsel's Salts*) are blood coagulants and help to stop dangerous bleeding from injuries. Birds cannot afford much loss of blood and should go through careful recuperation after such experiences. Every dietary supplement, especially vitamins and minerals, assumes great importance after a loss of blood.

Some severe bleedings fail to respond to either of the above coagulants. In such injuries, the writers cauterize the wound but only as a last resort. Perhaps the easiest cauterizing agent is the glowing tip of a lighted cigarette. If quickly touched by a clean cigarette tip, the bleeding usually stops.

ENTERITIS

Perhaps the most important and most deadly of all illnesses affecting finches is *infectious enteritis*. This insidious disease is caused by overcrowding and a dirty environment. It is most prevalent in new importations which have not been properly acclimatized according to the principles set forth in Chapter 3. The quickest remedy is complete isolation for affected individuals, application of first aid, and the addition of a bird remedy containing sulfamethazine.

COLDS AND PNEUMONIA

Several softbills and many finches suffer from the common cold which, if left without treatment, may develop into pneumonia. In both illnesses, the writers apply first aid, sulfamethazine and Aureomycin as described above, and one of the more effective cold remedies on the market. An inhalant is usually most helpful.

SINUS DISORDERS

Many finches and softbills suffer from sinus disorders. Usually these problems occur as aftereffects of colds, but they are extremely hazardous. The most recognizable symptom, outside of watery eyes and clogged nostrils, is a distressing impacted sinus condition which usually results in a large and swollen nodule which in turn impedes all natural drainage functions of mucus and other effects of colds. Sinus impaction in its most extreme manifestations will show a large nodule of hardened mucus. This nodule may be easily treated and removed by a slight prick of a pin or needle upon the affected area. In a very short period of time, the nodule will have attached itself to the resulting scablike development and may be easily removed by gentle massage. *Care must be taken to remove all the impacted material, or the condition may recur.*

ASTHMA

One discouraging aftereffect of a cold is *asthma* which is very difficult and time-consuming in its treatment. Asthma is easily recognized because of chronic wheezing and laborious breathing. Treatment may be prolonged over a six month period. Eyes may be watery because of sinus sluggishness. Treatment consists of a decongestant cold remedy and the administration of a strong inhalant as frequently as possible each day. Inhalants should be mild enough to prevent damage to tender respiratory membranes but strong enough to dispel the problem. There are several inhalants on the market designed for birds. Some clog and damage electric vaporizers. Since an electric vaporizer is the most efficient ministration, and the most highly recommended, the directions for the inhalant should clearly state that it will not clog vaporizers.

MOLDS

Occasionally conditions arise which resemble asthma but which are caused by various molds. Cleanliness and disinfectants are the best preventatives for molds. Foods often become dangerously moldy if not given frequent attention. This is a precaution which particularly must be observed if any food containers are in close proximity to water.

Symptoms vary. Most molds cause a general unthriftiness and, in some cases, diarrhea. Some antibiotics are effective, but most treatments fail.

SOUR CROP

A sour and impacted crop can cause many problems. The usual cause is a digestive upset which is easily treated by a teaspoon of baking soda in a quart of water for two days. Another rare cause is a mold which defies treatment.

GOING LIGHT

The frequently used term *going light* is usually given to any sick bird which is rapidly losing weight. This condition may apply to nearly any adverse problem since it is a *symptom* and *not a disease*. As mentioned before, any illness usually causes a drop in body temperature and a loss of appetite. The loss of weight is astonishing and death quickly ensues. *Going light* is also a symptom of tuberculosis, but this disease is extremely rare in finches and softbills.

CONSTIPATION AND DIARRHEA

The symptoms for both diarrhea and constipation may be similar. Loose droppings may be caused by either condition, and both may be symptoms of other disorders. If not caused by another ailment, the treatment for both conditions is the same because it involves a laxative effect which clears the digestive tract and enables natural functions to progress as originally intended.

The writers offer a treatment consisting of two tablespoons of black strap molasses mixed with one quart of distilled water. This solution clears the digestive tract and offers quick and easily absorbed food value.

The above treatment must be considered only if a careful examination fails to disclose other ailments.

SHOCKS AND HEART ATTACKS

The most frequent causes of these two conditions are rough and inexperienced handling. In many cases, the first attack is fatal. Both shock and a heart attack may occur before or during treatment for injuries. There is no cure, but a preventative or precautionary measure is to handle injured birds very gently. A recuperative measure is to develop slowly and gently a general muscle tone through proper exercise.

81

Recuperating from a broken leg, this active Japanese Tumbler instinctively knows the best treatment is non-use. Recovery is usually complete in less than two weeks.

SWOLLEN OIL GLAND

Every bird has an oil gland located at the base of the upperside of the tail. This gland secretes an oil which is used in preening and grooming. Occasionally this gland becomes clogged and swells up with a backlog of oil. The result is an inflammation which may even resemble a tumor. Treatment consists of gentle pressure by toothpick or matchstick until the backlog is removed from the gland.

FITS

The most frequent victim of fits is the pet Mynah Bird and other caged softbilled birds. In nearly all cases, the cause is improper diet and lack of adequate exercise. Refer to Chapters 1 and 2 for proper preventative measures. For treatment, immediately institute a corrected diet which is simplified as much as possible and which has a preponderance of dietary supplements.

Another cause of fits in Mynahs or other tropical birds is over-exposure to sun. Mynahs and many tropicals have jungle habitats and are nearly always protected from direct and harsh sunlight. Many bird owners, not realizing this principle, will put their caged pets out in the sunshine for a few hours now and then. Since there is usually no sheltering shade, the danger becomes very severe. Most birds recover if given first aid, but, if exposure has been too great, the result may be death.

BUMBLEFOOT

Bumblefoot is a painful disorder which occurs not very often in the softbill or finch groups. Feet become swollen with cheeselike and lumplike deposits. The only instances in either group that the writers can recall are badly treated caged birds or those highly active Cardinals and softbilled birds which have clipped wings when they are imported. The resultant inactivity and their ignorance of domesticated diets along with poor offerings can quickly bring about this condition. Usually the dietary imbalances involve foodstuff too rich for such curtailed activity. Too many mealworms and too oily a Mockingbird food are the most frequent causes. Importers may cope with this problem with simplified diets and must pluck the clipped feathers so that regrowth need not wait until the next moult. Three feathers at a time should be the maximum extrication. This is a long and slow process, but it is the safest for the birds.

Treatment for bumblefoot consists of cutting a small incision lengthwise in the affected areas and gentle pressure to expel the substances. A strong astringent and possibly a blood coagulant must be applied frequently. This is a very painful experience and should not be done all at once if there are several nodules. Subjection to prolonged and extensive treatments may result in shock or heart failure.

Clipping overgrown upper mandible on Necklaced Laughing Jay Thrush. Note position of head. No pressure is exerted but the lower part of the skull gives a good basis for a hold. Palm of hand enclosed over back immobilizes wings.

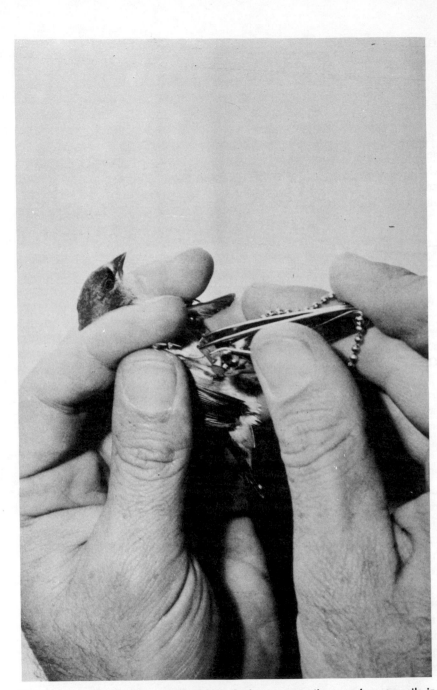

Strawberry Finches and all species of Nun finches customarily grow long toenails in aviaries with perches of too great a diameter. Clipping toenails is a simple task which gives the birds far more comfort and avoids dangerous entanglement in wire.

BROKEN BONES

Birds recover rapidly from broken bones. The treatment is very simple, but the outcome is not always dependable. Broken legs rarely show any problems after a week's recuperation, but broken wings often show a deformity which sometimes affects flying ability.

Most broken bones in birds show reasonable healing in a week's time. The only treatment offered by the writers is first aid to overcome shock and bleeding, if any, and forced inactivity. The inactivity is forced by a closely confined hospital cage with one perch placed near the floor. Foods and drinking water are conveniently close to discourage extra activity. Birds with broken bones have a natural adeptness for favoring the affected part and will welcome the inactivity.

Splints and slings usually become far more of an irritation than an aid. The writers avoid them wherever possible. If a splint becomes necessary, it may be made from scotch tape or a large feather quill. Broken wings may be loosely held in a sling to help insure proper settings for severe breaks, but most slings are of questionable benefit.

Most broken bones can be avoided by the removal of any dangers which will ensnare or impale a bird. Elimination of any cause for panic may prevent serious and fatal head injuries which usually defy treatment.

OVERGROWN BEAKS AND TOENAILS

Fast growing toenails are chronic conditions with many birds, but overgrown beaks are very rare unless caused by a deformity. Those birds which are most affected by overgrown toenails will be mentioned during individual coverage of the birds. Many dangers from entanglement become severe problems when toenails are not properly groomed.

The treatment is very simple. Fingernail clippers are useful in clipping the overgrowths. The writers usually leave toenails slightly longer than the normal growth to prevent clipping into a small vein. This preference requires more frequent clipping, but it prevents bleeding which is far more hazardous. The beak, if grown too long, should follow the average pattern. If toenails or beak happen to be cut too short and bleeding does occur, application of hydrogen peroxide or iron sulfate will check the dangerous bleeding.

MOULT

A normal moult should not be considered an ailment. It is a natural late summer phenomenon intended to replace feathers. The usual period for the moult is six weeks. Songbirds rarely sing during this period. Not *all* feathers are shed during the moulting period, but the number of replacements is really quite astonishing. The bird's appearance during the moult is usually unkempt and dishevelled and is punctuated by an abundance of pinfeathers.

The moulting period requires extra food value. A standard canary moulting food and other dietary supplements should be offered to finches during this period. Softbills will ordinarily not take a moulting food for

85

canaries. The best supplements are liquid vitamins and additional minerals added to the foods. Mineral supplements are usually powdered and must be sprinkled over food supplies.

Soft or out-of-season moults usually occur to *caged* birds rather than *aviary* birds. Very rarely do out-of-season moults occur without a traceable cause. For caged birds, the reason is usually too much heat or an abundance of sunshine through glass. Sunshine is beneficial for most birds, but it is changed when it comes through glass. Birds in such environments moult constantly and suffer the resultant debility which requires adequate dietary supplements. Sometimes an out-of-season moult is the result of harassment by a bullying companion.

FEATHER PLUCKING

The usual result of any bully is a feather plucked victim. Feather plucking becomes an insidious habit resulting in chronic shabbiness. In many cases, the feathers, if plucked often enough, refuse to replace themselves. Such victims are very unsightly. Certain species seem more prone to feather plucking addictions than others. These will be mentioned in individual coverage. Finches and softbills are rarely afflicted by the tiresome habit of plucking their own feathers, but some seem to be afflicted with a desire to be plucked.

Feather pluckers can be horrible bullies. By plucking feathers, these culprits slowly drain away the stamina of their victims. Usually, when the vitality is at a low ebb, the bully will pounce upon the victim in an all-out effort at extermination. If the bird fancier has not been foresighted enough to anticipate such an attack, the bully will usually be successful.

MITES

The customary mite problem in aviculture is confined to the red mite; but softbills, especially those from South America, often bring in some unusual mites, lice, and other vermin when they are imported. The writers consider it a matter of practice to spray all softbilled birds as soon as they arrive and to apply a very thorough disinfectant to all the shipping containers.

Red mites cluster in corners and crevices during the day and creep out at night to feast upon bird blood. A really heavy infestation can quickly reduce a bird to an anemic condition or, in extreme cases, can cause the death of full grown birds and nestlings. The season of prevalence is during hot summer months.

Eradication is quite simple nowadays if the bird fancier will persevere in weekly treatments. Several sprays are on the market. The writers prefer any of the several aerosol sprays which do not require removal of birds or food to be effective. There are many other types of mite eradicators available. Most pet shops carry a reliable stock of different kinds to satisfy all preferences. Pyrethrins are the safest of all mite killers. They are slow, but they are very safe.

Badly kept birds soon result in some of the unsightly conditions shown here. The Strawberry Finch at left has overgrown toenails, a frequent occurrence in many finches which usually can be traced to perches of too great a circumference. Small birds such as these should be given small twiggy branches in addition to perches.
The Strawberry Finch in this picture also exhibits a very dark brown overall plumage which is contrary to the natural coloration. This condition is called melanism. Dietary deficiency is the usual cause of this condition which affects many species of finches. Corrected diet, sunshine, and an ample supply of greens usually restores the natural color over a gradual period of time.
The Silverbill, second from left has a large neck area barren of feathers caused by a friendly or an aggressive feather plucker. After a time of constant plucking, the feathers may not replace themselves. Note the white spots on the back of the head. This is not a pied factor but an indication that the feathers have been replaced many times at intervals so short that pigment production is failing.
The shaggy Gold Breasted Waxbill, third from left, is also the victim of a feather plucker and should be isolated until all feathers have been replaced.
The Lavender Finch on the right like the Strawberry on the left, also has melanistic plumage; but it is still in a mottled stage. Although a dietary deficiency is indicated, there are no other signs of impaired health.

EGG BINDING

A very frequent problem with breeding birds is the rapidly exhausting state known as *egg binding*. When unable to expel an egg, any bird is likely to expend all her strength and die in a very short time. Symptoms are extreme weakness, a frequent straining attempt to expel the egg, and puffiness. A bulge above the vent will usually locate the stubborn egg. This problem is usually associated with caged birds which have not had adequate exercise, but other causes may also arise. Inadequate diet and a lack of calcium usually are the bases of such conditions if exercise has been sufficient.

Shafttail Finches from Australia are among the most popular of all members of the finch family. Soft shades of grays are perfectly contrasted with a long tapering black tail, large black bib, and black lores to give an oriental appearance. One species has an orange beak; another has a coral beak. Shafttails are good breeders, and they are peaceful as well as hardy. Photographed at Palos Verdes Bird Farm.

Treatment for egg binding is a simple procedure if caught before life's energy is expended. First aid principles and a mild household oil injected into the vent are usually successful in ejecting the egg. The writers do not believe in oral oil applications. Mineral oil is particularly damaging since it coats the intestinal tract.

Two complications of egg binding are soft shelled eggs and a ruptured egg sac. Both may be prevented by adequate diet, and both are extremely serious for birds. Soft shelled eggs indicate lack of adequate calcium which, for finches, is usually available in a good health grit. In softbilled birds, it indicates a lack of mineralized dietary supplement.

Ruptured egg sacs are extremely rare in finches and softbilled birds. In this most serious condition, the hen expels the egg along with the egg sac membrane or oviduct. Treatment consists of forcing the egg through the opening and returning the membrane into the vent. Whenever touching the delicate membranes, the fingers should be moistened by a saline solution.

PUTTING TO SLEEP

In rare instances, sick birds fail to respond to treatment. If the bird is in obvious pain or is a likely disease carrier, it is far more humane to put it to sleep than to prolong the suffering. Perhaps the least drastic method is to put the bird in a paper sack and hold it tightly over an automobile exhaust pipe for a few moments to render a painless asphyxiation. In many cities the local humane society can assist you in this unpleasant task.

SECTION II

CHAPTER 6

Australian Grassfinches

Australia's magnificent Grassfinches have always been the most popular family of finches. This family contains several of the most beautiful birds ever to take readily to captivity. As a group, Australian finches travel very well, arrive in excellent condition, and are easy to acclimate. None of them are as reasonably priced as the more common African or Indian finches, but all are worth the extra cost. Australian finches possess not only beauty of color but also matchless designs and shapes which are most pleasing to the eye. Most have clear, bright colors which are uniform in shade and which are sharply drawn and contrasted with neighboring colors.

Four finches will not be covered in this chapter. One, the Sydney Waxbill, will be covered in the chapter on Waxbills; and the other three (Pictorella, Chestnut Breasted, and Yellow-rumped Mannikin) will be covered in the chapter on Mannikins.

Australian Grassfinches are among the best of breeding finches, and there are several aviary bred strains now in existence. It is important for the future of these birds in the avicultural fancy that full attention be given to producing fully domesticated strains of all the various species because an Australian ban, long rumored, has gone into effect, prohibiting exportation from that continent of all forms of livestock. It is possible that there will never again be available the numbers and quality of wild trapped birds.

Grassfinches are very easy to feed. The standard finch diet plus greater quantities of spray millet are the basic fare. Some will eat a certain amount of live food, especially when rearing young. Mealworms, the standard domestic fare, are taken if the birds have followed the examples set by more insectivorous birds, but they must be strictly rationed to be useful. Aphis or Greenfly is very useful if available. Few aviculturists in the United States have used gentles or maggots extensively, but European authorities say that most, if not all, Grassfinches will avoid them. The writers try to fill this need by a dish of insectile mixture, but the birds must be taught by others to use it. This must be accomplished before the nesting period if the breeder desires consistent feeding of this food to the young.

All birds in this chapter are reasonably hardy but should be protected from temperatures below 45° and from excessive dampness.

The breeding season of Australian birds is just the opposite of ours because seasons are reversed. Therefore, almost all birds in this section start nesting operations in September or October and seldom show an inclination to change even in most aviary bred strains. A concerted effort to change the breeding season may be successful after several generations. Winter breeding increases the danger of egg binding, but maximum flight space and a good cod liver oil nestling food help to overcome these dangers.

SHAFTTAIL OR LONGTAILED GRASSFINCH (*Poephila acuticauda acuticauda*)

The Shafttail Finch of the Northern Territory and Northwestern Australia has great loveliness, being slender and sleek with a smooth design and sharp color pattern in the overall size of six to seven inches. The beak is bright orange. The head is a soft gray with black lores giving an oriental appearance. A large circular bib flares downwards from the lower part of the beak onto the upper chest area. The rest of the body is a soft, pleasant blend of pale grayish brown, darker on the upperparts and paler on the lower parts. The ventral area fades to near white. The black tail is long and tapers to two bare central shafts. A broad black bar on each side extends down to the legs and is flanked on each side by white. The legs and feet are red-orange.

Sexes are difficult to distinguish, but, if lined up side by side, females have noticeably narrower and smaller throat patches. This cannot be determined by holding the bird in the hand because, when the bird tilts its head upwards, it naturally stretches the throat bib so that it looks more narrow. There are many in-between sizes upon which behavior must be the most reliable factor in determining sex. The male sings a trifling song but extends the black feathers of his bib in a major effort. He also does a comic little jig and a hop before his intended mate. His beak is also slightly larger than that of the female.

The Shafttail is a perfect example of exotic pattern and contrasts which permit a bird of somber and quiet colors to achieve an ultimate in beauty. Colors are uniform and smooth while delineations are sharp and clear-cut.

As an ideal aviary bird, the Shafttail leaves nothing to be desired. It is hardy, peaceful, and requires simple care. Even though it is good in a cage, it is infinitely more lovely in an aviary because it is also a very active bird. In rare instances, a pair may show a desire to be lord and master over other birds in the aviary, but they never cause any real trouble.

Shafttails are ideal breeders. They have helped to enhance the reputation of all Australian birds, although conditions must favor them before they will show much interest. Removal of overbearing bullies and peacefully interfering birds such as Zebras and Society Finches is to be recommended.

91

Incubation is thirteen to seventeen days, and both birds help care for the average of four eggs. Both birds also feed their young with great energy. When young emerge from the nest after eighteen to twenty-three days, they are dull gray with dark tails and small irregular bibs. The beaks at first are dark gray but color soon appears at the base of the beak.

The nest selected is most often a canary-type nest which is covered over with nesting material. An enclosed finch box is sometimes preferred.

The diet is standard and does not require the complication of live food. However, since the writers offer mealworms to all who will accept them, there are many individuals which do feed their young with some live food. Nestling food is offered long before the nesting season begins so that the birds will become used to it. It is wrong to assume they will immediately take to a new food as soon as it is offered.

HECK'S GRASSFINCH OR CORAL BILLED SHAFTTAIL (*Poephila acuticauda hecki*)

The Coral Billed Shafttail is the same in every respect as the Shafttail except it has a bright coral red beak and is therefore more attractive. It is most difficult to obtain because its natural range is much more localized in northern Australia than the widespread Shafttail.

Hybrids between the two always produce coral bills which shows the genetic dominance of this form. It is an ideal hybrid to produce, and the offspring are fertile.

PARSON FINCH (*Poephila cincta cincta*)

The trim and neat Parson Finch, of slightly more than four inches, from Queensland and New South Wales is well named. It is very much like the Shafttail except for the following characteristics: black beak instead of orange; square, short tail instead of long tapering tail; and a pale brown chest instead of soft pale gray. In addition, the plumage is slightly less attractive because it appears to be flatter and somewhat harder than that of the Shafttail, and there is more of a brown tint even in the wings than on the Shafttail. The body contour is not so streamlined as that of the Shafttail. The absence of the long tapering tail and the heavy chest account for this difference.

The broad black bar on the flanks is present, and the feet and legs are reddish-orange.

There can be no doubt of the close relationship between Parsons and Shafttails, but the Shafttail is undoubtedly the most attractive. A whitish rump separates this bird from its very close relative, the Diggle's Finch.

Parsons are somewhat better tempered than Shafttails, but a few individuals are definitely spiteful.

Though sometimes difficult to sex, the same procedure in sexing Shafttails is followed for Parsons. Nesting procedures are the same as for Shafttails except that Parsons are slightly more insectivorous. In Southern California at least, the Parson seems to be even more prolific than the Shafttail.

DIGGLE'S OR BLACK-RUMPED PARSON (*Poephila cincta atropygalis*)

The only difference between this and the Parson finch is a black rump, a paler body color, and an extreme rarity which is probably due to its restricted Northern Queensland range. Undoubtedly some of the Parsons available are of this species; but, since the name of Diggle's Finch is not well known, the name of Parson sells it without any further question.

MASKED GRASSFINCH (*Poephila personata*)

The shape and size of the Masked Grassfinch of tropical northern and northwestern Australia is the same as the Shafttail except the two central tail feathers lack elongated bare shafts. The black tail nevertheless is long, pointed, and elegant.

The rather large beak with its squarish base is very prominent because of its bright waxy yellow coloring. Contrasting with this is a dark brown mask covering the forehead and lores, surrounding the eyes, and then tapering down to the throat. Although the eyes are deep wine red, they are not prominent against the dark brown background.

The basic overall coloring is a warm and soft pale brown with a shading of pastel rose-fawn. Upperparts are somewhat darker than the underparts, and the ventral area fades to a near white. The rump is decidedly white. The black bar on the flanks follows the same shape and size as that of the Shafttail, and this is just one of the several features that indicates the close relationship between the two birds. The legs and feet are, like those of the Shafttail, red-orange.

Though difficult to distinguish, most males show a larger brown facial mask than females. This is particularly noticeable on the forehead between the eyes. Also a prominent distinction is the beak which is usually brighter and larger in males. For those in-between birds, behavior is the only real test, and, since there is no black bib, it is not so easy to detect puffed out throat feathers during the song. The dance, however, is a positive indication of masculinity. Many authorities have suggested that the black bar on the flank is also a good sexual indicator with males having bolder and broader bars, but the writers have never checked this feature.

Masked Grassfinches are very peaceful and very beautiful. They are particularly lovely when seen with Shafttails because, despite many similarities, they still show a pleasing contrast with those birds. They are very fast flyers, and it takes a considerable amount of experience to avoid injuring them when trying to catch them in a net. Also, because of this fast flight and a tendency to panic easily, they are not ideal for a cage.

There have never been as many aviary bred Masked Grassfinches as there have been Shafttails, but there have never been as many adults available either. Their cost is slightly higher than that of Shafttails, and they are not as well known. Coming from northern Australia, they have a more restricted range than do Shafttails and are therefore apparently not as plentiful. Also, because of their more wild nature, they are less readily coaxed into nesting activities. When once they do start, they are on a par with Shafttails.

Both sexes help in building the bottle-shaped nest. The male displays constantly to his mate while trying to coax her to accept marital responsibilities. He waves his head back and forth, puffs out the feathers on his throat with his primitive little song, and frequently bows up and down.

When the female decides to accept these responsibilities, she lays an average of four eggs. The male shows his gratitude by helping her to incubate the eggs, but it is more a show of his devotion to her than an instinctive call which prescribes a certain number of hours' duty per day. Incubation goes on for fourteen days after which both parents spend most of the time feeding and tending their offspring. The young emerge after approximately eighteen days and are fed for another week by their parents before they are self feeding.

At this time, the young have dark gray beaks and more gray than brown on the upperparts. The rump is pale but is not white.

During all this time, Masked Grassfinches show every consideration for other birds in the aviary. They are neither aggressive nor inquisitive, but, on the other hand, their shyness will not permit interference without the danger that they will abandon their nesting project.

The writers have always held these lively and lovely little birds with great affection and perhaps even more so because their distinct charms have often been overlooked in aviculture. They are hardy, easy to acclimate, and require very little care.

WHITE EARED GRASSFINCH (*Poephila leucotis*)

The White Eared Grassfinch is a very rare form of the Masked Grassfinch which shows pale white ear patches and a generally paler shade of brown. The beak is also somewhat paler. Everything else, including description, breeding, and care, is the same as for the Masked Grassfinch. The White Eared Grassfinch has a remote North Queensland distribution.

LADY GOULD OR GOULDIAN FINCH (*Poephila gouldiae gouldiae*)

Much has been written about the Lady Gould which is easily one of the most bright and most beautiful of all birds in the world, but no words can really bring a visual picture to mind. We writers on birds easily get carried away; and, even when we describe this bird in accurate language, the person who has never seen this breathtaking and unbelievable creature cannot help but bring to mind a mental picture of a garish Christmas tree or a brilliant Easter egg. In truth, the bird is far more beautiful because it has the undisputed mastery of Mother Nature's unrivalled excellence in all forms of art; and this bird, it would seem, was designed for all bird lovers to admire. It is also, quite happily, an ideal avicultural subject.

The writers freely admit that ordinary or even extraordinary words cannot adequately describe this bird. Fortunately, the color camera can give a much better graphic image, but even the scope of this invention and the complexities of color reproduction cannot convey the true picture of the Lady Gould Finch. Painstaking effort and color reproduction have come as close as possible in this book to give a pictorial reproduction of the Lady Gould. Unfortunately, printers' ink, even in color, is sometimes hard and cannot convey the glowing warmth of this beauty. Therefore, let us try to reduce it to basic terms by saying that the bird is always lovelier in person and even more delightful to own.

The Lady Gould from Queensland to northwest Australia tries to include all the better colors of the rainbow, plus a few more, in addition to a graceful shape. It is five inches long including a long and taper-tipped tail of one and one-fourth inches. The two central tail feathers are almost bare shafts on the tips which give added elegance to the shape.

The male is the more beautiful sex. Females are duller and paler editions of the male particularly as regards to the greatly reduced intensity of the chest.

The following description is for the male Black Headed Gouldian: the bill is a pearl color with bright pinkish-red on the tips, the frontal sides of the upper mandible, and the outer half of the lower mandible. The entire facial area is a sharp and precise circle of black starting at the rear of the crown and extending downward to include cheeks and throat. The black eyes are surrounded by a pale turquoise-gray fleshy eye ring. Surrounding the black facial area is a finely drawn line of brilliant turquoise, narrow on the throat and more extensive on the rear of the crown. The upper parts, including the back, neck, and wings, are uniformly bright green shading into bright glossy turquoise-blue on the rump and elongated tail coverts which form a V-shaped area covering most of the main parts of the blackish tail but excluding the two long central shafts.

The dazzling underparts start with a brilliant and beautiful shade of light purple in a wide band extending across the chest from just under the fine line of turquoise to the middle of the chest. This is followed by an equally bright shade of rich deep yellow extending down to the abdominal areas where it gradually fades into white. The underside of the tail is grayish. The feet and legs are pinkish. Everything in this color scheme is perfect and shows sharp contrast where it is the most effective.

As mentioned before, the Lady Gould is an ideal avicultural subject. Experiences of many, however, have shown that there are some exceptions even where all recommendations as to care and feeding have been followed. Some will become ill and drop over dead despite all precautions. In many instances, these exceptions can be traced to overpampering which produces nothing more than hothouse flowers doomed when they must face the outside world.

Often, those least experienced in bird-keeping have the greatest success with Gouldians because they have not yet learned how to pamper their birds and have not added too many other birds to their collections to produce detrimental personality clashes.

In all but the rarest instances, the Lady Gould is overly peaceful and almost lethargic. It is far more likely to be the object of a bully's onslaughts than to become a bully itself.

The care and diet are simple even for breeders, and some of the mysterious problems which arise can often be traced to overly rich or inadequate diets. The writers have had most success by keeping Goulds in moderate-sized aviaries in an uncrowded population with a very simple diet and a sensible temperature control.

For imported birds, the temperature for the first two or three days is a minimum of 70° F. and a maximum of 85° F. with a warm light twenty-four hours a day. This procedure rapidly restores any difficulty encountered by long-distance shipment. Also the light bulb entices those which are not feeling well after such a journey to stay in close proximity to food supplies placed just below the light. If any do not show improvement, they can quickly be noticed and set aside in a hospital cage with a commercial preparation for birds containing sulfamethazine substituted for drinking water. In a short period the temperature is lowered gradually to normal ranges in which there is protection only from fast drops. Anything lower than 45° should be considered a danger point at any time.

The diet consists of the standard finch mixture which is high in small yellow finch millet. That which is available in the United States is called small Australian millet. White proso millet is omitted from this finch mix by some successful breeders, and the amount is increased by other successful breeders. In addition, unlimited amounts of spray millet are given. If the reader feels that this is an expensive diet, he must also consider that the value of the Lady Gould is also considerably above average. A good mineralized health grit, a dish of niger (thistle), extra oat groats during acclimation, a commercial dietary supplement, and cuttlebone, are available along with plenty of fresh water at all times. If water supplies are heavily chlorinated, a wise procedure is to hold water for twenty-four hours or to boil and cool it before putting it into aviaries. Green but ripening seeding heads of various wild grasses are always offered.

Mealworms are offered but most Gouldians must learn to accept these after following the examples set by other birds which already like them. Mealworms are a very rich source of protein, but too many tend to cause liver problems, and it is just as well that most Gouldians do not become overly fond of them. White ants or termites serve as part of their natural diet but these are not available in the United States.

Green food and seeding grasses, introduced slowly at first, are happily accepted and are highly beneficial.

Too rich a diet causes liver problems and other disorders. An inadequate diet causes even more trouble. There is no reason why such a simple and well-tested diet as listed above should not be followed.

Importations of Lady Goulds to the United States and Europe mainly come from two sources: Australia and Japan. Those from Australia are not available at the time of writing because of an Australian ban prohibiting export of all forms of native livestock. The writers, prior to this ban, imported hundreds of Lady Goulds annually from Australia. These always arrived in better condition and passed the acclimation period along with other Australian finches faster than any variety of birds received from any other country. Australian bird shippers are to be commended for their excellent care in preparing livestock shipments.

Lady Goulds from Japan pose several problems. Despite excellent packing and complete attention to every detail, Japanese Gouldians are not really successful in being transplanted to the United States.

All Lady Goulds from Japan are raised in captivity. There are no wild Gouldians native to Japan. Therefore, it is wise upon receiving them to put all Japanese Gouldians into large uncrowded cages rather than spacious aviaries. Gradually they can be transferred to larger and larger cages until they feel at home in large flights.

Also upon receiving them, it is wise to mix all food in the bottoms of shipping cages, after surface hulls and droppings have been removed, to the new food available. Even so, despite all precautions, many of these birds become thin and die before the acclimation period is over. They are very slow in accepting our foods, but even the precaution of ordering additional food to extend the orientation over a much longer period of time, though of considerable help, has not erased the problem.

Heavy feeding of greens to which they almost invariably have become accustomed has helped this problem.

Still there is one more solution necessary. Though a printed discussion is out of order on this point, the writers are aware of extensive work on this problem and feel that the solution is very near. The Japanese bird dealers and fanciers are acutely aware of the problem and have been lending every effort to the solution.

Those Gouldians of Japanese origin which do survive often become among the best breeders and the hardiest of all the Gouldians, *but it does take a long time.*

The nesting period is usually Australia's late spring, which is December, and these highly individualistic creatures usually refuse to change to our seasons despite many generations of aviary bred specimens. Many, however, will delay nesting operations until January or even February. In most cases, Australia's calendar seasons still prevail. Two nests per year are advisable.

Breeding Lady Gould Finches is a subject for specialization in aviculture. As much has been written by experts in favor of colony breeding as in favor of single pairs per breeding aviary. Most agree that flights of at least six feet are advisable for each pair; and, if other Gouldians are to be included, the population should never be crowded in any way. Mixed collections help to perpetuate the reputation of the Lady Gould as a poor breeder. They seldom will try to compete with other birds in the number of successfully reared chicks. Moreover, Zebras and Society Finches have a high degree of friendly curiosity and a desire to assist which is most discouraging to Gouldians.

Most successful specialists in Lady Goulds maintain several pairs of these helpful Society Finches in individual cages to take over the hatching of eggs and rearing of youngsters of Gouldians who desert the nests. This is a most successful practice which falls short of being ideal only when the young Gouldians are to be weaned. Gouldians feed their young longer than do Societies, and there is often a tendency for Societies to assume their project is finished before the young Gouldians are completely self-feeding. Their attention is turned to rearing a new family at this time, and so the wisest course is to remove female Societies at this time because males will in such cases continue to feed as long as the young Gouldians wish.

Interest in nesting operations is evident when the male steps up his amorous advances by doing the typical little hopping dance for his intended mate. At the same time he stretches his head up into the air and sings a little song which is not audible in an area of noisy birds. Even so, the performance is quite noticeable because the feathers on his chin move about in such a manner that a palpitating *Adam's apple* comes to mind. If he happens to be in a quiet area, his song can be heard. Though it cannot compare with his many other qualities, the Gouldian's song is not without charm. The writers never demand performances from their birds, and so they were agreeably surprised upon hearing it the first time.

Although the female seemingly does little to encourage these vocal efforts, she rarely disparages them. The male feels his song is really quite adequate and spends as much time as possible vocalizing in her presence. The female becomes much more interested when the male starts to shake his head at her. She wags her tail in appreciation and mating soon ensues.

After the courting period, the pair selects a nesting site. They usually show more preference for a box of five inches by five inches and six inches deep with the upper half of the front completely open. Dried grasses are carefully woven into a pleasant little nest inside. The writers always start the nests for the birds because many individuals are not interested in nest building. The average number of eggs is four or five and often more, and the incubation period seems to range from fourteen to nineteen days. Females a year or older are safest for breeding success. Younger birds often become egg bound.

Young stay in the nest for approximately twenty-three days, but this may vary considerably. The reasons for this variation in age before leaving the nest are not fully understood. Some sound ideas are set forth as explanations, and one or more could easily be satisfactory. Among these are variations in parental feeding, variations in food value offered to parents, and variations in selection of foods (some may be avoided even though offered.)

A curious phenomenon about the chicks are three fluorescent turquoise spots at each corner of the beak. Though the plausible explanation has been advanced that these spots are to guide parents to open-mouthed hungry chicks during night feeding, it has never been proved. The spots disappear about a week after the chicks emerge from the nest which is also the time they usually become self-feeding.

When the youngsters emerge they are vastly different from their beautiful parents. Their overall coloring is very dull and rather dreary. The upperparts are drab green, and most underparts are dull gray with a faint tinge of pale buff. Head colors are absent, and the beak is dull blackish. Adult coloring is assumed in blotches. They do not fill out into full adult plumage until six to eight months. Not all attain adult colors at the same age either. Many may wait until they are a full year of age.

Though there are plenty of successful exceptions to this rule, youngsters should not be moved until they color up completely. This is the period of greatest sensitivity in the lives of Gouldians, and they may die unexpectedly at any time for no explainable reason. Removal to another aviary presents adjustments which may not be surmountable, especially if there are differences in food and water involved.

RED HEADED LADY GOULD (*Poephila gouldiae mirabilis*)

The red-faced form of the Lady Gould is even more beautiful than the black headed form. The only difference in males is a very rich deep red head and facial area which superimposes most of the area of the black headed variety. The throat, which flares downward and slightly outward, is still black as is a fine black line separating the turquoise band from the red on the crown and sides of the face. This division between turquoise and red sustains the sharply contrasting color separations of the Lady Gould.

Females show much variation in the amount of red on the head. They may have the same amount of red area as the male, though it is much paler; or they may have the red restricted to tinges on the crown and sides of the cheeks applied onto the black faces.

The dominant and recessive relationship between Black Headed and Red Headed Lady Goulds is apparently often misunderstood according to the opinions of the experts. This misunderstanding is due to a curious phenomenon. In the wild state, black heads outnumber red heads four to one. Both forms travel together and are therefore not isolated geographical races. From this fact, one would naturally assume that black heads are dominant to red heads. However, opposite to what might be expected, black heads from all reports breed true; and red heads show some black faced among the offspring. This fact alone establishes red heads to be dominant since some are obviously split to black. Splits show the color of most dominance. The only plausible explanation is that the Red Headed Gouldian is a far more recent and dominant mutation which, in the evolutionary process, is destined some-day to envelop and replace the black headed variety.

YELLOW HEADED LADY GOULD (*Poephila gouldiae armitiana*)

The yellow-faced variety of Gouldians marks the beginning of the deterioration of the beauty of this lovely bird insofar as domesticity is con-cerned. This mutation occurred in the wild state but is of such great rarity that it never became established until man's incessant search for change and for rarity firmly established it in avicultural circles. Though always con-sidered rare, it is nowadays quite readily available due to the prowess of Japanese fanciers who now export this color variety to all parts of the world wherever people show an interest in aviculture.

Since the mutation cannot possibly have been perpetuated because of beauty, rarity of the newer color variation can be the only explanation. In appearance the Yellow Headed Lady Gould is just like the red headed variety except that a dull rusty-orange replaces the rich and brilliant red. If the mutation had been a true yellow face, there would have been ample reason for perpetuating it. Even though the domestic form of this mutation is noticeably duller and does not approach the brightness of the natural aberrant, the natural mutation is poorly named. No one can truthfully describe the face as more than a rusty-orange. This facial shade seems to unbalance the other sharp, vivid, and flamboyant colors.

Though many will not agree, the writers would prefer to see the yellow headed and all future mutations erased from the avicultural scene. The beauty of the Lady Gould in either the black faced or red faced form cannot be surpassed by any further mutations. In existence now is a non sex-linked lutinistic mutation which replaces the green upperparts with yellow and which dilutes all other colors. An albinistic aberration changes the green and yellow to white with the other colors very pale. Another mutation is the blue backed variety which replaces blue for green and white for yellow with all other colors diluted.

STAR or RUFICAUDA (*Poephila ruficauda* formerly *Bathilda ruficauda*)

The showy Star Finch is one of Australia's most popular finches. It ranks only slightly below the Lady Gould in price range. The size is nearly four inches long including a one and one-fourth inch tail. Stars are very good breeders and take to captivity very readily. Though they seem perfectly at home even in cages, they are much more suited to aviary life. They are peaceful but not shy and usually stay in a good display area so that the bird lover may closely observe their many charms. They are quite hardy after acclimation but should be protected from temperatures lower than 45° F. Captivity causes some slight fading of the bright yellow chest and varying degrees of red facial fading. Many aviary bred specimens fail to approach the vividness of wild birds, and the writers have seen a few which completely failed to develop red faces. These individuals also had ill-defined spots and bleached chests.

The Star Finch is a very cheerful singer and compares favorably with the Green Singing Finch. The pretty warble, though far less frequently uttered, has more variety than the shorter and squeakier song of the Green Singing Finch. Little mention has ever been made of the Star's song, but the writers feel that this considerable talent adds to the many other outstanding attributes of this ideal bird.

The latin name *ruficauda* refers to the rufous tail which is attractive but which is certainly not the most outstanding characteristic of the varied color scheme.

A very bright red centers on the beak and spreads over the facial areas of the forehead, throat, and cheeks. The male shows much more extensive and brighter red than does the female which makes the determination of sex quite simple.

The upperparts are olive with some dull red-brown on the tail and rose-red on the uppertail coverts where a few white spots tinged with red also occur. The underside of the tail is a dull grayish shade. Feet and legs are flesh colored.

The upper chest and throat are olive changing to bright yellow below. The yellow fades gradually in abdominal areas through the undertail coverts.

The face and chest are superimposed with a galaxy of white spots which are small on the facial areas and larger and further spaced as they radiate onto the chest area.

Females often show less bright yellow on the chest compared to males.

Stars are devoted parents. In the breeding season, which may start in November or which may in some instances be delayed until February, the bird fancier should provide a variety of sites as well as a variety of nests. A canary-type nest is often preferred as a base; but like most Australian finches, Stars will cover over the top. Males do much of the nest building, and females do most of the incubation. However, the male often sits with the hen. The average clutch is three to four eggs. The young demand enormous quantities of food which the parents very faithfully provide if the diet is correct. During this period, plenty of spray millet and mealworms are just as important as the basic diet of finch mixture and dietary supplements. The writers always feed insectile mixture in separate feeders, and, if the Stars have learned to eat it, this will be invaluable while rearing young.

Fledglings are dull green on top and paler on the undersides. The tail is dull gray. In a few weeks red starts to appear on the face. Body coloring and

101

white spots develop until the young resemble hens in every respect except that the spots are usually a trifle smaller. During this period, sex cannot be determined; but a few telltale streaks of red soon appear on the crown in areas beyond the normal reaches found in the female. These can safely be classed as males. Full adult plumage comes at about nine months of age.

The Star is rapidly becoming as domesticated as the Zebra Finch, but its price will probably always be much higher especially for brightly colored specimens.

Mutations, though still extremely rare, have begun to appear in Stars also. Yellow Stars lack the olive coloring which is replaced by yellow. White Stars show a pinkish face with most of the remaining color being white. Neither can possibly compare with the original, and the writers hope that bird fanciers everywhere will concentrate upon trying to breed domestic strains approaching the vividness of wild trapped birds.

AUSTRALIAN FIRE FINCH, also called *Crimson* or *Blood Finch* (*Poephila phaeton*, formerly *Neochmia phaeton*)

The richly colored Australian Fire Finch, which is five to five and a half inches long including the long and rather wide tail, is in no way related to African Fire Finches. The only similarity between the two is a red coloring which is infinitely more uniform and glossy in the Australian Fire. Apparently the name of this northern tropical Australian Fire Finch is used only in America. In England it is called the Crimson Finch, and in Australia it is called the Blood Finch.

The name of Blood Finch is perhaps most appropriate because it aptly describes the shade of red and also indicates the character of this bloodthirsty little red demon. Everyone will admire its beauty, but, unless it is given an aviary to itself or is housed with large and equally aggressive birds, few people will appreciate its behavior. The murderous intent is directed to any bird it can bully. Even though many birds may escape bloodshed, they are so psychologically subordinated that most of their personalities are destroyed. Therefore, the writers cannot recommend too strongly that Australian Fire Finches be isolated to one pair per aviary. In this isolation, their rich beauty can be fully appreciated, and their quite reliable breeding prowess can result in valuable offspring. There are some exceptions of course, and the writers have had several individuals which were peaceably disposed even to Gouldians, but there is little point in taking unnecessary risks with this species. Some are very prolific and good breeders while others show rather poor results.

The very active Australian Fire Finch is highly coveted and rather expensive. In both sexes it is a beautiful bird even though the female is far less colorful. Both sexes display gloss and are nearly always in good feather.

The male has bright crimson on the head, throat, and breast. The top of the head, back, and wings are still crimson but are mixed with brown and are, therefore, much less vivid. The wings are rather darker brown and show a shade approaching chestnut. The rump is again bright crimson, but the tail feathers show the brown mixture which dulls the richness. The beak is vivid red and matches the shade of the face. Underparts are mostly bright red shading into a very dark blackish shade covering the undertail coverts, ventral area, and tapering to a point in the central abdominal area. Small white spots on the sides of the chest and flanks are prominent. The feet and legs are dull orange-yellow.

The tail is long and beautifully proportioned. The two central feathers are longest with the shortest and outermost feathers extending to just half the length. All other tail feathers are well spaced graduations between these two extremes presenting one of the most attractive features of this bird.

Hens are less colorful with duller shades of red and a dull brownish abdomen. The large facial patch of bright red is very prominent. The throat and chest are much paler and duller with the white spots not as outstanding as in the male. The upperparts are dull brownish. Females, by the way, are never as readily available as males.

After a sensitive acclimation period, the Blood Finch is hardy, partly because of its aggressive nature and partly because of the sensible fulfillment of its highly insectivorous nature. Ailing birds are difficult to save, but their condition can easily be maintained if mealworms are rationed. Blood Finches gladly over-indulge in mealworms, but the sincere aviculturist will try to offer a variety of small insects in an attempt to curtail such extravagant imbalances.

Breeding pairs prefer nesting sites in the vicinity of five to six feet above the ground. The mating display shows a wagging fan-spread of the beautiful tail and a slow movement of the head from side to side on the part of the male. Usually the male holds a piece of grass in his beak during this performance. He also may raise the feathers on his head and neck to accentuate the expression of ardor. If the female is indifferent to such an elaborate display, the emotion may turn into a murderous attack upon her as punishment for her refusal of his most honorable intentions.

If all goes well, four eggs are deposited in the bulky nest of dried grasses and, if obtainable, bark and leaves. The male incubates during the day while the female takes over in the evening. Both birds join each other during the early dusky hours of evening. Reports of incubation vary from fourteen to twenty-one days. Males do much of the incubating and more of the feeding during the nesting period. Young usually leave the nest when they are twenty-one days old.

Young have black beaks and a medium brown basic shade with only a slight diffusion of crimson over the back and wings with dark brown flights. The tail is dull crimson and the underparts are dull, but lighter, brown. Beaks soon show slight traces of red.

Youthful males, which otherwise look like hens, show a spare feather of bright red in areas which females show brown as soon as three weeks after leaving the nest. Adult plumage is never acquired sooner than two months of age.

During the nesting period, the insectivorous nature of these birds is most readily apparent. Mealworms must be fed along with such other forms as gentles, fresh ant eggs, egg food, or even ground meat. Success in breeding is most dependent upon the quality and quantity of live food during this period. In most cases, this factor also decides the question of whether or not the nesting project is even to be attempted.

The Pale Crimson or White Bellied Crimson Finch (*Poephila albiventer*) is an extremely rare relative from Northern Queensland. It is paler and has a white abdominal area as well as a blue tipped beak.

OWL or BICHENO FINCH (*Poephila bichenovi* formerly *Stictoptera bichenovii*)

The crisply patterned and active little Owl Finch is one of Australia's everpopular avicultural subjects. Other popular names are Double-bars, Double-banded Finch, or Black-rumped Owl. The Owl Finch comes from northwestern Australia and the Northern Territory. A closely related subspecies from tropical northern Australia to New South Wales is the White Rumped Owl or Ringed Finch (*Poephila bichenovi annulosa*) which shows a

The Owl Finch from Australia is also called the Double Bar or Bicheno's Finch. A crisp and beautiful pattern attracts attention even though the brown and white colors may be considered by some to be somewhat less than spectacular. Hardy and very charming, the Owl Finch is also a fairly good breeder if given the right conditions. Photographed at Palos Verdes Bird Farm.

white rump as the only differing feature. There are several subspecies, but these two show the most important differences. Dominance of the White Rumped variety is apparent because all crosses have white rumps.

The size is approximately three and a half inches, making it the smallest of the Australian finches.

Though not overly endowed with color, it is a very attractive bird of distinct and sharp contrasts. Basic colors are white, grays, and dark browns which often are near blacks, all arranged in a most eye-catching pattern.

The top of the head and an encircling band around the face and under the throat as well as another band encircling the lower part of the chest are very dark brown but not quite black. These bands contrast vividly against the bright white underparts of the male and the slightly less bright underparts of the female. The width and boldness of these bands indicate the most prominent differentiations between the sexes. Males show bolder and more masculine bands than do females. In determining these differences, it is necessary to observe both birds side by side on a perch. If they are held in your hand, the bands show varying widths because of different head angles. If the bill points upwards, the band broadens slightly.

The upperparts are very dark brown with innumerable small white spots neatly arranged on the wings. The eye is black, and the beak is silvery gray.

Added to the pleasing appearance is a friendly and delightful personality as well as a peaceful congeniality to all other birds. As an aviary bird the Owl Finch is not often surpassed. It is a good breeder if conditions are right and is hardy after a rather delicate acclimation period. The temperature, however, should not drop below 45° F. Owl Finches spend a considerable amount of time in close proximity to the ground. Outside of Cuban Melodious and African Fire Finches, few other finches are so inclined.

Owl Finches prefer open nests to enclosed boxes in most cases, and the average clutch is four eggs. The parents are inclined to be a little too peaceful though they are nevertheless devoted to the task of rearing their offspring. Aggressive or meddlesome companions in the aviary may cause desertion of eggs or young. The incubation period is twelve days, and the addition of live foods is important while young are in the nest. During the first four months the young, before assuming adult plumage, are far more neutral in color than their parents. The whites are dull and dusty, and the browns are mostly a dull grayish shade. The two bands show very faintly.

ZEBRA FINCH (*Poephila castanotis* formerly *Taeniopygia castanotis*)

The Zebra Finch is the most popular and most readily available of all finches, and the price is very low. Its degree of domesticity rivals that of the Society Finch. Not only is it a very attractive bird, but it is also the easiest to breed. Most bird fanciers start with a pair of Zebra Finches and are quickly encouraged by the successful rearing of youngsters.

Usually this flush of initial success encourages the novice fancier so much that he or she rushes out to buy as many pairs of different finches as possible confident of being blessed by an avicultural green thumb.

The Zebra Finches go merrily on producing clutch after clutch of young while the other birds stand by observing. Soon the green thumb becomes tarnished while trying to entice other birds into the nest and the Zebras out.

Despite the fact that Zebras leave the bird fancier rather frustrated with their tendency to over-produce, these are joyful and amusing birds with a very pleasant appearance.

The original or wild Australian variety is the Gray Zebra. Like all varieties now available, the size of the Zebra is four inches including the tail of one and one-fourth inches. Another similarity in all varieties at present is a bright red-orange beak, paler and more orange in the female, and dark orange feet and legs. The basic colors are gray on the upperparts and buff-white from the chest through the undertail coverts.

Males have a large oval patch of bright rust-red bordered on the front side by a fine line of black which starts at the eye giving a tear stained effect. White borders this line and extends over to the beak where another fine black line tapers down almost to reach the other black line. This pattern gives a small white elongated triangle in between beak and eye. Fine zebra-like bars of black and grayish-white extend from the chin to the chest and become bolder at the chest. The center of the lower boundary is an irregular concentration of black which is a sharp contrast to the buff-white on the rest of the underparts. The sides of the chest and flanks have a broad band of bright chestnut spangled with prominent white spots. The underside of the tail is dull slate.

A slight shade of brown is added to the gray of the wings. The rump has a white band flanked by black, but the division is irregular and not sharply divided.

Elongated uppertail coverts reach nearly to the tip of the regular and stiffer tail feathers almost completely hiding them from view. The longest feathers are on the bottom next to the tail and the shortest are on top. Those in between are of graduated lengths. They are banded with black and white in bold one-eighth inch bands.

Females are drab by comparison, and lack the zebra markings on the chest, the chestnut and white flanks, and the rust-red cheek patch. The central tear-stained marking on the lower facial area and the banded tail are the only patterns. Her only color relief from the gray of the chest, head, and upperparts and the buff-white underparts is the orange in the beak, feet, and legs.

Zebras nest in a standard finch box using dried grasses, nesting hair, and any feathers which happen to be available. The simple diet requires no live food or any addition to the standard feeding outline. Eggs hatch in about twelve days, and the young leave the nest between two and three weeks of age.

Overzealousness and impatience in breeding frequently result in rapid desertion of eggs so the parents can start a new nest after separating the clutches with a new layer of nesting material. The beaks are blackish but quickly gain pale orange starting at the base.

Young Zebras mature in about two months and can be sexed about three weeks after leaving the nest. Up to this time, they closely resemble females; but males will develop a few lines of the zebra throat and chest markings in the area which later will be the black concentration at the lower boundary.

Zebras mutate and give us different color varieties quite frequently. Two have been established long enough to be almost as reasonable in price as are Grays.

Silver Zebras are diluted in color shadings, and the gray is replaced by an attractive pale silver gray. There is considerable variation in the shading of individuals. In many instances, Silvers are larger and more attractive than Grays to which they are dominant. Dilutes, in Zebras at least, are dominant to darker colors.

White Zebras are bright white with outstanding contrasts in the orange feet and legs and the brighter beaks. There are no pattern markings to point out sex, but the male has a decidedly richer red shade in the beak than does the female. Young are very much like females but lack the gloss which enhances the whiteness. Young frequently have, for a short while, traces of grayish-black on the tips of many wing and tail feathers. White Zebras are recessive to the other mutations.

Other mutations are still rather rare, in the United States at least, but are becoming more available all the time. The differences in the varieties are often very slight, and disagreements have prevented a complete standardization of popular names, therefore several varieties are confusing. To add to the puzzle, there are often minor variations in individuals of the mutant varieties.

Marked White or Chestnut-Flanked Zebras are distinctive and attractive. They have all the pattern markings of Grays and Silvers in diluted shades, but the basic overall coloring is white. Because it is a sex-linked mutation, there are always many more females available. The black tear-stain mark below the eye is the one feature which indicates a difference between females of the White and Marked White varieties.

The Penguin Zebra, sometimes called the White Bellied Zebra, is also distinctive. All the underparts are white with only a faint hint of the zebra markings on the chest if they are present at all. The tail is mostly white with faint gray bars instead of the bold black of the Gray Zebra. Upperparts are silver-gray in the male and darker in the female. The most prominent feature of the female is a larger white area replacing the cheek patch of the male. Penguin Zebras can be gray or fawn.

Mutant Zebra Finches—recently developed color varieties. Left, male "Blue Zebra"—gray parts have a bluish-gray tint with lighter underparts and diluted cheek patch. Center, male Cinnamon Zebra Finch with gray parts replaced by a definite cinnamon shade, brightly shaded accent markings, rust-orange cheek patches, chestnut flanks, and sharply contrasting zebra stripes on chest. Right, female Blue Zebra—distinctly different from gray variety with blue-gray shadings replacing gray in the normal variety. White underparts are brighter and lighter with white in place of absent cheek patches. Photographed at Palos Verdes Bird Farm.

Pied Zebras show a mottling of white against the dark upperparts. This factor can occur and be noticeable in nearly any variety of Zebra.

The Blue Zebra, one of the newer mutations, has not yet been set for the modifying factors of uniformity and good body type. Many individuals are, therefore, still rather poor. Selective breeding will in time correct this weakness. This is not a blue bird. It is much like the Silver Zebra except for a faint hint of a pale blue shade mixed with the gray. The writers have had many highly variable individuals of this variety. In most, the cheek patch is a very faint pastel chestnut. In some, color has disappeared entirely leaving a silvery-white in its place.

The Fawn Zebra is a mutation similar to the Silver Zebra except for a pale fawn shade replacing the silver-gray. This is a sex linked mutation. In the United States many Fawns are sold as Silvers because, as mentioned before, there are wide variations in shades of Silvers, and most bird fanciers and dealers have thought this was just one more of the differences in shading.

Cinnamon Zebras are now called Dark Fawn and are sex linked recessives following the cinnamon inheritance in canaries. For the first ten days the eyes are reddish and afterwards turn black. Except for a rich, dark fawn on the wings, a definite pale cinnamon shading on the upperparts, and a more blackish central chest concentration, the outward appearance is similar to silver. Cinnamon coloring has always appealed to the writers; and, therefore, this is their favorite variety among these mutations which are so similar as to be obscure and confusing.

Cream Zebras are examples of combined factors. The Fawn variety is paled by the addition of the further dilution of silver to produce a pallid but still pleasantly diluted Fawn.

There are several other mutations in existence, but most are extremely rare. Albinos are white with pink eyes. Lightly variegated White Zebras closely resemble white and are usually called white. Zebra fanciers in England have formed a Zebra Finch Society and are working towards standardizations of the popular names as well as the clarification of the ideal features of each variety. Undoubtedly the work will be difficult especially since many confusing and contradictory ideas from various fanciers in all parts of the world must be considered. The goal is to publish standards and ideals as well as genetic information.

Zebra finches are valuable to aviculture. They are the best recruiting agents for the fascinating hobby of aviculture, and they are excellent foster parents for many of the rarer and more undependable finches. Only the Society excels in this latter talent. For more experienced fanciers, the Zebra offers a chance for interesting studies on genetics.

PLUMHEAD or CHERRY FINCH (*Aidemosyne modesta*)

The Plumhead Finch, which ranges from Queensland to Victoria, is sometimes called the Modest Finch. Compared to most of the far more attractive Australian finches, the latter name is suitable. However, it is far more beautiful than many finches from other parts of the world. The more frequently used name of Cherry Finch is not suitable because there is no hint of true cherry coloring in its modest color scheme.

The four to four and a half inch Plumhead has, as its brightest feature, a richly vinaceous and glossy plum color in a patch on the forehead and crown. The male repeats the same coloring in a small chin bib. Females have smaller crown patches and lack the bib, and the shade is usually paler.

Upperparts are dark earthy-brown tinted slightly with a dull wine shade to give an added bloom. The tail and wings are darker than the back, and a tinge of metallic green, which is not bright, adds a little extra to the shoulders. White mottling, irregular and indistinct, vies with the brown for dominance on the rump. The wings have some distinct and clear white spots in the scapular region. The overall upper coloring is not really smooth or uniformly shaded.

The underparts are basically dull white with long, slender bands of dull purplish-brown on the sides of the chest and flanks. These bands are broader at the sides and diminish in size as they reach the central areas of the chest and abdomen. They nearly meet in the chest area but do not come even close in abdominal areas.

Plumheads are good breeders if conditions are right but are not among the more popular of Australian finches. Their coloring lacks richness and sharp patterns, and they are not by any means the least expensive. Furthermore, many have a distressing characteristic of dropping over dead for no apparent reason. The general condition of the bird may be excellent and the diet and environment apparently quite satisfactory. Usually there are no telltale signs of illness. The writers feel that when the authoritative answer to this enigmatic problem is discovered, the burden of blame will be placed on the over-use of rich live foods such as mealworms.

During the nesting period live food is usually necessary. A good grade of insectile mixture which is not too oily is helpful, but the birds must become accustomed to it before nesting starts. Small forms of live food are particularly useful. Mealworms are suitable if they are carefully rationed. Three to six per day are permissible while young are in the nest.

Plumheads prefer bundles of grasses to enclosed boxes, but personal preferences may vary. Usually they prefer to build rather near the ground. A planted aviary and tall strong grasses will be as helpful as an artificially arranged thicket of leafy branches at the most secluded end of the aviary.

Immature birds are dull brownish-gray above and whitish-gray below.

DIAMOND SPARROW (*Steganopleura guttata* also classified as *Zonaeginthus guttata*)

The beautiful Diamond Sparrow is another of nature's blessings dedicated to Australia. Though it is not really a sparrow, it is larger than most birds which aviculturists call finches and is rather a stocky bird. The square, short tail adds more body size to the overall length of just under five inches.

The writers do not know if it is as plentiful in the wild state as most sparrows or if the size prompted the name. They are, however, quite sure that it is an ideal avicultural subject. It is a good breeder in the right surroundings and is peaceful and steady, sometimes almost lethargic, in an aviary. Because it is rarely overactive, there is no tendency to panic as do many finches if disturbed. It is also reasonably hardy if temperatures do not fall below 45° F. It is far from being common and is priced, in most cases, comparably to Gouldians.

The color scheme lacks wide variation, but it is suitably varied with contrasting patterns to produce a thoroughly attractive bird with just enough bright accents to place it in the category of the unusual.

The beak is red with a silver-gray cast covering all but the thin rim around the base. In this area, the red is brighter. The tip of the beak is also lighter and brighter. The eye is reddish-brown surrounded by a bare faintly red ring.

110

The lores are black and a fine black line surrounds the eyes. The rest of the head and neck are dull gray fading to pale silvery-white on the lower cheek and throat areas.

Back and wings are neutral grayish in color blended with a tinge of brown. The short, square tail is black. A large area covering the rump and tail coverts is such a brilliant and glossy red that it looks as if it had been heavily lacquered.

The underparts are sharply contrasted blacks and whites. A broad black chest band extends down the sides. This area, though partly obscured by folded wings, is heavily dotted with large white spots. The lower chest area, abdomen, vent, and undertail coverts are white.

Females have brighter red beaks with less of the dulling cast of silver-gray. They also have, in many individuals, larger white spots on the sides. Though very difficult to differentiate, females often have narrower heads and slightly narrower black chest bands. These differences cannot be determined by holding a single bird in the hand. Both birds must be carefully observed side by side.

The unusual courting display is always the best indication of sex. The male holds a long piece of grass in his approach to the female. Then he stretches his head as far upwards as possible while standing very upright. After this gesture he happily bobs up and down in clown-like hops. The female who receives such an ecstatic display usually reciprocates by trying to appear as bored as possible, but she usually stays fixed in the nearby position instead of abandoning his advances. If she should flee from his show of admiration, he tries it on any other female who happens to be nearby. If the female accepts, nestbuilding soon starts.

There will be no serious aggressiveness if there is no overcrowding in the aviaries. The nest is either a larger than standard finch box or a spherical shape of woven grasses with an elongated neck. If at all possible, it will be hidden from view in thick foliage. Insectile mixture as well as some live food should be given during nesting periods.

Incubation stretches from twelve to thirteen days with both sexes participating, and the young remain in the nest for periods of eighteen to twenty-two days with only slight variation beyond this point.

The young, upon emergence from the nest, may not be self feeding for three weeks. They are much duller than their parents even though their dark crimson rumps are readily apparent. Gray marks the upperparts and the chest band. The white underparts are duller than those of the parents, and the beak is slate gray with a shade of flesh coloring at the base. The grayish flanks show indistinct darker and paler striations. Mature coloration comes very slowly.

Diamond Sparrows should not be kept in close confinement because of an easily acquired tendency towards feather plucking. Once the tendency develops, it may never be cured.

At the time of this writing the Diamond Sparrow has visibly mutated only once. This variation shows fawn replacing the gray areas and darker fawn replacing black areas. The red rump remains the same. Though this mutation is undoubtedly very attractive, it is extremely rare and will not be available to the public for many generations of Diamond Sparrow breeding seasons.

PAINTED FINCH (*Emblema picta*, also classified as *Zonaeginthus pictus*)

The Painted Finch of slightly more than four inches in length is from New South Wales to Southern Australia. It is now rare in the United States and Europe, and it is rather expensive.

Though very attractive and highly coveted by fanciers, it does not even approach the flamboyance of the Lady Gould. The male has a bright red facial area which covers the forehead, surrounds the eyes, and covers the cheeks and an extensive throat area. Upperparts are bright red-brown darkening on the middle of the back. The rump is bright red but not so vivid a color as that of the facial area. The tail is also brown.

The underparts are mostly black enlivened with large white spots on the chest and flanks. A prominent red streak runs lengthwise down the chest to the vent.

The long slender beak is black on the upper mandible, tipped in red, and red on the lower mandible with a silvery-blue tinge in the lower corners near the head.

The female is easily distinguished because the facial red is restricted to the eyebrow and a narrow forehead area. Moreover, the beak is less bright, and the white spots are smaller and extend up into the throat. The hen also shows duller browns than does the male, and the red streak on the underparts is less extensive and more poorly defined.

The Painted Finch is peaceful and somewhat shy in captivity. It is hardy after an acclimation period during which it is sometimes slightly more delicate than many Australian finches. The Painted Finch lives on a simple diet of seeds, but it also likes a small amount of live food. It spends more time near the ground than do most finches.

The writers have frequently owned Painted Finches but have never enjoyed them to the same extent that they have cherished and admired most other Australian Finches. Undoubtedly, some of the desire for ownership of many bird fanciers stems from the rarity of this species.

The shyness of the Painted Finch often extends to slowness in enthusiasm for breeding. When breeding responsibilities are accepted, however, Painted Finches are usually, but not always, good parents. The display of the male consists of the beak being held at angle approximating 60° and singing a monotonous little song while wagging his head from side to side. He does not bob up and down, nor does he hold grass in his beak.

112

If available, the parents usually choose a large box with the top half of the front cut away. If they are given a grassy hammock, they frequently prove to be poor nest builders. If possible, they add small stones, lumps of soil, or even charcoal to the bottom of the nest. This curious practice is probably for ballast and is shown by several Australian finches in the wild but not frequently reported in captivity. Painteds in the wild also prefer to nest in colonies with communual nests.

Incubation may range from thirteen to sixteen days depending upon how soon the female starts setting in earnest. The young leave the nest between the ages of three to four weeks. They usually are self-feeding in about ten days.

The young are dull in color with black beaks and only a slight shade of red on the rump. Otherwise they are like females. The spots on the chin are very small, and males, even at this early age, are usually showing larger and less dense spots. Adult plumage is started very rapidly, even as quickly as two weeks after fledging.

There are several races of Painted Finches. The differences show more numerous spots in some and very slight color variations in others. The only mutation known by the writers to be recorded is called the Yellow Painted Finch wherein the red areas are replaced by a pale rusty-orange shade.

FIRE TAILED FINCH (*Zonaeginthus bellus*)

Both species of Fire Tailed Finches have always been rare in captivity. The price has always been very high, and neither species is really colorful. The great rarity helps to overcome this last feature, and many bird fanciers are always ready to try their luck with this unpredictable bird.

It is sensitive to dampness and easily falls prey to enteritis and respiratory problems. Like the Plumhead, the Fire Tailed Finch sometimes has a tendency to drop dead for no *apparent* reason.

The Fire Tailed Finch from Tasmania and New South Wales is a very active and shy bird of four and a half to five inches. It will almost always hide from spectators if the opportunity presents itself. A considerable amount of patience and time are needed to overcome this unfortunate trait.

This species is reasonably hardy after an uncertain acclimation period, but the temperature should never fall below 45°. In the wild state the Fire Tailed Finch travels in small flocks averaging ten or twelve birds. Beyond this, the species is not gregarious. During the nesting period, a wise procedure in anticipation of the greatest possible breeding success is to isolate one pair per aviary because in the wild state many individuals stake claims to certain territories in much the same manner as do Robins and Mockingbirds. Even with these precautions, the Fire Tailed Finch is not considered a good breeder. The nest of dried grasses is enormous and has a side opening protected by a funnel-like entrance. Despite the shyness of this species, the nest is usually out in plain view. Eggs usually number three to five, but the bird fancier is overly fortunate if more than half of this number hatch. If he succeeds in rearing any young, the bird fancier can be considered very lucky.

The diet is the standard seed mix and insectile mixture which may require every subterfuge to induce acceptance. Live food is recommended, but mealworms should be rationed. Small forms of live food are more advisable. Greenfood and seeding grasses are also advisable.

The male has brown upperparts with an olive-green suffusion on the back. A very prominent feature is a myriad of finely drawn dark brown bars over the head, back, and wings. The bars are stronger on the back and on the dark wings. Subordinate bars also mark the facial areas. Underparts are also barred with finely drawn dark lines on a grayish background. Males show blackish abdominal areas, and the hen exhibits a continuation of the barred effect. Feet and legs are brownish with a flesh tint. The tail shows a considerable amount of black which is cluttered with paler brown bars.

The three outstanding features are the beak, facial mask, and rump. Both beak and an extensive area covering the rump and uppertail coverts are bright red, but the base of the beak is considerably more pale. Some individuals show variation in beak coloring. A blackish facial mask covers the forehead and lores and extends through the eye area where it tapers to a point above the cheeks.

Except for the difference in abdominal areas, sexes are very similar. Immature birds lack the boldness of the finely drawn bars and are more dull and neutral in the overall shading. The red rump area is also considerably smaller.

The Red Eared Fire Tailed Finch (*Zonaeginthus oculatis*) from the southwestern area of Australia has a red ear patch behind the eye and just below the taper of the black mask. The lower chest and abdominal areas are more boldly barred with black and a whitish shade.

CHAPTER 7

Parrot Finches

Nearly every bird fancier has heard about Parrot Finches, but only a few have ever had experience with them. Their beauty has been extolled in many bird books, and their great rarity has almost made a legend of them. Therefore, when any become available, there is always a ready and eager market awaiting them. Prices for all except the Pintailed Nonpareil are always very high.

If the bird fancier excludes the rarity of these birds, he is quite likely to discover their virtues are nearly equaled by their disadvantages. The writers feel they are somewhat over-rated as *ideal* avicultural subjects.

The *beauty* and *rarity* of Parrot Finches cannot be questioned, but on these two counts there are many peers in other families. Though the Pintailed Nonpareil presents considerable difficulty at first, the others ask only for reasonable care after the acclimation period.

The greatest disadvantage to members of this family is their extreme shyness and a tendency to panic at even the most cautious approach. There is not much pleasure in owning a beautiful bird if it is forever dashing into hiding to avoid observation. Owners of Parrot Finches must be aware of the ever present danger of panics in which these fast-flying birds may injure themselves while flying headlong into wire netting when they are disturbed. For these reasons, they are not safely or happily kept in cages.

Parrot Finches all come from a widespread range in the Southwest Pacific Islands ranging from Burma to the Philippines. Some species are quite localized in their individual ranges.

The Red Headed Parrot Finch is the most difficult to obtain at present because it is protected in New Caledonia which is its greatest stronghold.

On the other extreme, the Pintailed Nonpareil has a very widespread range and is despised as a rice field pest.

Availability is always erratic even though none are considered to be rare in their native ranges. Few natives are conscious of lucrative foreign bird markets, and the birds have a keen natural instinct for survival which makes capture difficult. Then too, many Parrot Finches are migratory and, therefore, even more elusive.

A trapper, explaining how he captured a large number of Tri Colored Parrot Finches, said that three weeks of patience and exasperation were required to capture the first specimen. After this trying period, subsequent trapping was greatly simplified because the captive bird was used as a decoy in luring birds to the scene of operation.

Young in the nest have phosphorescent spots at the corners of the beaks, as in Lady Goulds, until they are weaned.

PINTAILED NONPAREIL (*Erythrura prasina*)

The Pretty Pintailed Nonpareil, sometimes called Longtailed Munia, is the most frequently available of the entire family of Parrot Finches. Though farmers of Malaya, Sumatra, Java, and Borneo are always happy to be rid of each shipment, bird dealers are reluctant to import them because of an extreme stubbornness on the part of the bird to change to domesticated diets. Orientation and acclimation are consequently very difficult.

The most effective procedure in acclimating Pintailed Nonpareils to domestic life is to follow the standard steps for all birds regarding temperature and environment with certain modifications. Dampness presents an additional hazard and should be avoided since these birds are frequently subject to respiratory problems. The dietary changeover requires more time and effort than required for most birds.

Pintailed Nonpareils are very fond of paddy rice and must be weaned from it slowly. Paddy rice and hulled oats must be soaked and fed together with proportions changing gradually until oats are readily accepted. Canary and white proso millet can be added gradually and fed dry after first being soaked. Seeding grasses are always helpful both during and after acclimation. Fresh ears of corn seem also to help divert attention from rice, but food value in this item is not ideal, and subsequent rationing is advised.

Pintailed Nonpareils are perhaps more insectivorous than most Parrot Finches. A variety of live foods can be offered, but mealworms should be rationed severely. Two per day are ideal. Over-use leads to obscure problems which undoubtedly account for many of the unexplained deaths which frequently occur. If these birds can be coaxed into eating a good insectile mixture, they will benefit greatly.

Freshly imported Pintailed Nonpareils are lovely birds. The body length of slightly less than three inches is enhanced by a long and tapering slender tail of two and one-fourth inches in adult males. The rather large beak is black, and the feet and legs are indistinctly yellow.

The natural coloring of adult males is dark, but vivid, and seems to have been mixed from a painter's palette. The bright blue of the face, throat, and forehead changes to green on the upperparts. The lores are darkened by black. The rump and upper tail coverts are bright red which becomes softly duller on the tail. The central tail feathers are darker and brighter, and traces of black and green subordinate the outer edges. The chest is dominated by

116

bright red which spills in a diluted shade over the central lower chest area into the abdomen. The sides are duller and mixed with paler shades which become dull buffish in the ventral area.

Unfortunately, most reds on this bird fade in captivity to a yellowish-straw shade. The balanced beauty is easily upset. As a matter of practice, the writers mix soya powder or carotene with the insectile mixture and sprinkle it over seeds to help maintain the red. Though this practice has proven success-ful with other birds which fade, the experiment cannot be termed conclusive with Pintailed Nonpareils because of a limited time factor and too few subjects.

Females and immatures have shorter tails and are less vivid in coloration. Reds are greatly diminished on the chest and are replaced by greens and browns. Greens are also quieter and darker. Blues on facial areas are nearly absent.

One of the subspecies (*Erythrura prasina coelica*), comes from Borneo and is much brighter than the above. Unfortunately, it is rarely imported.

Pintailed Nonpareils are very difficult to coax into nesting activity, but the incubation period is approximately two weeks, and young are in the nest about three weeks. They are weaned in about ten days.

RED HEADED PARROT FINCH (*Erythrura psittacea*)

The Red Headed or Red Throated Parrot Finch is probably the most attractive and ideal member of the family, but it is also the most difficult to get and presently is the highest priced.

The beautifully proportioned reds do not fade in captivity, and the personality is far more stable than that of the Tri Colored Parrot Finch. After acclimation, it is reasonably hardy.

Protected in New Caledonia and limited in other ranges, the Red Headed Parrot Finch is now very rare in aviculture. Fortunately, several aviary bred strains are helping to prevent an avicultural extinction. The high price placed upon these birds helps to insure proper consideration for their require-ments. They are better breeders if they are given a spacious aviary to them-selves.

Red Headed Parrot Finches are simply patterned in bright red and bright green. The dark eyes, black beak, and grayish feet are the only contrasts. Red covers the rump and tail in rather a dull shade. An extensive facial area of a bright red shade includes an area to the top of the crown which flares outwards to encircle a large cheek area and drops onto the upper chest area. They are sleekly shaped and have a sharply pointed tail which, however, is not as elongated as that of the Pintailed Nonpareil. The overall length is four and a half inches. They are very peaceful and should be protected from overbearing birds even though their constant activity affords some escape from bullies.

Hens have slightly less red on top than do males. Although they are slightly duller, the distinction is very difficult. Males occasionally whistle a

117

little song, but they are very shy, and observation is difficult. Young are pale gray-green below and dull green above. Some scarlet appears on the throat, face, and tail.

Though they are rather poor breeders in most cases, good pairs can be really prolific. A variety of nests should be offered even though the most preferred will be a wooden nest box of rather larger than standard size. Incubation is usually thirteen or fourteen days followed by nineteen to twenty-three days before fledging. Any disturbance may cause desertion. Feeding, if possible, should be accomplished from outside the aviary. With these precautions, Red Headed Parrot Finches often become reasonably good breeders.

The diet is standard except for heavier percentages of canary, spray millet, greenfood, fresh fruit, and rationed mealworms.

TRI COLORED PARROT FINCH (*Erythrura trichroa*)

The Tri Colored Parrot Finch has greater diversification in color but somehow is a trifle less noticeable than the Red Headed Parrot Finch. The reason is that red contrasts more sharply with green than does blue. At the time of writing it is more readily available because it is not protected by law in its natural ranges and is therefore also lower in price.

The blue facial area is less extensive on the throat than in the Red Headed Parrot Finch, and no blue extends into the chest. The reddish tail and rump coloring is not as bright as in the Red Headed Parrot Finch, but it nevertheless is a dominant color feature.

Females are slightly less bright than males especially in the blue cheeks. Immature birds lack blue on the head. Several species of this bird show few if any variations in color.

The Tri Colored Parrot Finch is an extremely fast flyer and is very shy. The bird pictured in this book was more difficult to photograph than any other bird.

Breeding information is the same as for the Red Headed Parrot Finch, but precautions against disturbances must be even more strictly observed.

FIJI RED HEADED PARROT FINCH (*Erythrura cyanovirens peali*)

The Fiji Red Headed Parrot Finch is also known as Peale's Parrot Finch and is a very rare prize in aviculture. Though it has a stockier and less shapely body and shorter tail than any of the above species, it nevertheless is a very pretty bird.

The main coloring is the same as in the Red Headed Finch, but the throat is black instead of red and is broadly bordered with blue just above the chest. The black on the chin flares outward and downward to encircle the lower portions of the bright red cheeks.

The writers and Mrs. Van der Meid attempted to photograph a particularly beautiful specimen of this bird belonging to Carl Papp. None of the several pictures were suitable for reproduction because of the bird's insistence in hiding his throat. The results were several pictures of the back of his head and several more in which the bird was leaning so far forward with lowered head that these features were not even visible. This bird's shyness parallels that of the Tri Colored Parrot Finch.

Females are similar, but the red is slightly less extensive and a shade duller. The blue on the throat is less vivid. Immatures are much duller and have some yellowish-horn coloring in the beak.

The general care in captivity is the same as for the Red Headed Parrot Finch. In the wild state, it seems to frequent flowering trees feeding on buds. A greater percentage of seeding grasses would be helpful in captivity. Fruit especially is required. Apples, figs, and soaked raisins seem to be the most beneficial.

Several subspecies show only slight variations. Both the Royal Parrot Finch (*Erythrura cyanovirens regia*) from the New Hebrides and the Samoa Red Headed Parrot Finch (*Erythrura cyanovirens cyanovirens*) show more blue in the body coloring. The subspecies *efatensis* and *serena* have blue napes and breasts.

OTHER PARROT FINCHES

The remaining members of the family of Parrot Finches are extremely rare in captivity either because of much duller coloration or because they are scarce and often nomadic in their natural ranges.

The Green Faced Parrot Finch (*Erythrura viridifacies*) from the Philippine Islands has a black beak, a red tail, and flesh colored feet. The rest of the body coloring is a bright green which is brighter and darker on the upperparts. Females have a buffish-green shade on the abdomen. The young are similar but have even more extensive additions of buff.

The Green Tailed Parrot Finch (*Erythrura hyperythra*), with its several subspecies, is frequently called the Bamboo Munia and Green Tailed Munia. It has a wide range which includes the Philippine Islands, Borneo, Malaya, and several neighboring islands. It is very shy and not very colorful.

Upperparts are green, and lowerparts are buffish. The beak and forehead are black, and the crown is blue. The feet are flesh colored.

The Pink Billed Parrot Finch (*Erythrura kleinschmidti*) is too rare in its natural range to be available for aviculture. The large beak is yellowish-pink, and most of the coloring is green. The facial area is blackish-blue with brighter dark blue on the top of the head. The rump and tail are red.

CHAPTER 8

Mannikins

The family of mannikins comprises birds of many descriptions ranging from Africa to Australia via India, Ceylon, Burma, and the Philippines with some representatives in between most of these places.

There is a great extent of diversification in generic characteristics, but, generally speaking, mannikins have short, thick beaks and heavier bodies than most waxbills. Most are very hardy and easy to maintain in captivity. As a rule mannikins are not as brightly colored as most popular finches in aviculture, but they still include some of the most inexpensive and the most numerous finches which are great favorites with bird fanciers.

Mannikins belong in the family *Ploceidae*. Generic names have undergone many changes and more changes are in store for the future. Unfortunately, some of the changes are slow to gain acceptance, and some may be held in dispute for some time to come. Most are at least confusing to aviculturists, but the trend is towards simplification in scientific nomenclature.

Some of the generic changes are as follows: *Urolonchura* has been changed to *Lonchura*; many *Munias* have been changed to *Lonchura*; *Spermestes* and *Euodice* have probably been changed to *Lonchura* though some authorities are still clinging to the old names.

Several birds have been deleted from this book because they are not yet known in aviculture and are not likely to gain a popular following even if they should become available.

SOCIETY FINCH or BENGALESE (*Lonchura domestica*)

The Society Finch, as it is called in the United States, ranks equally with the Zebra Finch in popularity and availability, and the price range is similar. It is a good breeder and an ideal foster parent for many of the rarer finches that are not steady enough to be called *reliable* parents. Society Finches are as good in cages as they are in aviaries and are good breeders either way. They are generally very hardy and sturdy but should not be allowed to breed in unheated aviaries during cold weather. If the climate is too cold, Societies are best kept indoors.

This charming little personality is four and a half inches long including the tail of one and one-half inches. The central tail feathers are tapered to a

Society Finches nest readily in cage or aviary. This woven wicker nest is ideal for many birds. Note the young bird cautiously peering out of the nest. Photographed in Carl Papp's birdroom.

blunt tip, and the outer feathers have graduated lengths to meet and enhance the central feathers.

The beak is thick and blunt in the mannikin tradition, but the color is variable and may range from dark brown to pinkish-horn color.

Many Societies have a canary type crest. Some are double crested and the writers have seen one specimen with several rosette crests on the sides of the neck and throat. In trying to breed cresteds, it is wiser to breed crested to crest-bred, the latter being non-crested but having one crested parent.

No two Societies are exactly alike in their mottled pattern. Coloring varies from pure white to dark chocolate-brown. The range of color is limited to dark brown, cinnamon, and a deft blend between the two. In most cases, there is a mottled mixture of white, but there are some selfs both in cinnamon and dark brown. Selfs contain no white in their feathers. The shading of cinnamon in some individuals may be diluted slightly.

Pure white Societies are far less attractive than White Zebra Finches because they lack the bright red-orange beaks, feet, and legs. The writers prefer the cinnamon to dark brown shades. Dark browns are dominant to both cinnamon and pure white and are, therefore, far more numerous. Pure white birds, which are recessive to both shades of brown, are somewhat weaker and less prolific than other color varieties. There is a tendency for blindness in whites if they are inbred or if they are not outcrossed frequently with a lightly marked chocolate and white variety.

Sexes can accurately be determined only by behavior. The male sings a squeaky little song to his mate while puffing out his chest and sticking his head high up in the air. This is an amusing little performance punctuated by short but vigorous hops. His tail sticks up at a much sharper clownlike angle during the display.

Close observation to determine sexes, no matter how acute, involves some guesswork. Some are relatively easy, but there are many in-betweens in appearance that defy detection except by behavior. Those which are distinguishable show bolder and more masculine beaks if they are males.

Societies prefer nest boxes or covered wicker nests. Incubation is thirteen days. If Societies are to be used as foster parents, the hatching date of the fostered eggs or chicks should coincide as closely as possible with the hatching of their own eggs. Societies are devoted parents, and, if the fledging time of foster chicks should differ from their own, there will be no objection or desertion. Also, they know no nesting season and will go to nest at any time of the year.

The only real problem with the Society Finch is that it is friendly and helpful to a meddlesome degree. When a Society sees another bird preparing a nest, it just naturally wants to assist. When the nest is finished, the Society will help incubate the eggs. The writers have had many Societies which traded nests from day to day with equally friendly Zebra Finches. Shy birds will often desert their nests because of this unwelcome intrusion. Therefore, the wise breeder of rare and shy birds will undoubtedly maintain several pairs of Societies to be used as foster parents in emergencies, but he will house them in a separate aviary or in individual cages.

The Society does not occur in the wild state. Though it is now a distinct and recognized entity, it was evolved by a series of hybridizations which occurred in captivity by the Chinese so long ago that the true parentage is no longer known. There were obviously several Asiatic finches used in the hybridizing. The Sharp Tailed and Striated Mannikins were most likely used, and possibly the Philippine White Breasted Mannikin or a similar subspecies was also used. The general shape of the Society is more similar to the Philippine White Breasted Mannikin than to the Sharp Tailed.

PICTORELLA (*Lonchura pectoralis*, formerly *Donacola pectoralis*)

Also called Pectoral or Pectoralis, the Pictorella is the most beautiful of Australia's mannikins and is surely one of the most attractive members of the entire family. This is a heavy bodied, short tailed bird of four and a half inches. The stout beak is a silvery gray shade, and the feet and legs are a flesh color.

A very dark brown, almost black, area covers the face and throat. Starting at the upper margin of lores, the boundary extends over the eyes and circles down to the sides of the nape and to the lower part of the throat.

The most prominent feature is a broad black chest spangled with large white spots. Females have smaller, flatter, almost rectangular spots.

The rest of the colors are subordinated to the above features and are difficult to describe because of their subtle changes in shade. The rest of the underparts are buffish with sides slightly scalloped in a dark brown shade. The upperparts can variously be described as warm and pale milk chocolate or pinkish-gray or frosty ash-brown. The dark facial area is bordered with a paler and more brownish shade which merges softly with the upperpart coloring. The wings and tail are darker, and there are a number of small white spots on the back and wings.

The Pictorella is a good steady aviary bird with a mild and peaceful disposition. It is hardy after acclimation, but dampness should be avoided to help withstand a tendency towards respiratory problems.

The Pictorella is a shy and rather poor breeder. Best results occur if each pair is given a separate aviary. Some live food and seeding grasses should be added to the diet during the nesting season. Nesting facilities should be provided in a variety of forms. Boxes are usually bypassed in favor of a receptacle that will support a carefully woven covered nest.

Males help to incubate during the day. The incubation period usually lasts from twelve to fourteen days. Young leave the nest between three and four weeks after hatching.

Youngsters are colored with dull brownish shades;the underparts are paler.

CHESTNUT BREASTED MANNIKIN (*Lonchura castaneothorax,* formerly *Donacola castaneothorax*)

The quietly colored but attractively patterned Chestnut Breasted Mannikin is one of Australia's three varieties of Mannikins. Though it is less attractive than the Pictorella, it still is one of the most beautiful of all Mannikins. Moreover, it is very hardy and peaceful.

The body of this four and one half inch bird is neat, compact, and sturdy in appearance. Rarely is a feather out of place, and there usually is a healthy glow to the warm shades of varying browns.

The pale grayish-horn beak contrasts with an extensive facial area of very dark brown. This facial area also covers the throat and is highlighted with small and very finely drawn streaks of golden-yellow radiating outward from the eyes. The crown and back of the neck are frosty, pale brown with small, dark brown streaks. The back is brown, and the rump is bright golden-brown. The tail is dark brown.

The chest is a very attractive shade of golden-brown which is too light to be called chestnut. A bold line of very dark brown separates the chest from the pale buff-white underparts. The flanks are irregularly barred with some dark brown markings.

Chestnut Breasted Finches are difficult to sex. The dance of the male in display is the most reliable indicator, and, fortunately, he dances often. Most males, however, have larger and more massive beaks than females and usually have a bolder and broader dark brown line across the lower chest.

As a breeder, the Chestnut Breasted is only fair. If they should decide to go to nest, these mannikins like to choose from a variety of nests. Incubation usually is from twelve to fifteen days, and the dull-brown young leave the nest between three and four weeks after hatching. Adult plumage starts to appear early in occasional feathers, but the change requires several months to complete.

The writers have always been fond of Chestnut Breasteds not only because they are attractive and have pleasant dispositions but also because their quieter coloring is a good subordinate accent for many of the more brightly colored finches. Up until the Australian ban went into effect, the Chestnut Breasted was always one of the lowest priced of Australian finches.

YELLOW RUMPED MANNIKIN (*Lonchura flaviprymna*)

The Yellow Rumped is the third of Australia's three mannikins, and there are no distinguishing features to make it outstanding in any way except that it is quite a good breeder. It is not popular because of its drabness and has seldom been imported.

The head, neck, and part of the mantle are dull, pale gray changing to brown on the back and wings. The rump and uppertail coverts are yellowish-straw color. The tail is basically brown with dull yellowish-straw on the two central feathers and the outer edges of the other feathers.

The underparts are dull buff with a brighter concentration on the chest. The buff fades to near white in abdominal and ventral areas. The flanks are darker and duskier. The size is approximately four and a half inches.

Sexes are alike, but the hen may be slightly smaller and have a slightly darker shade on the top of the head. The surest indicator is the dancing display of the male.

Breeding information is the same as for the Chestnut Breasted. Young are dull brown above and dull buff below. The gray of the head and yellow of the rump are both absent.

SPICE FINCH (*Lonchura punctulata*)

There are several subspecies and several popular names for this inexpensive and readily available *Munia*. There are some slight variations in size and shading. The most widely used popular name is *Spice*, but it also is frequently called *Nutmeg Finch* and *Spotted Munia*. In some countries Spice Finches are called *Rice Birds* and are considered pests.

The subspecies *lineoventer* from India is the most frequently imported. It is slightly over four inches long including the tail which is slightly more than one inch long. The pattern and coloring are simple. Though it lacks glamour, it has a pleasant appearance and is a good contrast for the more colorful birds. The beak is black, and the head and all upperparts are deep, rich brown. The underparts are dull white with a lacy network of dark brown

124

Two Munias: on the right, the well-known Spice Finch from India; on the left, the seldom imported, smaller, and less colorful Spice Finch or Spotted Munia from the Philippines. Photographed at Palos Verdes Bird Farm.

scallops on the edges of the feathers. These scallops are boldest on the chest and start to fade on the abdomen. The ventral area and undertail coverts are dull off-white. The feet and legs are blackish-gray. In mature birds of good plumage there is a faint overcast of yellow on the rump.

Spice Finches are difficult to sex but are far easier than many finches in which sexes are similar. The beaks of males are distinctly larger and bolder. Males also dance their hopping little jigs and try to sing a bit.

Breeding success comes a little easier with the Spice, but it cannot be called prolific in captivity. Pairs usually choose a standard nestbox especially if the thoughtful bird fancier will add some nesting material and start the work. The addition of some live food helps also to stimulate interest in breeding. If not accustomed to live food beforehand, they may not bother to feed it to chicks.

Incubation is usually twelve or thirteen days. When the youngsters emerge from the nest, they are overall dull, smoky brown. Mature plumage starts to appear in blotches early in life, but maturation is rather slow.

Spice Finches are extremely hardy after a short acclimation period. Usually they are very peaceful, but a few individuals become aggressive with smaller finches. Because they usually can fend for themselves, Spice Finches are often kept successfully with larger birds such as Java Rice Birds and many Weavers. Some fanciers even include them with a few Budgerigars, but this may be risky.

Because of their hardiness and low price, Spices are excellent for beginners.

The Philippine Spice Finch (*Lonchura punctulata cabinisi*) is occasionally imported. In the Philippine Islands it is usually called a Rice Bird or Spotted Nun.

It is a pleasant little bird somewhat smaller and duller in color than its Indian cousin. The size is approximately three and three-fourths inches including the one and one-fourth inch tail. The upper mandible is dark gray, lighter and pearl-shaded at the base. The lower mandible is pearl gray. Eyes are red and brown. The entire head and all upperparts are dull, medium brown with finely drawn paler streaks running lengthwise. The rump has a slight overcast of yellow overlying the basic brown. The shade is more lemon than found on the Indian Spice. Both sides of the tail are grayish-brown.

The scaled underparts on chest, sides, upper abdomen, and undertail coverts are less prominent than found on the Indian Spice. Contrast is lessened because the white is somewhat dusky while the brown is less dark. Removal of one of the scaled chest feathers for close observation shows the pattern structure. Half the feather is downy undercoating. The shaft is pale off-white surrounded by an area of brown. The central area of the web is white, and the tips of the webs are brown.

The lower abdominal area extending to the vent is buff-tinged white.

The Philippine Spice is also very hardy and usually inexpensive, but it is not as good a breeder as the Indian Spice. Sexual differences are the same as in the Indian Spice, but detection is more difficult.

The Malay Spice Finch (subspecies *topela*) is duller than the Indian Spice, and the Javan Spice (subspecies *punctulata*) is very boldly scalloped on the chest.

BLACK HOODED NUN (*Lonchura ferruginosa*)

Three members of the nun family are important in aviculture: Black Hooded Nun, Tri Colored Nun, and White Headed Nun. Apparently they are called Nuns only in the United States and certain areas of Europe. In England they usually are called mannikins. In ornithology both popular and scientific names have been rather badly jumbled. Regardless of which scientific names the writers choose from the puzzling selection, protests are likely to be forthcoming.

The darkly colored Black Hooded Nun is four inches long including the one inch tail. Though dark and somber, it is trimly shaped and patterned with conservative dignity. The large mannikin beak is silver gray. A black hood entirely covers the head, neck, and upper chest area. The rest of the bird is a rich, dark brown, often glossy, with a blackish concentration extending from the center of the abdomen to the ventral area. The rump is a richly glossed red-brown, and the tail covert feathers are like soft, glossy bristles in a paint brush.

Black Hooded Nuns are dark brown with black head and silver beak. A high gloss and uniformity in color add beauty, but the main charm is a subordinating contrast to other more colorful finches. Owned by William Lasky.

This bird is very frequently imported and is very low in price. It serves as a pleasant, though subordinated, contrast to the more showy finches. After a short acclimation period, the Black Hooded Nun is very hardy. It requires meager care and is very peaceful.

Sexing is very difficult. In the extremes, males have larger and more masculine beaks than females. Most are, unfortunately, in the in-between category which makes detection impossible. Behavior is a sure sign. The male sings poorly and dances comically to the hen, but the display is not frequent. However, Nuns rarely rear young in captivity. Young are completely clothed in drab, indistinct grayish-brown.

The bird's natural good grooming does not extend to its bluish-gray feet and toenails. Heavy, unsightly scales quickly develop on legs and feet, and the toenails grow phenomenally and require frequent clipping. If neglected, the toenails become hazardous because of frequent entanglement in branches or wire netting.

The most frequently imported subspecies is *atricapilla* from India.

The Philippine subspecies *jagori* is very slightly smaller and has a warm brownish tinge added to the black hood which seems to add more of a velvet texture. It is not frequently available because all shipments from the Philippines seem to be very sporadic and all too infrequent.

TRI COLORED NUN (*Lonchura malacca*)

The Tri Colored Nun from India and Ceylon has one simple change which removes all of the somber darkness of the Black Hooded Nun. The

127

chestnut breast and flanks are replaced by bright white. The black concentration on the central portion of the abdomen remains. The Tri Colored Nun is like the Black Hooded Nun in flashy, formal attire. Everything else is the same as in the Black Hooded Nun except the price which is usually only slightly higher.

WHITE HEADED NUN (*Lonchura maja*)

The White Headed Nun is not as readily available as either of the above and is a little more costly. The body shape and coloring is similar to the Black Hooded Nun except for a white head. The white is softly tinged with traces of brown on the crown, and the change from the white to the brown on the body is softly blended instead of sharply divided. The paint brush bristles of the rump and uppertail are even brighter red-brown than those of the Black Hooded Nun.

White Headed Nuns are easier to sex than the two previous Nuns because females have a dull, dusty appearance on the white head. This feature can be misleading because, if the ages differ, there may be minute variations. The writers also check differences in beaks as a further precaution.

This species requires the same meager care as described for the Black Hooded Nun.

A close relative, the Javan White Headed Nun, has a very dark brown chin and throat. It rarely reaches the United States.

There are several mannikins from a wide range in the Far East which are seldom imported. In some cases, they are not particularly attractive; in other cases, there may be little interest in exporting them from the country of origin. Occasionally, some of tnese birds are included as substitutes in large shipments. All should receive the same care as given to the Spice Finch and Black Hooded Nuns.

STRIATED MANNIKIN or WHITE BACKED MUNIA (*Lonchura striata*)

The widespread Striated Mannikin has several races and minor variations. A broad white band across the rump and an even broader white band across the lower chest and abdomen are finely striated with brown. Facial, throat, and upper chest areas are blackish. The rest of this four inch bird is dark, dusky brown with fine white striations. The pointed tail is also blackish.

The Sharp Tailed Mannikin is represented by two subspecies of Striated Finches: *acuticauda* and *subsquamicollis*. The Sharp Tailed Mannikin shows less black and more brown in the face, throat, and upper chest. The tail is longer and more sharply pointed.

The Dusky Munia (*Lonchura fuscans*) is completely dark and dusky brown. The beak is dark brown on the upper mandible and silver gray on the lower mandible.

The White Bellied Mannikin (*Lonchura leucogaster*) is approximately four inches long including the one inch tail. It is shaped remarkably like the

Society Finch. The basic color is dark chocolate-brown with fine white feather shafts giving a striated effect on the back, wings, and rump. There are buffish margins on the brown tail feathers. The abdomen is white with brown spots in the outer areas and a few smaller spots in the interior of the white area.

Sexes are very difficult to determine. Immature birds are much paler.

The race described above is the Philippine subspecies *everetti* which is really a paler brown with less of a blackish shade than other races. Apparently rare, even in the Philippines, it is seldom imported. When it is available, it is usually a substitution and seldom exceeds two percent of the shipment.

Though they have never noticed any reference to such a possibility, the writers believe the White Bellied Mannikin must be one of the birds used in producing the Society Finch.

INDIAN SILVERBILL (*Lonchura malabarica* or *Euodice malabarica*)

Neither the Indian nor African Silverbill could be considered attractive; both are inexpensive, hardy, and good breeders. They require little care and will rear their young on seed alone.

The Indian Silverbill has a silver-gray beak and a white area covering rump and uppertail coverts. The upperparts are brown with very dark tail and flight feathers. The underparts are whitish with a shade of buff. The throat and undertail covers are white without the shade of buff. Indian Silverbills show greater contrasts and are therefore more attractive. The overall size is approximately four and a half inches including the sharply pointed tail.

Reasonably difficult to sex, males usually have larger and more masculine beaks. The males sing pleasant little warbles and dance their funny, hopping jigs. The standard finch box is preferred, and incubation is twelve to thirteen days.

AFRICAN SILVERBILL (*Lonchura cantans* or *Euodice cantans*)

The African Silverbill is the same as the Indian variety except for a uniform buffish-brown on upper as well as lower parts. The wings and tail are only slightly darker than the general body coloring. The rump is brownish instead of white.

The two species freely hybridize, and offspring are easily recognizable because they have pinkish rumps.

BRONZE WINGED MANNIKIN (*Lonchura cucullatus*, formerly *Spermestes cucullatus*)

The lively little Bronze Winged Mannikin from Africa lacks a bright and quickly noticeable color scheme, but it has a few distinctive features which make it a popular aviary bird. It is hardy after a short acclimation period and is usually readily available at a very reasonable price. Much of its charm lies in its small three and one-fourth inch size, which includes a one inch tail, and in its gregarious and friendly manner. Its constant activity and unobtrusiveness are strong points in its favor. During the breeding season it may show protective signs of aggressiveness, but on the average it is very peaceful.

The diet is mostly seeds and a little greenfood. Live food is helpful during the breeding season, but parents must become accustomed to it beforehand.

The Bronze Winged Mannikin does not have the heavy appearance found in several mannikins. It is neat, trim, and well-groomed. The beak is typically mannikin in shape but a little smaller in proportion than most. The upper mandible is black and the lower is pearl-gray.

The head, neck, and upper chest are dark brown with a bronzed metallic cast concentrated mostly on the crown. The back and wings are dull, dark brown; a sizeable metallic deep green patch occurs on the shoulder area and again on the sides of the chest. A large area covering rump, uppertail coverts, undertail coverts, flanks, and sides are boldly and irregularly scalloped with brown on white. These irregularities help to relieve monotony of the otherwise too well-tailored and rather dull pattern. Underparts are white except for the previously noted features, and the tail on both sides is a very dark brown almost approaching black. The sharp division between the white underparts and the dark brown, rounded bib of the upper chest is one of the most outstanding features.

Sexing is very difficult. Though there is often a difference in the size of the beaks, it often is too slight to be noticeable. Also, the skull of the female is slightly narrower. If both sexes are held in the hand and viewed in the right light, the male can be distinguished by the richer bronze gloss on the crown. Behavior is the most reliable sign. Males dance and try to sing for the females.

The Bronze Wing is a better breeder than most mannikins although many are very slow to start. Both birds help in building the nest. Incubation lasts approximately twelve to thirteen days. Both parents feed the young. Fledging time is about three weeks. Youngsters are mostly dull brownish with no traces of the bronzed areas. Underparts are grayish.

There are two races of Bronze Wings. The one described here is the West African subspecies *cucullatus* which is the one frequently imported. The subspecies *scutatus* covers a wide range in Eastern Africa but is not often found in aviculture. The glossy green patch on the sides is either absent or much smaller. There are also barely noticeable paler browns on the head.

BLUE BILLED MANNIKIN or TWO COLORED MANNIKIN
(*Lonchura poensis bicolor* or *Spermestes poensis bicolor*)

The Two Colored Mannikin from Africa is very similar to the Bronze Wing except for the following differences: a larger beak which is all blue-gray instead of having a darker upper mandible and a paler lower mandible; a color separation on the upper chest which is lower and not as rounded; a color which is more glossy black than brown; scalloping which is restricted to the sides and, though less extensive, is bolder and more uniform. The glossed areas are more extensive, and the body is just a trifle heavier.

A subspecies, *Lonchura poensis poensis* or *Spermestes poensis poensis*, is usually called the Black and White Mannikin. It is the same as the Two Colored Mannikin except that the rump and uppertail coverts are scalloped with black on white.

Both of these African birds are very rare in aviculture and far less plentiful in the wild state than the Bronze Winged Mannikin.

Care, feeding, and breeding information are the same as for the Bronze-Wing.

RUFOUS BACKED MANNIKIN (*Lonchura nigriceps* or *Spermestes nigriceps*)

The Rufous Backed Mannikin from Africa is also called the Chestnut Backed and Red Backed Mannikin. In general characteristics and appearance, it resembles the Two Colored Mannikin, but it has a chestnut color on the mantle and part of the wings.

A subspecies (*minor*) is the same but slightly smaller.

The Rufous Backed is also rarely imported.

BIB MANNIKIN or DWARF MANNIKIN (*Lonchura nana* or *Spermestes nana*)

The Bib Mannikin, which is the smallest mannikin, is about three inches long and comes from Madagascar.

It is very rarely imported and is not particularly interesting. Except for a small black chin and throat bib, the colors are dull and muddy-brownish on the upperparts, grayish on the head, and pale grayish-buff on the underparts.

MAGPIE MANNIKIN (*Amauresthes fringilloides*)

The rarely imported Magpie Mannikin from Africa is nearly five inches long. It is rarely imported because it occurs out of the regions from which bird shipments come. Though lacking a dainty appearance, because it is heavily built and has a large beak, it is nevertheless a rather handsome bird. It is hardy and aggressive and should be kept with larger weavers and whydahs, Java Rice Birds, and other birds of similar size and disposition.

The large beak is grayish-horn, and the head and throat are glossy black with metallic shadings. Underparts are white and are tinged with buff in the lower areas. The sides have irregular shadings of black which gradually turns to brown on the flanks. The back and wings are varying shades of brown with some centers of the feathers blackish and some feather shafts white. The rump and tail coverts are shaded with dark gray mixed with brown, and the tail is dark gray with a hint of brown.

Females have slightly smaller beaks, less bold appearing heads, and slightly less bright white on the chest.

CUTTHROAT or RIBBON FINCH (*Amadina fasciata*)

The very popular and readily available Cutthroat is the most frequently imported of Africa's mannikins. It is an ideal aviary bird, a good breeder, and very hardy after a very short acclimation period. The size of four and a half inches long, including the one and a half inch tail, affords some danger of aggressiveness to smaller birds. This is not a tendency found in all Cutthroats, but it would be wiser to give them plenty of room in uncrowded aviaries if they are to be housed with waxbills. The most likely time for such traits to appear is during the nesting season.

The writers do not consider Cutthroats to be ideal cage birds. Too many are likely to be confined in cages which are too small. Many feather problems may develop. One common complaint is melanism in which a smoky shade of dark gray overcomes the natural colors.

The thick mannikin beak is pale horn in color. Small bristles at the base of the beak and near the lores extend downwards to the corner of the mouth. This is perhaps an indication that the Cutthroat likes to catch insects in flight.

A precise and bright accent on the male is a broad ribbon of red cutting across the throat and extending far onto the sides of the neck. The rest of the color pattern is an irregular mosaic camouflage of rich earthy shades of pinkish-browns with buff, gray, and blackish accents.

The top of the head, back, and rump are irregularly striated with brown and near black. These striations are faint on the head and bolder on the back and rump. The shoulders, scapulars, and secondary flight coverts have pale tips on the feathers with flattened V-shaped dark markings to separate the two shades. The outer sides of the flight feathers show a paler shade of brown. The dark tail has dusty-white tips on both of the upper and lower sides.

The underparts have a basic pale pinkish-brown deepening on the lower chest and upper abdomen before fading to pale off-white on lower abdomen and ventral area. The undertail coverts return to pale brown with some dark circular striations. The chest and sides have some dark curved lines to provide a continuation of the forest camouflage pattern. The markings in these areas are similar to those of the shoulders.

Females lack the red-ribboned throat and have fainter striations. The camouflaged effect is less pronounced because of less bold dark markings.

Immature birds resemble females but can easily be distinguished because the pinkish-brown is still absent. They are duller in color and have the thick, fleshy corners of the mouth characteristic of most youngsters. The appearance of pinkish-brown on the chest with no development of a red throat ribbon is a good indication that the youngster will be a female. Females are always in the minority because many of the supposed females turn out to be immature males.

Cutthroats are delightful in many ways. The males are particularly amusing because they thoroughly enjoy displaying, and they sing and dance as often as possible.

A good pair is really prolific if not disturbed. A box slightly larger than the standard finch nestbox is ideal, but they also do well in the standard size.

The average clutch is four, and incubation may run from twelve to fifteen days. Fledging time is between three to four weeks.

Alexander's Cutthroat (subspecies *alexanderi*) from Abyssinia has more bold black markings both above and below. It is quite rare in aviculture. A South African subspecies, *meridionalis*, is similar to Alexander's Cutthroat except that the bill is smaller. It is also rarely available. Prices on both these subspecies are far higher than for the common Cutthroat, and color variations are slight. Therefore, in most instances, there will be little extra demand.

RED HEADED FINCH (*Amadina erythrocephala*)

The very attractive Red Headed Finch from South Africa is seldom available. Females are particularly rare. It is very hardy, heavy bodied, and large. The overall size of five inches includes a one and three-fourths inch tail. There is a tendency to become aggressive with small birds. These birds feed on a standard finch or parakeet diet with the addition of some live food.

There is a very obvious relationship to the Cutthroat. The beak is the same; and the mosaic camouflage pattern is only slightly changed.

The head of the male is a glossy, deep rust-red which is brightest on the forehead, crown, cheeks, and throat, and then fades into gray on the neck. The female lacks this red. The eyes are dark, and the lores are like gray felt. The row of bristles at the corners of the mouth are like those of the Cutthroat.

The neck, back, shoulders, and wings are a warm shade of grayish-brown. The secondary scapulars and wing coverts have pale spots caused by pale tipped feathers with fine dark lines separating the two shades. The lower rump has fine dark lines and broader pale bars. The tail is grayish-brown.

The underparts are very attractive with brighter contrasts. Starting at the lower extremities of the reddish throat, fine whitish bars near the tips of the feathers are banded on both sides by fine lines of deep brownish-black. The bars become broader and brighter as they reach the chest where they become elliptical in shape. Along the sides these markings become quite large and are spaced farther apart. The spots disappear in the central area of lower chest and abdomen. The base coloring below the white spots is a pale, earthy brown fading into off-white at the lower part of the abdomen and a dusty, dull buff mottled with darker gray on the undertail coverts.

The dull grayish underside of the tail is brightened with broad white margins at the tips.

CHAPTER 9

Waxbills

Of the twenty-eight species of Waxbills all are native to Africa except for the Sydney Waxbill of Australia, the Green Avadavat or Green Strawberry of India, and the Strawberry from India and other parts of the Orient.

Most waxbills are very pretty and well designed despite the lack, in most cases, of bright colors. Contrasts, unusual accents, precise patterns, and subtle changes in shading abound in this family. Nearly all waxbills are small. Many are nervous, alert, and ever active; and their sharp, rapid movements add a lively charm in a mixed collection.

As a rule, waxbills are very peaceful. A few become mildly quarrelsome during the breeding season, and a few become habitual feather pluckers if crowded.

Only a few members of this family can be considered good breeders. Unlike Australian Grassfinches, those waxbills which come from areas of reversed seasons are quite willing to change to our season after the first year. Even the comparatively easy ones must be given special attention to satisfy the characteristic insectivorous nature. If live foods are not provided, there is little chance for successful breeding. Nestling food is also advisable. The general procedures in breeding waxbills are outlined under Fire Finches and Cordon Bleus.

Live food is advisable at all times of the year even though waxbills can exist on a diet of seed alone. Mealworms are the most readily available and most widely used, but they must be rationed. Other useful live foods are aphis, fruit flies, gentles (or maggots), live ant cocoons, and enchytrae (or white worms).

Since most live foods, except mealworms, are not available commercially or in a reliably steady supply, the writers especially try to teach waxbills to take an insect mixture to fulfill the need for live foods. This mixture, along with mealworms, usually fulfills the requirements. Other live foods are helpful in stimulating interest in nesting and usually necessary for insuring the lasting interest in feeding youngsters.

The general conception is that waxbills are delicate, but the writers feel that the only delicacy occurs during the acclimation period. It is the dealer's responsibility to put all importations through the initial and most danger ridden acclimation period and the bird fancier's responsibility to meet the needs of the longer and easier test of complete adaptation to climate.

Both of these aspects of bird care are explained earlier in the book, and so there is no need for repetition except to say that if both phases are judiciously carried out waxbills will be as hardy as any other finch.

The waxbill family contains many of the most popular and most readily available of all aviary subjects. The season of availability is from spring through fall for those birds of the Senegal area which are the least expensive and best known. Importations from South and East Africa are infrequent and usually come in late spring or early summer.

INDIAN STRAWBERRY (*Amandava amandava amandava*)

Also known as Red Avadavat, Bombay Avadavat, or Tiger Finch, the Strawberry from India is one of the greatest favorites with bird lovers. It is inexpensive, peaceful, hardy, and nearly always available. The coloring is attractive, especially in its in-color phase, and the male has one of the most pleasant of all singing voices among avicultural finches. Though the song is small and often lost in an aviary, it is easily heard in a cage. In its out-of-color phase, it has a dull ineffective coloring which somehow still attracts bird fanciers.

The Indian Strawberry is slightly over three and a half inches long including a tail of one inch. It, along with its subspecies, has the only seasonal color variation in the waxbill family.

While in color during spring, summer, and fall, the male has a rusty-red on the head, chest, abdomen, and rump. The upperparts are dull brown, and white spots are sprinkled generously on the wings and chest. The beak in both sexes is red.

Females and males out-of-color are very similar. The red fades into a dull and dark yellowish straw shade in all areas except the rump. The white spots disappear from the chest but remain on the brown upperparts. Sexes are distinguishable during this phase because the rump is duller, and the spots are smaller in females.

Immature Strawberries are soft and dull brown with a paler shade on the chest. The white spots are absent.

Strawberries are difficult to breed; but, if conditions are right and sufficient insectile and live food are given, many become surprisingly prolific.

Usually there is some fading of color in captivity; but, if Strawberries are kept in aviaries planted with insect attracting shrubs and flowers, the color is more likely to stay bright.

CHINESE or ORIENTAL STRAWBERRY (*Amandava amandava punicea*)

The male Chinese Strawberry from Java, Indo China, and various parts of the Orient is prettier than the Indian Strawberry because it has a richer shade of red. Everything else in this subspecies is the same except that it is a trifle smaller and is usually a little higher in price.

GREEN STRAWBERRY or GREEN AVADAVAT (*Amandava formosa,*
formerly *Stictospiza formosa*)

The beautiful Green Strawberry from India is not often available and is considerably higher in price than the other Strawberry Finches.

In captivity many individuals become severe feather pluckers. This is a difficult habit to overcome; and, if plucked often enough, the feathers may not return. A good preventative measure is to give these birds plenty of uncrowded aviary space and a variety of live food. Such an environment is also conducive to breeding success.

The bill is red in a very bright but very deep shade. The total length is approximately four inches including the one-inch tail. In the male, the upperparts are a bright shade of dark green, and the rump is slightly paler. The tail is blackish.

Underparts are yellow, brightest on the abdomen and chest. The sides and flanks are boldly marked with alternating black and white bars. This easily is the most prominent feature. The face, cheeks, and throat are a dull smooth shade of greenish-yellow.

Females are much duller in every respect except for the bill. The green areas are shaded with gray, and the yellow areas are quite drab. The flank and side bars are no longer brightly contrasting. The black is greatly reduced in intensity and width.

The writers admire the unusual and attractive appearance of the Green Strawberry but do not recommend it for beginners or for crowded collections. Although it is hardy after a rather delicate acclimation period, there is a tendency for a few individuals to be afflicted with respiratory problems in damp climates. The main reason for a reluctant recommendation is, of course, the tiresome feather plucking.

AFRICAN FIRE FINCH or SENEGAL FIRE FINCH (*Lagonosticta senegala*)

Of the several species of African Fire Finches the Senegal or Common Fire is the most frequently imported, the lowest priced, and still one of the prettiest. It sometimes is called the Ruddy Waxbill.

As with most Fire Finches, it is extremely delicate until it is acclimated. After that period, it becomes very hardy. Most importers separate Fire Finches from other finches upon arrival because of the necessity for extra care for the first two or three weeks.

Fire Finches are among the most calm of all finches. They rarely panic; and, when a dealer tries to catch one in a net, most will circle the aviary and fly down to the floor. In fact, Fire Finches spend a great part of time near the ground and are much happier in a planted aviary which has some growing grasses. They are gregarious, happy, and peaceful but will protect their nests.

Many fanciers who live in areas free from predators, and this includes cats, turn their Fire Finches outside their aviaries in the summertime. They rarely stray away and often will nest in the garden. Recapture is usually no problem if a safety door has been built on the aviary. A supply of seed placed inside the vestibule and an open door will easily entice them back inside. Accidental escapees are also easy to recapture because of their desire to get back into the aviary to be with other birds.

This Fire Finch is three and three-fourths inches long including a tail of one and three-eighths inches.

The adult male has a red bill with a faint black stripe down the centers of both upper and lower mandibles. A yellow eye ring is very prominent, especially in birds two years old. The deep glossy red on the head and chest fades into dull brown at the lower end of the abdomen, vent, and undertail coverts. The underside of the tail is dark brownish-gray. Several white spots mark the red sides of the chest. Feet and legs are light brown.

The upperside is mostly brown starting in the center of the rear crown. The rump is bright red, and there are traces of red near the shoulders. The wings and tail are darker brown.

Females are nearly all brown, paler on the undersides and darker on the uppersides. The eye ring is absent, but the bill is the same as in the male. Red forms an illdefined eyebrow and covers the lores and rump. The white spots on the sides and flanks are slightly more numerous than in the male and are sprinkled on the chest. However, because of the duller background they are less distinct.

Immature birds are like the female, but they lack the red eyebrow and white spots. By the time these features start to appear, the youngster, if a male, will also have a few red feathers in the chest.

The distinction between youngsters and adult females is very important because females are always in far shorter supply than males. Errors on this point are all too frequent. Fortunately, the young show signs of maturing after six weeks and are usually fully colored at ten weeks.

Fire Finches are probably the best breeders in the waxbill family. Incubation is usually twelve or thirteen days, and young leave the nest anywhere between seventeen to twenty-one days. Weaning time varies from one to two weeks on the average after the young have left the nest.

Live food should be given during the nesting season, but in planted aviaries the parents will usually gather a sufficient supply if the competition is not too great.

There are several very similar subspecies scattered over Africa. Differences in most are very slight and include minor variations in shades of reds, browns, and/or size of spots. Most of these differences are so slight that they would pass unnoticed in the eyes of aviculturists. One, however, from South Africa not only has larger spots but is also much hardier in shipping and acclimation.

137

BAR BREASTED FIRE FINCH (*Lagonosticta rufopicta*)

The Bar Breasted Fire Finch, infrequently available, is very similar to the Common African Fire Finch; but the spots are far more numerous and larger on the chest, particularly in the female.

In this species the female is very much like the male except for a paler shade of red on the throat and facial areas.

Another distinguishing feature to avoid confusion with the Common Fire Finch is a blackish shade on the outer half of the tail and a reddish shade on the inner half. By nature, it is more shy than the Senegal Fire Finch, but this trait is far more noticeable in a planted aviary.

JAMESON'S FIRE FINCH (*Lagonosticta jamesoni*)

Jameson's Fire Finch, also called Jameson's Ruddy Waxbill, is frequently confused with the Blue Billed Fire Finch even though ornithologists classify it as a separate species. At any rate, both African species are very similar, and aviculturists and dealers could be excused if they group both birds into one category. It is not as frequently imported as the Common Fire Finch, nor is it as brightly colored. In most cases, it is also higher priced.

Jameson's Fire Finch is three and three-fourths inches long including the one and one-half inch tail. The beak is slightly longer than that of the Common Fire Finch and is a deep pearl blue-gray.

The male has a dull rose shade on most of the head except for a grayish-brown concentration on the crown. The back is a dull reddish-brown changing gradually to a deep rich red on the rump, uppertail coverts, and nearly half of the tail feathers which show red on the outer webs and black on the inner webs. When the tail feathers are folded, the black is not visible. The lower half of the tail is dull black.

A charcoal black on the underparts starts in the center of the abdomen and extends all the way back to the tips of the underside of the tail.

Females are duller editions of the male. The head is more brown than red. The wings and back are brown, and the rump is red though subdued and less extensive than in the male. The tail is black on both sides with some red on the upper side. The chest, abdomen, throat, and eyebrows are a paler shade of rose subdued by a brownish tinge. The charcoal shade of the female's abdomen is absent and is less conspicuous on both the undertail coverts and the undersides of the tail. The ventral area is pale buffish with a rose cast. Contrasts in the female are greatly reduced in comparison to those of the male.

BLUE BILLED FIRE FINCH or DARK FIRE FINCH (*Lagonosticta rubricata*)

Several subspecies of the Blue Billed Fire Finch include Shelley's, Bates', Reichenow's, Uganda, and Kenya Blue Billed Fire Finches, but differences are only slight. The entire species, in fact, is difficult to distinguish from Jameson's Fire Finch.

For the most part, the several races show a darker shade of red on the head and breast than Jameson's. Ornithologists have separated the two species mainly because of a difference in the second primary flight feather. The first feather is vestigal and does not seem to count from the aviculturist's viewpoint, but the second feather is very slender because the inner web is cut back in a graduated manner so that it is noticeably changed from that of the Jameson's. To be sure of the correct identification, however, one should have both birds in hand so that comparison can be made side by side.

The remaining Fire Finches depart drastically from the generally conceived idea of avicultural Fire Finches. All so far are very rare in aviculture, but some are exceptionally beautiful and would be ideal if they could be made available. A few are not known in aviculture and are omitted from this book.

BLACK BELLIED FIRE FINCH (*Lagonosticta rara or Estrilda rara*)

The Black Bellied Waxbill or Black Bellied Fire Finch is very similar to Jameson's Fire Finch except for the following characteristics: the black of the abdomen and tail extends up into the breast; the red has more of a wine-colored shade; and no white spots appear on the sides of the chest and flanks. The wings are dark brown. The bill is black on the upper mandible and crimson on the lower mandible.

Females have gray on the sides of the face, chin, and throat. Immatures are dull grayish-brown except for the crimson uppertail coverts.

The average length is four inches, and it comes from parts of Africa which are remote insofar as avicultural shipments are concerned.

VINACEOUS FIRE FINCH (*Lagonosticta vinacea*)

The quietly lovely Vinaceous Fire Finch is one of the most distinctive members of the African Fire Finch family. Also called the Black Faced Waxbill, this very rare and highly coveted species has most features of the Common Fire Finch except for a dominant black face on the male.

The Vinaceous Fire Finch is a very handsome species with great dignity in its conservative color scheme. The eyes are reddish, and the grayish-olive beak also shows a tinge of rose.

The male has a quiet gray forehead and crown which offsets a black facial area surrounding the eyes, cheeks, and throat. A very narrow band on the forehead is also black. The basic coloring on the rest of the bird is a dusky vinous coloring with various accent shadings. The upperparts are richer, and the underparts are softer in a slightly paler shade. The flights are shaded with brown, and the visible parts of tail feathers are more boldly shaded with crimson. Most hidden or underlying parts of tail feathers are blackish.

The sides of the chest and flanks are dotted with small white spots. Abdominal areas show a duskiness which increases to black on the undertail coverts.

139

Females lack the black facial and throat areas. The white spots on the sides are present, but much of the lovely vinous shading is replaced or subdued by neutral shades of brown.

BLACK FACED FIRE FINCH (*Lagonosticta nigricollis* or *Lagonosticta larvata*)

The Black Faced Fire Finch is also an extreme African rarity. It is much like the Vinaceous Fire Finch in basic pattern, but a heavy shade of dusky gray on both sexes is mixed with the vinous shadings in all areas except the rump, uppertail coverts, and tail. There are three races which show slight variations.

CORDON BLEU (*Uraeginthus bengalus*)

The beautiful Cordon Bleu adequately fulfills the many reasons for its high ranking popularity. It is one of the few finches with a beautiful shade of sky blue. The shape is gracefully simple and seems designed for its highly active but peaceful nature. Cordon Bleus are inexpensive and usually available.

Cordon Bleus are usually imported from Africa in the spring until late fall. They are hardy only if carefully acclimated. For two or three weeks after importation, Cordon Bleus must receive every consideration in their new environment and above all must not be overcrowded. They are subject to enteritis during this period of delicacy. In this period, the same care should be given to African Fire Finches; but the Cordon Bleu is really somewhat easier to acclimate than the Fire Finch.

The four and three-fourths inches of length includes a long slender tail of two inches in the male. The tail of the female is slightly shorter. The beak is a soft shade of rose darkening to gray at the tips. It looks as if it has been sealed in a silvery cast.

The male has a lustrous sky blue on the face, cheeks, and much of the underparts. A dusky, dark tan covers the center of the lower chest, abdomen, vent and undertail coverts. The uppersides of the tail coverts and tail are blue. The rest of the upperparts including the top of head and neck are mouse brown. A very bright accent is a vivid maroon patch almost elliptically shaped and diagonally placed across the cheek.

The female lacks the cheek patch and has less extensive blue on the chest and sides. The shade of blue is also somewhat paler.

Cordon Bleus are so charming and pretty that they always are among the first of African finches to catch the eye of newcomers and are therefore responsible for kindling the first interest in many bird fanciers. The writers are fully as fond of the Cordon Bleu today after having handled thousands as they were when they were captivated by their first few pairs long ago.

Many fanciers successfully breed Cordon Bleus, but many others are disappointed. Breeding success is erratic and is dependent upon many factors. They will usually do very well if given a variety of small live foods as well as mealworms. They like planted aviaries and as much seclusion as possible. Overly friendly and helpful birds such as Zebra and Society Finches as well as overbearing bullies should be removed.

Both sexes help to build the nest, but the hen sits during the twelve to thirteen day incubation period. Young leave the nest after about fifteen days and are weaned during the next ten days. Immatures are like females and are very difficult to distinguish except for darker beaks, but the maroon cheek patch starts to show at an early age of approximately five months.

There are several races or subspecies of Cordon Bleus. Ornithologists call all three species Cordon Bleu and designate this one as the Red Cheeked Cordon Bleu. Aviculturists prefer a little broader distinction in species but do not pay much attention to subspecies because the variations are only slight.

The race described above is *bengalus* from Senegal. Most shipments of African birds are from this area, and *bengalus* is therefore the most frequently imported.

The Abyssinian Cordon Bleu (subspecies *schoanus*) is infrequently imported and is therefore considerably rarer in aviculture as well as more expensive. It shows more extensive blue on the abdomen and a paler shade of brown above.

BLUE WAXBILL or ANGOLAN CORDON BLEU (*Uraeginthus angolensis*)

The Blue Waxbill, also called Blue Breasted Waxbill and Angolan Cordon Bleu, is much like the Cordon Bleu. It is far less frequently imported but is a very desirable avicultural subject. The cost is usually a little higher.

Males are distinctively different in that they lack the maroon cheek patch and have slightly more extensive blue on the underparts. The shade of blue is also slightly paler but far more lustrous. The beak is slightly darker than that of the Cordon Bleu. The body is also slightly shorter and stockier than that of the Cordon Bleu.

Females are very similar to Cordon Bleu females, but female Blue Waxbills have darker beaks.

The Blue Waxbill is a more prolific breeder in captivity than the Cordon Bleu, but requirements are the same.

Judging from a large number of shipments, the Blue Waxbill seems hardier than the Cordon Bleu and requires a shorter acclimation period.

BLUE CAPPED CORDON BLEU (*Uraeginthus cyanocephalus*)

If it should ever become readily available, the Blue Capped Cordon Bleu would be a welcome addition to aviculture even though it is somewhat shyer than the Cordon Bleu. Those few aviculturists fortunate enough to receive any have reported very favorably on this attractive bird. It has a narrow range in Eastern Africa; and, though it is not considered rare on a local basis, bird shipments are very infrequent from these areas.

141

The male is distinctive in that the entire head and neck are blue instead of having brown on top of the head and nape. The female is very much like the female Blue Waxbill but is paler and sometimes has blue on the forehead. Youngsters are paler than females and have dusky bills.

RED EARED WAXBILL (*Estrilda troglodytes*)

The Red Eared Waxbill is the most numerous of African importations and is, therefore, understandably called the Common Waxbill. Unfortunately, the Common Waxbill name is also applied by ornithologists and by residents of Africa to the St. Helena Waxbill which is similar but a very distinct and different species. The popular name of Black Rumped Waxbill recognizes the distinction between the two birds, but another popular name of Gray Waxbill is not only unfair but totally misleading.

The lively and softly lovely Red Eared Waxbill is just three and one-fourth inches long including a highly active tail of one and one-fourth inches. The ever active nature of this little bird is most evident in its constantly moving black tail.

This vivacious tail twitcher is best observed in a small flock perched in a small bare tree or branch. The pertness and activity will charm even the most non-esthetic person in the world.

The basic coloring is pale brown with a faint rose cast. The uppersides are darker and more brown, and the undersides are paler with the rose shading far more visible especially in a concentration on the abdominal areas. The undertail coverts are very pale. Newly imported adults are always brighter in color than those maintained in captivity for any length of time.

The beak is red, and the red extends in a conspicuous eyebrow extending through the lores, around the eyes, and tapering backwards to the back of the head.

Males have broader and bolder eyebrows and a deeper shade of red on the beak. The abdomen is especially a good sex indicator because the male has a much greater concentration of rose in this area.

Upon careful observation, a very faint barred effect of darker and paler browns will be noticed in far less prominence than is found in the St. Helena Waxbill.

Red Eared Waxbills are easily acclimated, hardy, very inexpensive, and usually available. They should be included in every collection of small finches.

Every group of advantages must have some drawback, and the Red Eared Waxbill is no exception. In this case, the exception is the nearly complete disinterest in breeding. Though several successes have been recorded, the percentage is very low.

The nest is built very low to the ground and, similar to many waxbills, has two compartments. One is for the female and eggs, and the one above is for the male for roosting at night. Incubation lasts for twelve to thirteen days, and a variety of small live foods must be provided for complete success. The young stay in the nest nearly three weeks, and, upon emergence, are dulled by dark grayish upperparts and light brownish-gray underparts.

After a few weeks, the young resemble females; but the width of the eyebrow is evident even though it is not completely filled out. Sexes can usually be determined even at this early age by the eyebrows and not in the similarity of the rosy abdomen.

Despite its prevalence, there are no subspecies yet recorded.

CRIMSON RUMPED WAXBILL *(Estrilda rhodopyga)*

The seldom imported and slightly higher priced Crimson Rumped Waxbill from East Africa is three and one-half inches long including a tail of one and one-fourth inches. It is similar in many respects to the Red Eared Waxbill but is less attractive. The general coloring is much flatter and harder than the soft and rosy warmth found in the Red Eared Waxbill.

The beak is black with a hint of red at the lower rims of the upper mandible. The red eyebrows are similar to those in the Red Eared but are more of a red than a rose shade. The browns are more harsh and unattractive than those of the rose tinted Red Eared Waxbill. Upperparts are dull medium brown, and underparts are pale buffy-brown. Faint striations of alternating darker and lighter shades cover most of the body, but they are most noticeable on the undertail coverts and to a lesser extent on the sides and back.

Some color compensation occurs in the dull red markings scattered on the wing coverts and in the more heavily concentrated rump area. The tail is dark brown, nearly black.

Females have narrower eye stripes, and immatures lack this feature completely for a few weeks. Breeding requirements are the same as for the Red Eared Waxbill, but success is even more rare.

One subspecies, *centralis*, is slightly darker in overall coloring.

ST. HELENA WAXBILL *(Estrilda astrild)*

There are several races of the St. Helena Waxbill spread over a large area in Africa which give it the suitable ornithological name of Common Waxbill; but the nominate subspecies, *astrild*, is the most outstanding. This South African species is called the Greater St. Helena Waxbill.

Four and a half inches long, including a tail slightly longer than one and a half inches, the Greater St. Helena Waxbill is really little more than a glorified edition of the Red Eared Waxbill; and the smaller subspecies are even less distinguished.

The general coloring is the same as in the Red Eared Waxbill, but there are noticeable differences. Prominent but finely drawn striations cover nearly all of the color scheme. Black covers the underside of the tail as well as undertail coverts and an area covering the ventral and central abdominal area. A strong tint of rose starts on the center of the chest and extends to the black area. The upper tail is dark brown. Feet are brownish-black. The red eyebrow and beak are the same as in the Red Eared Waxbill.

143

Males have bolder and more distinct bars than females. Usually, if mature, the eyebrows of males are bolder and broader than those of females. Beaks are deeper red in the males, and the abdominal rose is richer.

St. Helena Waxbills have the charming tail twitching mannerisms of Red Eared Waxbills but are much better breeders. They are less readily available than Red Ears and are higher priced. They are hardy after a short acclimation period.

For best breeding success, St. Helenas ask for a sizable aviary with protection from overly friendly birds such as Zebras and Societies or bullies and from overly inquisitive bird fanciers. Otherwise, they desert easily. Live food is necessary. Incubation is twelve or thirteen days but does not always start with the first egg. Chicks are in the nest a little over three weeks, and when they fledge they show only a few traces of barring on the head and no shades of pink or red.

The Pintailed Whydah parasitizes the St. Helena Waxbill's nest, and the young of both species are remarkably similar.

The race known aviculturally as Lesser St. Helena Waxbill is the subspecies *angolensis*. It is far more frequently imported than the above but is less distinctive. The size is nearly one half inch shorter, and colors are slightly less bold. The black area in the center starts near the vent, and the rose starts at the center of the abdomen.

The several other subspecies show very minor variations in size and shades of coloring.

The St. Helena Waxbill has been introduced into many of the islands in the South Pacific area and South America.

ORANGE CHEEKED WAXBILL (*Estrilda melpoda melpoda*)

The attractive Orange Cheeked Waxbill is one of Africa's most popular and inexpensive waxbills. It is a very fast flyer as well as being constantly active; and it, therefore, is a vivacious addition to any collection. The disposition is gregarious and peaceful.

The size is three and three-fourths inches long including the one and one-fourth inch tail. The two most prominent features are a bright coral red beak and a large orange cheek patch which covers lores, eyes, and most of the facial area.

The rest of the head is quietly colored starting with dark gray fading to pearl-gray on the throat and chest. The central abdominal area has a concentration of orange against a pale gray background. The sides are tinted with a brownish shade. Undertail coverts are gray, and the underside of the tail is grayish-black. Feet and legs are brownish-horn color.

On the uppersides the coloring is mostly a shade of pale but dull brown. The rump is red and the upperside of the tail is grayish-black.

The female has a paler beak; and, if age and all other conditions are equal, she will have less orange on the face and abdomen. These last differ-

144

ences are not wholly reliable because the orange fades after the birds have been in captivity for any length of time.

Newly imported birds show very bright and extensive orange and can easily be sexed by the greater amount of orange on the face of the male.

Though sometimes delicate in the beginning, Orange Cheeks are easy to acclimate and are very hardy thereafter if not crowded.

As breeders, Orange Cheeked Waxbills are usually disappointments. They build flimsy nests and feed their young in a halfhearted manner. The male joins the female on the nest, but the hen does all of the serious incubating. Incubation time is twelve to fourteen days after which the parents prefer to feed a variety of live foods. Nests are often placed near the ground in planted aviaries.

Youngsters are quite dull. The beak is gray, and no orange is present for the first few months.

A rare subspecies of very limited range (*tschadensis*) is paler than the above.

GOLD BREASTED WAXBILL or ORANGE BREASTED WAXBILL
(*Estrilda subflava subflava*)

The lovely Gold Breasted Waxbill from Senegal is the smallest of Africa's waxbills and is as variable as a desert sunset. No two males are exactly alike in the red and red-orange shadings of the chests. The size is three inches long including the one inch tail. The bill is reddish.

Males have a dull brownish shade on the upperparts with orange tail coverts and a blackish tail. An orange-red eyebrow covers the lores and extends backwards over the eye nearly one-fourth of an inch. A golden yellow starts below the eyes and on the throat extending through the tail coverts overlaid with a bright orange on the undertail coverts. The chest and abdomen are fired with a variable mixture of orange and red-orange. The richness of the shading depends upon age. The maximum brilliance is attained in the second year. The sides show a faint barred effect of yellow alternating with brown.

Females lack the orange eyebrows and have dull straw colored chests with only a trace of orange or dull red on the undertail coverts. Barring on the sides is either absent or just barely visible. Females are nearly identical to female Strawberry Finches except for a slightly smaller size, orange uppertail coverts, and a trace of orange on the undertail coverts.

Gold Breasted Waxbills, also called Zebra Waxbills, are usually better breeders than most waxbills; but success varies with individuals and is highly dependent upon environment. Small live foods are advisable.

Incubation is twelve to fourteen days, and young leave the nest after about three weeks. Youngsters look like females, but the red eyebrows soon start to appear in males.

Gold Breasted Waxbills are not only the smallest of waxbills, but they are easily among the prettiest. Moreover, they take readily to aviary life and are hardy as well as peaceful, which classes them as ideal. In cages or completely shaded aviaries, Gold Breasteds sometimes show melanistic problems in that the overall coloring turns dark brown.

SOUTH AFRICAN GOLD BREASTED WAXBILL (*Estrilda subflava clarkei*)

The seldom imported, rare South African Gold Breasted Waxbill is slightly larger by one-fourth inch than the Senegal Gold Breasted Waxbill; but it is less colorful. Females in both subspecies are similar except for size.

Males have bolder zebra markings on the sides but lack all reddish shades on the chest. Orange coloring is reduced to a paler shade. Altogether this is a less attractive bird, but its rarity greatly enhances its demand.

LAVENDER WAXBILL or LAVENDER FIRE FINCH (*Estrilda caerulescens*)

Some authorities class the Lavender Finch with the Fire Finches and give it the name of *Lagonosticta caerulescens* mainly because of the white spots on the sides. Regardless of its final classification, the Lavender is one of the most popular of avicultural subjects. It is frequently imported, reasonably priced, and quite hardy if given reasonable care.

The Lavender is three and a half inches long including a tail of one and one-fourth inches. The beak is blackish with a pearly cast and pale lavender rose on the sides.

The basic color is a soft and smooth gray with a lustrous deep red covering the lower back, rump, both sides of the tail, undertail coverts, and ventral area. There are numerous small white spots on the sides and flanks.

Lavenders are very difficult to sex; but, if the birds are mature, females show less vividness and less extensive red on the back and ventral area. Differences in age and length of aviary life usually affect these slight differences and often make sexing impossible.

Two mishaps of captivity are a tendency towards feather plucking and a frequent tendency towards melanism. Both can usually be overcome by housing the birds in spacious uncrowded aviaries which allow plenty of sunshine. Habitual feather pluckers should always be isolated. Otherwise the Lavender is peaceful. Though hardy after a short acclimation period, Lavenders should be kept in temperatures above 45° F. In the writers' Southern California aviaries the temperature often goes below 45° F. with no visible ill effects, but these lower fluctuations are exceptions rather than the rule.

Lavenders are not reliable breeders, but they are always worth a try. Live foods, in a variety, and small worms, if possible, are necessary in rearing young. Young lack the white spots and have duller red areas.

PERREIN'S WAXBILL or BLACK TAILED LAVENDER (*Estrilda perreini perreini*)

Two species of this rarely available avicultural subject are found in a more southerly African area than the frequently imported Lavender Waxbill.

Both are very similar to the Lavender Waxbill except for a black tail and grayish beak. The rump and upper tail coverts are red as in the Lavender.

The second race (subspecies *incana*) is paler and is from an even more restricted area in Eastern South Africa.

FAWN BREASTED WAXBILL (*Estrilda paludicola*)

Fawn Breasted Waxbills are seldom imported and seldom requested by aviculturists. Though they are very pleasant aviary subjects, hardy, peaceful, and reasonably attractive, they are far less distinctive than many other waxbills and usually are higher priced.

These modest little finches are more heavy bodied than most waxbills. Prominent features are a bright red bill and a bright red rump. The rest of the bird is drably colored with brownish upperparts and a pale, neutral straw shade on the undersides. Some grayish shades highlight the sides of the face and the top of the head. The tail is blackish, and the abdominal area has a pleasant tinge of dark rose.

The writers have never hesitated to import a few of these charming birds during their rare periods of availability. Most dealers have a difficult time engendering enthusiasm for these waxbills and sometimes use popular names which, though applicable, are already given to other birds. The most frequent misapplication is, understandably, Red Rumped Waxbill.

Sexes are very similar, but the writers have found some success in selecting as females those birds which have paler beaks and less colorful abdominal areas. Insofar as the writers know, this species has rarely been bred successfully in captivity. Young are similar to parents but have black beaks and an absence of the reddish tinge in the abdominal area.

There are several races showing only slight variations. All come from various areas in East Africa.

BLACK CHEEKED WAXBILL (*Estrilda erythronotos*)

The long-tailed and dignified Black Cheeked Waxbill is a very beautiful bird in its precise and smoky color scheme. It is an Eastern and South African rarity seldom available and usually rather expensive.

The four and a half inch length includes a long two-inch tail. It is somewhat large compared to most waxbills but is nevertheless beautifully proportioned and gracefully borne. The dignified and active demeanor is not overactive and clownish nor is it so quiet that it is lethargic. The personality is perfect.

Overall coloring is subdued and dusky. Upperparts are smoky-mauve with the wings showing many distinct and precise narrow bars of alternating lighter and darker shades than the general upperparts. The tail is black above and grayish-black on the underside.

The rump is dull and subdued red which reaches around to brighten the smoky undersides especially on the sides and, to a lesser degree, on the abdomen. The chest also shows an almost hidden trace of dull rose-mauve.

Black Cheeked Waxbills from South Africa, are rare and rather expensive. Though subdued in color, they are nevertheless very attractively patterned and have more dignity than most waxbills. Photographed at Palos Verdes Bird Farm.

A large blackish cheek patch starts from the lores, stretches like a long eyebrow past the eyes, and dips downwards to cover the entire cheek area. The beak is mostly black, but the base is a pearl-gray. The feet are black.

Black Cheeked Waxbills are unfortunately not considered good breeders. Their shyness entitles them to an aviary by themselves; and, if possible, it should be planted to try to encompass all their desires which are not yet completely known in aviculture.

These rare birds are very difficult to sex and cannot be distinguished unless both sexes can be compared. In most cases, except those impossible in-betweens, the male has bolder and more contrasting markings on the wings; but an experienced eye is needed to tell the difference. There may be other differences such as shading in the cheek and abdominal areas, but they have eluded the writers. Behavior, of course, is the truest test.

Though considered delicate in most temperate climates, the writers have never had the slightest problem with them. Of course, because of their rarity and rather high cost, the writers may have given them extra care; but they have never lost a single bird during acclimation. Live food is needed, and an insect mixture is helpful. Another bird already accustomed to the insect mixture is helpful in luring these birds to this food.

The different races show minor variations in dusky shadings which in some instances makes the task of sex differentiation even more difficult if shipments include mixed subspecies.

BLACK CROWNED WAXBILL (*Estrilda nonnula*)

The rare Black Crowned Waxbill from South Africa has a bright and cheerful personality as well as a very attractive and unusual pattern. It is three and three-fourths inches long including a tail of one and three-eighths inches. It is peaceful, very active, and reasonably hardy after a somewhat delicate period of acclimation. Since it is also somewhat expensive, it is usually given a very careful acclimation period with all necessary precautions to insure its survival. Afterwards it gets along well with no additional care than that given to all waxbills.

One drawback to its general health is a proneness to respiratory problems. Damp environments should be avoided. If the bird fancier will observe this precaution and protect the bird from aggressive bullies, he will have no problem with the Black Crowned Waxbill.

The beak is black with a fine line of red on both sides of the upper mandible and at the base of the lower mandible. A crisp black cap covers the entire forehead and crown and curves downward to include the eyes. The nape, back, shoulders, and scapulars are smoky-gray; and the flights are black but not as intensely black as the cap. The tail on both sides is black. Feet and legs are also black.

Underparts starting just below the cap are pearl-gray.

To prevent a somber appearance and to provide just the right color contrast a bright red accents the sides and covers the rump and uppertail coverts.

A further feature to add pattern is a faintly barred effect on the smoky-gray of the scapulars and shoulders. These bars are dusky-black alternating with a paler grayish shade.

Sexes are extremely difficult to determine. Behavior is the only true test. The writers placed six Black Crowned Waxbills in a cage and searched for distinguishing differences. The only difference they could see was a very, very slight difference in the barring on the wings. Those individuals with bolder bars were assumed to be males as in the case of St. Helena and Black Cheeked Waxbills. The assumption coincided with behavior in some individuals, but this test is by no means conclusive. Bannerman states the mantle and back of the female is brown rather than gray, but the writers found no trace of brown.

Sex determination can be even more confusing if the Black Crowned Waxbill happens to be shipped with its very similar relative, the Black Capped Waxbill. The differences between the two are slight enough that one could easily persuade himself that one species is the female and the other the male.

Immature birds lack the barred effect and have a dull brown on the back and wings and a dull, dusty buff on the underparts. The beak has far less red, but the black cap, red rump, and black tail are present.

BLACK CAPPED or BLACK HEADED WAXBILL (*Estrilda atricapilla*)

The equally rare Black Capped Waxbill closely resembles the Black Crowned Waxbill in appearance as well as characteristics. The Black Headed Waxbill has more of a scarlet rump and darker underparts than the Black Crowned. The red on the flanks is more extensive, and there is no red on the upper mandible.

SYDNEY WAXBILL (*Estrilda temporalis,* formerly *Aegintha temporalis*)

The pretty but unassuming Sydney Waxbill is the only waxbill native to Australia. It also has been introduced into many islands in the South Pacific. Before the Australian ban this peaceful species was usually readily available from Australian exporters but not in great demand from bird fanciers, nor has it ever been really low priced. It is also quieter and less active than most waxbills and quickly becomes calm and poised in an aviary. Though it cannot be called a frequent breeder in captivity, it certainly is more reliable than many waxbills.

Though it ships well, the acclimation period is somewhat touchy because of a tendency towards respiratory problems in damp areas. Otherwise and after this slightly extended period, it is more than reasonably hardy.

The first impression one gets from the Sydney Waxbill is that it looks smaller than it really is, but this is an illusion caused by the subdued general coloring. The body is larger than most waxbills of a similar four to four and a half inch size. The tail is a little more than an inch long.

The bright and dominating accents are red on the rump and uppertail coverts, beak, and on a long and broad eyebrow. The beak also has some black on the top of the upper mandible. The eyebrow sits mostly above the eye compared to that of the Red Eared Waxbill and is far more rectangular in appearance because it ends bluntly rather than tapering to a point.

The rest of the bird is washed in soft, dull gray with a noticeably paler area on the throat and chest. A soft warm golden-olive concentration occurs across the nape and on the shoulders, and the wings are soft grayish-green. The feet and legs are flesh colored, and the tail is grayish-black with a tinge of brown.

Sexes are very much alike, but the eyebrow of the male is bolder and longer. In fully mature males, the concentration of golden olive on the nape is richer; but several slight variations in birds from different areas occur to make this feature an indeterminate sexual factor. Behavior and the male's display are the truest test.

Immature birds are very dull and dark. They lack the red eyebrow, have only a tinge of red on the rump, and have a mostly black beak.

A seldom available subspecies is the Lesser Sydney Waxbill (*Estrilda temporalis minor*) which is less than four inches long. It resembles the Sydney Waxbill except for paler shades on the face and underparts and black on the undertail coverts.

DUFRESNE'S WAXBILL *(Coccopygia melanotis melanotis)*

Dufresne's Waxbill from South Africa is rather a rare prize for avi-culturists. Seldom available because of its eastern and southern distribution in Africa, it always finds a ready market when it is imported. The acclimation period is sometimes difficult; but afterwards, Dufresne's Waxbill is hardy except for a sensitivity to cold weather.

This small and elegant bird is peaceful, alert, and very active. It has the rapid tail-twitching habit of the Red Eared Waxbill. Though not considered a good breeder, it is, nevertheless, a very worthwhile addition to any collection of small finches; and young have been reared several times.

The size is a shapely, though fulsome, three and a half inches including a tail of one and one-fourth inches. Many individuals become feather pluckers if overcrowded, but they rarely victimize any except their own kind.

Though most of the colors are subdued, the uniformity of shading and sharpness of contrasts give a most attractive appearance. The upper mandible of the beak is black, and the lower mandible is red. The feet and legs are black.

The head and nape are smoky-gray shading into a distinct but soft black on an extensive area including the cheeks, sides of face, and throat. The lower boundary of black is sharply divided from a pale pearl-gray which covers the chest. The abdomen shades into an indistinct straw color which extends through the tail coverts. The underside of the tail is dull gray.

On the upperparts, a dull shade of grayish-olive covers the back, wings, and sides. The olive sides are normally covered by the wings. Undersides of wings are gray.

The rump is red which, though somewhat subdued, contrasts brightly with the other colors. The upperside of the tail is black.

Females are like males in every respect except for the lack of the black cheek areas. Sexes are therefore easily distinguished.

Dufresne's Waxbill, sometimes called Swee Waxbill, likes a considerable amount of live food. A variety is advisable, and the major part should be small insects rather than mealworms.

In nesting, Dufresne's must be supplied with a variety of small insects if they are to rear chicks successfully. For this purpose they do better in a planted aviary where the insects are available naturally. The nest is usually higher than six feet from the ground, and the birds dislike disturbances. Incubation is from twelve to fourteen days, and young leave the nest usually sometime during the third week. For a short time youngsters have both mandibles dull black but otherwise look like females with less green on the wings. Adult plumage is assumed in the next three months.

The Abyssinian Yellow Bellied Waxbill *(Coccopygia melanotis quartinia)* is a subspecies of Dufresne's Waxbill. The male lacks the black area of the face and throat but has a more distinct yellow abdominal area. Except for

151

this additional yellow, it closely resembles the female Dufresne's. There is just a hint of barring on the mantle and wings. Females are similar but have far less yellow on the abdomen.

Another subspecies is the Kenya Yellow Bellied Waxbill (*Coccopygia melanotis kilimensis*) which is like the Abyssinian subspecies except for a slightly smaller size and more of an olive shade in the mantle. Two other races are the Angolan Yellow Bellied Waxbill (subspecies *bocagei*) and the Uganda Yellow Bellied Waxbill (subspecies *nyanzae*).

VIOLET EARED WAXBILL (*Granatina granatina*)

The very rare, expensive, and lovely Violet Eared Waxbill from South Africa is a very close rival of the Lady Gould as far as great beauty is concerned. Though far less flamboyant and showy than the Lady Gould, the Violet Ear compensates for the lack of brightness by showing a rich glow and intensity of shading which is really quite indescribable. The deep warmth and rich gloss cannot be captured by the most expert of photographers. The illustration in this book was taken from Butler's **FOREIGN FINCHES IN CAPTIVITY.** It gives a good likeness of the well-proportioned and long-tailed gracefulness of this five to five and a half inch bird, but the coloring of the print cannot begin to do justice to this beautiful creature. It is regrettable that a suitable subject was not available for photography at the time of writing. A good color photograph would doubtless have captured far more of the richness in this bird's coloring.

The male has a deep rich reddish-brown on the head, back, and wings. The variation is from chestnut on the head to a darker more brown shade on the primary flights. The upper tail coverts are brilliant deep blue, and the tail is a dark grayish-black edged on the tips and sides in dark blue.

The forehead is vivid blue and a long chin and throat accent is black. The beak is a bright shade of wine red, and the reddish eye is surrounded by a bright red eye ring. A large flaring cheek and facial area is purplish-blue in a richness which defies description. The chest and underparts are a beautiful shade of burgundy-brown becoming progressively less bright on the abdomen and ending in a dark dull shade under the vent. The underside of the tail is dark, dull blue.

Females are far less showy and duller in coloration. They fall into the category of being merely attractive. Upperparts are dull, pale brownish. The cheek patch is much paler, and the blue of the forehead is just barely present. The black of the throat is reduced to a pale gray which changes to a bright fawn tinged with red on most of the underparts. The wings are duller, but the tail and bright blue uppertail coverts are similarly bright as in the male. The beak is like that of the male but is less bright.

Males have a very pretty song which unfortunately is not frequently heard.

The Violet Eared Waxbill is one of those rare and overrated birds which, like Parrot Finches, is known mostly from overly effusive written material.

Some disadvantages must be mentioned to be completely fair. It is not a good breeder even though success has been attained. It cannot successfully withstand excessive dampness or rapid drops in temperature. The lowest safe temperature is 45° F.

The writers are careful in coaxing Violet Ears into an all inclusive diet during the acclimation period. The diet includes the standard finch mix, greenfood, seeding grasses, a few mealworms carefully rationed, and an insectile mixture, the use of which is taught by a bird previously conditioned. With this diet, the writers have considerably eased the problems which usually are reputed to be particularly difficult. Normally, Violet Ears are reported to be difficult to maintain in good condition due to sudden unexpected deaths for no apparent reason. The writers have been pleasantly surprised at the comparative ease of keeping these birds but freely admit that much of the credit probably goes to Southern California's mild climate. And, of course, the careful tutoring to include the insectile mixture is also most helpful.

Anyone who is fortunate enough to own a pair of Violet Eared Waxbills is quite likely, because of their cost as well as rarity, to give these birds the requirements they deserve. If so, the acclimation period is relatively short as well as successful.

Incubation time is twelve to fourteen days, and young fledge in about three weeks looking much like females except that they are duller. Sexes can be determined after about three months.

PURPLE GRENADIER (*Granatina ianthinogaster*)

The extremely rare Purple Grenadier from East Africa is larger and somewhat less shapely than the Violet Ear because of its heavier body.

The male has its head and beak of the same basic coloration as the Violet Ear, but the cheek patch is greatly reduced in size. The black throat patch and blue forehead are absent. The back and wings are more brown than the head. The rump is cobalt blue and the tail black. Underparts from the chest through the undertail coverts are vivid purplish-blue, but there are some uneven chestnut markings which detract from the overall uniformity.

The female is brownish, pale on the underparts and tinted with chestnut on the head. A white patch surrounds the eye, and white spots are sprinkled on the underparts. The rump is blue, and the tail is blackish-gray.

There are some slight variations in three subspecies.

PYTILIAS

There are four species and several subspecies of the genus *Pytilia*. All are from Africa, and all are rather difficult to get. Though Pytilias are waxbills, all show a considerable departure from what most people regard as typical characteristics of waxbills. The bodies are heavier, and the beaks are longer and narrower.

Pytilias are highly insectivorous and should be fed as much of a variety as possible. Mealworms are very good but should be rationed. Three meal-

153

worms per day is sufficient, but the number should at least be doubled during nesting. Insectile mixture is usually very readily accepted. The writers have frequently used the Melba Finch to induce other birds to try the insectile mixture. Usually when interest is shown by one bird, other birds are quick to follow the example.

MELBA FINCH (*Pytilia melba melba*)

The beautiful but rather rare Melba from South Africa is the prettiest member of the genus and is a delight in many ways. Also called the Green Winged Pytilia, the Melba is a heavy bodied bird nearly five inches long including the slightly less than two-inch tail.

In recording the description, the writers placed a male in a small cage nearby. He settled down immediately with no sign of panic. To our surprise, the bird quietly and happily started to warble a lovely and melodious song. The long and unhurried larklike trills are unlike those of any other finch. The quality of the song can favorably be compared to the songs of many well-known softbilled musicians.

The long, narrow, and sharply pointed beak is coral-red to match the similarly colored bright head and extensive throat areas. A soft dove-gray divides the red, surrounds the eyes, and covers the lores. The same shade of gray covers the lower crown and neck areas and gradually changes into dark olive-green on the back, wings, and rump.

The upperside of the tail and uppertail coverts are dull red with a brighter concentration near the base. The underside of the tail is blackish.

A rich golden-olive wash on the throat and upper chest borders the lower boundaries of the bright coral-red. A slight shading of olive follows on the chest overlying the basic gray which covers the rest of the underparts. Irregularly shaped white spots are tightly packed on the lower chest area. Fine lines of black mixed with the gray add further contrast. On the sides and flanks the spots become larger, almost forming bars of white alternating with gray. The abdomen fades to a dull grayish-white, and a faint trace of indistinct olive is added to the undertail coverts.

Females lack all red on the facial area and have no golden-olive wash on the lower throat and upper chest. Their replacement is soft gray except for barlike white spots on the throat and upper chest.

Immature birds are like females except for the addition of a yellowish-brown shade and the absence of spots and bars on the underparts. Mature coloring is complete at about three months of age.

Melba Finches are calm and ideal aviary birds usually being neither shy nor aggressive with other birds. Males will often show some aggressiveness towards each other if they are competing for a mate. In most instances far more males are imported than females, and this competition may become bothersome if sexes are not equal. Extra males which are subjugated may be victimized by being feather plucked. There are certain individuals which upon first meeting a prospective mate, may chase the female too much. The writers had to separate one pair when the male attacked the female in a vicious rage because she ignored his display.

Melba Finches are often purported to be delicate and addicted to feather plucking. The writers have experienced neither problem. The acclimation period is rather touchy, but these birds usually adjust quickly. There is possibly a tendency for many people to overfeed mealworms which ultimately may cause problems.

As breeders, Melbas are disappointing. They haphazardly build nests usually about six feet off the ground, but often quickly tire of the project. Undoubtedly they would do better in large planted aviaries where they can catch small insects. Seclusion is important because it lessens the danger of desertion. In the wild state the Paradise Whydah lays its eggs in nests of Melba Finches.

Both birds sit during the fourteen day incubation period. The parents feed lots of live food; and, as usual with chicks who receive a large percentage of live food, the youngsters leave the nest in a comparatively short time. The fledging time is between two and three weeks, and youngsters are not completely self feeding for three more weeks.

There are several subspecies of Melbas. The Senegambian Melba (*citerior*) has red around the eyes and on the lores. The red is also a paler shade, and there is a less heavy concentration of spots on the underparts. The Tanganyika Melba (*grotei*) has the red of the throat extending onto the chest. The Kenya Melba (*soudanensis*) is generally darker. Red covers the lores and closely surrounds the eyes, but it does not extend as far backwards as does the Senegambian race. There is some barring on undertail coverts. Two other subspecies are *belli* and *jessei*. Except for the Senegambian Melba, the subspecies are too rare in aviculture outside of Africa to be well-known.

ORANGE WINGED PYTILIA or RED FACED WAXBILL (*Pytilia afra*)

The dark and rather dully colored Orange Winged Pytilia has too many popular names. In addition to the two most widely used names, Red Faced Waxbill and Orange Winged Pytilia, it is also called Golden Backed Pytilia, Crimson Faced Waxbill, and Weiner's Finch. Fortunately most are passing into disuse.

This Pytilia is four inches long including a tail of one and one-fourth inches. It is shaped very much like the Melba.

The long red bill of the male has dark grayish tinges at the base of the beak. In the female the beak is grayish with some orange on the lower mandible. The male has a deep red covering a large area on the head including the forehead and part of the crown, cheeks, and throat. The female lacks this red and has in its place a gray slightly shaded with olive in the facial area and a heavier shading of olive on the forehead. The top of the head in both sexes is grayish-olive, and the throat is gray with only a slight cast of olive.

The back, wings, and most of the rump is deep, dull olive with a brighter shading of dull burnt-orange on the outer webs of the flight feathers. When the wings are folded, this becomes a prominent feature.

The tail, uppertail coverts, and the lower part of the rump show a dull red. The tail pattern is similar to that of the Melba in that the central feathers are all red and just the outer webs of the side feathers are red. The rest of the tail feather coloring, hidden on the upperside and visible on the underside, is black.

The underparts are dull, dark olive with a slight concentration of a tinge of burnt-orange on the chest; but this is dull and weak compared to that on the wings.

The center of the abdomen is white in an irregular pattern. Many of the long chest feathers are irregularly and broadly striated with wavy white markings in an ill-defined attempt at color variation. The undertail coverts are dull grayish-black with some white striations.

This is a difficult bird to describe. It is unusual, different, and attractive in a subdued way. Mainly, it is quite rare and can command attention on that basis alone. As with Melbas, males seem to outnumber females in importations.

Breeding is similar to information given for the Melba. It goes to nest more readily than does the Melba, but it gives up just as quickly and as easily.

AURORA WAXBILL or CRIMSON WINGED PYTILIA (*Pytilia phoenicoptera phoenicoptera*)

The seldom available Aurora has a simple color scheme compared to other members of this genus. Though rather quietly colored, it is nevertheless attractive. It is a heavy-bodied bird approximately five inches in length including a tail of nearly one and one-half inches.

The basic coloring is soft gray contrasted by a darker slate-gray beak. A bright crimson marks a broad band starting near the shoulders and covering most of the primary flights. This same shade covers the rump and tail feathers in much the same manner as described for the Orange Winged Pytilia.

The basic gray is not uniform. The undersides as well as the top of the head and nape are finely barred with alternating shades of slightly paler and slightly darker grays.

The female is less bold in appearance because of less distinct bars.

Auroras cannot by any means be called good breeders, but they are a little better than either of the above two species. The procedure is the same.

The Abyssinian Aurora (subspecies *lineata*) has a reddish-brown beak and has a brownish tinge on the upperparts. The White Nile Aurora (subspecies *emini*) is much the same as the West African race described above.

RED FACED AURORA (*Pytilia hypogrammica*)

Also called the Yellow Winged Pytilia, this species is extremely rare in aviculture. It is similar to the Aurora except for two major variations. The

156

outer webs of the flight feathers are dark golden-yellow instead of red as in the Aurora. The male has a red facial area similar to that of the Orange Winged Pytilia except it is somewhat brighter. The female lacks the red face.

TWIN-SPOTS

The small family of Twin-Spots from Africa embraces three genera and just a few species. These are extremely rare in aviculture, but nearly every bird fancier who covets very rare birds hopes to own some of them. They are said to be excellent aviary subjects and hardy. All the different Twin-Spots are very attractive and unusually patterned.

To include this group in the chapter on waxbills is perhaps incorrect, but there are many similarities between Twin-Spots and Pytilias which cannot be ignored. The size and shape of their bodies is similar. The diet is equally insectivorous, and the beaks are similarly shaped.

Breeding success has been achieved several times with various species, but each breeding is a noteworthy and infrequent achievement.

The general care is the same as for members of the Pytilia group.

PETER'S TWIN-SPOT (*Hypargos niveoguttatus*)

Peter's Twin-Spot is often called Peter's Spotted Fire Finch and Peter's Ruddy Waxbill, but these names are very misleading and suggest a much closer relationship to the well-known African Fire Finches than is actually the case.

The male has a slate-gray beak. The forehead, crown, and nape are grayish-brown darkening to brown with a faint tinge of red on the back and wings. The rump and uppertail coverts are deep red, and the tail is both red and blackish. A large and distinctive area of rich crimson covers all facial areas, the sides of the neck, and the throat down to the chest. The rest of the underparts are black with large white spots scattered prominently over the sides of the chest and flanks. These spots are much larger than those found in Fire Finches. The male also has a bright but fine-lined eye ring of greenish-blue.

The female has greatly reduced areas and intensity of red in the face and throat areas. Black underparts are slightly paler, but each white spot is encircled in dark black.

GREEN BACKED TWIN-SPOT (*Mandingoa nitidula*)

The male has a bright red face patch, and all of the uppersides and the rest of the head and throat have a dark shade of olive green. The rump is a paler shade which is slightly tinged with yellow, and the wings are dusky. The tail is black on the outer parts and olive-green in the center. A large area from the breast to the lower abdomen and the flanks is black with prominent white spots. The ventral area is pale olive-buff.

The female is paler and lacks the red face patch. Instead, this facial area is dull orange.

157

A subspecies, Schlegel's Twin-Spot (subspecies *schlegeli*), has some orange-red on the chest and throat of the male. Another subspecies (*chubbi*) has golden-olive on the same area.

BROWN TWIN-SPOT (*Clytospiza monteiri*)

The five inch Brown Twin-Spot is especially distinctive and attractive. Sexes are very similar except for a difference in the color of a small throat patch. The beak is pearl-gray near the base and slate-gray on the outer half. The head is gray changing to brown on the back and wings. The rump and uppertail coverts are dark red, and the tail is blackish on both sides. All the underparts from the upper chest through undertail coverts have a very attractive chestnut as basic coloring. The large white spots are exceedingly numerous. Below the vent and on the undertail coverts the spots become alternating bars of chestnut and white.

The male has a small crimson throat patch, and the female has the same patch in white.

DYBOWSKI'S TWIN-SPOT or DUSKY TWIN-SPOT (*Clytospiza dybowskii*)

The two dominant features of the Dusky Twin-Spot are the white spots on a black background starting on the lower chest and extending to the abdomen and through the flanks and a broad swath of deep crimson starting on the broad mantle and covering the back, rump, and uppertail coverts. The rest of the bird is clothed in slaty, dusky shades. The female has a gray background instead of black for the white spots.

CHAPTER 10

Whydahs

All whydahs are from Africa and are rather closely allied to weavers. This is a family of flamboyance and contrasts from the very plain to the unbelievably exotic and beautiful which is nearly comparable to the metamorphosis of the lowly caterpillar to the lovely butterfly. All males go through a seasonal change of plumage. When in color during the breeding season, the nuptial plumage of most members is very beautiful. Most have long tails to enhance their courting displays, and the one predominant color is black.

When the males are in eclipse plumage, they are said to be out of color. During this period they lose all their long tails and colors. The result is an uninteresting and unattractive sparrowlike drabness. Females, having no plumage change, retain their sparrowlike appearance at all times.

Whydahs are all presumed to be polygamous, but there is no proof of this. In flocks in the wild state, males are greatly outnumbered by birds which appear to be females. It is known, however, that a good percentage of these out of color birds in the flocks are immature males who do not come into color until the second year. Even so, it seems the females actually do outnumber the males. This lends credulity to the idea of polygamy.

Importations, however, usually contain more males than females. This fact brings to light a peculiar personality difference in the sexes. The imbalance cannot be selection on the part of the exporters because a major percentage of those birds sent from Africa are birds out of color, and the differences are too slight for large scale selectivity. The reason for the predominance of males in shipments is that they are bolder and less shy than timorous, hiding females and are therefore more easily trapped.

The family is divided into two basic groups: parasitic and non-parasitic. The parasitic members include those species from three genera: *Steganura*, *Vidua*, and *Hypochera*. These birds lay their eggs in other birds' nests and thus relieve themselves of the many burdens of parental responsibility. Non-parasitic species are those from the genera *Drepanoplectes* and *Coliuspasser*.

The courting displays of all members are highly interesting and in many ways similar. The most spectacular and most advanced is that of Jackson's

159

Whydah. For most members, the display makes use of the long tail in ribbon-like flutterings during the frequent skyward sallies and rapid returns. After descent, the male hovers in a slow and graceful flight over the female. These charming marital advances are usually so irresistible and fanciful that few females prove invincible.

Whydahs are easily managed in aviaries. The diet is the simple, standard finch fare. Greenfood and some live food are advisable. Though they take kindly to captivity, none of the whydahs are good aviary breeders.

Most whydahs spend much time on the ground scratching like poultry for germinating seeds and possibly certain insects. Males with long tails show a careful regard for their tails while on the ground and hold them gracefully aloft to prevent damage.

After a short acclimation period, whydahs are very hardy; but some of the more popular varieties cannot stand extreme cold. Generally speaking, it would be wiser not to allow temperatures to drop below 45° F. Some individuals are affected by respiratory and sinus problems in damp climates.

Once in a while, certain individuals do not come into color during the season and others may not go out of color. Most are inconsistent about the seasonal color changes in that the changeover may vary several weeks one way or the other, but to have complete seasonal lapses regarding changes is not a sign of the best of health. The aviculturist whose birds completely ignore the seasonal changes should check diet as well as environment for possible imbalances. The most frequent exception is the Red Collared Whydah which often undergoes partial metamorphoses. Many Red Collareds lose color but retain the long feathers during the eclipse plumage phase.

In Africa, many whydahs, especially those of the genus *Coliuspasser*, are called "Widow Birds" because of the assumption of long tails and a pre-dominant black costume which resembles "widows' weeds."

PARADISE WHYDAH (*Steganura paradisaea*)

When in color the male Paradise Whydah is an amazing sight. Though the coloring is predominantly black, the addition of two very long and broad tail feathers never ceases to evoke expressions of lavish admiration. Regardless of how many years the bird fancier has kept birds, he or she could never cease to enjoy watching this charming creature whether he is perched in a dignified pose or whether he is in his peculiar graceful and fluttering flight.

The diet is the standard finch mix plus greenfood. Some mealworms are helpful if the birds will accept them.

Paradise Whydahs are nearly always available during the African importation season, and they are usually very reasonable in price. Naturally, males in color are somewhat higher in price than those out of color; but, considering the assurance of receiving a male and of not having to wait impatiently for the development of the nuptial costume, the price increase is modest.

Male Paradise Whydah in full color and maximum tail growth of fourteen inches. The black tail has a mildly corrugated texture which accounts for the barred appearance of the tail. Photographed at Palos Verdes Bird Farm.

The male in color, usually for a six month summer and fall period, has a body length of approximately three and a half inches exclusive of tail. Two large paddle-shaped, black tail feathers are two and three-fourths inches long. Each has a long hairlike appendage extending from the shaft. The paddle-shaped feathers are situated above two very long and quite broad central tail feathers. The two flamboyant central feathers are black and show a slight and minute corrugated effect which in certain lights gives the misleading appearance of darker and lighter striations. Eventually these central tail feathers may reach fourteen inches in length. During the first year, however, the male Paradise Whydah does not come into color. The second year the nuptial pattern is complete except for the absence of the two long tail feathers. Each year thereafter, the two central feathers appear, shorter at first and becoming progressively longer each year until the maximum length is reached.

The writers once had an interesting color variation in a male Paradise Whydah. The two long central tail feathers were snow white. At first the abnormality was attributed to inadequate diet or to other reasons which sometimes cause new feathers to be abnormally pale, but the white feathers occurred year after year which refuted all suppositions except that of a mutation.

Black covers the back, wings, tail, head, and beak. The black head extends to the back of the crown and cuts a sharp dividing line to the lower cheek area after which it cuts into a V-shaped area on the throat.

A glossy chestnut-brown collar extends around the neck and chest and gradually fades into a pale buff which covers the abdomen and vent.

Males out of color and females are very similar. The beak is a pale horn color. Underparts are a drab and pale buff. The upperparts are sparrowlike with indistinct variations in the shadings of feathers. On the head two wide bands start with the nostrils and extend backwards to the hind limits of the crown. These bands are dark and blackish on males out of color and paler and less bold on females and immatures. The male also seems to be slightly larger. Pale buffish streaks separate the dark bands, giving the appearance of long trailing buff eyebrows on the sides. There is one long pale streak down the center of the forehead and crown.

The tail in males in the out of color phase and in females is two inches long. The head seems larger and flatter and is perched upon a longer neck than most members of the family.

The Paradise Whydah is peaceful even with small waxbills and is a perfect subject in mixed collections. However, a few have been known to eat eggs of other birds. The dominance is in appearance rather than in disposition.

One of the greatest accomplishments in aviculture is the breeding of Paradise Whydahs. Because Paradise Whydahs parasitize Melba Finches in the wild state, successful breedings in captivity are rare. Though there is much controversy as to whether the Melba is the only victim, the acceptance of other species as hosts is very rare indeed. A very good account of a first breeding in the United Kingdom appears in the October, 1955, issue of Foreign Birds. The breeder, Mrs. Lloyd, said the female Paradise Whydah laid her eggs in the nest of an African Fire Finch.

The display is always a delight to watch. The male hovers in flight over the hen in a slow motion manner. Frequent sallies up into the air are intended to be irresistible to even the most reluctant female, and the exotic magic usually is effective.

BROAD TAILED PARADISE WHYDAH (*Steganura orientalis*)

The Broad Tailed Paradise Whydah is distinctly different from the Paradise Whydah. It is not frequently available in the bird trade and usually is a little higher in price. There are several races of this species with variations so minor that the aviculturist need not be concerned.

The male in color has a slightly heavier body than the Paradise Whydah. The two paddle-shaped feathers are three and a half inches long. This is about three-fourths of an inch longer than in the Paradise Whydah. The hairlike appendage from the shaft extends at least one inch.

The two long tail feathers are much broader and fuller but do not reach the maximum length as found in Paradise Whydahs. There are two long hair-like strands emanating from somewhere within the tail trailing about five inches in length. The writers have never noticed these in the Paradise Whydah.

The coloring is the same as in the Paradise except the brown on the nape and chest is a glossy shade of chestnut extending down onto the lower chest.

Males out of color and females are similar to the Paradise Whydah; but they are distinguishable by a slightly larger body, shorter neck, and a larger, more rounded head. Differences in sex are the same as for the Paradise Whydah.

The Broad Tailed Paradise Whydah is equally peaceful and ideal in mixed collections in comparison with Paradise Whydahs.

PINTAILED WHYDAH (*Vidua macroura*)

The very attractive and hardy Pintailed Whydah from Western Africa is smaller than the Paradise Whydah, but it is very pugnacious to small birds during the in color phase. Therefore, it is best that they be housed with weavers and other birds similarly able to fend for themselves rather than with the smaller defenseless waxbills.

Pintailed Whydahs are usually available and are reasonably priced. They are slender, well-proportioned birds; and adults always have red beaks whether they are in nuptial dress or in eclipse plumage. Youngsters have grayish-black beaks and closely resemble youngsters of St. Helena Waxbills who are the hosts of the parasitic Pintails.

The male in color has a black cap which extends through the eye and continues to the nape of the neck. There is also a little black patch under the chin. Black continues again on shoulders and primary coverts. The black of the shoulders extends in a broad bar down to the sides of the upper chest area. Most of the flights are black, but a broad white band extends across the primaries and scapulars.

Except for the tail, the rest of the bird is white. The white undersides of flight and tail feathers are carefully shaded with grayish-black to give very soft accents.

Four long slender tail feathers, usually nine inches in length, are black. Like the Paradise Whydah, the male does not come into color the first year. In the second year the tail seldom reaches a length beyond six inches.

All long-tailed Whydahs have a graceful flight. One would think the added effort of supporting long tail feathers would make the flight labored and cumbersome, but the effect is quite the opposite. The flight is somewhat slower because of the long tail, but the appearance is one of beribboned elegance seldom found in other birds. The color picture of a Pintailed Whydah in flight in this book is a very remarkable study showing not only the artistry of a very talented photographer but also the bird's masterful technique of attracting attention from prospective mates. In the nuptial display, the flight up into the air is very high; and the drop to the ground is very fast. The hovering display is also fascinating and unusually animated.

When out of color, the male is not aggressively dominant. He is modest not only in disposition but also in dress. While out of color, the male Pintailed Whydah closely resembles the female. Sexes are nearly impossible to detect during eclipse plumage, but males have bolder head stripes than females. The beak is red, though somewhat less bright than during the in color phase; but the rest of the coloring is a haphazard and cluttered mixture of buffs, browns, and blacks in sparrowlike drabness. The total length is four and one-fourth inches including a tail of one and three-fourths inches.

Two irregular and wide black stripes extending from the forehead to the back of the crown are flanked by tan stripes. An ill-defined black stripe extends backwards from the eye and fades out at the back of the head.

The back, wings, and tail are mostly black with a careless arrangement of pale brown marking the outer edges of most of the feathers. The underside starts with a pale buff on the throat and fades to a dull white extending from the lower end of the chest through the undertail coverts. Several blackish spots are sprinkled on the chest. The underside of the tail is grayish fading to whitish on the outer margins.

The Pintailed Whydah has very seldom bred in captivity. Presumably it would accept species other than the St. Helena Waxbill as host; but, since its aggressiveness with these small waxbills precludes it as a safe companion, it seldom would have the opportunity of finding a host to its liking. A large wilderness aviary with one pair of Pintailed Whydahs and several pairs of St. Helena Waxbills, African Fire Finches, and Bronze Winged Mannikins would undoubtedly give the best chance for success and would furnish the mild mannered waxbills secluded retreats from the overbearing tendencies of the male Pintailed Whydah while in color.

QUEEN or SHAFTTAIL WHYDAH (*Vidua regia*)

The unique and rarely available Queen Whydah from South Africa shows an obvious relationship to the Pintailed Whydah because of a very similar pattern, but it has distinctive differences.

The male in color differs from the Pintailed Whydah by having buff on underparts instead of white and by having the four ten-inch long central tail feathers wire-like, bare shafts with spatulared feathery tips which are elongated, narrow, and particularly exotic.

The body is slightly smaller than that of the Pintailed Whydah; and in the out of color phase, as well as in females, there is more of a buffish tinge than in the Pintailed. The dark head stripes are nearly absent.

Queen, or Shafttail, Whydahs are hardy and are more peaceful than Pintailed Whydahs; but they are less peaceful than Paradise Whydahs. Queen Whydahs are very beautiful birds and are much in demand by aviculturists, but there are no records of breeding success. The Violet Eared Waxbill is presumed to be the usual host of this parasitic species.

FISCHER'S WHYDAH (*Vidua fischeri*)

Fischer's Whydah is an avicultural rarity from Eastern Africa where it is presumed to be parasitic on both the Purple Grenadier and the Violet Eared Waxbill.

There are certain characteristics which show a relationship to both the Pintailed and Queen Whydah. It has been described as a Queen Whydah with a reverse color scheme, but this is not quite accurate. The shape and size are very similar to the Queen. The color scheme is, for the most part, reversed. The four central tail feathers have no bare shafts. Instead these feathers are like those of the Pintailed Whydah except for being narrower.

The male in color has a yellowish cap covering the forehead and crown. The rest of the head, throat, mantle, back, and chest are black. The remainder of the underparts are yellowish through the undertail coverts. The undersides of wings and tail are similar to those of the Pintailed Whydah. The wings and most of the tail are blackish. The rump and uppertail coverts are buffish with blackish streaks. The central tail feathers are yellowish, and the bill is red. Feet and legs are rather orange in shading.

Males out of color and females closely resemble Queen Whydahs during the eclipse plumage phase but have less black in the markings.

The disposition is very similar to that of the Queen Whydah.

RESPLENDENT WHYDAH (*Vidua hypocherina*)

Also called the Steel Blue Whydah and Longtailed Combassou, the Resplendent Whydah is another avicultural rarity from Eastern Africa. Little is known of its habits in the wild; but, like other members of the genus, it is presumed to be parasitic.

165

The Queen or Shafttailed Whydah is a moderate rarity in the Whydah family. Related to the Pintail Whydah and resembling it in many ways, the male Shafttail Whydah has bare shafts with spatulated tips on four long tail feathers. This specimen is going out of color and has already lost three long tail feathers. The black areas are already fading into brown. Owned by William Lasky.

The male in color closely resembles a Combassou. It has four long tail feathers shaped like those of the Fischer's Whydah, but they are colored black. Except for some white on the sides of the rump, at the tip of the tail, and on the undersides of the wings, this bird is glossy black with iridescent purples, blues, and greens.

Out of color males and females resemble the Pintail Whydah during its plumage eclipse except the beak is brownish-horn instead of red.

COMBASSOUS, genus *Hypochera*

The Combassous, also called Indigo Finches and Steel Finches are classed with the Whydah family because of similarities in nuptial dress and a parasitic habit practiced by several whydahs. The main difference from other parasitic whydahs is the lack of elongated tail feathers. When they are out of color, Combassous resemble Paradise Whydahs in miniature. Combassous are frequently described as Whydahs without long tails.

The question of the parasitic nature of the Combassou has long been more of a supposition by ornithologists rather than a recorded fact. Aviculturists who have been successful in rearing young report that Combassous prefer to be parasitic but also will actually take over a disused nest and rear their own young. The main question still to be answered is the comparison

Members of the Whydah family: left, female Paradise Whydah; center and right, male Combassous showing corresponding smaller size. The Combassou in center is in full glossy black color while that on the right is in process of coming into color. Combassous do not develop long tail feathers characteristic of most Whydahs. Photographed at Palos Verdes Bird Farm.

of percentages of young reared by parasitic means with those reared by their natural parents.

Theorists may come up with some interesting suppositions once these percentages are established. One theory may perhaps go along these lines: that the Combassou is less advanced in its evolution than other parasitic whydahs since the parasitic habit is not fully entrenched, that in time it will become fully parasitic, and that eventually it may come to have a long tail.

There are several species and subspecies of Combassous scattered over very wide ranges in Africa. Variations on many are so slight that confusion and frequent disagreement cannot help but exist. Females of most species are practically indistinguishable.

The only frequently imported species is the inexpensive and popular Senegal Combassou (*Hypochera chalybeata*). Others may come along from time to time but do not arouse much enthusiasm except with aviculturists who are interested in rarities or in ornithological matters. The commercial importer is usually concerned only with the above species.

The Purple Combassou (*Hypochera ultramarina*) has been imported from Abyssinia and shows white patches on the sides of the rump while in color. The iridescence is noticeably more purplish.

The South African or Brown Winged Combassou (*Hypochera amauropteryx*) is noticeably different but perhaps less attractive. The wings and tail are dull brownish, and the iridescence is greenish. The beak, feet, and legs may vary from yellow-orange to coral-red.

SENEGAL COMBASSOU (*Hypochera chalybeata*)

The Senegal Combassou, measuring three and three-fourths inches in length including a tail of one and one-fourth inches, is usually called the Combassou or Steel Finch. The popular name of Indigo Finch is not widely used in an avicultural sense.

The male in color has pale horn-colored beak, feet, and legs. All the other coloring is a shiny metallic black showing reflections of purples and blues. In an aviary the male in color is a marvelous contrast with a White Zebra. Fortunately the male is usually in color nearly eight months, but the change-over times are not always consistent. At the time of writing (May) the writers have Combassous in full color as well as some showing only a few blotches of black on the chest.

When completely out of color the male resembles the female who in turn is quite like nothing else except a miniature and somewhat duller female Paradise Whydah. The head is somewhat smaller and the neck slightly shorter in a comparison between the two. The only possible sex distinction during the out of color phase is a sharper contrast in the males showing alternating paler and darker head streaks. This distinction has checked positively in most cases, but final tabulations are still inconclusive.

The pattern of the head is dominated by two broad brown stripes extending from the nostrils to the back of the crown and separated and flanked by pale buffish stripes. A black line extending backwards from the eye fades out near the back of the head.

As in most whydahs, the brown back, wings, and tail are cluttered with some pale markings on the edges of the feathers and darker markings in the centers. The entire effect is muddied with sparrowlike drabness.

The underparts are a drab, dull whitish shade with a preponderance of buffish-brown on the chest. The underside of the tail is brownish.

The many Combassous owned by the writers over the past several years have always proven hardy after acclimation, but they seem less inclined to withstand cold or damp weather than the average run of waxbills. The writers therefore suggest that temperature drops below 45° F. may be dangerous.

The Senegal Combassou is presumed to be parasitic upon Fire Finches in the wild state; but, in captivity, it has also placed its eggs in the nests of Cordon Bleus. In even the wildest stretch of the imagination, no one would call the Combassou a frequent breeder in captivity.

Only in a few isolated instances known to the writers has the Combassou revealed any of the tendencies which have unfortunately labeled it as overly aggressive. The frequent inspection of other birds' nests is sometimes bothersome, but the tyrannical individual is the exception rather than the rule.

JACKSON'S WHYDAH (*Drepanoplectes jacksoni*)

The writers have never had the opportunity of measuring the actual size of the very rare and showy Jackson's Whydah from Kenya; but, if memory serves correctly, the heavy body is somewhat larger than the White Winged Whydah and would therefore be about five or six inches long excluding tail. The luxuriously flamboyant and heavy tail is approximately twice the body length during the in color phase. It curves in a graceful arc like the tail of a cock domestic chicken.

The plumage is mostly glossy black particularly on the long and broad rooster-like tail feathers. The wings are brownish and have pale scalloped edges. The longer, squarish feathers on the neck form a weaver-like ruff which is raised in the fantastic display to the female. The beak is grayish and black.

The female is drab and sparrowlike in the typical female whydah manner. The male during the out of color phase is similar but slightly larger and more brownish.

Jackson's Whydah is a great showman and seemingly has borrowed characteristics from several birds. In addition to rooster-like tail feathers and a weaver-like neck ruff, this fascinating creature has borrowed the tactics of Bower Birds and Birds of Paradise to carry out his nuptial display.

The basic pattern of all Twinspots is the same as the sketch at upper left. Twinspots, though rare and expensive, are ideal aviary birds. Fischer's Whydah, second from left, is also very rare and extremely handsome in yellow and black. It belongs to the same genus as the Pintailed Whydah and is somewhat aggressive.

Jackson's Whydah, right and second from right, is one of the finest of all avicultural subjects. It is not only a very handsome species but is endowed with a flamboyant and interesting character. The small sketch at right shows the upraised tail feathers in its ebullient courting display.

The writers once had the experience of witnessing the lavish nuptial display of Jackson's Whydah in a zoo in Germany. It was quite an elaborate spectacle. The aviary had several patches of grass which grew several inches high. The male chose one of these patches and stamped out a circular area leaving an upright tuft of grasses which became the locale of the display. He sallied up into the air and dropped back to the ground brandishing his tail feathers in an upraised and fanspread manner. A few of the lower and more central tail feathers stayed in their natural position, and the writers have made a sketch of this display position to be included alongside the drawing of the male in a natural stance during the in color phase.

The frequent sallies into the air successfully attracted the female who approached in a properly demure manner. The male then stayed mostly on the ground but continued a series of strutting leaps into the air along with the raising of tail feathers in peacock pride. During this display, the female moves around just enough to keep the tuft of grasses between the two birds. She tries to pose as a bored sophisticate but cannot help viewing the display with awestruck admiration.

Jackson's Whydahs are rarely available and are usually rather expensive. After acclimation they are hardy. The diet is the simple finch diet with a little live food.

Success in breeding this species (the only member of its genus) is a rare achievement. This species as well as all those of the following genus is non-parasitic.

GIANT WHYDAH (*Coliuspasser progne progne*)

The beautiful Giant Whydah from South Africa is another prize for aviculturists. It is seldom available and rather expensive; but it is hardy, easy to acclimate, peaceful with even the smallest finches, and requires simple care.

The male in color is one of the most lavishly ornamented of all Whydahs. The body is approximately seven inches long, and the long flowing tail may reach up to eighteen inches. Of the eight to twelve long feathers, the two central ones show the greatest length; and the remainder are graduated. The wings are a greater than average length to support the weight of the tail in its curiously graceful, undulating flight.

The beak is pale bluish white, and the wings show a shoulder patch of red which fades to red-orange in captivity. Most of the wing feathers have brownish outer margins. Otherwise the male in color is jet black with an appearance of velvet in most areas and a shiny gloss in others.

Both the male in eclipse plumage and the female are drab and sparrow-like, but the male is larger than the female. The pattern is typical for most whydahs except the basic coloring has more of a grayish shade in the buff and the head stripes are greatly reduced. Some of the wing patch coloring is retained. The wings are somewhat darker than the average whydah pattern. The writers will never forget their first sight of Giant Whydahs.

They were out of color and seemed particularly uninteresting, but they had such high price tags that one could not help but study the birds carefully to determine the reason for such an exorbitant cost. Upon looking back, the price would be extremely reasonable these days.

As breeders, Giant Whydahs are seldom successful. Those successful breedings on record were usually accompanied as much by luck as by sensible management. Giant Whydahs, and all members of this genus, are non-parasitic. Tall grassy areas are preferred for nesting sites. Incubation time is twelve to thirteen days. Young leave the nest after fifteen to sixteen days. Both parents may feed the young; whereas, with most whydahs, the male ordinarily refuses to accept any parental responsibility whatsoever. Of course, the male may not have time to assist in rearing young if he has enough females to indulge in his polygamous nature.

Youngsters are similar to hens but show less dark markings. Sexes can be separated at an early age because males grow faster than hens.

Even though breeding in captivity is seldom accomplished, the male's display is a frequent occurrence. He flies up into the air and returns to hover slowly over the hen. The undulating flight enhances the rippling suppleness of the long tail feathers.

During the rainy season, males become so heavy with drenching that they cannot fly. Wild birds are easily caught by hand in this manner.

Delamere's Giant Whydah (*Coliuspasser progne delamerei*) is a subspecies with a very limited natural range. It is very rare. It is said to be distinguishable because its tail feathers are longer and more pointed, but less wide, than those of the Giant Whydah.

RED COLLARED WHYDAH (*Coliuspasser ardens ardens*)

In a way, the Red Collared Whydah is an overly simplified and junior version of the Giant Whydah. It is, of course, far less outstanding and smaller; but it also is less expensive and more readily available than the Giant Whydah. Nevertheless, it is a very handsome and an extremely desirable bird for mixed collections of birds larger than the average waxbill.

The male in color has a body length of three and a half inches exclusive of tail. The multiple tail feathers, usually twelve in number, are uniformly three-eighths of an inch wide. Those which have been shipped to the writers have had a tail length of six and a half inches, but they have not kept them long enough to determine whether or not the length increases with age. In maximum growth, the tail feathers should reach at least a length of eight inches.

The beak is black; and the overall coloring is velvety black with a prominent orange-red half collar which extends across the throat and pale brown, fine margins on the secondary flight and covert feathers. The shade of red fades slightly in captivity. The Red Collared Whydah is a handsome bird and is unusual as well as rather rare. It is not as peaceful as the Paradise

Whydah, but the writers house it with weavers and larger finches with no damaging effects.

Males out of color and females are pale brown with dark brown streaks especially prominent on the back. Males are larger than females and have longer tails measuring one and a half inches when out of color. The male is not as white on the underparts, and the light eye patch is missing.

Red Collared Whydahs are extremely hardy and easily acclimated; but, in cold and damp climates, they should be kept inside for a few weeks. Males are far more abundant in shipments than females. The diet is very simple, but some live food is preferred. This species is not parasitic and has been bred in captivity.

The male Red Collared Whydah is one of those birds which often does not go fully out of color or which often does not come completely into color. In this respect, it is the most inconsistent of all whydahs ever owned by the writers.

An important subspecies is the Long Tailed Black Whydah (*Coliuspasser ardens concolor*), which, though very seldom available even in its West African range, is different from the Red Collared. The red collar is completely absent, but other characteristics are the same.

RED NAPED WHYDAH (*Coliuspasser laticauda*)

Many authorities classify this East African bird as a subspecies of the Red Collared Whydah, but the writers will go along with Mackworth-Praed and Grant in reporting it as a separate species even though there are many similarities and an inevitable confusion. It is very rare in captivity.

The head is red on the upperparts, and the tail is wider but not as long. The red collar is wider. All other characteristics are similar except the tail is rather rigid and stiff by comparison.

A subspecies, *Coliuspasser laticauda suahelica*, has a longer tail.

RED SHOULDERED WHYDAH (*Coliuspasser axillaris*)

Another popular name for the rarely imported Red Shouldered Whydah is Fan Tailed Whydah. It is non-parasitic but is almost certainly polygamous.

The male in color is velvety black with red or orange-brown epaulette-like shoulder markings, bordered by buff. The beak is a bluish-horn shade. The tail is short even in the male during the nuptial phase.

Females and males out of color are like most whydahs in their drabness, but the male shows some bright orange in the wing.

Several races show very slight variations in size of beak, wing measurements, and shoulder coloring. The shoulder shades in some vary to orange-yellow.

MARSH WHYDAH (*Coliuspasser hartlaubi*)

This is a medium-long tailed species mostly black except for a yellow shoulder patch followed by buffish primary and secondary coverts. It is very rarely imported and far less interesting than most members of the family.

YELLOW SHOULDERED WHYDAH (*Coliuspasser macrocercus*)

The rarely imported Yellow Shouldered Whydah from Eastern Africa will undoubtedly never arouse much interest with aviculturists. It is very similar to the White Winged Whydah which is somewhat easier to get and less costly. The tail is of medium length, somewhat broad and graduated, and stiff rather than long and fluttery. Overall length is about nine inches.

The basic color is black including the beak, feet, and legs. The only color variation is in the wings. A broad shoulder patch is yellow, and the edges of the wing feathers are rimmed in a pale brownish shade.

Females and out of color males show some yellow in the shoulder area. The male is larger and has bolder markings above. Otherwise they follow a typical whydah color and pattern.

YELLOW MANTLED or YELLOW BACKED WHYDAH (*Coliuspasser macrourus*)

The extensively distributed Yellow Mantled Whydah is fairly often imported and is slightly more interesting than the above species. The tail is more fan-shaped, and the yellow covers the back and mantle as well as shoulder areas. The shade of yellow is not perfectly bright, but it is an improvement over the Yellow Shouldered Whydah.

Females and males out of color are typical for the genus. Both are dull and poorly marked. The upperparts are broadly streaked with black. The male, however, is slightly larger.

Females of Yellow Shouldered Whydahs and Yellow Mantled Whydahs can be differentiated by duller streaks on the upperparts of the Yellow Mantled Whydah.

WHITE WINGED WHYDAH (*Coliuspasser albonotatus*)

Like the preceding four species, the White Winged is not a truly interesting bird. When one thinks of Whydahs, the thought image is long fluttering tails and exotic adornments. Though the tails are slightly extended on males in color, they cannot be called long. There is also a lack of imagination in the color scheme. The White Winged is smaller than the preceding four and is somewhat rare in captivity.

The male in color is six inches long including a tail of two and three-fourths inches long. The rather long beak is pearl-gray, and the all over coloring is black except for the following markings on the wings: white underwing coverts, bright yellow shoulder patch, white primary coverts and those parts of primary flights covered by the coverts, and buffish margins on the secondary covert feathers. One subspecies (*eques*) has cinnamon on the shoulder.

The female and male out of color are grayish-brown, pale on underparts and darkly streaked on upperparts. The yellow patch remains during the out of color phase.

The White Winged Whydah is very hardy; but, because of size, it should not be housed with small finches. This is true also of the preceding four species. The diet is standard for all whydahs. The non-parasitic White Winged Whydah has been bred in captivity.

CHAPTER 11

Weavers

The very large family of weavers has some of the most popular of aviary subjects. Nearly all undergo a seasonal change of plumage thus showing a close alignment to whydahs. Many males in nuptial plumage are very beautiful; but many are bypassed by aviculturists because they are dull, uninteresting, and often unpleasantly aggressive. Only a comparative few are available. The writers have included only those birds which are imported for aviculture.

Weavers are often gregarious and fraternal colony birds carefully building huge masses of a nest which has many apartmental compartments. In captivity, many weavers are assiduous in exercising their nestbuilding talents; but very few follow through to the actual rearing of youngsters. The writers feel certain that more success could be attained if the aviculturist would house colonies of these birds rather than individual pairs of various species.

The talent for weaving is really surprising in these birds. Their proclivities for nestbuilding extend far beyond the mere placing of a piece of material into a packed-up mass of grasses. Each strand of grass is carefully and intricately woven into place. Extrication is not a simple tug. Instead, it becomes an exasperating unravelling process full of complications which cannot help but lend admiration to the construction talents of this wonderful family. The nests are usually covered over to protect them from rain.

Several weavers have red in their native color schemes which turns to orange in captivity. Both colors are beautiful, but the fading in captivity indicates the absence of certain live foods which afford the production of red pigments. The Orange Weaver was obviously named from captive specimens because, in the wild state, males in color show a vivid red instead of a bright orange. The absence of these pigments in no way affects the general health of the bird. Weavers are an unusually hardy lot after acclimation and are among the longest-lived of all aviary birds. The bright colors of nuptial plumage are not assumed until the second year.

Most weavers cannot safely be housed with small or mild finches such as waxbills, Australian Grassfinches, small mannikins, serins, or mild-mannered whydahs. For the most part this group encompasses the bolder finches which must be separated from the smaller birds.

Weavers are very hardy and require the simplest of care. Some live food is advisable and is necessary if breeding success is to be achieved.

They are apt to panic in cages but are ideal in aviaries.

Most weavers out of color are extremely difficult to sex. In many cases, either before coming into color or after going out of color, there may be traces or spare feathers showing the male's nuptial coloring. These birds are assuredly males. To help eliminate guesswork, weavers should be carefully searched on the rump and undertail coverts for these traces of nuptial coloring because these areas are often the first to show colors as well as the last to lose them. Usually males are purported to be somewhat larger than females; but the difference, if any, is so slight that it cannot be used as an accurate sex distinction.

In most cases, females are singularly undistinguished and, like female whydahs, are drab and sparrowlike. Males out of color are the same. Incubation time is twelve to thirteen days, and the young fledge in fourteen days.

With the exception of the Baya Weaver, all weavers with which aviculturists are concerned are from Africa.

ORANGE WEAVER (*Euplectes orix francisciana*)

The Orange Weaver is also called the Orange Bishop, Red Bishop, or Little Bishop. It is probably the most popular member of the weaver family with aviculturists because of its attractiveness, low price, and usual availability. The natural range is a broad area from east to west across central portions of Africa.

This species, even though not quite four inches long including a one-inch tail, is a little too aggressive to be housed with small waxbills or Australian Grassfinches. It is excellent with whydahs, larger mannikins, and most of the popular weavers of similar size.

The male in color is a flashing beauty. The beak is grayish-horn with black tips. The head is velvet-black to the back of the crown. A brilliant sweep of orange covers the nape of the neck, the lower facial area, throat, and chest. The feathers on the nape have a tinge of red and are somewhat longer than the average. Furthermore they are slightly recurved giving a fleecy ruff which is erectile during the display.

The back and scapulars are a deep and less bright orange-red. Flights and coverts are brown with pale margins on the outer edges of the feathers. The rump and elongated, lacy, and filmy upper and lower tail coverts, covering most of the brownish tail, are the same brilliant orange as found on the nape and chest. The lower chest and abdomen are black.

In the wild state Orange Weavers have brilliant red replacing the orange. Those newly imported males in color show the same red and are sometimes sold as entirely different birds, but after a moult in captivity the red fades to orange. The brilliance is hardly reduced, and the orange still is vivid enough against the velvety black to produce one of aviculture's most brightly colored and most popular birds.

177

The name Orange Weaver was quite obviously given to birds which had been out of color for at least one season in captivity. Not many Orange Weavers in native red coloring are available in the bird trade. For some unknown reason, males in color do not make satisfactory adjustments after travelling. Though most weavers are inordinately hardy, Orange Weavers in native coloring must be regarded as delicate and difficult.

The writers prefer to import Orange Weavers in eclipse plumage and await the development of nuptial plumage even though females usually outnumber males in such importations.

Males out of color and females are streakishly brown on the upperparts and warm buff on the underparts. The eyebrow is straw colored, and the outer margins of the dark feathers on back, wings, and tail are pale buff. The buff on the underparts fades to dusty white on the undertail coverts. The underside of the tail is a dull grayish-brown. Undertail coverts are very long and extend nearly to the end of the tail.

When out of color, the Orange Weaver has a high degree of smooth uniformity compared to the Napoleon and most other weavers. The shades of tans and browns have a warm earthy appearance in comparison.

There are several subspecies of the Orange Weaver. The ornithologically typical race (*orix*) is different from the usually available avicultural race. *Orix*, from South Africa, is called the Grenadier Weaver. It is similar in appearance but slightly larger and somewhat stronger. The chin, throat, and sides of head are black. The orange extends from the top of the crown instead of the back of the crown.

The Zanzibar Orange Bishop Weaver (*Euplectes nigroventris*) is very much like the Crimson Crowned Weaver. It is smaller than the Orange Weaver, and all its underparts are black. The crown and forehead are orange as in the Crimson Crowned Weaver. The undertail coverts are orange. This species is very rare in captivity because of its limited East African range.

CRIMSON CROWNED WEAVER (*Euplectes hordeacea*)

The Crimson Crowned Weaver, also called Black Winged Red Bishop and Fire Crowned Weaver, is very much like the Orange Weaver. It is four and a half inches long including a tail of one and one-fourth inches and, therefore, is larger than the Orange Weaver. The orange on this bird starts at the top of the head instead of the back of the head as in the Orange Weaver. On the underside the orange is less extensive and less circular. It stops at the lower portion of the neck instead of covering most of the chest as in the Orange Weaver. The beak is larger and darker. The throat has black extending about three-eighths of an inch below the beak, and the black facial area is somewhat more attractively proportioned.

The orange collar is fleecy, recurved and erectile.

The velvety-black underparts are more noticeably extensive on the chest area. The thighs are buff. The elongated tail coverts on both sides and the

178

large rump area are bright orange. The brownish tail is one-fourth of an inch longer and is not covered by the tail coverts. A deep, dull orange is mixed with the brown in a larger area covering the back, shoulders, and part of the wings. The wings are the same as in the Orange Weaver.

In the wild state or in newly imported birds, the orange is brilliant red.

The female is like a large female Orange Weaver.

The rather aggressive Crimson Crowned Weaver is not often available and is usually higher in price than the Orange Weaver.

NAPOLEON WEAVER (*Euplectes afra afra*)

The Napoleon Weaver from West Africa is also one of the Bishop Weavers. It is perhaps next to the Orange Weaver in both popularity and availability. It is similar in requirements and habits, though a little less aggressive than the Orange Weaver. The Napoleon is a pleasant and color-contrasting companion to the Orange Weaver even though it lacks the added glamour of the fleecy recurved ruff and elongated, filmy tail coverts. The basic colors of black and yellow are bold, bright, and very pretty. The size is approximately the same as the Orange Weaver.

The male in color shows a similar pattern of brown in the wings with paler edges to the feathers as in the Orange Weaver. The tail also is brownish. The rest of the colorings are nicely divided yellows and blacks. The beak and a large facial area are black, the pattern of which includes a narrow forehead band and a line through the eyes which encircles a large cheek area and cuts downward to include a broad throat area extending almost to the upper chest. Black starts on the lower chest area and extends to the ventral area. On the underparts, yellow covers the undertail coverts and a broad band across the chest. The flanks show yellow irregularly bordering the black. A prominent yellow covers the lower back, rump, and uppertail coverts. Most of the upperparts of the head, except for the narrow black forehead, are yellow; this bright color extends to the shoulders and connects with the broad chestband.

The females and males out of color are shaped and sized like the Orange Weaver, but the basic ground color of yellowish-straw is less warm than that of the Orange Weaver, and it is more cluttered with dark streaks on chest and back than the Orange Weaver. An eyebrow is more distinctly yellowish.

Sexes are extremely difficult to determine while males are out of color. The male is said to be slightly larger than the female, but the difference is so slight that it has missed the writers.

In nuptial display, the nape feathers are somewhat erectile; but they do not show the recurved fleecy appearance of the Orange Weaver.

There are several races of the Napoleon Weaver. None are as frequently imported and none are as attractive as the nominate race. One subspecies from South Africa, known as the Taha Weaver, shows all the underparts black as with several of the other subspecies.

YELLOW BACKED or YELLOW SHOULDERED WEAVER
(*Euplectes capensis*)

Seldom imported, and not always admired, is the Yellow Backed Weaver. Most of the coloring is black except for a broad patch of yellow on the rump and another on the shoulders. The flights show pale edges.

Nearly six inches in length, this species, as expected, is usually considered aggressive.

LITTLE MASKED or ATLAS WEAVER (*Sitagra luteola* or *Ploceus luteolus*)

There are several species of weavers bearing certain similarities to the Little Masked Weaver, but this is the smallest and one of the prettiest. Though none of this group is frequently available, there is a good colored picture in this book which can be used by the reader in sorting out the differences from the other species.

The Little Masked Weaver is not quite four inches long including a tail slightly over an inch in length. In size, it is comparable to the Napoleon and Orange Weavers; but it is much more peaceful.

The dominant coloring is a bright yellow covering all the underparts and much of the head. The beak and a large facial area are black. In this species the black covers the forehead to the forepart of the crown, drops down to the eyes, flares backwards surrounding the cheeks, and then drops into the throat.

The shoulders are deep yellow tinged with brown; and the wings, though overcast with a slight greenish-yellow shade, are typically weaverlike brown with paler outer margins. The female is much duller in color and has no black on the head.

The West African Little Weaver (*Sitagra monacha*) is very similar but slightly smaller. The nape and underparts are brighter yellow, and the back shows no streaking. The two species are frequently confused, but the West African Little Weaver is very rare by comparison. If it were not for this rarity, the writers would be inclined to identify the species pictured in this book as *monacha* instead of *luteola*.

HALF MASKED or VITELLINE WEAVER (*Plesiositagra vitellinus* or *Ploceus vitellinus*)

The Half Masked Weaver is one of the more frequently available of many confusing and very similar species, most of which are generally called Masked or Yellow Weavers. It is pretty, but it attracts much less attention than the Orange or Napoleon Weaver.

The approximate size is four and a half inches including a tail of about one and a half inches. It is slightly larger than the Little Masked. It has a shade of reddish chestnut on the crown and at the base of the throat. The black facial mask is confined to a very narrow forehead band and a very small chin area. The wings are decidedly more brownish.

180

Other Masked Weavers with descriptive differences are listed below. Most are now very rare in aviculture; but, with many African changes forthcoming in the 1960's, several may become available. All require the simple care afforded all weavers covered so far in this chapter.

Heuglin's Masked Weaver (*Plesiositagra heuglini* or *Ploceus heuglini*) lacks chestnut on the crown and has more black on the throat. The tail is shorter, and the body is slightly larger.

Tanganyika Masked Weaver (*Ploceus reichardi*) has a more extensive black area on the forehead and throat, and the chest and flanks are tinged with chestnut.

Masked or Cabanis' Weaver (*Ploceus intermedius*) is also called the Abyssinian Weaver. The overall size is nearly six inches long. The black facial area is perhaps even slightly more extensive than in the Little Masked Weaver and far more so than in the Vitelline Weaver.

The Southern Masked Weaver (*Ploceus velatus*) shows more black on the throat area than the Vitelline Weaver.

The Slender Billed Weaver (*Icteropsis pelzelni*) does not go through a nuptial change of plumage. The bill is more slender than the foregoing, and the yellow has more of a golden chestnut tint. The black facial area is similar to that of the Masked Weaver.

The Loango Slender Billed Weaver (*Icteropsis subpersonata*) has an olive tinge on the mantle, back, and scapulars. It is slightly more chestnut shaded below. Otherwise it is similar to the above and is extremely rare in its native range.

Ruppel's Weaver (*Ploceus gabbula*) is a departure from the above species in that the black mask is replaced by chestnut.

The Southern Brown Throated Weaver (*Ploceus xanthopterus*) has a chestnut face and throat area. The forehead is yellow.

The Golden Palm Weaver (*Ploceus bojeri*) has the entire head, nape, and throat orange with no mask.

RUFOUS NECKED WEAVER (*Plesiositagra cucullatus* or *Ploceus cucullatus*)

More than six inches long, the attractive Rufous Necked Weaver is best kept with budgies and medium sized hardy softbills. It is much too aggressive and too large to be housed with small or medium sized finches. The personality is unfortunate because it otherwise is an ideal aviary bird. It is extremely hardy and very long lived.

The male in color differs from the above patterned birds by having the entire head and V-shaped throat termination very dark brown. This coloring is so intense that it almost appears to be black. The nape fades to a reddish-brown or rufous shade. The beak is black, and the eyes are a dominating bright red. The underparts are bright yellow, and the upperparts show the typical weaverlike pattern in a more striking contrast of darker back. The

181

wing feathers have pale yellowish edges. The rump is yellow, and the tail is rather short.

When out of color, the male does not revert to the drabness of the female. The brightness is greatly reduced, and the head fades to an olive-yellow shade. The bill fades to a pale horn shade.

Females nearly undergo a change of plumage during the breeding season. The head assumes a slight cast of olive, and the underparts are more yellowish.

The writers always offer sunflower seed to large birds such as this species, and it is surprising how many they take. The diet otherwise is the same for all weavers. Live food is very much appreciated, but overindulgence in mealworms can cause trouble.

The personality problem may lead the bird fancier to try these birds in planted aviaries along with softbills, cardinals, quails, and doves. This is a mistake because it leads to rapid defoliation. The writers once included a pair of Rufous Necked Weavers in a large planted aviary because no other space was available. The birds were delighted with a pine tree in the aviary and ignored all the large-leafed shrubs. They stripped the pine tree and built a neat, compact nest which had a basket-like firmness because of the drying pine needles.

Unfortunately the pine needles were insufficient to finish the job. The birds rearranged the needles while waiting impatiently for the tree to grow a new supply. As soon as the tree grew a new crop of needles, the birds stripped the tree and began work on a new nest. The tree, discouraged by such a procedure, decided life was not worthwhile and promptly died. As is usual with this species, the hobby of building nests did not lead to laying eggs or rearing young.

There are several subspecies of the Rufous Necked Weaver and several other species extremely similar in pattern and coloring. One subspecies, the Abyssinian Weaver (*P. c. abyssinicus*), has been kept in captivity. The Gambian Black Headed Weaver (*Sitagra melanocephala*) is considerably smaller but larger than the Niger Black Headed Weaver (*Sitagra capitalis*).

RED BILLED WEAVER (*Quelea quelea*)

The Red Billed Weaver is often available and is very attractive. It is an extremely hardy bird and requires the very simplest of care, but it is too aggressive for small waxbills and Australian Grassfinches. The writers keep it with large finches such as other weavers, Java Rice Birds, and the larger or more aggressive whydahs. In many instances, if no other space is available, the Red Billed is housed with budgies whose diet and personalities are perfectly acceptable as companions. It likes mealworms and other live food but can do without them.

The size of the Red Billed Weaver totals four and one-fourth inches including the tail of one and one-fourth inches.

The male in color has a large and very deep red bill and eye ring. A large black facial patch includes the eye, encircles a large cheek area, and ends on the throat. The wings show the typical weaver pattern of brown feathers with pale edges. The tail is blackish, and the feet and legs are reddish.

On all the rest of the bird a very becoming shade of rose overlies the basic tan of the out of color phase. This rose cast fades considerably on the lower chest, abdomen, and sides.

The male out of color still retains a reddish shade to the beak, but it is paler. Females are similar to most weavers except they are larger and have a larger beak of pale yellowish-buff. The beak of the female is slightly smaller than that of the male.

The Red Billed Weaver usually is not considered a breeder in captivity due to its quarrelsome nature. In the wild state it breeds in colonies.

A close relative, Russ' Weaver, lacks the black facial patch and shows just a hint of a shadow around the outline. Most authorities consider it a dimorphic variety of the above. The writers do not particularly care for Russ' Weaver because it gives the appearance of not having completed the color change. The facial patch is rose, often with a slaty shading. Comparably, Russ' Weaver is fortunately too rare to be considered important in aviculture.

Another closely allied species is the Poker Headed Weaver or Red Headed Quelea (*Quelea erythrops*). This species, now rarely available, is similar except that the head, throat, and nape of the male in color is red. The beak is blackish, and the black facial patch is missing even though there is often a blackish chin patch which may extend into the throat.

SCALY CROWNED WEAVER (*Sporopipes squamifrons*)

The charming Scaly Crowned does not undergo a change in plumage during the breeding season, and sexes are always difficult to determine. The male has a slightly bolder mustache. It is a rarely available South African species. The price is usually rather high, but the unusual pattern and pleasant disposition makes the increase worthwhile. The writers have always been exceptionally fond of this benign but somber little bird which can safely be kept even with the smallest waxbills. During the breeding season, however, it is wiser to keep them with slightly larger birds.

The overall size is four inches long including a tail of one and one-fourth inches.

The main charm is in the contrasting blacks and delicate white edges on a basically gray bird. The beak has a pale pink on the upper mandible and a whitish shade on the lower mandible. A broad black walrus-typed mustache begins just under the beak and contrasts nicely with the otherwise white throat. The lores are black. A fascinating pattern marks the area of the forehead and crown as well as the wings and tail. Each feather is black with fine white outer margins to give a prominent but fine-lined scaled effect. Because the feathers on the forehead and crown are very small, the effect is one of minutely executed detail work. The wings and tail have the pattern in a bolder effect because the feathers are larger. Only those wing feathers visible when the wings are folded are patterned. Most of the flight feathers are dull gray.

The rest of the bird is a uniform and smooth gray which is paler on the underparts and darker on the upperparts.

The Scaly Crowned Weaver is hardy after a rather strict acclimation period. It is, however, never quite as hardy as most weavers.

Another member of the genus is the Speckle Fronted Weaver (*Sporopipes frontalis*) which has several races with paler and darker shadings. Though this species is perhaps more often available in its east to west central African distribution, it is rarely available on the avicultural market. It is less popular because it is less attractive.

The Speckle Fronted Weaver is larger than the above and has a cinnamon shading on the top of the head and neck. There is just a slight dark mustache dropping from the corners of the lower mandible. This line then curves upward to outline the lower cheek area. The top of the head is finely dotted with white. The whitish edged feathers of wing and tail are brownish, and the underparts are pale beige. The beak, feet, and legs are whitish-horn.

MADAGASCAR WEAVER (*Foudia madagascariensis*)

The Madagascar Weaver from Madagascar, Mauritius, Seychelles, and St. Helena Islands, is practically never available nowadays even though it was once common in the field of aviculture. It is common in its wild state. This is a beautiful though quarrelsome bird with most of the coloring being a superb red.

Attractive differences are shown with black on the beak, on a streak covering the lores and extending through the eyes, and on the centers of the feathers of the back, wings, and tail. The feet are flesh colored.

The female is brownish with the centers of the feathers on the upperparts blackish.

The Comoro Weaver (*Foudia eminentissima*) from Comoro Island is very similar except for the following differences: larger black beak, abdomen and lower underparts tawny-buff, and a brownish-olive basic back coloring. This species is even more quarrelsome than the preceding and must on all accounts be separated from weaker birds.

BAYA WEAVER (*Ploceus philippinus*)

The rather poorly decorated Baya Weaver is not often imported if dealers have their say. Bayas are somewhat plain and uninteresting and are usually available only because they are substituted for other more desirable species.

The male in color assumes a bright yellow cap on the head which gives rise to a popular name of Golden Crowned Weaver. The chest is golden-buff; a dark mask includes a large facial area, chin, and throat; and the rest of the bird looks like most weavers out of color.

184

When out of color, sexes are practically indistinguishable. Their main features, yellow head and chest, disappear leaving streaky and dull sparrow-like patterns.

Baya Weavers, of which there are several slightly varying species, do not occur in Africa. The most frequently available race is the Indian race described above. Several subspecies occur in a large Asiatic range, but importation is infrequent. All are rather large, nearly six inches, and are not peaceful. They excel in building nests and are more interesting from this standpoint than from color.

The illustration is taken from Butler's *Foreign Finches in Captivity*. However, the bird in the picture is much prettier than the bird in reality. The face is dull brownish instead of black, and the chest shows less yellow.

CHAPTER 12

Quail Finches, Java Rice Birds, Sparrows, and Rose Finches

The grouping of these birds into one chapter does not indicate any relationship whatsoever. There just seems to be no other place to put them. They are not members of any previous group nor are they members of any following group. This, then, is a chapter of miscellaneous birds.

Ornithologically, the Quail Finches are placed somewhere between the mannikins and waxbills, but they are sufficiently unique to be included in neither family.

Java Rice Birds are often called munias, and they would normally be classed with the mannikin family. However, the general characteristics are greatly different.

Sparrows are closely aligned to weavers but are somewhat different from the aviculturist's general conception of weavers. Only one species of this large family is important in aviculture.

Rose Finches are in turn rather closely related to some sparrows; but, as an avicultural family, they also stand alone.

QUAIL FINCH (*Ortygospiza atricollis*)

The strange Quail Finch has adopted not only the markings of quails but also the terrestrial habitat of most quails. Not frequently available, the Quail Finch from Africa is considered a curious rarity in the field of aviculture. There are several races with slight differences. All are interesting and quietly attractive. If given satisfactory accommodations, the Quail Finch will breed; but the accomplishment is considered rather an exception. Small live foods, in addition to the standard finch diet, are necessary in rearing young.

Quail Finches are rather shy and spend a great part of their time hiding in grasses. They seem to dislike perches and open aviaries. If disturbed, they often panic in the same manner as quails. They fly quickly upwards without regard to aviary roofs. Such a tendency is rather hazardous.

186

The coloring of Quail Finches has mainly been given for protective measures. Though dulled by earthy browns, grays, and dusky shadings, they are nevertheless attractive in a subdued way. The total length is approximately three and a half inches including a very short tail. The upperparts are dusky brownish, and the underparts have fine white bars on the dark upper chest and flanks. The lower chest and areas adjoining the flanks are bright chestnut. The central abdominal area is a pale grayish which pales to white in the ventral area. The male has a blackish area covering the forehead, throat, and face. The female shows dusky brown in these same areas. The female has more of a buffish shade in the barred areas. The beak coloring shows some variation. The upper mandible may vary from red to black, but the lower mandible is always reddish.

Variations in different races are rather minor with darker or lighter shadings. The most important variation is a bright white underlining the eyes and chin.

The writers have never had many Quail Finches because of a lack of suitable environment. There is little point in keeping these charming little creatures unless the aviary is just right for them. They prefer a dust bath instead of the usual liquid facilities, and the food supplies must naturally be placed on the ground. Concrete floors are totally unsatisfactory. Unless the floor is of soil, turf, or peat, Quail Finches may show a proneness to foot problems.

JAVA RICE BIRD (*Padda oryzivora*)

Java Rice Birds are among the most readily available, hardiest, and most popular of all finches. Their low price and smooth velvety plumage are major factors for their popularity. Many bird fanciers have started their hobby with the purchase of a Java Rice Bird. In the United States the Java Rice Bird as a caged household pet is perhaps exceeded in number only by Budgerigars and canaries.

The writers prefer to see Java Rice Birds in nice big aviaries where their great beauty is maintained with ease. In cages, these birds often become scraggly derelicts with frayed tail and flight feathers and thinning head feathers. In such conditions, no one would term the Rice Bird as beautiful. Most of the beauty of the Rice Bird stems from the smoothness and sharp contrasts in coloring. Feather problems quickly destroy this beauty.

The overall size of the Java Rice Bird is a heavy-bodied five and a half inches including the tail, which is slightly over an inch long. Since Rice Birds are large, they should be housed with weavers, Cutthroats, Whydahs, Saffrons, and similarly sized birds rather than small defenseless birds. A few individuals become complete bullies with small finches, and there is no point in creating a hazard. The Java Rice Bird is also a good companion for Budgerigars. The dietary requirements are very simple and either the standard parrakeet or finch diet is acceptable. Live foods and fruit are not required.

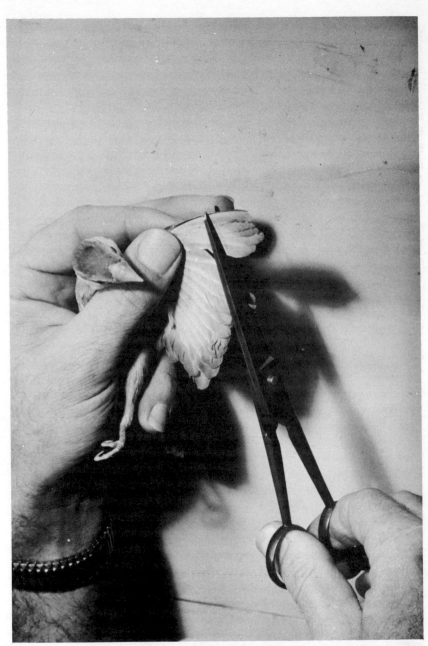

Pattern for slowdown clipping for aggressive birds. This young Java Rice Bird can now go with smaller finches without fear of bullying. Clip both wings to reduce aggressiveness.

The Gray Java Rice Bird is the most attractive of the three color varieties. It is also the original, or wild type, and is the least costly. The head is glossy black except for a large, very white cheek patch covering most of the facial area below the eye. A prominent, fleshy eye ring is red; and the huge beak shows a deep rose-pink concentration near the upper and lower bases which fades gradually to whitish at the tips. The feet and legs are also pinkish. The tail is black, and the undertail coverts are white. The body is gray. On the back, wings, and chest, the shading is a uniform soft slate-gray. The abdomen is buffish-gray fading to a whitish shade in the ventral area. The overall effect is one of smooth, uncluttered uniformity with pleasantly balanced contrasts. In good plumage, the Java Rice Bird has a lovely sheen which cannot help but attract admiring glances.

The White Java Rice Bird is completely white in a glowing, glossy sheen except for the rose, red, and pink found in the beak, eye ring, feet, and legs. In some individuals an occasional dark feather indicates a nearly suppressed pied factor, but most people still call these individuals White Javas. White Javas are beautiful contrasts to Gray Javas; and, though more costly, they are no longer expensive. The White Java is a mutation which occurred in captivity. It is not an albino. Immature White Javas often show extensive areas of buffish-grays which later change to white upon maturation.

A third variety, the Calico, or Pied Java Rice Bird, appears to be a mixture of the two previously described varieties. As in Society Finches, there are almost no two individuals alike. Pieds may be predominantly dark or predominantly light, but the most attractive is a nearly equal division of colors. Those leaning far to the basic gray pattern are usually unattractive because of the destruction of the beautiful and classic uniformity found in the Gray Java Rice Bird. The Calico, or Pied Java Rice Bird, is also the result of a mutation in captivity. The price is usually midway between the prices of the gray and white varieties.

Since both the White and Calico Java Rice Birds were developed in captivity, these varieties have acquired the reputation of being better breeders than the Gray Java Rice Bird. This is an unfortunate misconception. Aviary bred Gray Java Rice Birds are excellent breeders in captivity. They almost outstrip the Zebra Finch in productivity. Trapped wild Gray Java Rice Birds, however, rarely show an inclination to go to nest. Since the number of imported, wild trapped birds greatly exceeds the number of aviary bred Grays, the average successful breeding is understandably completely out of balance. Aviary bred Gray Java Rice Birds are considerably more expensive than promotionally priced wild trapped imports, but they are always worth the extra cost to the bird fancier. Unfortunately, no one can look at a Gray Java Rice Bird and accurately determine whether it was raised in captivity or was trapped in the wild. In this instance, the reliability of the dealer is all-important.

A standard parakeet nest box is ordinarily preferred by Java Rice Birds. It is usually stuffed with dried grasses and lined with small feathers or nesting hair. Incubation time is thirteen to fourteen days, and the chicks usually leave the nest in three weeks.

Sexual characteristics are not easily determined; but, if a male and a female are held beak to beak, the male will show a larger and more massive beak, especially at the base. The female has a more slender beak with a sharper angle at the tip. Usually the hen has less color on the beak and on the eye ring, but such variations may also be attributed to age.

Immature Gray Java Rice Birds are dull grayish with just a faint hint of rose in the beaks. Before they begin to acquire adult plumage, usually starting at four months of age, Rice Birds can be finger tamed in much the same manner as Budgerigars. The wing must be clipped to prevent flying and to remove some of the natural independence. The Java Rice Bird is one of the few finches which can be finger tamed without resorting to hand feeding before the weaning period.

A finger tamed Java Rice Bird can be considered a delightful pet provided the bird fancier does not require additional talents such as singing or talking abilities.

GOLDEN SPARROW (*Auripasser luteus*)

The Golden Sparrow, from Africa, is the only sparrow of sufficient importance in aviculture to rate an admirable standing; and even this standing is given with a great deal of equanimity. The Golden Sparrow is reasonably attractive and frequently available in African importations, but its aggressive personality precludes it as an ideal companion in mixed collections. It can be mixed only with larger and more aggressive weavers, Java Rice Birds, Cutthroats, and birds of similar size and disposition. Moreover, it is not a good breeder in captivity. In all honesty, this is one species which the writers try to avoid. Regardless of the extreme affection which they feel for many birds, the writers hold the Golden Sparrow in a category of complete indifference.

The total size is four and a half inches long including a tail of one and three-fourths inches. The male has a predominant black beak and dark eyes which contrast sharply with the yellowed brightness of head, neck, and all underparts extending through the tail coverts. The undersides and uppersides of the forked tail are grayish. The rump is dull yellow with some brown. A marked color contrast occurs in the pronounced brown of the back and wings. The brown is mildly mixed with streaks of yellow. The wing coverts and primary flights are mostly grayish.

The overall pattern of the male is rather attractive, but the female is a neutralized and colorless bird. The yellow is greatly dulled, and the brown on the wings is only slightly darker than the dull head and chest. The beak is a pale horn color.

The Golden Sparrow is extremely hardy and requires meager care. It is very fond of mealworms but can do without them.

ROSE FINCHES (genus *Carpodacus*)

Rose Finches enjoy a widespread range throughout much of the world in their slightly varying species. They take kindly to captivity and breed well; but captivity, unfortunately, does not enhance their charms. In all species the rosy shadings fade to a dull yellowish-straw shade. Moreover, most are aggressive birds and cannot be kept with small finches. They do well with larger weavers, Java Rice Birds, and similar personalities.

Without their attractive rosy hues overlying heads and chests, the Rose Finches are perhaps even more sparrowlike than the female English Sparrow. Those received from foreign countries are usually sent as substitutions for other more desirable aviary subjects. Those native birds cared for by aviculturists are usually rescued nestlings or injured individuals. In all fairness to the species, these hand fed youngsters become delightfully tame and enchanting pets. Even without their rosy coloring, they command an interest because of their individualistic personalities. The writers have reared many nestlings of the California Linnet by hand and have been more than repaid by the show of affection.

The species most frequently available are the Scarlet Rose Finch of Western Europe and India (*Carpodacus erythrinus*), the Purple Finch of Northeastern America (*Carpodacus purpureus*), and the California Linnet or Mexican Rose Finch (*Carpodacus mexicanus*).

The writers have had considerable experience with the California Linnet which happily abounds in many California areas. This species is a tireless singer; and, though it is not the best avian musician, it at least seems to be constantly rehearsing. The song is very cheerful and not unlike that of the Chaffinch even though it is somewhat harsh. Nevertheless, the California Linnet is the best singer in the genus. The writers do not know about other species, but the California Linnet has often been used in hybridizing with canaries. The offspring are not very colorful, but they are among the most frequent of all singers.

Purple Finches and California Linnets are protected by law and may not legally be kept in captivity without a permit. However, bird fanciers may obtain such required permits in the event of disabilities of individuals which would mean an inability to survive in the wild state.

The diet for these birds is usually parakeet mix; but they should also be given plenty of greens, fruit, and some live food. With proper color-inducing foods, someone may yet manage to maintain the natural color in captivity; but the color food generally used for canaries does not accomplish the desired result.

CHAPTER 13

Miscellaneous Central and South American Finches

CUBAN MELODIOUS (*Tiaris canora*)

The very small, alert, and attractive Cuban Melodious Finch, from Cuba and nearby islands, has many of the vivacious charms of waxbills; but it is far more aggressive and should be mixed either with larger birds or with equally aggressive birds. In a collection of waxbills, the average individual of this species during the breeding season will soon have the entire flock either subjugated or feather plucked. Not every individual is of such a disposition, and there are many varying personalities, but the bird fancier must exercise caution in adding the Cuban Melodious to an average collection.

The Cuban Melodious is a Grassquit of about three and a half inches in length. It is slightly more plump than most waxbills and, like the Fire Finch, spends a great deal of time on the ground hunting for seeds and small insects. As an aviary bird it is excellent in every respect except for the above-mentioned aggressiveness. It is steady and quite tame, more than reasonably hardy, and shows off very well. The acclimation period is usually very short.

The male has an unusual head pattern which never fails to attract attention even though the rest of the coloring is rather subdued. Intense black covers the beak, cheeks, lower facial area, and throat. This area is surrounded with a broad circular frame of bright yellow starting with a fine yellow line above the eye and circling downwards in a broadening sweep to include the upper chest area. In a way, this facial and head pattern reminds one of a wild pansy; and this may have prompted the poetic expression that finches are like "flying flowers."

The rest of the bird is dull by comparison. A less intense shade of black on the chest becomes a contrasting border to the yellow, but it fades to grayish-olive on the lower chest and abdominal areas. The upperparts are a dull olive-green.

The female has a brown facial area instead of black, and the brightness of the yellow is greatly reduced. Chest areas are grayish-olive. Females are never as plentiful as males; and, since immatures resemble females, careful selection of a pair is very important.

The Cuban Melodious is a very good breeder in captivity if the insectivorous nature of this bird is satisfied. Mealworms are important, and more are necessary than for the average finch, but overfeeding will cause problems. While young are in the nest, the Cuban Melodious can be given twelve mealworms per day without harm. Other live foods in variety as well as an insectile mixture are highly recommended.

Both sexes incubate during the twelve to fourteen day incubation period. After the young are weaned, they should be removed from their parents to prevent harm if their parents want to go to nest again.

As a rule, no more than one pair per breeding aviary should be permitted. In the wild state these birds claim certain areas and males fight furiously if these territorial claims are violated. In non-breeding aviaries, the Cuban Melodious is more peaceful; but a large number will inevitably result in quarrelsome personalities and the inevitable feather plucking.

The popular name of Cuban Melodious is rather badly chosen. Though this finch sings happily and often, its song cannot be called melodious if compared to several other more gifted songsters. In fact, the term "melodious" is used widely only in the United States. In most countries this bird is simply called Cuban Finch.

CUBAN OLIVE FINCH (*Tiaris olivacea*)

The less attractive and far more aggressive Cuban Olive Finch is nearly four inches long. It has several very similar subspecies in a rather wide range. In addition to Cuba, this bird is found in nearby islands, Mexico, Costa Rica,

The male Cuban Olive Finch is mostly dark and dusky olive-green with bright yellow markings above the eyes and at the corners of the lower mandible. The beak is shiny black.

Panama, and Colombia. Its less colorful pattern and aggressiveness preclude a high degree of popularity even though it is a good breeder. The song, though rather weak, has been described as sweet.

The Cuban Olive is slightly larger than the Cuban Melodious; the basic colors are the same, but the pattern is far less attractive. The bright yellow is present on the male but is much reduced and is arranged in a less imaginative pattern. Yellow forms a prominent but short eyebrow and a small chin patch which dips into a lengthened mustache at the corners of the lower mandible. A slight yellow mark also occurs below the eye. The beak is black, and the rest of the coloring is identical to the Cuban Melodious.

The female is, like the Cuban Melodious, very dull by comparison. The yellow is greatly reduced in brightness, and black is absent.

Breeding information is the same as for the Cuban Melodious. The Cuban Olive, however, nests rather low in shrubbery if given the chance.

JACARINI FINCH (*Volatinea jacarini*)

The four inch Jacarini from Cuba, Mexico, Central America, and South America, is not often available and not highly popular. However, it is a very peaceful and pleasant, though somewhat shy, aviary bird. It is not a good breeder, but breeding information is the same as for the Cuban Melodious. The Jacarini is sometimes called the Blue-Black Grassquit.

The male somewhat resembles the Combassou but is less attractive. The beak is black and more slender than the pale beak of the Combassou. The basic color is glossy black, and the only departure is a patch of white on the scapulars and a usually hidden patch of white on the sides of the chest.

In some avicultural literature, Jacarinis are said to go into an eclipse plumage. Though the writers have never had more than two or three dozen of these birds, they have never seen a Jacarini undergo a plumage change.

The female is indistinctly marked and quite dull. The upperparts are brownish, and the underparts are a pale and dull mixture of grays and whites.

BLACK CRESTED FINCH or CRESTED BUNTING (*Lophospingus pusillus*)

The very beautiful Black Crested Finch is incorrectly called the Pigmy Cardinal and, in the United States, the Crested Bunting. It is not a true bunting; and, even if it were, the name Crested Bunting has already been given to an Indian bird which is seldom seen in aviculture. The name of Pigmy Cardinal probably refers to the very attractive crest and black pattern of the Green Cardinal and was possibly given to create enthusiasm of bird fanciers who had never seen it. However, there is no need for "gilding the lily" with fancy names because this is a very charming and attractive bird. It is not often available and is offered at rather a high price, but it is always quickly accepted by the discerning fancier. The overall size is somewhat more than four and a half inches including the rather long tail but excluding the crest.

194

Black-crested Finch or Crested Bunting, formerly called Pigmy Cardinal. This is a very attractively-patterned finch of medium size. Though somberly attired in black, white, and gray, this species commands attention because it is shapely and has a very attractive crest. This specimen, in a heavy moult, does not show its true beauty. Owned by William Lasky.

The basic color scheme sounds dull because it consists of black, white, and gray; but the precise and pleasing arrangement of these colors along with a beautifully proportioned body, long tail, and prominent crest, lifts this bird into the realm of extraordinary beauty. In a black and white picture, this handsome bird resembles a Green Cardinal with somewhat more attractive proportions and sharper color contrasts.

The male has a long feathered black crest which is nearly always erected. The black coloring starts at the crown and continues through the nape to the back. The rest of the head is white except for a broad swath of black covering the lores, eyes, and cheek areas and a strong black throat patch. The rest of the bird is a pleasant and uniform shade of gray which is darker on the upperparts and lighter on the underparts.

The female is slightly less bold in color because the blacks and whites are less intense and are shaded with a grayish tinge. The black throat patch is absent.

The Black Crested Finch is a good breeder if its desire for insects during the breeding season is satisfied. In addition to seeds, this species should be offered a variety of live food and insectile mixture. Mealworms are indispensable during this period. This finch may become slightly aggressive in the breeding season but is peaceful at all other times. Much of the aggression is directed towards its own offspring if the youngsters are not removed during succeeding nests.

Incubation time is usually twenty-two days. The young fledge in a very short time, usually less than two weeks; but the weaning period may last as long as a month. Females feed the young at first, but the male takes over just before fledging time and continues through the variable weaning period. Youngsters resemble females but have short crests and rather streaky chests. Adult plumage is attained during a variable period which may extend from six months until the second moult.

The Black Crested Finch is a very desirable aviary bird and should be included in every collection if it is available.

CRIMSON PILEATED FINCH (*Coryphospingus cucullatus* or *Coryphospingus cristatus*)

The Crimson Pileated Finch of South America is a distinctive and quietly colored finch of moderate beauty and shy disposition. It is not often available and is rather highly priced, but the ardent aviculturist is not likely to bypass it. In an aviary, it will often hide in any underbrush available.

This species can be reared in aviaries but such an accomplishment is not often achieved. Incubation is approximately twelve days, and the nest is cup-shaped. Males do not seem as hardy as females. The mortality rate is rather too high. Many individuals tend to drop dead from no apparent reason; but, upon investigation, the cause is usually found to be improper diet. The diet is a simple finch mix, greenfood, insectile mixture, and a variety of small live foods. Mealworms must be rationed because Pileated Finches easily form a fondness for this live food which quickly becomes excessive and undoubtedly causes most of the problems which lead to the inexplicable deaths. Nevertheless, mealworms are very important during the breeding season.

The male has a basic coloration which is best described as brownish with a dull tint of rose. The shade of rose becomes more red and more prominent on the chest and abdomen. The beak is black, and a prominent eye ring is white. The size is nearly five inches, but it is very peaceful even with the smallest finches.

The crest is a flat and horizontal feature composed of bright red hairlike or brushlike feathers bordered on the sides by a dark brownish-black line which, while rather fine, is prominent. The crest is quite unique and is the most distinctive characteristic of this somewhat somber bird. The recumbent crest is usually lying flat against the crown, but it sometimes is halfway erected during a show of emotion.

The female shows a greatly subdued tint of brown with nearly all the tint of rose missing except on the rump.

GRAY PILEATED FINCH (*Coryphospingus pileatus*)

The Pileated Finch or Gray Pileated Finch is the same as the above except the basic coloring is soft and quiet gray instead of rose-tinted brown. The upperparts are a much darker shade than the underparts, and the predominating crest remains a bright red bordered on the sides by black. The female is brownish, particularly paler on the underside and fading to white on the abdomen. The crest is a bright shade of chestnut.

This species is not as popular as the above species, but it is still a charming and unobtrusive bird. Not often available, the price is usually rather high. The personality and care are the same as described for the Crimson Pileated Finch.

SAFFRON FINCH (*Sicalis flaveola*)

The robust and hardy Saffron Finch from South America is a very good breeder and has a lustrous glow which few birds can match. The Saffron is a large finch of five inches including the tail of nearly two inches. It is aggressive to small birds and must be kept with larger finches. The Saffron is also a satisfactory companion for Budgerigars, and it thrives on parrakeet mix but also likes fruit, greens, and mealworms. It will also take a finch mixture in place of the parrakeet mix. Mealworms and oats must be rationed because the Saffron easily becomes overweight.

The male glows with a bright shade of golden-yellow which overlies the entire color scheme. The forehead and crown are rich golden-orange. The chest and underparts are a very bright shade of yellow, and the upperparts are dark and dusky-greenish with sulphurous-yellow edges. The bill is basically a horn color with a dark shade above and an orange-horn below. The eyes are dark brown, and the feet and legs are a flesh color. The yellow of this bird is vivid and gives the impression of a smoldering sulphurous glow.

The female, which is imported in smaller numbers, is dull by comparison. The golden-orange is absent on the forehead and crown, and the yellow underparts are less bright.

Immatures take several months to acquire adult coloration and cannot be sexed until some streaks of golden-yellow appear on the crown. The basic grayish-buff in the beginning slowly gives way to streaks of yellow which gradually envelop the entire body.

Saffrons are not only easily acclimated but are also very prolific breeders. They prefer a standard parrakeet nestbox and lots of dried grasses. The male proves his ardor by an extremely vigorous, though tuneless and rather harsh, song. Incubation time is twelve to thirteen days, and the young leave the nest in about two weeks. Mealworms must be increased during the nesting period.

There are several species of the Saffron Finch which are considerably less well known and not often available. Also, they are less attractive with greatly reduced areas of yellow and more dark markings.

CHAPTER 14

Buntings

Those American Buntings which are native to the United States cannot be legally kept in captivity in the United States. Many are trapped in Mexico and South America and sent to European bird markets where they are very highly regarded. One, the Painted or Nonpareil Bunting, has often been described as the "gem of the avicultural world."

The diet should consist of a much greater percentage of canary seed for most of these birds. Otherwise, the seed mix can be a standard parrakeet mix instead of the usual finch mixture. All these birds can handle the larger seeds quite well though both mixtures are completely acceptable. Buntings also like spray millet and should be given fresh fruit and live food. Mealworms, though very important, are rather too greedily accepted and should be rationed.

Buntings cannot be considered to be good breeders. They prefer planted aviaries where their nests can be hidden in shrubbery. The nests are small and cup-shaped and usually are built low. Incubation time is usually thirteen days with fledging time twelve to thirteen days.

RAINBOW BUNTING (*Passerina leclancheri*)

The male Rainbow Bunting, sometimes called Leclancher's Bunting, is an exceptionally pretty bird; but the female is very dull by comparison. There is no seasonal change of plumage. Females are very seldom available, possibly because Mexican exporters consider them too colorless to be saleable. As a result, many people not knowing of the great color difference often buy two males assuming they have a pair. This is perhaps a natural mistake because one would assume from viewing a flight full of Rainbows that the sexes would be approximately equal.

Rainbow Buntings must have plain canary seed in large portions. Mealworms can become an obsession with them and must be rationed to two or three per day. The average fancier's experience with Rainbow Buntings is that they rarely live a full natural lifespan in captivity. The writers feel the reason is the bird's own preference for certain dietary items to the exclusion of a well-rounded selection. The writers offer a good selection of fruits, greenfood, insectile mixture, and wherever possible a variety of live foods.

Usually other birds who already accept such a well-rounded diet are necessary to coax them onto the insectile mixture.

Unfortunately the Rainbow Bunting is not quickly acclimated because of its dietary idiosyncrasies. Once the proper adjustment has been made, it is only reasonably hardy and must be protected from cold weather below 45° F. This is a very difficult species to breed. The only chance for success is in planted aviaries, and the Rainbow is unfortunately inclined to be shy and to hide his beauty in the underbrush.

Since the Rainbow Bunting is not native to the United States, it has no restrictions against keeping it in captivity. However, at the time of this writing, Mexico will allow no further export of these birds. They therefore may become very scarce if the Mexican ruling is long-lived.

Rainbow Buntings are rather heavy-bodied compared to waxbills, but they are very pleasantly proportioned, and their rather long tails add just the right balancing effect. The overall size is five inches. They are peaceful and quiet, almost lethargic, in aviaries.

The male's extremely attractive and uncluttered color scheme never fails to attract attention. The dominant colors are a very pleasant shade of rich blue on the upperparts and a bright, cheerful yellow on all the underparts from the chin through the undertail coverts. The blue has been described as both turquoise and cobalt, but the writers feel it is more of an exquisite blend between the two shades and is further enhanced by a high gloss. The forehead and crown are bright green, but this shade is overpowered by the shade of brighter blue. A tinge of green is also slightly added to the blue on the back, but this may totally escape the observer. The wings and tail are darker and duskier. A prominent eye-ring is pale yellowish and is a dominating feature surrounding the large, dark eye. The beak is a dark bluish-gray shade. The chest shows a strong concentration of bright and glossy orange on the basic yellow, but this shading may fade slightly in captivity. The extent of fading in captivity is fortunately negligible. The feet and legs are gray.

The female is very dull by comparison. The basic overall coloring is a drab grayish-green with a tinge of soft blue on the wings, uppertail coverts, and tail, and a slight shading of yellowish-green on the underparts. The beak, large eye-ring, size, and shape are similar. Despite her uninspired color scheme, the female is a pleasant sight because of a pleasantly proportioned body and tail and because of her quiet relaxed manner.

The writers are extremely fond of the lovely Rainbow Bunting but should like to caution the bird fancier to avoid this species unless he is willing to give the slight extra attention to diet required to maintain its long life and good health.

PAINTED or NONPAREIL BUNTING (*Passerina ciris*)

The beautifully colored Painted Bunting is an elusively shaded bird which constantly succeeds in contradicting the most expert of photographers.

The soft shadings seem to change with each photograph and with each painting. Moreover, the shading changes appreciably in captivity which merely adds to the elusiveness of this lovely creature. Several subspecies show slight differences to add to the confusion.

The Painted Bunting is a native of the United States and cannot legally be kept in captivity within the confines of this country. However, it is trapped during the migration season in Mexico, Cuba, and South America and sent in great quantities to European markets where it is very highly regarded as one of the great beauties in aviculture. The writers particularly and enviously remember it in the Paris bird markets where the asking price was high but still very worthwhile, especially to bird fanciers to whom it was denied. The Painted Bunting or Nonpareil Bunting is also sometimes called the Mariposa.

The overall size is five and a half inches including the long tail. The general proportion is pleasantly distributed like the Rainbow Bunting over a handsomely heavy-bodied bird with a reasonably long tail. The size is slightly larger.

The upperparts are the most variable. The head down to the shoulder is brilliant purplish-blue. The beak is grayish, and the black eye is surrounded by a fine eye ring of fleshy-orange. The back, wings, and tail are bright, glossy green of varying shades. The mantle and back show a bright chartreuse shade. A dull purplish-red bar extends across the scapulars, and the wing coverts are dark green followed by dark flights. The tail is mixed green and red, and the rump and lower back are bright red. The underparts, from chin to undertail coverts, are a brilliant red which fades somewhat in the ventral area. This coloring fades to dull pink, orange, or even dirty yellow, in captivity. There is no seasonal change in plumage.

The female is very dull by comparison. It has a basic coloring of dull grayish-green, darker on the uppersides, and paler and more yellowish on the undersides. The abdomen shows traces of green.

Painted Buntings are quarrelsome with their own kind and to close relatives but are peaceful with other species. They are quite hardy but are difficult to breed.

INDIGO BUNTING (*Passerina cyanea*)

The Indigo Bunting is another native of the United States and cannot be kept legally within the confines of its borders. Many are trapped in Mexico or other more southerly countries and shipped to European markets. It is sometimes called Azulejo in its Spanish speaking ranges.

This species is easy to acclimate and is hardy afterwards. It is not a good breeder but becomes a good aviary bird because of its calm demeanor. Males particularly stay out in the open, but hens seem rather shy. The overall size is five inches long. Males undergo an eclipse plumage and lose nearly all their coloring.

200

The Indigo Bunting is a migrating species denied to American aviculturists, but it is a popular favorite in European aviculture. This large finch is hardy and good looking in the deep blue of the male.

The male in color is dark and rather dusky blue all over, but the shadings vary somewhat, and there is an attractive glossy sheen. The head has a violet shading, and the tail is blackish. Dull brownish bars cross the wings.

The female is mainly dull brownish with tinges of blue in the wings and rump. Underparts are more of a buffish shade. When out of color, the male resembles the female but shows more extensive blue shadings.

LAZULI BUNTING (*Passerina amoena*)

The five and a half inch male Lazuli Bunting is much like the male Indigo Bunting except for paler shades of blue and a total departure of underpart coloring from the top of the chest through the undertail coverts. The coloring of the underparts ranges from a brownish-orange shade on the chest to fading whitish on the abdomen and undertail coverts. There are also two whitish wing bars.

The female has brownish upperparts and head which fade to a buff on the chest and a white in the abdominal and ventral region. There are usually a few traces of blue on the upperparts. The male during eclipse plumage is very much like the female.

The native Lazuli Bunting is also illegal in the United States but popular in Europe. It is difficult to breed and not quite so hardy as the Indigo Bunting.

201

VERSICOLOR BUNTING (*Passerina versicolor*)

The rare Versicolor Bunting is illegal in the United States and is seldom found in Europe. It is a poor breeder and possibly the most delicate member of this group. Males have a very attractive nuptial plumage and an off-season coloration during which time they resemble females. The size is about four and a half inches.

The male in color has a greatly subdued appearance because of its very dark coloration and lack of contrasts; but the actual coloration, though difficult to describe, is really quite rich and beautiful.

Basically, the coloring consists of smoky shadings of purples, blues, mauves, near blacks, and an occasional touch of dull crimson.

The lower crown, nape, and throat are dark crimson with a purplish-mauve and a blackish shade covering the forehead, forecrown, cheeks, and a narrow collar without black at the lower end of the nape. This purplish-mauve also covers the rump and uppertail coverts. The back shows a purplish-blue, and the wings and tail are similar but more blackish. The underparts are mostly a purplish-red.

The female is a dull bird with grayish-browns which are darker on the upperparts and paler on the underparts.

YELLOW BUNTING or RED HEADED BUNTING (*Emberiza bruniceps*)

Buntings occur in many parts of the world other than the southern areas of the United States, Mexico, and Central America. Furthermore, the birds called Buntings embrace more than the genus *Passerina*; but few have attained a very high avicultural status. The writers doubt that very many buntings of other genera could approach the avicultural desirabilities of the species listed above. This belief, however, does not prevent other species from becoming available from time to time. Some become available because of exporters' substitutions and others because of specializing aviculturists' demands. Two of those, which become reasonably important because of the above reasons, curiously, have the same popular name of Yellow Bunting.

From India comes the first subject, the Yellow Bunting, which is frequently called, for some inexplicable reason, the Red Headed Bunting even though the head is not red.

The Red Headed or Indian Yellow Bunting is imported usually as a substitute for other birds which may be out of stock. After arrival, this bird is most frequently sold as a promotional bird with such a low price that few can resist it. Those who cannot resist this bird's low price often wonder what to do with it after they acquire it.

Because of the size of this bird, which totals approximately seven inches, it is best housed with large finches and can even be mixed with Budgerigars.

After viewing many of the more popular finches, most people will not call this bird beautiful. There is a lack of precision in the distribution of colors, and the shades of coloring are not the most desirable.

The entire head, throat, and upper chest of the male are a rich brown instead of red; and the nape fades to a buffish-brown which extends to the mantle. The back and wings are brown with paler edges; the brownish rump is dulled by gray; and the brown tail is darkened by black. The underparts are variable shades of yellow.

Females are grayish-brown muddled with dark streaks on the wing and traces of green on the back.

This species is one of those birds which the writers try to avoid even though it is lively and hardy and requires a very simple diet. The standard parrakeet mix with greenfood and a few mealworms provide an adequate diet.

A close relative, the Black Headed Bunting (*Emberiza melanocephala*), from Europe and India, is similar in size as well as pattern. The head of the male is black, and the throat is yellowish. The black head fades in the winter. The female has a brownish head and buff underparts, and she also fades somewhat in winter.

YELLOWHAMMER or YELLOW BUNTING (*Emberiza citrinella*)

The Yellowhammer of Europe is the least colorful of the buntings in this book, but it is not the least colorful of the family. This bird is offered to American importers but not often ordered. With those European fanciers who prefer their own native birds, the Yellowhammer is a familiar favorite. The total length including the long, rather forked tail is approximately six and one-fourth inches.

The male shows a basic coloring of yellow cluttered with patternless streaks and spots of brown. There are two long and prominent brown streaks running through the head and an irregular brown border around the ear coverts. The upperparts are far more heavily marked with brown than the underparts.

The female is similar except she is paler.

In the wild state, the Yellowhammer is occasionally regarded as a good singer; but it makes little effort towards singing very much in captivity.

CHAPTER 15

European Finches

This chapter by no means includes all of Europe's seed-eating birds which are important in aviculture. The European Goldfinch, which is the most popular of all, will be included in a later chapter.

European finches become available in the United States during the month of November and the early part of December. The period of availability is usually very short. Only the Bullfinch is apt to be somewhat expensive.

EUROPEAN BULLFINCH (*Pyrrhula pyrrhula*)

The lovely European Bullfinch is an unusually shaped bird which is a very popular favorite with bird lovers. Importation into the United States is prohibited, but many Bullfinches are admitted annually by government appointees who identify incoming shipments.

The writers have never had many Bullfinches, because of the above mentioned prohibition. European shippers, not familiar with our laws, have nevertheless included an occasional pair with shipments of other birds.

Bullfinches require a different diet than do most finches. Anyone fortunate enough to own Bullfinches should bend every effort to furnish a satisfactory diet to these birds. Without the correct diet, the Bullfinch is quite likely to die from otherwise undetermined causes. The bird fancier must take the cue from the habits of the Bullfinch in the wild state. Small berrylike fruits, buds, and insects are eagerly sought by Bullfinches in addition to a seed mix which contains both canary mix and parrakeet mix. Live food is necessary but should not be confined to mealworms alone.

Bullfinches have a strange and heavy-bodied shape. The overall size is somewhat less than six inches, and there appears to be no neck. The head is broad and flat and looks small from a profile angle. There is no dipping into a neck from any side.

Black covers a medium-large beak, the lores, an area under the eyes, a small chin area, and a large cap extending from the forehead to the nape of the neck. Soft gray starts at the black cap and covers most of the upperparts. A grayish-white bar crosses the scapulars, and black flights and tail become very prominent. The underparts of the male including a large facial area and cheeks are a very beautiful shade of smooth rose-pink fading to dusty grayish-white in the abdominal area, ventral region, and both uppertail and undertail coverts. The feet and legs are blackish.

The female is the same except for a lovely and soft shade of gray replacing the rose-pink underparts.

Bullfinches are very beautiful but are not completely hardy unless careful acclimation and a correct diet are observed. Though not highly active, they are sometimes aggressive to smaller birds. In the wild state, they pair for life.

The highly coveted Siberian Bullfinch (subspecies *pyrrhula*) is similar but larger. There are many other Bullfinches scattered around the world, but none have become available to aviculturists in satisfactory numbers, and none are as attractive as the European and Siberian Bullfinches.

CHAFFINCH (*Fringilla coelebs*)

The quietly colored and mild-mannered Chaffinch from Europe is five and a half inches long including a slightly forked tail of two and one-fourth inches. The long canary-like beak is a pale, fleshy-horn color with dark tips. At first glance the male seems to have a dull warm brown over most of the body, but there are slight variations which offer a mild diversification.

A broad white shoulder bar with some sporadic white markings highlight the dark grayish wings. The tail is also a dark shade of gray. The top of the

The Chaffinch from Europe is quietly colored and lacks a distinct pattern, but the subtle shadings are softly attractive. Though larger than the average finch, the Chaffinch is peaceful and pleasant. It is inexpensive and a vigorous singer in its short season if given proper accommodations. The song is most voluble in planted aviaries.

head is a paler shade of gray. Dull off-white shades the ventral and abdominal area, and the underside of the tail is gray and white. The face, throat, and underparts are a dull shade which is composed of blended rose, gray, and brown. During excitement, the head feathers can rise in a slight crestlike effort.

The Chaffinch is a difficult bird to describe. In addition to the basic description, there are attractive blue-gray tints on the top of the head and neck. A faint trace of green appears on the neck, wings, and tail and prominently on a large rump area. This shade is a soft moss-green which, while subdued, is curiously almost glossy. One must study the Chaffinch carefully to comprehend its subtle shadings and the shy but pleasant contrasts. It is perhaps not fully appreciated because of a lack of bright and showy colors, but it deserves every consideration.

Females are more subdued and in every way less contrasting. Females are very seldom imported because they are not offered by European exporters.

Males are hybridized with canaries and other European finches. Chaffinches are very hardy and easy to acclimate. They seem to fare well whether they are fed on parrakeet mix, finch mix, or canary mix. Greenfood is necessary, but live food is usually ignored.

The real surprise of the Chaffinch is the enormity of its springtime song. The writers have followed this cheerful song in several European countries expecting to find a bird the size of a large thrush, but it always turned out to be the unassuming Chaffinch. There is perhaps more volume than melody, but the cheerfulness is unsurpassed. Unfortunately, the song is far less spontaneous and not often heard at its best in captivity.

There are other species of Chaffinches from various parts of the world, but they are not available in American aviculture.

EUROPEAN LINNET (*Acanthus cannabina*)

The plain looking and peaceful European Linnet has a very pretty song and is frequently paired with a Canary to produce hybrids which surpass the songs of both Linnet and Canary. From the standpoint of appearance, however, the Linnet is one of the least colorful of the popular birds in aviculture.

In the wild state the male Linnet shows a slight seasonal plumage change by sporting varying traces of deep and dusky reddish-maroon on the forehead and chest. These traces soon fade in captivity and never quite return. The rest of the coloring is a dull brown which is darker and streakier on the upperparts and paler and smoother on the underparts. The blackish wing feathers have white on the outer borders of the primaries.

The female is very similar but is slightly paler and has more streaks on the chest. The white borders on the flights are less extensive.

The writers feed canary mix, niger, oat groats, greenfood, and a little insectile mixture. Oat groats are heavily used during the acclimation period and then tapered off to a reasonably small amount. If the Linnet is to be kept

Though it has a dull color scheme, the European Linnet deserves every consideration because of its superb song. There are plenty of other finches to provide color, but add a European Linnet to your collection for melody. Photographed at Palos Verdes Bird Farm.

in a cage, the amount of oats must be less than if it is to be kept in an aviary.

Linnets do not travel well, and the acclimation period is quite difficult. The loss of weight during the shipment and immediately thereafter is dangerous, and the birds affected show very little cooperation in making the adjustment. The writers add a liquid appetizer to the water and administer a sulfamethazine remedy for the first two days to curtail any possible infections.

LESSER REDPOLL (*Acanthis rufescens*)

MEALY REDPOLL (*Acanthis linaria*)

Both the Lesser Redpoll and the Mealy Redpoll are very rare in American aviculture. Both are rather closely related to the European Linnet, but the disposition is a little less peaceful during nesting. Redpolls have more color and less song than Linnets and are somewhat smaller. The reddish areas unfortunately fade in captivity. In Europe they are popular.

The male Lesser Redpoll, before it loses its color, has a deep red on the crown which changes in captivity to a bronzed shade. The underparts are also red in a less intense shade. Basic colors beyond this are buffish-whites and dusky-browns haphazardly arranged and streaky. Upperparts are darker than the underparts. The female is duller.

The Mealy Redpoll is slightly larger but still smaller than the Linnet. It is also paler.

The European Greenfinch is a large and sometimes aggressive finch cloaked mainly in a dark and dusky grayish-green. Yellow, bright on the flights and subdued on the lower chest, give the bird its only brightness. The female is greatly subdued to a grayish-olive. This species is inexpensive but not very popular.

EUROPEAN GREENFINCH (*Chloris chloris*)

The dusky European Greenfinch is a rather large heavy-bodied bird totaling six inches. The shape is robustly handsome. The head and beak are also somewhat large. The basic coloring is uniformly soft and smooth. Dull and dark olive-green shaded with gray covers the entire bird becoming paler and slightly tinged with yellow on the abdomen. A prominent yellow bar marks the flight feathers.

The female is similar but lacks the yellow wing bar, and the general shading is grayer. The beak on both sexes is a pale horn color.

The Greenfinch is not a popular bird except with those fanciers specializing in European birds. These fanciers usually are interested in song and are disappointed because the Greenfinch is not a talented songbird. Moreover, the nature of this bird is quite aggressive during the breeding season; and it must be housed with larger birds.

Greenfinches are very hardy and are good breeders in an aviary. The acclimation period is short, and the diet is simple. Though they will exist on parrakeet mix, they will thrive if also given canary mix, some oat groats, a few sunflower seeds, and plenty of greenfood.

Should an illness develop, the bird will fail very rapidly if not given immediate attention. The loss of weight is quite astonishing. First aid and a sulfamethazine remedy are the first requisites. These usually check the problem.

BRAMBLING FINCH (*Fringilla montifringilla*)

When the Brambling Finch is imported, it usually is substituted for some other more desirable bird. Such substitutions are unfortunate because they are usually sent in the same shipping box with other European finches. Even though shipments by air are delivered in a short time, the very aggressive Bramblings will have caused a tremendous amount of damage particularly to Chaffinches. The damage ranges from frayed and torn feathers to an outright bloody scalping.

The Brambling is an inordinately hardy bird and requires the very simplest of care. It is overly fond of mealworms, but will live on parrakeet mix or canary mix and a little greenfood. A few sunflower seeds are also appreciated. It must, of course, be housed only with larger birds; and, even then, it should be frequently checked for aggressive tendencies.

The Brambling Finch is rather attractive, but it always looks as if someone forgot to put the finishing touches on the head. The back, neck, and head, except for chin and throat, are glossy black with buffish tips to all the feathers. These dull tips are broader during immaturity and during slight seasonal variations. When the color starts to return, the bird fancier always hopes it will complete the job and show a glossy all-black head; but it never quite does.

The wings and tail are dark blackish-brown with pale feather edges. The shoulders are paler brown followed by a narrow buffish-white bar above the scapulars. The underparts, starting at the chin and extending to the abdomen, are a pale shade of chestnut tinted slightly with orange. It fades as it approaches the abdomen and becomes whitish on the remaining underparts.

The female is duller and browner.

The shape and size are nearly the same as the Greenfinch. The writers try to avoid the Brambling Finch if possible.

CHAPTER 16

Goldfinches, Siskins, and Serins

All members of the three generalized groups have certain basic characteristics in common showing a somewhat close relationship. First of all, from the aviculturist's viewpoint, the most important similarity is the importance of the singing voice. All of these birds sing better than the average seed eating bird to be found in aviculture. Naturally there are variations in the quality and styles, not only in different species but also in individuals; but all these birds can rightly be classed as singers.

The male American Goldfinch (*Spinus tristis*) in nuptial coloring is very attractive in its dominant bright yellow body and black cap. The black wings have both yellow and white edges. This charming species is unfortunately denied to American bird fanciers. It migrates to Mexico and may possibly be shipped to European fanciers from some of the Mexican exporters.

The winter plumage of the American Goldfinch is far less attractive for the male. He loses his attractive colors and looks like the drab greenish female.

Not all members of the three groups have been included because some are not available for aviculture and because others lack interest as cage or aviary birds. Some of the most popular avicultural subjects are found in this chapter.

There are two basic diets for the birds covered in this chapter. Many birds require the specialized diet for the European Goldfinch which is detailed under the writing for that species. Each species requires the same diet. Variations, if any, are noted during the coverage of the species.

The second diet is described under the Green Singing Finch which requires the standard finch diet with a little extra attention given to canary song food and its major component of niger. Each species requiring this diet is referred to the Green Singing Finch for dietary information.

Some of the birds in this chapter hold interest only for specialized branches of aviculture. There are many aviculturists who concentrate upon the individual quality of song, and certain members covered in this chapter will be the only birds to hold their interest.

Other fanciers may be more interested in hybridizing members of this group with canaries. This is a highly specialized branch of aviculture. It is a particularly interesting branch because the hybrid offspring from such matings often excel both sides of the family in singing ability and frequency of song. Most of the offspring, except as otherwise noted, are mules or, in other words, are infertile and incapable of reproduction. In hybrid breedings the female is usually the canary, and the male is usually the outcrossed species.

EUROPEAN or BRITISH GOLDFINCH (*Carduelis carduelis britannica*)

The European Goldfinch is one of the truly delightful birds of the entire world. It is very pretty, hardy, a fine songster, and a reasonably good breeder. It is one of the most popular cage birds in Europe and is well known to American fanciers. Among its greatest fans are people who were born in Europe and now live in America.

The overall size is about five inches. The long, slender, and sharply pointed black-tipped beak is well designed for probing into thistle blossoms for its favorite seed which is called niger. A fine blackish line surrounds the beak, and the lores are blackish. A large facial area of bright red encircles the top of the crown and eyes and encircles downward to include the chin and part of the throat. A broad whitish, crescent-shaped swath covers the rest of the facial area followed by a narrower crescent-shaped band of black encircling the overall facial area from the crown to the sides of the throat. The nape, back, mantle, and chest are dark and dusky-brownish. The abdomen fades to whitish, and the undertail and uppertail coverts are also whitish. The forked tail is black with some white tips. The black wings have some white spots at the tips, and a broad band of bright yellow cuts across the flights.

The vivid red face often fades drastically to a dull yellowish shade with only a few flecks of red after a few months in captivity, but the red always returns after a moult in a rich shade which is only slightly paler than the original. Usually, it is the caged pets which fade the most.

The sexes are very similar; but the general conception regarding the distinction is that males show more red on the head, are slightly larger, and have a more pointed beak. The writers have not found these to be reliable indicators because of many individual variations. Instead, they spread the wing and check the forepart between the shoulders and the bend of the wing. Adult males always have black in this area, and adult females show grayish-brown. Immatures are like females, but those who are already showing red

212

on the faces will also show more or less black borders on the tips of these very small feathers. As they become older, the black becomes more extensive.

As breeders, European Goldfinches do better in planted aviaries. The nest is cup-shaped, and incubation time is about thirteen days as it is for all members of this genus.

When first imported to the United States, the standard acclimation procedure is followed; but the diet consists almost exclusively of niger and oat groats. The writers also empty the sunflower seed hulls from parrot cages and aviaries. Goldfinches love to pick through these hulls and find many bits of seeds which the parrots have overlooked. In this manner, the need for hemp seed, the sale of which is illegal in California, is removed. Even if hemp seed were legal here, the writers would never use it because it sometimes is a dangerous seed if it has lain in storage for any great length of time; and over-use is quite likely to cause overweight in birds. The sunflower fulfills all the food requirements found in hemp seed.

Not until spring do the Goldfinches take to canary mix. At that time the consumption of oat groats should be reduced, but the niger will always remain their first preference. A standard canary song food should also be given as well as greenfood. During the nesting period, a standard nestling food becomes important.

The European Goldfinch takes kindly to captivity and is quite long-lived. It is generally peaceful but likes to engage in harmless battles with its own kind.

Those fanciers in America who were born in Europe, particularly Yugoslavia, spend a great amount of time in selecting their birds. They carefully search for a reddish feather on the nape of the neck, and they insist that the bird will be a better singer if he has such a feather. The writers must confess they have been unable to verify this, partly because they fail to re-cognize any red on the feather indicated and partly because those who might have such a red feather are the first ones selected.

The European Goldfinch has been introduced into Australia where it flourished to such an extent that Australian exporters, up until the time of the export ban, were exporting them to many parts of the world. The European Goldfinch also has been introduced into certain eastern areas of the United States where it is carefully protected. No Goldfinches can legally be sold in those areas for fear they will be trapped by American dealers.

The Siberian Goldfinch (*Carduelis carduelis major*) is highly coveted though much less readily available and higher in price. The only difference is a noticeably larger size. Another similar goldfinch, the Himalayan Goldfinch (*Carduelis caniceps*), occurs in India. The writers once received what was called an Oriental Goldfinch from Hong Kong which was very similar except that the red face, a major feature of beauty, never appeared; and the yellow in the wings was very dull even after a considerably lengthy period.

The European Siskin is a small, stocky bird of cluttered and indistinct coloring. The dark cap and blackish streaks are contrasted by grayish-green in paler and lighter shades. These vigorous little songbirds are not really melodious, but their cheerful efforts are at least commendable.

EUROPEAN SISKIN (*Spinus spinus* or *Carduelis spinus*)

The European Siskin is a popular avicultural subject because it takes kindly to captivity, becomes quite tame, has a pleasant little song, and is readily available for importation during the month of November.

Not many people would describe this bird as beautiful because its basic dusky green coloring is darkly, haphazardly, and heavily streaked. The upperparts are darker, and the lower parts are somewhat pale. The most distinctive features are a large blackish patch sitting atop the rather flat head, a small black chin patch, and prominent black areas in the wings. The horn colored beak has a sharp black tip. The body is slightly plump, and the tail is short. It is rather a small bird about four inches long.

The female, which is rarely available for export, is duller and lacks the black cap. The European Siskin is often used for hybridizing with canaries.

The diet is the same as for the European Goldfinch; but, after the acclimation period, oat groats and other fattening foods should be fed very sparingly because this little bird easily becomes overweight.

BLACK HEADED SISKIN (*Spinus icterica*)

The Black Headed Siskin from South America is more distinctively attired than the European Siskin and also has a better song. This species is not to be confused with the far more beautiful Black Hooded Venezuelan Red Siskin, a description of which follows later in this chapter.

The Black Headed Siskin is not often available, as is the case with many South American birds; but it is an attractive species which usually receives the consideration it deserves. It is far more attractive than the European Siskin because the entire head, beak, chin and throat are conspicuously black. The underparts are yellow, and the upperparts are very similar to the European Siskin in that they are dull and dusky-greenish with dark, haphazardly arranged blackish streaks. Rump and uppertail coverts are bright yellow. The size is slightly larger, and the proportions are more pleasing because of the longer tail and less plump body.

The female is dull greenish and grayish on the upperparts and pale yellowish on the underparts. The black on the head is absent.

The diet is the same as for the European Siskin; and, if carefully administered, helps to insure a long life to this bird which is often considered delicate. The main dietary item is niger, which is rather expensive but which cannot be ignored if one is to keep siskins and goldfinches in good health.

The Black Headed Siskin has also been used to hybridize with canaries. At one time, such hybrids were produced with the ultimate object of producing a black canary, but the plans never materialized.

The Black Headed Siskin from South America is a very attractive species which is not often available. The female lacks the black head and is more subdued in color.

215

A similar Siskin is the Mexican Black Headed Siskin (*Spinus notatus*) which is slightly smaller and has a more extensive black on the throat and chest. There is also more black in a better-defined pattern across the wing coverts. If it is sold in the United States it, in all probability, will be sold as the Black Headed Siskin.

COLOMBIAN BLACK SISKIN or COLOMBIAN BLACK HEADED SISKIN (*Spinus psaltria columbiana*)

In many ways the Colombian Black Siskin can be surpassed in beauty only by the Venezuelan Black Hooded Red Siskin. This beautifully proportioned bird also has precise and brilliant markings. Unfortunately, it is seldom available. The diet is the same as the foregoing, and the writers class this charming little bird among their favorites in this family.

The underparts are a uniform bright yellow starting on the chin and fading only slightly on the ventral area. The upperparts are jet black from the forehead through the tips of the tail. The divisions are sharp and well-defined. The eye is surrounded by a pale eye ring which serves only to enhance and accent the overall color scheme and pattern.

The head is smaller, the tail is longer, and the overall proportions are more pleasing and more slender. The overall size is approximately four and a half inches. The female is less attractive with a dull greenish-gray shade replacing the black, and the yellow is greatly reduced.

There are some subspecies which are rarely available in aviculture and which are somewhat less attractive because of the color schemes which are rather cluttered by comparison. Moreover, some are native to the United States and are thereby prohibited by law.

MEXICAN GOLDFINCH or MEXICAN SISKIN (*Carduelis mexicana* or *Spinus mexicana*)

The Mexican Goldfinch is similar to the above except for the following differences: a red is on the rump and uppertail coverts; there are white edges on the upperwing coverts, on the scapulars, on the rather prominently marked secondary flights, and on the somewhat more poorly marked primary flights; and the eyes are not surrounded by black. Other characteristics are the same.

This species is illegal in the United States because it is native to the western areas. It is imported into Europe from Mexico or northern South America. The diet is the same as for the European Goldfinch, but some may also like a little finch millet.

VENEZUELAN BLACK HOODED RED SISKIN (*Spinus cucullatus* or *Carduelis cucullata*)

Easily the most vivid and beautiful member of the Siskin Family is the Venezuelan Black Hooded Red Siskin. Now very rarely available because of a ban by the Venezuelan government which prohibits trapping, this species, if available at all, commands a very high price. Several years ago it was imported in great numbers to hybridize with the canary in producing the Red Factor Canary. Subsequent generations of canary breeding have instilled the red factor coloring in canaries, but the demand for Red Siskins has nearly depleted the native supply.

The hybrid produced by a male Red Siskin and a female canary is not always fertile, but it is a lovely bronze shade.

The path for canary breeders has not been an easy one. Selective breeding to eliminate infertile mules from first crosses has succeeded admirably, and second crosses (hybrid by canary) have brought beautifully shaded red-orange canaries even though the song is substandard. Subsequent selective breeding has brought back a good canary song.

The male Hooded Siskin is richly clothed in brilliant red and vivid black. Black covers the head, nape, and throat as well as the shoulders, flights, and tail. The rest of the bird is red, slightly shaded with blackish on the back and then shaded to white on the abdomen. The female is mostly gray with shadings of red on the chest, flanks, scapulars, and uppertail coverts, and black on the tail, flights, and a bar on the upperwing area. The total size is about four inches.

The initial acclimation period is rather touchy, but afterwards it becomes quite hardy. The diet is the same as for the European Goldfinch.

GREEN SINGING FINCH (*Serinus mozambicus*)

Easily the best known, one of the prettiest, and one of the most frequently available members of the Serin family is the Green Singing Finch from Africa. The writers have a difficult time expressing their thorough admiration of this charming species. Though it lacks the precise division of coloring found in most of the waxbills with whom it is usually associated, the Green Singing Finch seldom fails to attract attention because of the bright yellow underparts and a cheerful little song.

The male is four inches long including a tail of one and a half inches. The canary-like beak is a grayish-horn color. The upperparts start with a grayish shade on the head. The feathers have darker centers and lack a smooth uniformity. The neck, back, wings, and tail are greenish-gray with the same pattern of darker centers. The rump is bright yellow, and a prominent eye-brow band which connects across the forehead is bright yellow. A patch of gray covers the lores and extends behind the eyes. Bright yellow covers the lower cheek areas and the entire underparts with a greater concentration on chin, throat, and chest. A narrow mandarin mustache flares outwards and downwards from the lower mandible. The underside of the tail is grayish.

The female is generally duller and less distinct in all colors and patterns. The only other difference is a necklace of ill-defined dark spots encircling the lower throat area.

Immatures are the same as females but are even less distinctly and less brightly marked. The necklace spots are smaller and are even more poorly defined. The chest is dull greenish-yellow. Fortunately, they can be sexed at an early age because young males will show a breakthrough on the necklace spots. If any of the spots are missing and are replaced by brighter yellow, the individual is undoubtedly a young male.

The Green Singing Finch thrives on the standard finch mixture and does not require the more expensive and exacting diet of the European Goldfinch. Canary song food with its major component of niger is rather an important part of the diet.

Green Singing Finches are ideal companions for waxbills because they lead the chorus of cheerful little calls and insignificant little songs of most waxbills by their own far more frequent and far more pleasant singing. They are inexpensive and, after a short acclimation period, are quite hardy. Though the hens try to sing once in awhile, their notes are less varied and less sweet than those of the male.

They are better breeders than the average waxbill but show slight aggressiveness during the breeding season. The nest is usually a bulky mass and requires a considerable amount of material. Incubation is from twelve to thirteen days. Insectile mix and live food should particularly be given during the breeding season and are definite requirements for the period of slightly more than three weeks while the young are in the nest. The Green Singing Finch has been crossed with canaries, but the accomplishment is a rare one.

There are several slightly varying subspecies of this finch coming from a large African area. The subspecies described above is *caniceps* and is the most readily available West African race.

YELLOW EYED or YELLOW CROWNED CANARY (*Serinus flavivertex*)

The Yellow Eyed (or Yellow Crowned) Canary is also called the St. Helena Seedeater and comes to aviculturists from South Africa, though birds from this area are indeed rarely forthcoming and only at a higher price.

This finch is a slightly larger cousin of the Green Singing Finch with a larger body, larger head, and bolder markings. The yellow eyebrow is noticeably broader, and the larger head is more attractive. The male is a far more vigorous singer than the Green Singing and is almost as good as the Gray Singing Finch.

Despite the larger size, the writers have never found the Yellow Eyed Canary to be any more aggressive than the Green Singing Finch. Furthermore, the writers have found it to be rather more hardy than the Green Singing Finch. The diet is the same as for the Green Singing Finch.

SHELLEY'S SEEDEATER (*Serinus sulphuratus shelleyi*)

The rarely available Shelley's Seedeater of Africa is one of at least three similar subspecies and is also called the Uganda Brimstone Canary. It basically resembles a very large Green Singing Finch, but the markings are less precise and somewhat less attractive. The yellow is not as bright and does

Bronze Winged Mannikins, left, are pleasant and hardy and are good breeders; but, except for a highly glossed bronze on the crown and shoulders, the color scheme is subordinate to most of the popular finches.
Shelley's Seedeater, right, is a very large cousin of the Green Singing Finch with a less precisely marked pattern and a blunt beak. It is never readily available and is costly compared to the Green Singing Finch. Photographed at Palos Verdes Bird Farm.

not show sharp contrasts against the green. The eyebrows are present, but the yellow cheek patches and the mandarin mustache are absent.

Shelley's Seedeater is five inches long including a tail of two inches. The large head is five-eighths of an inch across, and the beak is large and thick. This bird has been well described as a "giant sized Green Singing Finch which is the size of a canary."

The writers have found this species to be very peaceful but quite difficult to acclimate and only half hardy afterwards. The song is pleasing but is less attractive than that of the Gray Singing Finch. The diet is the same as for the Green Singing Finch, but for best results should also include elements of the diet for European Goldfinch.

The two similar subspecies are Sharpe's Seedeater or Kenya Brimstone Canary (*Serinus sulphuratus sharpii*) and the Brimstone Canary or Sulphury Seedeater (*Serinus sulphuratus sulphuratus*).

CAPE CANARY (*Serinus canicollis*)

The rarely available Cape Canary of Africa, sometimes called the **Gray Necked Serin**, is slightly less than five inches long. It is hardy, peaceful, and a reasonably good singer; but it is not really a pretty bird. The writers have never been particularly impressed with this species.

The Cape Canary is shaped somewhat like a domestic canary except for a shorter tail. The coloring is mostly a dull, dusty yellow. There is a hint of a grayish collar extending rather broadly to the sides of the throat. The upperparts are dully streaked with yellow and dark grayish markings. A pale grayish shade surrounds the ventral area. The female is similar but duller, particularly on the underparts.

The diet is the same as the Green Singing Finch, but a little canary mix is also appreciated.

GRAY SINGING FINCH (*Serinus leucopygius*)

The unimpressive appearance of the Gray Singing Finch is balanced by an outstandingly pretty song which surpasses the other members of the genus. Unfortunately, the attributes stop with the song. It is, even so, exceeded in availability and perhaps popularity only by the Green Singing Finch insofar as members of this genus are concerned.

The Gray Singing Finch from Western Africa, sometimes called the White Rumped Serin, is smaller than the Green Singing Finch by about half an inch. The body is more slender, and the head is somewhat smaller. The coloring is cluttered and plainly unattractive. Dull gray is the basic shading, and underparts are paler. Sexes are alike in appearance, but differentiation is not difficult because the male is a frequent singer while the female does not sing.

The Gray Singing Finch is hardy and is easily acclimated. Moreover, it is rather a good breeder, but it is extremely aggressive to all small birds. Though it is greatly outsized by weavers, Java Rice Birds, and other similar birds, it can well fend for itself. The height of the aggressiveness is, of course, during the breeding season.

Breeding and dietary information is the same as for the Green Singing Finch.

BLACK THROATED SINGING FINCH or BLACK THROATED CANARY and YELLOW RUMPED GRAY SINGING FINCH
(*Serinus atrogularis*)

The writers must apologize for their own confusion of two rarely available birds both of which closely resemble the Gray Singing Finch except for yellow rumps. These two very close relatives are, from all indications, subspecies of *Serinus atrogularis* with one slight difference: one has a blackish chin while the other has a whitish throat and chin. Ornithologists, avicultural importers, and bird fanciers all share the same confusion with mixups in scientific names and a myriad of popular names.

The writers have had experience with only one subspecies of this group. The European exporter labeled it with the interesting and inviting name of Black Throated Canary. Some of the writers' lack of desire for the Gray Singing Finch obviously extended to this disappointing bird when it arrived because of its readily apparent relationship to the Gray Singing Finch.

In a short while, the very pleasant difference of a less aggressive personality from that of the Gray Singing Finch was noted. The color scheme, while still drab and uninteresting, was at least more diversified than that of the Gray Singing Finch; and, most important of all, the song was still exquisite and only slightly less delightful.

The overall size is four inches including the one inch tail. This is slightly larger than the Gray Singing Finch. The basic color scheme is a mixed-up gray with indeterminate streaks and shadings. The wings have paler outer edges, and a paler shaded eyebrow is present. The underside is a faded buffish shade with ill-defined streaks on the chest and sides. The yellow on the rump gives the only color relief, and the black chin markings were the only characteristics to apply the name of Black Throated Canary. An added difference is a shade of brownish-buff replacing the faintly blue shade of the gray found in the Gray Singing Finch.

After studying Mackwords-Praed and Grant's second volume in the first series of *African Handbook* of *Birds*, the writers can only assume that this subspecies is the very limited subspecies *somereni* which is limited to the African area of the Belgian Congo to Uganda. The series of South African birds, not published at the time of writing, may change this opinion. In the meantime, these aviculturists gladly bow to the contributions of the many dedicated ornithologists whose contributions are far more important than their minor disagreements.

The Yellow Rumped Gray Singing Finch is the subspecies sent to bird fanciers from Angola which has a whitish area on the chin and throat. The species name *angolensis* broadly used in avicultural literature seems to be incorrect. Either subspecies *xanthopygius* or *reichenowi* of *Serinus atrogularis* could fall under the popular term of Yellow Rumped Gray Singing Finch since it otherwise shows only slight variations in shading.

The diet is the same as for the Green Singing Finch.

EUROPEAN SERIN (*Serinus serinus*)

Usually available along with November shipments of European birds, the European Serin is not too well known among American fanciers and is not likely to become really popular. The writers have always imported several of these birds each year to satisfy the demands of specialized fanciers who hold them in very high regard, not only as singers but also as potential hybridizers with canaries and other European singing finches.

The European Serin, like the European Linnet, has a touchy acclimation period. The diet is the same as for the European Goldfinch and the European Siskin. Though it cannot begin to compare with the beauty of the European Goldfinch or even the somewhat indistinct attractiveness of the European Siskin, the writers will always remember the cheerful song and liveliness which enriched and added much joy to visits to some of Italy's most ancient monuments. The sleepy Italian village of Tivoli with its ancient Villa de 'Este was far more enlivened by the cheerfulness of these serins than by the

The European Serin is another of Europe's favorite singing finches. Not endowed with a particularly attractive color scheme, this small songbird has a cheerful song and pleasant disposition.

famed fountains. The writers would probably import some of these birds each year even if there were no requests for them.

In appearance, the European Serin is particularly nondescript. The background is variably olive-greenish and olive-yellowish heavily streaked with greenish-black markings. The head is rather flat and sits on rather a long neck. Sexes are difficult to distinguish, but the male has more yellow on the chest. The size is only slightly larger and more slender than the European Siskin.

CANARY (the true wild species) (*Serinus canarius*)

A larger cousin of the European Serin is the true wild canary from the Canary Islands, the Azores, and Madeira, which is usually accredited with being the basis for the entire bird fancy. The much loved and much changed domestic canary evolved from this drab and unattractive serin.

The original species is now very rare in aviculture. The most recent claim to fame, even though the prolonged incident occurred many years ago, was a lowly souvenir pawn sold to tourists visiting the Canary Islands. Native vendors sold yellow-dyed serins to tourists as real canaries. It seems such a shame that the original should have to assume a false face to maintain an interest for humans. Bird lovers would probably appreciate the wild canary if it should ever again become readily available in aviculture. The term "wild canary" is frequently given to many siskins and serins wherever they occur throughout the world.

The true wild canary is approximately five inches long and rather closely resembles the European Serin except for a smoother and more uniform coloration of darker olive-green.

The diet is the same as for the European Goldfinch except for a larger proportion of canary mix which should also be given right from the beginning.

ALARIO FINCH (*Alario alario*)

Closely related to the Serins but not really a member of the family, the Alario Finch from South Africa has an unusual color scheme. The male has a black head which gives it the popular name of Black Headed Canary. Black not only covers the entire head, neck, and throat; but it also stretches onto the sides of the chest and occurs again in the flight feathers. White extends from a collar on the nape throughout the rest of the underparts. Except for the black on flight feathers, the rest of the coloring on the back, wings, and tail is brown. The size is about four inches.

The female is much duller and lacks a definite pattern. White areas are replaced by brownish-buff, and the browns are reduced to a drab and colorless shade of grayish-brown. A description is particularly difficult, but a painting from Butler's *Foreign Finches in Captivity* included in this work will save needless words which would result in an inadequate description.

The Alario Finch is very rare in American aviculture but seems to be appreciated more in European aviculture when it is obtainable. It is pleasant

223

and peaceful and has a quietly pretty little song. It has been hybridized with canaries to produce some really fine songsters.

A subspecies, the Damaraland Alario (*Alario alario leucolaema*), is even more rare. The male has white on the head forming an eyebrow as well as covering the forehead, chin, throat, and a spot on the ear coverts.

The diet is the same as for the Green Singing Finch but should also include rather more niger.

CHAPTER 17

Warbling Finches and Seedeaters

Although there are sixteen species of the genus *Poospiza*, all coming from South America, only a very few have been kept in aviculture either in England or the United States. The writers have had experience with only one species, the Ringed Warbling Finch, but have drawn upon excellent accounts of the first successful breedings by the Keston Foreign Bird Farm of the Chestnut and Black and the Pretty Warbling Finches. Detailed accounts of these first breedings were given in the journals of the Foreign Bird League and the Avicultural Society as well as in the excellent book *Foreign Bird Keeping* by E. J. Boosey, one of the partners in the Keston Foreign Bird Farm of England.

Warbling Finches are recent advents upon the avicultural scene, and the awards for successful first breedings of the three species so far bred in captivity all go to English aviculturists. Mr. Allan Silver first bred White's Warbling Finch in 1937. The Keston Foreign Bird Farm succeeded in breeding the Chestnut and Black Warbling Finch in 1955 and the Pretty Warbling Finch in 1960. These successes are in the traditional ratio of first breeding successes because English aviculturists have always been foremost in the strictest attention to necessary details regarding the many facets of aviculture. The success of English aviculture cannot be regarded as mere good fortune nearly so much as the regard for the proper consideration of the native requirements of the birds prominent in aviculture.

The Warbling Finches so far kept in aviculture are all good sized birds which seem rather spiteful to smaller and more peaceful finches such as waxbills and Australian Grassfinches. The writers suggest housing them with larger and less defenseless birds.

The basic diet is either a finch or parrakeet mix with a high percentage of canary seed, but the highly insectivorous nature must be considered if breeding success is the desired goal. Warbling Finches have aptly been described as very unlike most finches in appearance as well as diet. While young are in the nest, the supply of live foods must be nearly unlimited. Fruits must also be supplied.

The Lined Warbling Finch closely resembles the Black Crested Finch except for the absence of the crest and the addition of a shade of chestnut on the rump. It is good looking but not greatly popular.

RINGED WARBLING FINCH (*Poospiza torquata*)

The quietly colored but handsome Ringed Warbling Finch instantly reminds one of the Black Crested Finch if the crest were absent. The basic color scheme is the same except for minor alterations. In addition to the absence of the crest, the black throat patch is missing leaving a very broad and prominent white throat as a very noticeable accent. The rest of the bird is gray, black, and white like the Black Crested Finch except for a touch of chestnut on the undertail coverts. The head is black except for a long stripe of white starting at the sides of the upper mandible and stretching backwards over the eyes and down the nape of the neck. This band is much narrower than the one on the Black Crested Finch. The broad swath of white on the chin and throat is bordered by a large black area on the chest. The size is slightly more than four and a half inches including the rather long tail.

The Ringed Warbling Finch is inordinately hardy and can withstand nearly any adverse treatment given it by the amateur aviculturist. It is not a beautiful bird by avicultural standards, but it is at least pleasant and reasonably attractive.

CHESTNUT AND BLACK or CHESTNUT BREASTED WARBLING FINCH (*Poospiza nigrorufa*)

The upperparts are slate-gray with a very faint trace of green. A stripe of creamy-white extends both above and rather far below the eye. Underparts are chestnut-brown on the chest and flanks showing something of an inverted "V" dividing the whitish central abdominal area. This species probably will attract more fanciers than any other member of the genus. The female is similar but has colors which are much duller. The overall size is about five and a half inches.

PRETTY WARBLING FINCH (*Poospiza ornata*)

The Pretty Warbling Finch is not really attractive. The upperparts are a dark blend of gray and brown, and the underparts have variously been described as buffish-cinnamon to light chestnut. There is a white stripe through the eyes, and whitish bars mark the wings. It resembles a smaller cinnamon colored Chaffinch. The female is paler on the underparts.

Other species which have occasionally been kept in captivity are White's Warbling Finch (*Poospiza whitei*), White and Gray or White Breasted Warbling Finch (*Poospiza melanoleuca*), and Bonaparte's Warbling Finch (*Poospiza bonapartei*).

The members of the genus *Sporophila* are often good loud singers but usually are not very pretty. Those with which the writers have had experience all came from South America, and many had such thick beaks and rather stout bodies that they quickly termed them "Miniature Grosbeaks." Though none were large, nearly all were much too aggressive to be kept with small finches. The writers housed them with weavers, Cutthroats, and Java

227

Rice Birds and had no trouble. In the spring, the volume of their vocal efforts was really quite astonishing considering their small size.

Those species from South America are never readily available because of the instability of South American bird exporters. During those sporadic periods when they do become available, these birds usually are sent in quite large numbers. As aviary birds they are extremely hardy.

The diet for most of these birds is a standard parrakeet mix and greens. Live food is always appreciated but is not really necessary except in the breeding season.

Females and immatures are, for most species, dull olive-brown, darker above and slightly paler below. Beaks are mostly blackish. The nest is cup-shaped following the pattern set by canaries.

The writers have had several species which they have been unable to classify despite a careful search through avicultural literature. Ornithological literature is not readily forthcoming for South American birds, and so the exact scientific and popular names cannot be given.

One rather prominent member was an all-gray bird with a large beak of bright orange-yellow. The song was especially good with this species. Another was all black except for white on the underparts starting with the chest. A fine white line surrounded the underside of the eye. Another smaller species was the same except for a shade of yellowish on the underparts. The grayish beaks on these two species were smaller and more slender.

Perhaps the prettiest was also the smallest. It had a bright chestnut coloring on the underparts. The uppersides were mainly grayish and brownish with the traditional small white patch at the base of the primaries. The beak was blackish. This bird was called the Fire Red Finch (*Sporophila minuta*), but the writers feel it was badly named. The other popular name of Ruddy Breasted Seedeater is far more appropriate. A similarly patterned member of the genus is the Lavender Backed or Chestnut Bellied Seedeater (*Sporophila castaneiventris*) which has chestnut on the underparts and lavender-gray on the head and underparts.

Another species following this general pattern is the quite rare Reddish Finch (*Sporophila bouvreuil*) which has been described as resembling a miniature Bullfinch. A shiny-black Bullfinch-like cap covers the forehead and crown. Upperparts are reddish-brown except for the blackish wings, and the underparts are reddish. A patch on the nape of the neck is a quite bright shade of red. The female is similar in pattern but shows greatly reduced colors. The black cap is missing, and the size is about three and a half inches long.

WHITE COLLARED SEEDEATER (*Sporophila torqueola*)

Perhaps the best known as well as the most distinctive member of the group is the White Collared Seedeater. The size ranges approximately four inches including the tail of nearly one and a half inches. The large and heavy beak is yellowish-horn in color. The large black head is contrasted by a bright white enclosing a large and flaring area on the throat. This white area starts on the chin and covers the throat extending below the cheeks to encompass a prominent white collar which stretches backwards to the nape of the neck. A broad black band extends across the upper chest, and the rest of the underparts are grayish-white. The underside of the tail is dull gray, and the remaining upperparts are grayish with a tinge of brown on the wings and tail. A small white patch marks the base of the primary flight feathers.

The female is dull olive-brown, paler on the underparts and duskier on the upperparts. The beak is usually blackish.

This species, with several races, generally extends over large areas including Mexico, Central America, and northern South America. It is a good singer but is very aggressive to smaller birds.

The scientific name is often listed as *Sporophila albigularis*.

BLUISH FINCH or BLUISH SEEDEATER (*Sporophila caerulescens*)

The very similar Bluish Seedeater is far less available. It comes from South America and is the same size and shape as the above species. The head is slightly less black and more grayish-blue. The throat is black with a line of white dipping from the corners of the lower mandible down to the throat. A white band crosses the lower throat area followed by another rather narrow black band. The female is similar to the female of the White Collared Seedeater.

LINED SEEDEATER (*Sporophila lineola*)

The Lined Seedeater from South America is also similar except for the pattern of the blackish head and the upperparts. The beak is blackish. A white line runs down the center of the head, and a large white patch extends across the lower cheek area. The chin and throat are black. The female is similar to the above females.

VARIABLE SEEDEATER (*Sporophila aurita* or *Sporophila americana*)

The Variable Seedeater from Mexico and Central America is sometimes called Hick's Seedeater or Lineated Finch, and so the term "variable" might be applied more to the scientific and popular nomenclature than to the appearance. The overall size is less than four inches. The small white wing patch is present, and the rump is white. A white collar is narrow on the throat but broader on the sides of the neck. The abdomen is white with gray shadings at the sides. The rest of the bird is black including a broad black band across the chest. The female is olive-brown as in the foregoing species. The Variable Seedeater has several races with black covering more areas than the nominate race. The subspecies *corvina* is all black except for some white in the wings.

229

CHAPTER 18

Cardinals, Grosbeaks, and Hawfinches

All the members of the groups of Cardinals, Grosbeaks, and Hawfinches seem to be connecting links between finches and softbills. These birds are omnivorous in that they require the diet of the average softbill as well as a basic seed mixture and other requirements of seedeating birds. In fact, the writers actually prefer to classify these birds as softbilled birds because the average bird fancier is quite likely to overlook the soft foods which these birds require and may give them just an average seed mix.

Cardinals are much more popular and much more readily available than members of the other groups. Moreover, they are very brightly colored, quite inexpensive, and are extremely hardy if given the proper diet. All are rather large and should be kept either with large finches or medium-sized softbills for best community results. All birds in this chapter may be quite aggressive toward smaller birds.

Cardinals basically fall into two groups: those with large, heavy beaks and those with slender beaks. All of the slender beaked cardinals are from South America and are the most easily obtainable for avicultural purposes. Those with large grosbeaks range from the United States through Venezuela. Those native to the United States and Mexico are legally denied to bird fanciers in the United States. The writers regard cardinals as being among the finest of all birds in aviculture.

The diet for all these birds should consist of many elements. A variety of fruits and greenfood are as important as live foods and either an insectile mix or mynah bird pellets. Parrakeet mix, sunflower seed, and health grit are equally necessary; and peanut butter is very helpful.

Grosbeaks and Hawfinches are not commonly available avicultural subjects, and their popularity is not in the forefront of aviculture. Cardinals, on the other hand, are always popular and delightful birds.

Breeding birds of this group will not forego live foods. The average incubation period is fourteen days, and young are in the nest for a similar period. The nest is usually a large and untidy cup-shaped affair. The female does most of the work of building, incubating, and rearing the young.

Because of the highly active nature of these birds, the writers consider them suitable only for large aviaries and never for cages unless they have been hand reared.

VIRGINIAN CARDINAL or RED CARDINAL (*Richmondena cardinalis*)

Probably the most beautiful member of this chapter is the Red or Virginian Cardinal along with its several very similar subspecies. Several races, usually grouped under the same popular name, are the Kentucky Cardinal, the Arizona Cardinal, the Mexican Cardinal, and, perhaps the brightest of them all, the Florida Cardinal. Since the laws of the United States prohibit trapping for domestic or for foreign avicultural purposes, those found in European bird markets are usually the Mexican Cardinal. All are so very similar that the above popular name is quite adequate and most frequently used. Because of a trade agreement with the Mexican government, the Mexican Cardinal is not legal in the United States. American aviculturists come into contact only with injured wild specimens if they are to remain within the law.

The writers have kept the Mexican Cardinal in captivity and have observed the Florida, Arizona, and Mexican Cardinal in the wild state. In addition, the species introduced into the wild state in Southern California and the Hawaiian Islands have been studied by the writers.

This is a difficult bird to photograph. It panics in a cage and quickly drops its usually erected crest thereby detracting considerably from its beauty.

Few birds are quite so beautiful and flamboyant as the cardinal in its wild state. The brilliance of the red male is a constant joy against a natural green background, and these birds seem to delight in showing themselves by darting across roads at the most opportune moments.

The male is a dazzling red except for a brownish-red shade on the wings. The luxurious crest of minute feathers adds a delightful shape; and the black triangular mask covering the forehead, lores, eyes, and chin adds a pleasing contrast. The beak is orange-red.

The female is mostly brownish with reddish shades on the wing, crest, and beak. The black mask is present, but the female is otherwise quite an unassuming bird. The overall size is nearly eight inches including the long tail. This is a beautifully proportioned bird with a heavy body.

In captivity the red richness fades drastically to a pallid pink. The writers conducted experiments to try to restore the original richness and attained a high degree of success by adding soya powder to the diet. Curiously, only those cardinals with large grosbeaks fade in captivity.

Virginian Cardinals are officially classified as songbirds by the law which prohibits holding them in captivity. This official status once again proves that not all lawmakers quite know the full details about the issues upon which they take firm stands. No one with any sense of hearing could comment favorably upon the song of this bird if he had heard other birds to which the bird fancier refers as songsters. However, the lack of song is not at all important for the aviculturist. The great beauty and easy care give a full measure of enjoyment not easily surpassed by other birds in aviculture.

The actual song during the breeding season is not one to be ignored. The most appreciative audiences are the cardinals themselves. The male is obviously happy with his meager talent, and the female seems duly impressed. The song is as pleasant as the trills and warblings of any happy bird, but it can hardly be described as symphonic.

The writers have successfully kept seven varieties of cardinals in one large aviary without trouble. The major signs of aggressiveness seemed to be directed towards birds with red in their basic color scheme; but, because the aviary was large, no harm resulted from the mild aggressiveness.

Youngsters have blackish beaks and dull grayish-brown plumage until the second year.

VENEZUELAN SCARLET CARDINAL (*Richmondena phoeniceus*)

The deeper shaded Venezuelan Scarlet Cardinal, sometimes called the Phoenix Cardinal, is of a similar shape and size in a comparison with the Virginian Cardinal except for the much larger and bulkier beak of silver gray. The black facial patch is absent, and the crest is longer and more gracefully recurved. The overall color is deep red with a darker shade of brownish-red on the wings. This may account for the popular name of Maroon Cardinal, but the color of maroon is completely absent in this bird's makeup. The infrequently used name of Vermilion Cardinal accurately describes the basic coloring.

The red coloring fades in captivity, but the writers have very successfully restored it by adding soya powder to the diet. This experiment was carried on for five years after the color had faded to a washed out pink shade. The restoration of color was nearly perfect.

Females are quite similar to female Virginian Cardinals except for the larger beaks and longer crests.

The Venezuelan Scarlet Cardinal is not often available but it is imported legally into the United States. After the difficult and time consuming acclimation period, this bird is very hardy and long lived. The acclimation period is difficult because most of the birds upon importation have clipped wings, and foot problems often develop during the regrowth period after the wing feathers have been pulled. Special care must be given to prevent damage to delicate pinfeathers during these periods because of the bird's natural inclination for great activity. The writers cannot understand the incredible and useless cruelty of clipping the wings of such active and flight loving birds as cardinals. No other cardinals have ever arrived in such a deplorable state, and certainly there is no possibility of finger-taming adult cardinals. Nearly every importation of Venezuelan Cardinals has followed the same pattern of clipped wings requiring prolonged acclimation periods. Cages must be kept scrupulously clean during this doubly difficult period, and fattening foods must be curtailed to prevent bumblefoot or other foot problems. The writers offer the various necessary foods in cafeteria style and try to have on hand a completely acclimated bird to induce acceptance of correct domesticated foods. The tendency to offer too many mealworms must be checked. Though readily accepted, they only add to the foot problems because of over-richness.

The Venezuelan Scarlet Cardinal is a truly delightful and lovely bird after the initial problems have been overcome. It is very hardy and an ideal aviary bird if housed with large finches or medium sized softbills. The huge and powerful beak, along with its rather large size, would naturally not lead the bird fancier to include it with small finches. This cardinal is quite peaceful, but there is no point in taking unnecessary chances.

BRAZILIAN CRESTED CARDINAL or RED CRESTED CARDINAL
(*Paroaria cucullata*)

The beautiful and brightly colored Brazilian Crested Cardinal is about seven inches long. The large size and heavy body are offset by a long tail and extremely attractive and well-formed crest of small but supple feathers. The

The Brazilian Crested Cardinal is an extremely hardy and colorful species and is ideal for the beginner. Inexpensive and usually readily available, the Brazilian Crested Cardinal frequently has a very pleasant song. The fiery red-orange crest contrasts pleasantly with white collar and underparts and gray upperparts. Cardinals are both seedeaters and softbill feeders. Owned by William Lasky.

233

crest is usually raised; but, like the Virginian Cardinal, it panics when introduced to the photographing cage and drops the pretty crest.

In its native areas, it is often kept as a cage bird; but the writers much prefer seeing such an active nature in an aviary. In cages the plumage frequently becomes frayed and shaggy, but in an aviary this bird is meticulous and immaculate in its grooming.

Occasionally the Brazilian Crested Cardinal is a very good singer, but the song is not frequent, and only a few individuals excel in this area. All males will do some singing.

The beak is much narrower than in the foregoing birds. This cardinal and all the following cardinals are not in the grosbeak class. The diet is the same, but the colors do not fade in captivity.

The Brazilian Crested Cardinal is the most popular cardinal in the United States and rivals the popularity of the Virginian Cardinal in other countries. Because of its beneficial insect eating nature, it has been introduced into the Hawaiian Islands. It is not yet as numerous as the Virginian Cardinal, but it is reported to be flourishing.

The very bright red-orange head is the brightest feature of this bird. The crest and a deep V-shaped throat area are included in the extent of the red-orange. The beak is horn colored with a dark grayish shade across the top of the upper mandible. The eye is dark. A whitish margin on the top and sides of the head is followed by a very pleasant shade of gray which covers the rest of the upperparts. Several wing feathers have darker margins to give an irregular pattern break. The underparts are bright white.

The female has a duller shade of red on the head, and the young have brownish upperparts and dusty white underparts until they reach maturity. The red on the head appears gradually and sporadically and is rather dull, but the color is all present before the brownish shade disappears on the upperparts.

The Brazilian Crested Cardinal has frequently been bred in captivity especially in planted aviaries. The live food ration must be greatly increased during this period, and it should consist of a variety instead of just mealworms.

POPE CARDINAL (*Paroaria dominicana*)

The beautiful Pope Cardinal, also called the Dominican or Red Headed Cardinal, closely follows the Brazilian Crested Cardinal in popularity. It usually is less expensive.

The size is approximately the same, and the distribution of the similar colors is identical to that of the Brazilian Crested Cardinal. Although it lacks a crest and is therefore less flamboyant, adequate compensation is given in the much richer shade of red on the head. The dark grayish wing feathers are edged in whitish-gray to give a noticeable variation in the upperparts. The beak is also similar except for darker tips on both mandibles.

The female is very similar but has a less bright shade of red and a slightly dusty shade of white. Youngsters have a brownish shade on the upperparts, dusty white underparts, and no red on the head. Adult coloration follows the same procedure as for the Brazilian Crested Cardinal.

The Pope Cardinal is equally as hardy as the Brazilian Crested Cardinal and closely follows the same diet and habits. It is a lovely bird and is especially suitable for novice bird fanciers. It also is one of the easier breeding members.

BLACK THROATED CARDINAL *(Paroaria gularis)*

The Black Throated Cardinal from South America is sometimes called the "Little Pope Cardinal" in the bird trade. It is not as well known as the Pope Cardinal, but it is much prettier. It is quite a bit smaller than the Pope Cardinal, rather less than six inches in overall length; but the basic pattern, diet, and habits are similar. The female shows less brilliance on the head and a paler shade on the throat.

The beak is a horn color with the outer areas tipped in black. The orange eyes are elliptically surrounded by a blackish-red shade. The head and most of the neck is brightly glossed in brilliant red. As in the Pope Cardinal, the crest is absent. The back, wings, and tail are glossy black; and these upperparts are therefore a better and sharper contrast than the gray of the Pope Cardinal. The underparts, like the Pope Cardinal are white except for the basic red V-shaped throat area which darkens to a near black in this species. The feet and legs are grayish-black.

The writers have had considerable experience with this beautiful species and consider it far more attractive than the Pope Cardinal or the following similar species.

YELLOW BILLED CARDINAL *(Paroaria capitata)*

The rather rare Yellow Billed Cardinal is similar to the above species in size, shape, and color; but it is less attractive. The beak is a shade of yellowish-horn, and the black is of a far less intense and less glossy shade. Otherwise, it is the same. The general habits are the same as for the Black Throated Cardinal, but it is considerably less hardy and more difficult to breed.

The female is rather paler in the facial area and shows a grayish shade on the mantle, but the distinction is somewhat difficult. Youngsters have gray beaks, brownish heads, and dusty-white underparts.

This South American slender-billed cardinal is more peaceful than most cardinals and does not lose color in captivity.

BLACK CHEEKED CARDINAL *(Paroaria nigrigensis)*

The Black Cheeked Cardinal is extremely rare in aviculture. It is similar to the Black Throated Cardinal except for a brownish-black band dividing the red across the lores, eyes, and upper cheek area. The head feathers are rather long, giving just a hint of a crest.

GREEN CARDINAL *(Gubernatrix cristata)*

The nearly seven inch crested Green Cardinal is a great departure from the cardinal family in color scheme. It sometimes is called the Yellow

Cardinal, but this name is nearly as incorrect as the popular name of Green Cardinal. It is about as accurately named as the Green Singing Finch. This South American slender billed species is full-bodied and long crested.

The green is neither well-defined nor bright. The male is more of a combination of bright yellows and blacks with subdued greens on the back and other subordinate areas. The beak is grayish-black and is darker on the upper mandible. The tall and slender crest, lores, and elongated biblike throat patch are black contrasted with bright yellow adjacent areas. The cheeks and rest of the body are basically dull olive-green. There is more yellowish on the underparts, especially around the vent and undertail coverts. The wings are more grayish with black markings on the centers of the wing and scapular feathers. The feet and legs are grayish-black.

Females are much duller and are especially wan in the black and yellow areas.

The Green Cardinal is probably the best breeder in the cardinal family. The diet and breeding information are the same as for all members.

This is a very handsome bird, but its attractiveness cannot compare with the beauty of other cardinals. Females are always less available than males; and, as a rule, the species is slightly less hardy than the average cardinal. A recommended minimum temperature is 45° F.

The beautiful Rose Breasted Grosbeak with its vivid reds, blacks, and whites is a superb songbird; but it is not available to American aviculturists. It now is also very rare in European aviculture, but it is easily maintained in captivity.

GROSBEAKS

Generally speaking, grosbeaks are not popular avicultural birds. Those outstanding and beautiful members are not available to most aviculturists, and the remaining members are easily outclassed by many other birds. All have very large beaks and should receive the same care as described earlier in this chapter. Only the more important species are included in this book.

ROSE BREASTED GROSBEAK (*Pheucticus ludovicianus*)

The beautiful Rose Breasted Grosbeak is a native of the United States and cannot be kept except in the case of injured specimens. Since it winters in Mexico, it sometimes is trapped in fair numbers and exported to Europe. It has the reputation for being the best singer in the group. The size is approximately eight inches.

The male has a bright and variable patch of rose on the chest. The underwing coverts are also splashed with pink. The remaining underparts, including the underside of the tail, are white. Head, neck, shoulders, and back are black. The wings and tail coverts are black with white spots. The rump is white, and the tail is black.

The female is a dull and streaky mixture of olive, gray, and brown on the upperparts and buffish on the underparts sprinkled with dark spots.

BLACK HEADED GROSBEAK (*Pheucticus melanocephalus*)

The Black Headed Grosbeak is also a native of the United States and cannot be legally kept in American aviculture. It is slightly larger than the Rose Breasted Grosbeak.

The male is golden-brownish-yellow on the underparts and on a band around the neck. The head is black, and the beak is grayish. The rest of the upperparts are black with bars of white in the wings. The female is similar to the female Rose Breasted Grosbeak.

GOLDEN MANTLED GROSBEAK (*Pheucticus chrysopeplus chrysopeplus*)

The Golden Mantled Grosbeak from Mexico is a very large bird with a grayish beak. Most of the plumage is bright yellow except for a whitish vent, grayish thighs, and black wings and tail sprinkled with white spots. The female is dull olive-green with muddy stripes and white wing bars.

GOLDEN BREASTED GROSBEAK (*Pheucticus chrysopeplus chrysogaster*)

The Golden Breasted Grosbeak is a South American subspecies of the above. It has a black back but otherwise is very similar.

GOLDEN BELLIED GROSBEAK (*Pheucticus aureoventris*)

The Golden Bellied Grosbeak is from Argentina and is mainly black with the customary white markings on the wings and tail. Bright yellow covers the underparts from the lower chest. The female is dark on the upperparts and yellowish on the underparts. This species is also very large but is a little smaller than the two species above.

237

PINE GROSBEAK (*Pinicola enucleator*)

The Pine Grosbeak is about eight inches long and is native to arctic regions. During the winter it migrates into Europe and Canada. It is not a popular bird because of the fading of the reddish shadings which cover the head, neck, back and the faintly tinted chest. The remaining upperparts are blackish except for paler wing bars. It is protected by law in the United States.

EVENING GROSBEAK (*Hesperiphona vespertina*)

The Evening Grosbeak is less than eight inches long and is native to the United States and Canada. It is a quietly colored bird with a few yellow highlights over a generally dusky color scheme.

The male has a bright yellow forehead which extends into a broad eyebrow stripe. The crown is blackish. The rest of the head is olive-brown. The same shade extends over the rest of the body becoming lighter and more yellowish on the flanks, rump, shoulders, and an area near the wings. Most of the wings are blackish but a broad white area covers some of the secondary flight feathers. The bill is dull olive-yellow.

The female is mostly dull grayish with some olive on the mantle and lots of black and grayish-white in the wings and tail.

It is protected by law in the United States.

BLUE GROSBEAK (*Guiraca caerula*)

The Blue Grosbeak from the United States winters in Cuba and Yucatan from which areas it is occasionally exported to the European bird markets. Another popular name is Brown Shouldered Grosbeak. The length is approximately seven and a half inches. The beak is black, and the male is uniform dark blue. Some brownish and black markings occur in the wings, and a broad patch of chestnut covers the middle wing coverts. Black covers a narrow band across the forehead and expands to include the lores and again to give a chin patch.

The female is mostly a dull and streaky brown.

This species is also protected by law in the United States.

BRAZILIAN BLUE GROSBEAK (*Cyanocompsa cyanea*)

Also called the Ultramarine Grosbeak or Blue Bishop, the Brazilian Blue Grosbeak is a very beautiful bird which is occasionally available to aviculturists. The size is approximately six inches long, and the disposition is much more peaceful than the species above.

The male has a black beak, feet, and legs; and the same black facial pattern is present. There is more black on the abdomen and in the wings and tail. The remaining colors are brilliant and rich cobalt blues of slightly varying shades. The female is dull brown with muddy variations.

LAZULINE or MEXICAN BLUE GROSBEAK (*Cyanocompsa parellina*)

The Lazuline Grosbeak is seldom available but is a good aviary bird. It is similar to the above except for the smaller size of approximately five inches.

238

BLACK TAILED HAWFINCH (*Coccothraustes migratorius*)

The glossy and attractive Black Tailed Hawfinch is a large and aggressive bird reaching seven to eight inches in length. The extremely large beak is a bright shade of orange-horn with blackish tips. The sexes differ slightly in coloring.

The male, except for reddish eyes, has the entire head glossy black followed by a pale and pleasant shade of gray starting at the nape and the throat. The back, rump, and uppertail are a darker shade of gray. The wings and tail are glossy blue-black, but many of the wing feathers have white tips while the flights have broad areas of white. The underparts are gray on the chest fading to white on the abdomen and orange-chestnut on the flanks. Feet and legs are orange.

The female lacks the black head. A band around the beak is dusky brown, and the top of the head is gray. There is less white in the flight feathers, and the center of the tail is grayish. The underparts are more grayish on the abdomen.

This Hawfinch is from China and Siberia and is no longer often available. It can be kept with large finches or medium-sized softbills.

EUROPEAN HAWFINCH (*Coccothraustes coccothraustes*)

The very pretty European Hawfinch is similar in size, habits, and disposition to the Black Tailed Hawfinch. The coloring is greatly different. A fine line of black rims the base of the beak and enlarges to include the lores and a chin patch. The rest of the head is bright chestnut fading to grayish-brown on the nape. The back is dark brown followed by a pale wing bar and blue-black flight feathers. The tail is brownish. The underparts are uniformly pale brown tinged with rufous.

The beak changes color with a change of seasons. In the winter it is a horn color tipped in black, and in the summer it becomes bluish.

The female is smaller and paler.

A subspecies is found in many parts of Africa, India, and the Orient.

CHAPTER 19

Doves and Quails

A few doves and quails hold the interest of finch fanciers and are fascinating inclusions in any collection. Both of these families are fully apart from finches and softbills, and each family maintains a high degree of interest in separate branches of aviculture. Each family has far more members than listed in this book. Those species in which finch fanciers are mainly interested are quite small and usually are called "miniatures." Most large doves and quails are not suitable companions for finches. The diet of the birds included in this chapter is the simple standard finch fare or millet. Sprouted seeds should be given during nesting periods. Quails require mealworms or some form of live food, but nothing else need be added. The birds will select those items required. Doves especially swallow seeds whole without husking them.

DIAMOND DOVE (*Geopelia cuneata*)

The charming and remarkably hardy Diamond Dove from Australia is seven and a half inches long including the long tail of four and a half inches. This bird is an excellent and inexpensive addition to any collection of finches. Rarely does it ever become a bully, and it is an excellent breeder. Moreover, its quaint coos and tail-fanning bows during courtship add pleasant personality accents.

This small dove has a black beak, pinkish cere, flesh colored feet and legs, and blackish toenails. The eye is red and black, and a prominent fleshy eye ring is red. The rest of the coloring is soft bluish-gray, darker on the upperparts and head and paler on the underparts shading to white on the abdomen and undertail coverts. Most of the color changes are gradual. Fine white spots on the wings are responsible for the name of Diamond Dove.

The tail is long with the central feathers showing the greatest length and greatest dominance. The side tail feathers show diminishing lengths; and, during the outspread fanned tail display which occurs during courtship, the general tail outline resembles an inverted V-shape. The feathers are mostly slender and rounded on the tips, but the outermost and shortest tail feathers may best be described as bluntly pointed. A broad band of white on the outer feathers on both the upper and lower sides contrasts sharply with the remaining slate-gray which covers the rest of the tail feathers.

Females usually have traces of dull brown instead of the bluish tint of the gray on the head and wings. The eye ring is paler and smaller; the head is often smaller; and the overall size is usually slightly smaller.

Young at first are dull brownish-gray with no bright eye ring or white wing spots. Horizontal striations of darker gray-brown mark the wings. The appearance during maturation gradually assumes the general appearance of the female until maturity is reached between eight months to a year of age.

Diamond Doves are very good breeders. They nest frequently and patiently may even commandeer feeding dishes if the proper facilities are not provided. Both sexes share the incubation period of approximately thirteen days. Young leave the nest remarkably early (eleven or twelve days after hatching), but they are fed by the parents nearly two weeks more even though a new nest has been started. The average clutch of young is two which nearly always become a pair. The customary nest receptacle is one designed for the large Yorkshire Canary. Since they are careless in building nests, the writers always add a nest pad lining which can be purchased in any pet store.

Some individuals become aggressive if more than one pair is present in each flight. This characteristic may apply to most doves. The writers have kept many species of doves together in harmonious breeding flights, but they cautiously include just one pair of each species and none which are closely related. Some of the larger species are hopelessly aggressive to all other doves and should be given flights to themselves.

ZEBRA DOVE (*Geopelia striata*)

The charming and quietly colored Zebra Dove, native to Malaya, is not often available on the bird market. This species has been introduced in the Hawaiian Islands and is now extremely prevalent near all human habitations. Zebra Doves are very excellent additions to any bird collections, but they are usually more costly and less easily bred than the Diamond Dove.

The general shape, size, and behavior quickly identify this species as a close relative of the Diamond Dove. The body is usually slightly larger and more bulky, and the coloring is quiet and subdued with earthy tones. Not quite as hardy as Diamond Doves, the general treatment and diet are usually the same.

The Zebra Dove is slightly larger than the Diamond Dove. An elliptical fleshy eye patch is bluish-green. The basic color is soft grayish-brown. Fine black striations on chest, sides, and flanks give the Zebra Dove its name. The back and wings also show striations, but they are rather broader and less pronounced. The facial area is grayish. Sexes are extremely difficult to detect by appearance. Behavior is the truest test.

INCA DOVE (*Scardafella inca*)

The Inca Dove is not often available to aviculturists, and it is not the most ideal of aviary subjects because of its characteristic wildness which refuses to disappear despite several generations of captive breeding. It occurs in Mexico and southwestern United States.

The Inca Dove has a dull pattern of nondescript and dark striations with dark wings. The basic coloring is a rose-shaded brown on the underparts and a more brownish shade on the upperparts. Flights are reddish-brown. Sexes are difficult to determine and must basically be differentiated by behavior.

CAPE DOVE (*Oena capensis*)

The beautiful Cape Dove from Africa is a quiet and docile aviary bird. It is not often available and is nowadays rather expensive. Cape Doves are very charming, very tame, and very excellent aviary birds in finch collections. The body size is approximately the same as the Diamond Dove, but the tail is much longer.

The male Cape Dove has a large black facial patch covering the forehead, sides of the face, and an extensive throat area. The beak is bicolored with a purplish-orange base and yellow tip. The rest of the coloring is mainly brownish-gray and silvery-gray with underparts shading to whitish on the abdomen. The lower back and rump are marked with a whitish band bordered with darker and more contrasting bands. The flights are reddish-brown showing a pleasant dash of color while the bird is flying. The underside of the tail is quite dark adding a further contrast.

The female is dull by comparison. She has a shorter tail and has no black on the face.

BUTTON QUAIL (*Coturnix chinensis*)

Technically, the variously closely related races of Button Quails are more correctly called Painted Quails. The real Button Quails are not related to the true quails and, if found in aviculture, are usually known by different names (sometimes reversed and called Painted Quails). There is not much use in trying to correct such a long standing avicultural error in nomenclature because the only result would be more confusion.

The avicultural Button Quail is well known by nearly every bird fancier and is an extremely delightful bird. It is tame, gentle, easily maintained, and a good breeder if conditions are correct.

Every finch collection should contain a pair of these charming creatures if the aviary has a suitable floor of sand or soil. They are hardy even on concrete floors and are usually kept in such easily cleaned aviaries while in the hands of dealers. In large numbers, quails must be in scrupulously clean aviaries. Infection from contaminated soil is a definite hazard which can probably kill off an entire flock. Where there are just one or two pairs as in the average collection, the dangers of such infections are very slight.

The size of the plump adult Button Quail is four and one-fourth inches including the hint of a tail which is composed of elongated tail coverts instead of the stiff tail feathers found in most birds. The feet and legs are

242

orange, and the small beak is mostly black with gray extending down the centers of the sides. The eye is a deep burgundy shade.

The male is very prettily marked. A broad flaring triangular bib, narrow in depth, is black followed by a white band on the underside and then by another black band. Along the sides of the bib a band of white is bordered by another narrow black band which in turn is flanked by still another faint white line which extends from the nostrils to just under the eyes.

The upper chest and sides are a soft and dark gray with a bluish tinge. The rest of the underparts are bright chestnut except for an elliptical bar of pale buff-white down the center of the lower chest to the central abdominal area.

The head has a broad band of dull gray from the forehead through the sides of the face down into the sides of the neck. The center of the crown, top of the neck, back, and rump are varying shades of brown and black with many feathers prominently centered in pale buff. This protective coloration is difficult to describe. The wings are mostly dull grayish-brown with only a few markings of the blacks and browns of the back to be found on the long secondary wing coverts.

The female lacks all of the distinctive markings of the male and has an overall cluttered pattern of earthy browns with black and buffish striations.

Youngsters are basically like females except for smaller size, noticeable slimness, and lack of smoothness in the incomplete extent of plumage. Mature colors come quickly, even before the young have filled out their lanky frames into the plumpness of adulthood.

The feathers of Button Quails are very soft and easily fall out during handling. The best way to hold one of these birds is to cover the flapping wings with the palm of the hand and to place the first two fingers on each side of the neck. The grip must be firm enough to be restraining but loose enough to avoid excessively dangerous pressure which may squeeze the life out of the bird. The Button Quail is quite hardy in the average aviary, but it detests being handled. When chased, frightened, or first released from carrying cages, its first impulse is to fly skyward. Without proper understanding of this basic characteristic, the bird fancier is quite likely to cause severe head injuries and possible scalping during the almost inevitable ensuing panic. Carrying cages should always be covered and padded to avoid these hazards.

Though they disregard all other aviary inhabitants, their peaceful and affectionate natures rarely extend to the introduction of other individuals of their own species. Whether the newly included species are male or female, the existing male inhabitants will always exert every possible harassment and attack to establish their dominance. These attacks may inflict severe damage if secluded refuges are not available. After a time peaceful gregariousness usually is established, and multitudes may live in close harmony after the dangers of the initial, cautious introduction.

For best breeding results, the writers have usually isolated one pair of quails per aviary although other inhabitants may run the full gamut of all types of finches, cockatiels, and certain types of Australian parrakeets. Softbills are not included because of a tendency to include eggs and offspring in their diets.

A secluded leafy shelter should be added to an obscure corner in the shelter. The writers usually use eucalyptus branches because the leaves remain intact even when dried, but various materials from different climatic environments are always available. The main consideration is the provision of a secluded thicket into which the female Button Quail may be coaxed to lay the majority of her eggs and to incubate without interruption or intrusion. Without such a private and secluded thicket, the female Button Quail may lay her eggs in every possible haphazard and widely distributed manner. The bird fancier is continually collecting the eggs in a bewildering exasperation, wondering what to do with them.

The female Button Quail usually lays far more eggs than she can incubate adequately. The eggs are large and astonishingly hard-shelled with a blue-green basic color spotted with brown. Usually fertile, the extras, beyond the usual six which are adequately incubated, can ordinarily be hatched in an incubator.

Newly hatched babies do not require hand feeding, but they must be taught the proper feeding procedure. In nature, either male or female will teach the feeding routine. This involves attracting notice to those items which are delectable and nourishing. Baby Button Quails are very tiny, but they are able to walk from the first moment of emergence from the egg. They easily pass to and fro through half inch aviary netting. At the first call note of alarm, youngsters dash under their parents and remain hidden in the plumage. The parent, hovering over youngsters, frequently belies the presence of youngsters and walks casually about as if they were not present. At any disturbance, however, the protective parent will stop abruptly. The youngsters, continuing the pace, often step out from under the parent.

These highly interesting, furry little bumble-bee sized creatures are fascinating and easy to rear without parental care. The writers have even hatched them under Budgerigars. The brooder should be circular to prevent the chicks from hiding in corners. In some cases, the writers have even used fish bowls for this purpose. Heat should be provided at a nearly constant range of 80° F. The diet should be a ground and powdery dietary supplement at first. The addition of dried flies helps to evolve a natural interest even though no food value is included in this item. Small mealworms or Enchytrae will fulfill the live food requirement. Frequent tapping of the container will call attention to the foods. In a very few days, the youngsters will learn to eat without being reminded. The writers have reared Button Quail and Valley Quail by this method, and the youngsters have always been incredibly tame pets. The characteristic wildness of quails is completely abandoned by all hand reared chicks. Many people have denied the possibility of tame quails, but the writers have known several species which become tame through hand rearing. It is indeed a great pleasure to have a friendly quail dog every footstep or fly to your shoulder in a show of affection. The writers will not easily forget such experiences.

KING QUAIL (*Coturnix japonica*)

The far less attractive but usually less expensive King Quail is often added to finch collections. This quail, which is at least twice the basic size of the Button Quail, is more often able to withstand the marauding onslaughts of many softbilled birds and may be included with Pekin Nightingales and Bulbuls. Newly hatched chicks may fall prey even to these birds and should be carefully guarded.

The basic appearance of mottled browns, blacks, and buffs, designed for protective coloration, is rather like a pale female Button Quail. Males have browner facial areas.

The eggs of this prolific species are astonishingly large and hard shelled. Like the Button Quail, far too many are laid in haphazard and careless locations to be successfully incubated. The female seldom gets down to seriousness until the last half of the clutch. Eggs are, at first, basically whitish

Two popular and fascinating miniature quails which are perfect avicultural subjects are the Philippine Button Quail and the Harlequin Quail. Males, pictured here, are more attractive than females. Photographed at Palos Verdes Bird Farm.

with large pale bluish splotches. The colors harden into dark bluish splotches after a short time.

King Quails are so easily reared that they have been liberated in several areas of the United States to be treated as game birds. They are rather smaller than native quails, and the ultimate object of shooting these charming birds is as repugnant to the writers as the deplorable shooting of any live bird or animal. Many naturalists shoot only with a camera, and the writers feel an inestimable admiration for these humane people. People who hunt with guns deserve quite another condemnation.

HARLEQUIN QUAIL (*Coturnix delegorguei*)

The rarely available Harlequin Quail from Africa is a very pretty bird rather closely resembling a large Button Quail. The size is nearly twice as large, and the cost is at least twice as much. This species has great charm but is usually reserved for quail fanciers rather than finch collections. The writers have occasionally had Harlequin Quails and have treated them the same as Button Quails with successful results.

SECTION III

CHAPTER 20

Pekin Nightingales, Related Species, and Jay Thrushes

PEKIN NIGHTINGALE (*Liothrix lutea*)

Easily the most readily available, inexpensive, and popular member of the softbill family is the Pekin Nightingale, sometimes erroneously called the Japanese Robin, which is a totally different bird. This lively, lovely, and hardy bird, which is neither robin nor nightingale, takes very kindly to captivity and has many admirers. It is often kept as a very active and feather-frayed cage bird, but it is far happier as an aviary bird.

The diet is the simple softbilled fare described in the chapter on diet. It also appreciates nectar food. Some fanciers consider this bird as partially seed eating. It readily partakes of certain seeds, but these usually pass through the bird undigested and offer no food value whatsoever.

During its season, it is an admirable songster.

The total size is five inches long including a forked tail of two inches with a slight spreading at the tips. The beak is red on the outer half and dull brownish-black on the basal half. The head is a dark olive shading gradually into a grayish-olive shade over most of the upperparts except for the following highlights. The tip of the tail becomes blackish; the outer fineline webs of the primary flight feathers are edged in bright yellow with about one third of the base length exhibiting a change in feather texture. These webs become slightly longer and show a deep rust-orange shade. The secondary flights have a yellowish bar spread across a small portion of the outer half of the webs near the secondary coverts. When the wings are folded, several fine lines of yellow show along the entire length of the flight feathers dominated by a deep rust-orange. This is a very attractive and prominent pattern.

Starting just behind the beak, a pale area covers the lores and draws a rather sharp dividing line between a dark and light area over and behind the eye.

Underparts are dominated by a broad and flaring fan-shaped bright yellow throat patch starting with the chin. The lower area of this throat patch is a deep rust-orange. The rest of the underparts are pale olive becoming very light in the area of the abdomen, vent, and undertail coverts.

Sexual distinction is difficult because some variations do occur in different seasons and because many individuals fade slightly in captivity. In full bloom, however, females have a paler shade of orange on the beaks and less of a flare on the yellow throat patch. The loreal area has a grayish tint. Many authorities look for a duller shade on the wings, but the writers have found this method less reliable and difficult to determine.

Some Pekin Nightingales have exquisite songs, but the average male merely sings nicely when compared to the superlative Shama Thrush or other noted songsters. The song season is not prolonged, but it does last past the spring. Unfortunately, it does not always sing in cages.

The breeding of the Pekin Nightingale is rather frequent compared to most softbills. There are certain preferences of the birds which, if furnished, will increase the chances for success. The aviary is best if planted and if a constant supply of fresh running water is given for frequent bathing during the nesting period.

The small cup-shaped nest is usually hidden in shrubbery only a few feet from the ground as close as possible to running water. Also unlimited should be a constantly available supply of live food. Although a variety of live foods should be offered, successful rearing has been accomplished with mealworms as the only live food available. Each youngster may consume up to the astonishing number of fifty mealworms per day.

Incubation is thirteen to fourteen days, and the young leave the nest in the same span of time. They grow very rapidly in the nest and reach maturity in a short time because of the live food.

Because of the highly insectivorous nature of this bird, it has been liberated in the Hawaiian Islands where it is thriving.

Most of the Pekin Nightingales found in aviculture originally came from India and Hong Kong.

SILVER EARED MESIA (*Mesia argentauris* or *Liothrix argentauris*)

The extraordinarily beautiful Silver Eared Mesia from India and southern Asia is related to the Pekin Nightingale but is considerably more expensive and not often available. This vivacious and active bird has a complicated and fascinating color pattern. The size is nearly seven inches long.

The bright yellow of the beak continues onto the forehead. Most of the head is black except for a large silvery-white cheek patch. The throat and a collar are a shade of rust-orange which is brighter on the throat. The rust-orange shades into olive and then gray for the remainder of the underparts and back. The rump and tail coverts are brilliant red, and the long square tail is dull black.

The wings have an excellent pattern. The narrow outer rim of the flights is yellowish-orange, and a large deep red area follows the gray bend of the wings. The rest of the wing feathers are grayish-olive.

The female is duller, especially on the tail coverts.

The care is the same as for the Pekin Nightingale, and the similar song is rather stronger.

There are several subspecies, all quite hardy, with slightly different shadings. In one, *tahanensis*, the forehead is more orange. This species ranges from the Himalayas throughout Indo-China and sometimes reaches Malaya. The subspecies *laurinae* from Malaya is larger and has more red with the female more nearly like the male.

The Silver Eared Mesia is a delightful aviary bird and one of the most desirable additions to any collection.

BLUE WINGED SIVA (*Siva cyanouroptera*)

The Blue Winged Siva is related to the Pekin Nightingale and the Silver Eared Mesia. It is a pleasantly active little bird, but it is far less colorful and known more by name than by personal experience. There are several quite similar subspecies, but none will probably ever reach the avicultural peaks of the above two species.

The total length is nearly six inches including a tail of approximately two and a half inches. The only dominant coloring is the blue in the wing and tail. The blackish eyebrow and pale eye ring accent a dull grayish head and neck. The back is brownish-gray with a bluish tinge, and the underparts are buffish-gray. The rump is brownish, and black is mixed with the blue of the wings and tail.

The Blue Winged Siva does not travel easily and has a difficult acclimation period. Afterwards, however, it is quite hardy and thrives on the standard softbill diet given to Pekin Nightingales. The writers do not consider it the most ideal of aviary birds, and those fanciers who are limited as to the number and scope of desirable species will probably overlook this species.

BLACK CHINNED YUHINA (*Yuhina nigrimentum*)

Very rare and somewhat difficult to acclimate, the Black Chinned Yuhina from Burma is a very lively and charming bird for a large cage or aviary. The writers feel that they should be kept in pairs instead of singly because of their constant and sociable activity, and they are much more entertaining and happy in pairs. Yuhinas are somberly colored and very small birds, but they have a distinctive crest which is erected in a frequent display of various emotions and any kind of excitement. The size is about four inches long.

The basic coloring is a dusky grayish-brown. The active crest and small chin patch are blackish, and the throat and abdomen are grayish-white tinged with buff. The long, slender beak is reddish. Sexes are very much alike, but the male has a pleasantly melodious call note which the female lacks. Visual distinctions show that the female often has more red on the beak, but this distinction is not always reliable. The crest of the female is usually shorter, but the difference is so slight that the individuals must be held in the hand for accurate differentiation.

The diet for this delicate softbill should consist of a mild honeyed mockingbird food instead of an oily food. Nectar, a variety of fruits, and small insects such as fruitflies complete the diet. Coaxing new imports to accept a mockingbird food is not always easy, but Yuhinas especially seem to like the honey in some of the new all-purpose basic foods.

Yuhinas cannot safely be kept with medium sized softbills. They get along well with small finches or small softbills such as Honeycreepers, but they are pugnacious to birds closely related.

Breeding is very rare. The nest is cup-shaped, and both sexes share in the incubation.

There are a few other Yuhinas and closely related Ixulus slightly larger than the Black Chinned, but they are even more rare in aviculture.

BLACK HEADED SIBIA (*Icioptilia capistrata*)

The handsome and hardy Black Headed Sibia from India is an ideal subject for aviculture. It is very easily managed on standard softbill fare. It is a good medium but slender size of nearly nine inches including the quite long tail. There is a half developed straggly and recumbent crest which is frequently partially raised. The disposition is peaceful even though it exerts its influence to assert its rights. The writers have always thoroughly enjoyed this engaging and beautiful bird. It enjoys the spotlight and poses in dominant positions for best viewing.

The slightly curved beak and entire head are black down to the throat. The encircling black cheeks break a diagonal line from the nape of the neck to the throat. All of the rest of the basic coloring is rich chestnut brown with a brighter concentration on the rump. The intriguing markings on the wings and tail add greatly to this bird's beauty. A broad band of bluish-gray serves as a margin for the long tail preceded by an equally broad band of black which runs up the sides of the tail in a narrow border to the base.

The variable wings are also heavily marked with this same almost indescribable shade of bluish-gray and are accented by some slate margins on the outer flight feathers. Secondary flights and shoulder feathers show considerable areas of bluish-gray with less slate to give just the proper accents.

Its ringing call and variable notes are pleasant, but it cannot be called a good softbilled singer. In some respects, the personality of the Black Headed Sibia resembles that of the Jay Thrushes, but it is distinctly different.

BABBLERS

The predominating family to which all the birds in this chapter are loosely related is the family of Babblers (*Timaliidae*). Speaking generally, the birds which are aviculturally called Babblers are rarely kept in captivity because of rather dull colors and lack of interest. Jay Thrushes are included in this group, however; and several are amusing and entertaining avicultural personalities. Moreover, several Jay Thrushes are readily available.

SPECTACLED JAY THRUSH or MELODIOUS JAY THRUSH (*Garrulax canorum*)

Though not particularly attractive in its overall shade of chestnut-brown, the Spectacled Jay Thrush has a dominating eye feature which invites attention. The dark eyes are surrounded by a pale circle of bluish-white extending into prominent and trailing white eyebrows. The shades of brown are slightly differing to show darker upperparts and paler underparts with a golden-brown on the chest and throat. The large and narrow beak is brownish-horn merging into a yellowish-horn at the base.

The Spectacled Jay Thrush is usually inexpensive when it is available. The major avicultural source is from Hong Kong bird markets. Though it is outclassed by many softbills, it is pleasant and hardy and is a charming song-bird. It is aggressive with small softbills and belongs in that awkward group of in-betweens which are rather difficult to place. This bird in an aviary spends much of its time on or near the ground, and in the wild state spends much of its time in low underbrush. It has been liberated in the Hawaiian Islands and is thriving in this adopted habitat.

It is pleasant and hardy and is easily managed on a simple softbill diet with a little extra raw meat or live food.

CHINESE JAY THRUSH (*Garrulax chinensis*)

Sometimes called the Chinese Mocking Thrush, the Chinese Jay Thrush is seldom available and is somberly shaded; but it is a wonderfully interesting aviary bird. Hardy and easily acclimated, this bird is usually inexpensive when it is sent from Hong Kong. It is excellent as a companion to the above species and medium sized softbills. It is smaller than most Jay Thrushes, but it is larger than the above species.

A small bristly forehead crest is black along with lores and a large throat area. A large cheek patch is white bordered by a blackish shade above and below. The beak is also black. The rest of the coloring is mauve-gray, darker above and slightly paler on the undersides.

The diet is the simple softbill fare, but it should include extra raw meat or live food.

This enjoyable species should be available more frequently.

WHITE CRESTED LAUGHING JAY THRUSH (*Garrulax leucolophus*)

Easily the most showy of all readily available Laughing Jay Thrushes, the hardy White Crested Laughing Jay Thrush from India and nearby areas is a constant source of admiration among large softbills. Active, amusing, and ever curious, this bird with its catcalling laughing sounds is easily managed in aviculture.

The standard softbill diet should include extra raw meat or an abundance of live food which may even include mice. The writers have kept these birds for several years and have been rather surprised that they have of their own accord gradually excluded every dietary item except the basic mynah pellets.

The heavy bodied size is eleven and a half inches including the tail of four and a half inches and the crest. The entire head and fulsome crest back to the beginning of the nape and including a large circular bib protruding down into the chest are white. A tinge of gray on the back of the crest becomes more concentrated at the back of the crown. The forehead, throat, and chest are brighter white. The eyes are reddish-brown and the beak is black. A sprightly black mask starts from the beak, includes the lores, surrounds the eyes, and encloses part of the cheek area.

The rest of the bird is dull brown with a brighter shade adjoining the white areas. The feet and legs are grayish. All of the feathers other than the tail and flights are soft and abundantly long to give a luxurious texture. The handsome crest of very fine feathers is especially bushy. In the female, the crest is slightly smaller and has more of a grayish extent.

WHITE THROATED LAUGHING JAY THRUSH (*Garrulax albogularis*)

The rather less attractive but equally hardy White Throated Laughing Jay Thrush from India has a disposition and size similar to the above. The head is large but not crested. The basic and predominant color is earthy brown in varying shades, darker on the upper side and paler on the lower side. The most outstanding accent is a broad and flaring bright white throat patch which starts directly under the beak and spreads out under the eyes to cover the entire throat area and adjacent sides. The long tail is pleasantly marked with broad white tips on the upperside and a pale grayish shade on the underside.

The bold and pleasant personality fits conveniently into the same care and restrictions applying to the White Crested Laughing Jay Thrush.

NECKLACED LAUGHING JAY THRUSH (*Garrulax moniliger*)

There are more than one species of the Necklaced Laughing Jay Thrush, and proper identification of the species pictured in this book is rather difficult since the writers acquired the birds through a trade rather than through a direct importation. The only reference material available to the writers is Smythies' **BIRDS OF BURMA** which lists a greater and Lesser Necklaced Laughing Jay Thrush. Salim Ali's **INDIAN HILL BIRDS** also lists the Necklaced Laughing Jay Thrush.

By an actual measurement, the birds pictured are presumed to be the Lesser Necklaced Laughing Jay Thrush. Though the picture shows an obvious variation in breadth of the necklace line, the writers have been unable to determine whether this is a sexual distinction or a subspecies difference.

The general personality of all three birds in the writers' possession is the same aggressive and carnivorous nature as described for the White Crested

Necklaced Laughing Jay Thrushes are large and aggressive. They are patterned in varying shades of brown and white. They do well with other aggressive birds of similar size. Though not the most attractive Jay Thrushes, these birds are active and raucous clowns.

Laughing Jay Thrush. Care should be the same, and the birds are equally as hardy.

Far less attractive than the White Crested Laughing Jay Thrush but nevertheless handsome and quite interesting, the Necklaced Laughing Jay Thrush is ten and a half inches long including a tail of four and a half inches. The long and powerful beak is grayish. The body is heavy, and the head is large. Dull brown covers most of the upperparts including the forehead, nape, back, wings, rump, and most of the tail. A long and narrow white line forms a thin eyebrow extending from the eye to the rear of the crown. This divides a large blackish area which covers the face down to the lower beak and extends to the lower part of the neck. A few whitish feathers give a silvery reflection to the black.

A broad, blackish necklace band connects on each side to the end of the black facial area and circles downward onto the chest. The throat area down to the necklace is pale buff. The chest areas below the necklace band have deep earthy shades of buff. The abdomen fades to off-white, and the undertail coverts are dull buff.

The underside of the wings and tail are grayish with broad dusty white tips preceded by broad dull black bands on the underside of the tail except for four central feathers which show only a hint of a blackish shade. The upperside of the tail shows the same white tips preceded by black except for the four central tail feathers which are all brown showing a trace of black on the second pair. The narrow outer rims of the three outer flight feathers are whitish giving an added pattern when the wings are folded.

The Greater Necklaced Laughing Jay Thrush (*Garrulax pectoralis*) is about an inch larger. Both species have several subspecies.

STRIATED LAUGHING JAY THRUSH (*Garrulax striata*)

Not often available because of an indistinct pattern and lack of interest, the Striated Laughing Jay Thrush is nevertheless large, handsome, very hardy, and excellent in aviaries. This bird extends from India to Burma and averages slightly less than twelve inches in length. The heavy body looks even more so because of long and bushy feathers which are especially prominent on the head and neck. The diet is the same as for the White Crested Laughing Jay Thrush.

The overall coloring is dark but rich and dusky brown, slightly paler on the underparts. Very fine but prominent pale buff striations occur on nearly all parts except tail and flights. The beak is blackish and rather shorter than found in most Laughing Jay Thrushes.

CHAPTER 21

Bulbuls, Chloropsis, and Fairy Blue Birds

Many of the birds in this and the preceding chapters comprise the backbone of the softbilled bird fancy. Many are very readily available at varying but reasonable prices. Fairy Blue Birds are avicultural aristocrats and bring high prices, but few birds are as exquisite or as beautiful. Members of the *Chloropsis* group become delightfully tame with very little effort. Most Bulbuls have very pleasant singing voices on a par with Pekin Nightingales, but none can compare with some of the superlative musicians to be found among the thrushes and solitaires.

Bulbuls and Fairy Blue Birds are easily maintained on the standard softbilled diet outlined in Chapter Two, and they require no extras. Chloropsis, slightly more delicate, must be given nectar if they are to remain in prime condition. Chloropsis, moreover, are not quite as sensible in their domestic feeding habits. Many become addicted to certain soft fruits such as banana and exclude other more important and well balanced items. Since they easily become tame by offering mealworms from the hand, there is a great temptation to overfeed this rich but important dietary delicacy.

Bulbuls show extreme hardiness after acclimation. Fairy Blue Birds, because of their great rarity and high price, are given every consideration and perhaps pampered more than they need.

All the members of these groups are charming and are admirable additions to any collection. Only such medium-large members as the Southern Black Bulbul need be checked for aggressiveness in the average collection. Most are too active for cage life, but a few species are remarkably poised and do well in cages provided they are given frequent exercise outside the cage.

RED EARED BULBUL or RED WHISKERED BULBUL (*Pycnonotus jocosus*)

The overall six and a half inches of the Red Eared Bulbul, with its tail of two and a half inches, is a handsomely proportioned and crested bird regularly available from India at a very reasonable price. This is a charming, easily acclimated, and quite hardy bird which is sometimes a good breeder in captivity if proper conditions are provided. It is peacefully companionable with a great many small to medium sized softbills and cardinals and is ideal for the novice fancier. The diet is the standard simplified diet for softbills, and the breeding information is rather parallel to that given for the Pekin Nightingale.

The major colors are dark and dull brown on the upperparts and white on the underparts. The beak is black. A very upstanding perpendicular crest, usually giving the impression of startled jauntiness, is three-fourths of an inch long. The numerous crest feathers and the rest of the brown on the head are darker brown, almost black. Immediately upon being caught in a net and held in a hand, the crest drops to a horizontal position. A bright tuft of bristly red feathers radiating backwards from the lower side of the eye and covering the ears enhances the basic white cheek area. A fine and well-defined line of blackish-brown starts at the corners of the lower mandible and connects to the nape of the neck encircling and separating the white cheeks.

The rest of the underparts are basically white starting with the throat and becoming slightly dulled by a tinge of brown on the sides, lower chest, and abdomen. A bright accent on the red undertail coverts completely dominates the dull grayish underside of the tail with its broad white tips. The upperparts, as mentioned before, are nearly all brown except for the broad white tips on the tail feathers.

Since there are several races of this bird with slight variations and since the length of the bristly red ear patches becomes less extensive after a moult in captivity, sexes are often difficult to distinguish. During the acclimation period, the writers earmark those individuals with large and brighter red areas over the ears as males and those with smaller red areas as females. Subsequent song tests for males have shown a higher degree of accuracy than any other method of sex distinction.

RED VENTED BULBUL (*Pycnonotus cafer*)

Perhaps the reason for the Red Vented Bulbul's high ranking second place in bulbul popularity is that it, like the Red Eared Bulbul, usually is equally available and similarly low priced. Moreover, it is just as hardy and thrives on the same diet. Slightly larger and only slightly less amicable, it nevertheless belongs in the same group of birds with personalities like the Red Eared Bulbul.

The dusky Red Vented Bulbul is far less colorful than the Red Eared Bulbul; but it has an infinitely more handsome, crisp, and well-tailored masculine silhouette. The well proportioned and fine feathered crest and wide flaring tail with its white tips enhance the general robust appearance.

The basic coloring of blackish-brown shading is darker on the head and shows paler margins on each feather of the back, wings, and breast. The beak is black. The lower abdomen fades to whitish to add contrast to a

256

The Red Vented Bulbul from India is a dull colored bird except for a chrysanthemum-like rosette of red feathers surrounding the vent. The main charm is a handsome shape with a trim crest and a long squared tail slightly spread near the white tips. Owned by William Lasky.

frivolous accent. A large rosette of slender and curly red feathers surrounding the vent gives a chrysanthemum-like texture.

Breeding success is as frequent as for the Red Eared Bulbul, and facilities should be the same as for the Pekin Nightingale. Aggressive traits during this period often become rather overbearing. Sexes are very similar. Behavior and the song of the male are the most reliable indicators. Females often show a slightly less extended crest, but this characteristic is not always reliable.

WHITE CHEEKED BULBUL (*Pycnonotus leucogenys*)

The less frequently available and smaller White Cheeked Bulbul with its even more simplified color scheme is one of the most delightful members of the very extensive bulbul family. The writers easily consider it among their favorites. Vivacious and ever active, the White Eared Bulbul is an ideal aviary bird for small or mixed collections. It is peaceful and quite hardy. Not easily bred, the incubation period is fifteen days, and fledging time is also fifteen days as is the case with most bulbuls.

The White Cheeked Bulbul from India is not so readily available as the Red Eared or Red Vented Bulbul, but it is more charming than either. Slightly smaller and of dull brownish coloration, the White Cheeked Bulbul has an extremely attractive crest and bright white cheek patch. Owned by William Lasky.

The Black Headed Yellow Bulbul from India is a little more rare and more delicate than many of the more popular bulbuls. The yellow eye and black head and beak contrast sharply to the deep olive covering the rest of the bird. This bulbul has charm and is interesting, but it frequently becomes sluggish in captivity. Because they become tame and confiding, it is a great temptation to overfeed mealworms to these bulbuls.

The beautiful dark brown crest is greatly and gracefully recurved and is one of the two outstanding features of this great charmer. The other predominance is the large circular white cheek patch. The beak is black, and a fine white line separates the brown upperparts from a blackish area covering the lores, surrounding the eyes, and spreading onto the throat. The rest of the head is also dark brown but in a slightly varying shade. Remaining upperparts are yet a different shade of dull brown except for a yellowish shade on the rump and pale tips on the tail. Underparts are a paler shade of less definite brown except for a yellow ventral area.

BLACK CRESTED BULBUL (*Pycnonotus melanicterus*)

The very calm and mildly dispositioned Black Crested Bulbul, also known as the Black Crested Yellow Bulbul, is not often available and is much

259

higher in price. It is a particularly tame bird which quickly learns that its keeper hands out such delicacies as mealworms or soaked raisins. This calm species is so completely poised and confident that the owner may frequently be obliged to step over it if it happens to be on the aviary floor when he enters. The Black Crested Bulbul is a very endearing bird to those fanciers who are fortunate enough to possess it. Its confiding charm is quite immeasurable.

The Black Crested Bulbul and all its races present a few complicating problems. The acclimation is rather difficult because it is slow to accept domesticated diets. Because of poor judgment, it may tend to accept the wrong dietary proportions which may lead to complications such as *avoirdupois* or severe imbalances. Great care must be taken in the proper acclimation and subsequent diet. Otherwise, this bird may drop dead from unseemly reasons. The olive shading which covers most of the body frequently fades in captivity to a washed out olive-gray. In general, this species is only half hardy.

The entire head, crest, neck, and throat are black dominated by a pleasant and confiding yellow eye. The rest of the coloring is olive-green, darker above and paler on the underparts gradually fading to dull yellowish-olive on the abdominal and ventral areas. The crest is rather sparse compared to the Red Eared Bulbul, but it is equally and perpendicularly erectile. The size is about the same as that of the Red Eared Bulbul.

BLACK BULBUL (*Hypsipetes madagascariensis* or *Microscelis psaroides*)

There are several slightly differing races of the Black Bulbul from India. This is a rather aggressive and large bird eight and a half inches long including the long and squarish fanned tail of three and a half inches. Not often available and not coveted by too many aviculturists because it is too large for small softbills and too small for the average collection of medium or large softbills, the Black Bulbul is nevertheless a very fascinating and engaging avicultural subject. The writers include it with Glossy Starlings, Spectacled Jay Thrushes, and birds of similar temperaments.

Though not very colorful, the Black Bulbul has a handsome and slender shape because of the rather long neck and long tail. Beak, feet, and legs are reddish-orange. The basic coloring is dark gray with a duskier shading on the wings and tail. The underparts are paler and fade to a whitish shade in the ventral region. Undertail coverts are gray streaked with white. The top of the head, including the spiny and poorly formed crest, is charcoal. A small charcoal patch rests below the eyes and on the chin.

Very hardy and easily acclimated, the Black Bulbul also shows great poise in cages or aviaries. It is a good singer from the standpoint of persistent frequency, and the melody is average for the family. The bird pictured in this book was entered in a National Cage Bird Show with no previous experience in a cage. Because of his extreme calmness, pride in his appearance, and joyful song while being judged, he casually won the coveted Kellog Trophy for Best Foreign Bird in Show.

There are many other bulbuls; but few, if any, beyond the species covered are given significance in aviculture. Some are never available; others are not glamorous enough to receive attention from bird fanciers. Any that might stray into the hands of aviculturists should receive the same care as given the above species.

GOLD FRONTED CHLOROPSIS (*Chloropsis aurifrons*)

The beautiful and charming Gold Fronted Chloropsis or Gold Fronted Fruitsucker, as it is often called, is one of the most enchanting and recommended members of all the softbill groups. It quite naturally becomes very tame and confiding in cage or aviary, and its inquisitive nature is one of great amusement. At feeding time, this well-poised bird meets the fancier at the door and with complete lack of fear will inspect hands, pockets, or any containers which might be bearing good things to eat.

The writers once had fifteen hand-reared and beguiling Gold Fronted Chloropsis and so thoroughly enjoyed the swarming attention that they found it difficult to stay out of the aviary. The birds immediately flew to shoulders, arms, and hands and began their probing searches to indulge their incessant curiosity. The complete confidence and lack of fear provided many of the most enjoyable experiences which aviculture has given to the writers.

Chloropsis are often called Leaf Birds or Green Bulbuls. Though allied to Bulbuls and Fairy Blue Birds, the various species of chloropsis are distinctly different not only in diet but also in appearance. The long, slender, and curved beaks indicate the most obvious distinction as well as the need for more fruit and nectar than required by the average softbilled bird. All have a bright glossy green as the major coloring, and nearly all males have pleasant songs. On the whole, chances for breeding success must be considered remote.

The size is approximately seven inches. The graceful beak is black; and an area covering the lores, lower cheeks, and throat is also black. A rich, glossy, royal blue is superimposed on the black on the sides of the chin and throat giving a tapering and divided bearded or mustached effect. Surrounding the black area is a halo of golden-orange, which is noticeable under the lower throat boundaries becoming rather faint on the sides and very prominent on the forehead and crown. The rest of the coloring is bright green except for a brilliant turquoise shoulder patch which is mostly hidden when the wings are folded.

The Gold Fronted Chloropsis is the most readily available member of the family and usually costs about three times as much as the Red Eared Bulbul, but it is one of the most worthy members of any collection. Reasonably hardy, it nevertheless is prone to respiratory ailments in some damp climates. There are several subspecies covering southeastern Asia, but the Indian race is the most frequently obtainable. Sexes are very much alike, but the female sings very little if at all. The blue on the throat is less bright and less extensive on the female.

261

HARDWICK'S or ORANGE BELLIED CHLOROPSIS (*Chloropsis hardwickii*)

Equally well known, even more attractive, but less readily available and higher in price, Hardwick's Chloropsis is another bright and shining star in the avicultural field. The main difference from the above species is a bright golden-orange covering all the underparts below the more extensive black throat area. The golden-orange is mostly missing from the top of the head, and the size is slightly larger. Sexes are alike except for paler underparts and a less bright mustache on the female.

JERDON'S CHLOROPSIS (*Chloropsis cochinchinensis jerdoni*)

Very seldom available, Jerdon's Chloropsis from India and Ceylon shows a marked difference in sexes. The male closely resembles the Gold Fronted Chloropsis except for the lack of the rich golden-orange on the forehead and crown. All the black area is haloed by a pale shade of yellowish-green. The female shows green instead of black on the facial and throat areas. The turquoise mustache is also considerably reduced. Several races showing rather considerable variations cover a wide geographical distribution. The nominate race *cochinchinensis* from Southern Indo-China and southeastern Thailand is called the Blue Winged or Yellow Headed Chloropsis. The sub-species *icterocephala* from Sumatra is called the Golden Headed Chloropsis.

There are a few other species and many subspecies of the Chloropsis group, but all are much too rare in aviculture to be considered important. Most are from areas which seldom if ever export birds. This is regrettable since most chloropsis are ideal avicultural subjects and show pleasing pattern variations.

FAIRY BLUE BIRD (*Irena puella*)

The very rare and delightful Fairy Blue Bird from India and many Asiatic areas is one of the most exquisite of avicultural gems. Expensive and highly coveted, this jewel quickly finds a home in leading zoos or aristocratic collections.

Nearly ten inches long, the heavy-bodied Fairy Blue Bird has the smallest feet in proportion to size of all birds known to the writers. Even the hummingbird, whose feet and legs are weak and tiny, cannot show such a difference in size ratio. The beak, feet, and legs are black; and the eye is bright red with black pupils. Sexes are very different. The male is rich and brilliant, and the female is quietly dusky.

The male shows two colors in his plumage: soft and velvety black and a richly shining lovely blue. A very interesting and boldly contrasting pattern encloses the blue upperparts. Encircling the topmost part of the crown and running down the center of the nape, the blue broadens to include the wide shoulders and tapers in the vicinity of the secondary wing coverts. Without a break in pattern, it includes the back, rump, and elongated upper and lower

262

tail coverts which reach nearly to the tip of the tail. He presents a breath-takingly beautiful appearance and has a bold self-confident manner which the illustration unfortunately does not convey.

The female is softly colored in an overall shade which seems to be a smoky blend of black and blue. She is dull in color but mildly handsome in appearance.

Not completely peaceful, the Fairy Blue Bird should be housed alone or with medium-large softbills. The writers know of no recorded breeding in captivity. Variations in the five subspecies are slight except for *tweedalei* of the Philippine Islands. In this race, the blue is duskier and less well-patterned.

The Black Mantled Fairy Blue Bird and subspecies (*Irena cyanogaster*) is also duskier and has a broad black mantle on the upperparts and blue extending from the lower chest through the undertail coverts. Handsome and valuable, it is unfortunately extremely rare.

CHAPTER 22

Waxwings

CEDAR WAXWING (*Bombycilla cedrorum*)

The Cedar Waxwing is a smooth and somber beauty. Its requirements are simple, and as an aviary bird it is ideal.

Native waxwings cannot be legally kept in the United States except in cases where there are injuries or other disabilities. When the bird recovers, the law says it must be released despite the fact that it will have been bypassed by its migrating flock and will be out of its real environment.

Those individuals with which the writers are experienced are birds which have fallen from migration. These exhausted and sometimes ill birds in most cases die unless bird lovers come to the rescue.

The first few days are extremely difficult and require an inordinate amount of patience and understanding, but the results are always worth the effort. Waxwings gradually emerge from their immobile stupor and show their gratitude by being the most tame and confiding of all wild birds.

At the moment of writing the authors have a waxwing which had fallen from its rigorous migration. Ill and exhausted, this hapless creature seemed not to care about its dubious future. It regarded the helping hands of the writers with a resigned suspicion for several days.

A complete lack of interest in food meant forced feeding. After the second day, the bird reluctantly accepted applesauce mixed with liquid vitamins from an eyedropper. Mynah meal was added the third day to balance the diet.

During these very frequent feedings the bird came to appreciate both the eyedropper and the hand which manipulated it. On the fifth day he eagerly accepted soaked raisins, bits of apple, and mynah pellets if they were offered from the hand. Previous to this he showed no interest in these foods. Mealworms were ignored. The natural diet includes far more fruit than animal matter. Berries are especially preferred.

At this time, the immobility ceased; and the bird began to enjoy his surroundings. He had not been caged during this time. The writers felt he would be happier perching on a large houseplant.

The finely combed smooth plumage and exquisite shape of the lovely Cedar Waxwing show very well here. Rescued fallen migrants are sometimes kept in captivity until recovery by American bird fanciers. Such birds become very tame, but trapped birds would have a tendency to panic in aviaries until they become accustomed to their surroundings.

He adopted this environment quite happily and occasionally moved to another plant nearby. He started probing into crevices of stems and leaves with considerable interest. The writers placed mynah pellets, soaked raisins, and pieces of apple in convenient locations; and from that time the bird was self feeding.

He now takes a great interest in all activity and almost seems glad to have dropped from the migration. Since his activity is confined to the houseplants and since he is extremely tame, the writers felt no need for caging him.

When another fallen migrant was introduced, the first, contrary to the writers' supposition, was decidedly hostile. He fought the intruder constantly for the first two days, jealous at the prospect of sharing his new environment. The intimidation display included fluffed feathers on chest and rump as well as menacing wings, outstretched head, and open beak. Later, he relented and coached the new arrival into accepting a domesticated diet.

Cedar Waxwings migrate in large flocks and descend to feed upon trees or shrubs which bear small berrylike fruits such as found on Pyracanthus or untrimmed Japanese Privet.

The Cedar Waxwing is five and three-fourths inches long including a two inch tail. The softly shaded plumage looks as if it had been finely combed. The blunt beak and feet and legs are black. The inside of the mouth is rimmed in black and otherwise pink.

A sharply drawn black mask covers the forehead and lores, surrounds the eyes, and extends backwards tapering and disappearing near the back of the crown. A fine line of white borders the lower rim of the eye. A small white mustache, deftly shaded with buff, is a pleasant accent to frame a very dark brown throat.

The black mask helps to enclose a shapely recumbent crest. The basic head coloring is soft olive-brown which also covers the neck, back and chest.

The back is a darker shade of grayish-brown shading to slate gray on the rump and tail. The tail is more blackish on the outer lengths ending in brightly tipped yellow.

The wings and flights are bluish-gray slate.

The underparts and sides fade to a pale grayish-olive around the abdomen. The vent is darker, and the undertail coverts are dull grayish-white. The underside of the tail is grayish-black tipped in dull yellow.

The six inner flight feathers have beautiful small appendages extending from the tips. These appendages account for the name and appear lacquered in a bright coral shade. They are stiff and show no feather-like structure in their one-eighth inch length and a width of less than one-sixteenth of an inch.

Sexes are alike, and immature birds show some stripes.

Waxwings are closely related to certain flycatchers, notably those of the genus *Ptilognys*.

In addition to the Cedar Waxwing, there are two other species in the family.

BOHEMIAN WAXWING (*Bombycilla garrulus*)

The Bohemian Waxwing of Europe and restricted areas of Eastern North America is slightly larger and more colorful. The undertail coverts have a reddish-brown shade. Flight feathers are tipped in white and yellow. The throat has more of a blackish shade.

EASTERN or JAPANESE WAXWING (*Bombycilla japonica*)

The Japanese Waxwing, which also occurs in other parts of Asia, is more colorful than the others. In size, it is between the other two. The tail is tipped in pinkish-red instead of yellow, and the lesser wing coverts show a tinge of dull red. The waxy coral appendages are missing, but the secondaries show a tint of rose on the tips.

CHAPTER 23

Niltavas and Flycatchers

Niltavas and true flycatchers are usually considered delicate, but the main problem experienced by the writers is a successful acclimation to a domestic diet. Their basic insectivorous nature is not easy to satisfy in the beginning and insectile mixture is completely ignored. Unless the insect food is alive and moving, there is usually no interest. Proper education is particularly slow with these birds, and the desperate stopgap substitution of large quantities of mealworms not only leads to dietary imbalances but also fails to elicit an interest in the inert insectile mixture. Importers have a very trying time with these birds which may partially explain their reluctance to import them even when they are rarely available. Skillful handling and an abundant variety of live foods are prime requisites in adapting these birds to aviculture. Breeding successes in captivity are practically nil.

For the most part, the birds in this chapter are not, despite their beautiful variations, standard avicultural subjects. Rarity, rather high prices, and difficulty in management tend to make them less than ideal.

On the other hand, the Tyrant Flycatchers, which are not true flycatchers but which merely share the popular term of flycatcher, are disregarded for completely opposite reasons. Extremely hardy and easily managed, the tyrants eagerly accept domesticated diets. Unfortunately, some are rather large in-betweens insofar as size and temperament are concerned and completely lack the delicate beauty of the true flycatchers. They have very ordinary and rather cumbersome shapes as well as uninspired color schemes.

RUFOUS or RED BELLIED NILTAVA (*Niltava sundara*)

All three species of niltavas are very rare in worldwide aviculture but are even more so in American aviculture. The most readily available and most colorful species is the Rufous Bellied Niltava. It is found in India which is one of the major exporting centers for birds. It also is native to China and Indo-China.

The size is approximately six inches. The sexes are very different. The shape is heavy-bodied and large-headed. Because of their dull coloration, females are very rarely available possibly because exporters feel they would not be saleable alongside the beautiful males.

Niltavas are noted for beautiful blues which highlight their coloring. They prefer insects, as do flycatchers, and berries, as do waxwings, as the principal diet. The male of this species has brilliant blue highlights on the crown, wing coverts, tail coverts, and rump with a subordinate deep blue on most of the remaining upperparts. Black marks the forehead, lores, facial areas, and throat. Dark brown dulls the flights. Underparts, starting at the upper chest range from reddish-orange to chestnut in the different races. The female is a dull olive-brown, paler on the underparts fading to a whitish shade near the vent and on the undertail coverts. The two most noticeable features are a large whitish chest patch and two blue spots on the sides.

The Lesser Niltava (*Niltava macgrigoriae*) also occurs in India as well as in Burma. It is slightly smaller than the above species (nearly five inches long) and is less colorful. The underparts, starting with a purplish chest, fade to ashy-gray. Bright blue adorns a patch on the sides. Otherwise, the male is rather similar to the above. The female is also smaller but is similar to the female Rufous Bellied Niltava except for the absence or noticeable reduction of the white chest patch.

The extremely rare Greater Niltava (*Niltava grandis*) is about eight inches long. It occurs in India, Burma, and other parts of the Orient. Both sexes have bright blue patches on the sides but otherwise differ completely. The male is more noticeably purplish on the back. The female is similar to the above species except for size.

PARADISE FLYCATCHER (*Terpsiphone paradisi*)

The flamboyant and exquisite Paradise Flycatcher is one of the world's most beautiful birds, but it seldom is available to aviculturists. Moreover, it is extremely difficult to coax over to domesticated diets. It is a creature of fragile loveliness and does not easily stand drastic temperature changes. Once fully acclimated, it is well poised and half hardy. The price is quite likely to be rather high.

The writers have not had much experience with this species or its extensive geographical races because of its great rarity in aviculture, but their experience probably exceeds that of most dealers or fanciers. Acclimation is probably one of the most difficult tasks they have ever attempted with birds, and end results are not completely satisfactory.

The standard size is about seven inches including the long and somewhat fan-shaped tail. The male has two long central ribbon-like tail feathers which may extend twelve to fourteen inches beyond the normal tail. A handsome and full-bodied crest of tiny feathers adds a cardinal-like shapeliness to the head. The male undergoes a color change which seems to indicate maturity differences. Immature birds in early stages resemble the female and lack the long tail feathers.

The fully mature male has a glossy black head which includes the neck and throat. Nearly all the remaining parts are white with many fine black accents on the upperparts. These black accents are mainly the feather shafts on the back, tail, and most of the wing feathers. When the wings are folded, the flights appear as a dull blackish shade. The inside of the mouth is a bright greenish-yellow.

The sub-adult phase is predominantly shiny chestnut-brown in coloration. The head is black, and the underparts are grayish fading to whitish on the ventral area. Females and immatures are similar but lack the long tail feathers. There are several races which show slight variations. The nominate race in Japan differs by having a purplish-maroon on the mantle of the adult male.

CELESTIAL BLUE FLYCATCHER (*Hypothymus coelestis*)

Very rare and very beautiful, the Celestial Blue Flycatcher is one of the finest examples of Monarch Flycatchers. Native to the Philippines, this lovely bird is one of the most difficult to obtain even during the sporadic periods when Philippine birds are available.

The size is nearly six inches, and one of the most prominent features in the predominant blue is a very attractive crest. The male is mostly blue with cobalt highlights on the back, wings, and tail. Purplish-blue occurs on the ear coverts, throat, and upper chest fading to bluish-white mixed with a green tinge on the lower chest and abdomen and to white on the undertail coverts. The female is much the same except for a shorter crest and duller colors.

The inside of the mouth is greenish-yellow and is quite similar to that of the Paradise Flycatcher.

JAPANESE BLUE FLYCATCHER (*Musicapa cyanomelana*)

The Japanese Blue Flycatcher is the most readily available of the group of Blue Flycatchers; but, even so, it is rare in aviculture. In the male, the face, beak, and a large throat area extending into the chest are black. Remaining underparts are white; and all upperparts including the head are a beautiful shade of blue with brilliant highlights on the crown, shoulders, and tail. The brown eyes are quite large, and the song is very pleasant. The female is dull olive-brown, paler below, darker above, and brighter on the rump. Some shadings of dull white occur on the chest and cover the lower abdomen and undertail coverts.

This flycatcher migrates to Malaya and Vietnam during the winter. Other extremely rare Blue Flycatchers include the many races of the Verditer Flycatcher and Azure Flycatcher.

TICKELL'S BLUE FLYCATCHER (*Musicapa tickelliae*)

Nearly six inches long, Tickell's Blue Flycatcher usually reaches the bird fancier from Indian importations. The basic coloring is blue with bright highlights on the forehead, on an eyebrow, and on shoulder patches. Wings and tail are bluish-black. Underparts are sort of a rusty orange fading to whitish on the abdomen and undertail coverts. The female is duller and paler.

MEXICAN SILKY FLYCATCHER (*Ptilogonys cinereus*)

Often simply called Ptilogonys, the quietly colored Mexican Silky Flycatcher is a rare and charming addition to any aviary. The predominant characteristic which attracts attention is a long slender body enhanced by a gracefully long and square tail and handsome crest. A casual but regal bearing and a penchant for perching in dominant and easily observed locations show further very admirable aviary traits. It is peaceful in a subtle dominance which has never, in the writers' knowledge, harassed any other aviary companion.

The overall size is nearly eight inches. Outstanding physical variations are yellow undertail coverts and a prominent white eye ring surrounding the large dark eye. The rest of the bird is softly and smoothly shaded in subtle variations of gray with a brownish tinge on the head, a bluish tinge on the back and small wing feathers, and a blackish tinge on the flights and tail feathers. Olive-yellow begins to show on the flanks contrasting with the white abdomen before merging into the quiet but rather bright yellow undertail coverts. A broad band of dull white crosses the central part of the tail.

The female is similar but shows much more extensive shades of brown. Several subspecies with slight differences may possibly becloud sexual distinction.

Silky Flycatchers take kindly to aviary life with remarkable poise and calmness. The diet, however, is extremely important. Lack of judgment on the part of the birds must be counterbalanced by the judicious skill of the aviculturist in catering to a rather delicate digestive system. The highly insectivorous nature of Silky Flycatchers might lead to overuse of mealworms which may eventually lead to problems resulting in sudden and mysterious deaths for no obvious reason. Live food is very important, but a variety of different insects as well as acceptance of a mild insectivorous mixture is recommended far more than the inadvisable offering of unlimited mealworms. As with most softbills, some fruit and available berries are necessary.

This species is slightly delicate and should be included only in advanced aviculturists' collections.

TYRANT FLYCATCHERS

The extremely variable members of the large family of Tyrant Flycatchers all occur in the Americas and may range from northern Alaska to southern Patagonia. Compared to most flycatchers, the average member of this family is coarse, unattractive, and heavy beaked. Bold and often abundant near human habitation, most members are well known in their natural state; but few are known aviculturally. The one exception perhaps is the Derbian Kiskadee Flycatcher which is covered below and which is one of the larger and less interesting but more readily available members of this group. Others generally well known in the wild state are the graceful Scissor Tailed Fly-

Two American Flycatchers which would not receive much attention from aviculturists even if they were permitted in captivity are the Wood Pewee (above) and the Phoebe (below). Though interesting in habits, the diet must be refined. A close relative, the *Ptilogonys*, is a much more desirable subject for the bird fancier.

catcher, the Phoebe, and the King Bird. All of these are illegal in the United States because of their native status.

Those from South America are admitted legally only if they are not resident in the United States. Though the Derbian Kiskadee Flycatcher is native from Texas to Brazil, it often has been imported and passed by inspectors though technically illegal. The writers do not particularly admire this bird, and so the knowledge of its illegality gave welcome reason for specific directions to exclude it if substitutions were necessary in South American importations.

DERBIAN KISKADEE FLYCATCHER (*Pitangus sulphuratus*)

The Derbian Kiskadee is also known as the Great Kiskadee or Sulphury Tyrant. Often surprised American dealers who receive it as a substitution will merely list it as a Tyrant Flycatcher.

The overall length reaches nearly nine inches. Both body and head are large and have unattractive proportions when compared to the medium-short tail. The rather large and cumbersome beak also helps to give a very ordinary and less glamorous appearance.

The beak is black, and a dull blackish head is marked with a broad band of white starting at the nostrils and extending over the eye down to the nape of the neck. Another line of yellow extends backwards from the whitish forehead on each side of the forehead to the back of the crown. Underparts start with white at the chin and cover the throat shading into a vivid yellow which extends through the undertail coverts in a somewhat faded shade. The eye is yellowish-brown, and the underside of the tail is brownish. Upperparts, starting at the lower nape, are dull brown including the tail. Color differentiations are not concise and do not offer the most pleasant contrasts.

Collections in which this bird is included should be composed of medium-large softbills with moderate aggressiveness. The writers have included it with Spectacled Jay Thrushes, Glossy Starlings, certain large thrushes, cassiques, mynahs, and softbills of similar dispositions.

The diet is composed of the standard softbilled fare if the bird is properly acclimated. It requires the most simple care of the entire family but likes extra raw meat and live food. There is some fading of the yellow in captivity indicating a lack of certain live foods which maintain color. Basically, this is an extremely hardy bird.

CHAPTER 24

Cuckoos and Roadrunners

Members of the Cuckoo family are rarely kept in captivity. Many are extremely difficult to keep alive because they will not readily take to domesticated diets. The orientation and acclimation period is therefore very strained and prolonged. Once past this expensive and difficult period, however, most members thrive in captivity.

Another reason for captive rarity is that very few specimens are offered for sale. This probably is because of the high mortality rate during the changeover to domesticated diets. Dealers, therefore, cannot afford to handle them. Zoos are the most likely places to see members of the Cuckoo family.

This large and varied family includes many beautiful birds of elaborate and brilliant color schemes as well as fanciful designs such as crests, wattled eyes, long tails, bare facial areas, and other unusual ornamentations.

Members are called cuckoos, coucals, Koels, Crow Pheasants, brainfever birds, and Malkohas and are found in most countries. Usually, however, they are secretive and solitary. Many of the most beautiful are found in dense jungles which also helps to account for their unavailability. Most are extremely carnivorous. Also, most or all are parasitic breeders which means that they lay their eggs in others birds' nests and destroy the eggs of those birds whom they parasitize. There are some marvelous pictures in various books showing very small parent birds trying desperately to supply food to a youngster five times their size. This must be a bewildering experience for the victimized parents even though they do an admirable job of rearing the young.

The writers have had experience with the Pied Crested Cuckoo (*Clamator jacobinus*) of India and the California Road-runner which is from a somewhat closely allied family.

PIED CRESTED CUCKOO (*Clamator jacobinus*)

The writers have had extremely difficult problems in trying to supply the Pied Crested Cuckoo with an acceptable domesticated diet. The highly carnivorous nature of this bird insisted upon live foods. Raw meat and mealworms were accepted but, of course, cannot constitute a complete diet. Mynah meal and mockingbird food were mixed with the meat to round out the dietary requirements.

273

The Pied Crested Cuckoo of India is rather a handsome bird approximately twelve inches in length. The upper half of the head including the good looking crest is very black. The rest of the upperparts are black, often glossy, except for the brownish tinged wings and white on the tips of the tail and on a wing bar. The tail especially is long and gracefully graduated. Underparts, including chin and lower cheek area, are white.

ROAD-RUNNER (*Geococcyx californicus*)

The comic but charming Road-runner ranges from fifteen to twenty-two inches in length including the very long tail which varies with different species and subspecies. A bushy and rangy crest adds to the awkward shape and a general appearance of startled alertness. The general color scheme of dusty-buff seems to be trying to exclude all glamour in favor of protective coloration. This seems a very wise adaptation in its desert environment of southwestern United States and Mexico.

Though keeping in captivity is illegal in the United States, the writers have accepted a few "gift" Road-runners for recuperative measures. One in particular was brought to the writers more dead than alive but turned out to be one of the most amusing tame pets ever cared for by the authors.

The Road-runner cannot be legally held in captivity except in instances of injury or illness. This Road-runner was brought in a starved and dying condition to the Palos Verdes Bird Farm. Mealworms revived an interest in food. Medication and convalescence followed. Six months of delightful experience followed before the bird was liberated. By this time the bird was completely tame and dogged everyone's heels like a puppy. It was a great comic with its extroverted and congenial personality, startled rangy chest, awkward gait, long heavy tail, and muddled pattern of colorless shades. It seemed something like an avian version of Ichabod Crane.

It showed its peculiar affection by dogging their heels whenever they entered its aviary.

The first aid diet at first consisted of huge doses of appetizers and liquid vitamins while it was in the hospital cage. Interest in mealworms soon showed that it would live. It often consumed up to fifty mealworms per day and, after several days of forced feeding, gladly accepted mynah pellets. For the six months that the writers had this delightful and peaceful creature in their possession before liberating it, the average diet consisted of mynah pellets, raw meat, and an astonishing number of mealworms each day. The writers were quite gratified that it gradually gravitated towards the mynah pellets as the prime source of food. Companions in the same aviary were Mynahs, Jays, Laughing Jay Thrushes, and Indian Red Billed Blue Magpies.

Nearly hidden in the dull and cluttered pattern of buffs and browns with numerous black markings is a very rich bronzed green covering the inner half of most of the feathers on the upper side. Not only does protective coloration tend to hide this beautiful shade, but the ludicrously awkward and comic shape also tends to deny it.

In the wild state the Road-runner spends practically all its time on the ground. It seldom walks but runs in a lanky and fast-paced gait. It principally lives on lizards or other desert wildlife, but its main claim to fame is that it kills snakes. Bold and fearless, it is one of the most important natural enemies of the poisonous and fearful rattlesnake. Not so well known is an equally useful trait to destroy harmful field mice. The writers consider it one of the best mousers in all the groups of softbilled birds.

Though this is a species which the law says is illegal, the writers feel a far greater responsibility to protect and to care for it even if the careless lettering of sometimes ill-advised laws is transcended. The writers feel that anyone who shirks the humane treatment and care of our wildlife is guilty of a far greater sin than ignoring a few misinterpretations of laws. Of course, the trapping and selling of protected species is a blatant defiance of the law. This is the purpose for which the various protective laws were originally intended.

Though closely related and allied to cuckoos, most of the Road-runners build their own nests and care for their own young. This fact attests to the great character which these birds exhibit in place of glamour.

CHAPTER 25

Drongoes, Minivets, and Bee Eaters

The birds included in this chapter are especially insectivorous and must have a greater percentage of a variety of live foods and raw meat than the average softbilled bird. All are quite rare, but all are highly coveted by specializing and intense bird fanciers. None of the birds in this chapter can be classed as completely hardy or as being easy to change over to domesticated diets. Novices should therefore bypass them. Even so, there are some fascinating and beautiful members in this group which deserve every consideration from advanced fanciers.

DRONGOES

All drongoes are very darkly colored. Some are dull, and some are heavily bronzed with a very deep and rich gloss. Of all the birds encompassed in the families of this chapter, the drongoes are usually the best known, most highly coveted, and most regularly available.

The Racket Tailed Drongo (*Dissemurus paradiseus* or *Dicrurus paradiseus*) from many parts of Asia in several slightly varying subspecies is truly a remarkable and fascinating bird. Like mockingbirds, this charmer with a beautiful natural song mimics other birds and includes their songs, whistles, and calls in its repertoire. In some instances, provided the imagination is adequately flexible and possibly stretched, the Racket Tailed Drongo has been known to utter a few words in its adaptable performance.

Though the writers never expect performances or demand an ability for imitating human speech, they have been very pleasantly surprised at the admirable aviary calmness of these birds and the willingness to share their talents to give their benefactors a very musical reciprocation. The melody of the song is indescribably sweet with an unaccountable fluidity which is matched only by the quality given forth in a similar manner by Solitaires and Clarinos. One individual particularly emulated the G.I. wolf call of a nearby mynah. Though he could not match the shrill and deafening volume, he engagingly included it in his song in one of the most charming manners ever experienced by the writers.

Many Shrikes are very beautiful birds which occur in many parts of the world. Some of those from Africa and various parts of Asia are among the world's most colorful birds, but they seldom become available to aviculturists. This Northern or Great Gray Shrike somewhat resembles the native Mockingbird in coloring and pattern, thereby frequently escaping detection by its unsuspecting prey. This species is often called the Butcher Bird.

The overall coloring is dull black. A straggly and unshapely recumbent crest adds a distinctive accent. The two outer tail feathers are greatly elongated with naked shafts beautifully spatulated in feathery tips. Sexes are alike, but the male is the real songbird, and the female is more shy and not as readily captured in the wild state.

The main size of the Greater Racket Tailed Drongo may reach fourteen inches including the standard tail length. The two outer tail feathers may extend another twelve inches. Variations do occur with different subspecies, but the most readily available race is the Indian subspecies described above.

The distinctive side tail feathers are rarely intact upon importation and do not often develop satisfactorily in confinement. Though this bird seems contented and happy in a cage, its tail feathers cannot develop properly or remain unbroken in a cage.

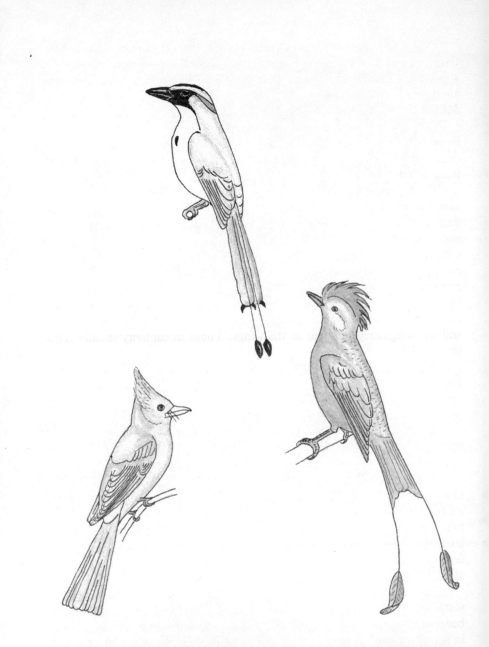

The Blue Crowned Motmot has the basic shape and bare central tail feathers with spatulated tips as found in most motmots. The Ptilogonys or Gray Silky Flycatcher has a handsome shape with its long tail and dignified crest, but its color scheme is greatly subdued. The diet should be refined for this shy and rare bird. The entirely black Racket Tailed Drongo is a fine songbird and an amazing mimic. The crest is straggly, and the long outer tail feathers are frequently and easily broken in captivity. These sketches are not drawn in any ratio to size.

The Lesser Racket Tailed Drongo is somewhat smaller and lacks a crest. Other drongoes lack the long tail feathers and are therefore less distinctive in appearance. Most are not as excellent singers as the aforementioned, and few are coveted by bird fanciers.

MINIVETS

There are four species of minivets which have been kept in captivity from time to time. The red brilliance of the favored species fades badly in confinement. Minivets are rather closely allied to shrikes and are highly insectivorous. All are very rare in captivity.

The Scarlet Minivet (*Pericrocotus speciosus*) of many Asian areas is nearly nine inches long. The male has black covering the entire head and throat, back, mantle, most of the wing feathers, and central tail feathers. Beak, feet, and legs are also black. A broad but irregular band of scarlet runs through the wings and covers the rest of the bird showing particularly beautiful underparts. The female of all species unless otherwise indicated has the same basic pattern except for the head in a much less attractive shading. Red is replaced by yellow which also takes over the forehead. Facial areas, chin, and throat are also yellow. Upperparts are grayish except for black in wings and tail and the irregular yellow bar in the wings. Those in captivity usually come from India.

The Orange Minivet (*Pericrocotus flammeus*) is also available during very infrequent importations from India. It is very similar in size and coloration except for paler underparts. It is also called the Scarlet Minivet by many authorities.

Short Billed Minivets (*Pericrocotus brevirostris*) are also very similar except for a smaller size (nearly seven inches), shorter beak, and more red on the wings.

The Small or Little Minivet (*Pericrocotus peregrinus*) also shows the same basic pattern but is not quite six inches long. Upperparts are grayish except for the scarlet rump and the irregular scarlet wing bar. The central tail feathers are mostly brownish-black and all but the two central feathers are edged in flaming scarlet. The rest of the pattern is identical except the female shows a strong whitish tinge to the yellow of the underparts.

BEE EATERS

The very extensive family of bee eaters includes many beautiful birds scattered through many parts of the world. None are widely kept in aviculture because of their highly insectivorous nature and a particular stubbornness in accepting domesticated diets. The diet in the wild state includes all types of insects rather than just bees. They prefer to hawk their prey in the wild state, and the writers feel that this preference should be recognized as a paramount reason to exclude this family from aviculture. Nests are usually located in extensive underground tunnels.

The best known member of this family is the European Bee Eater (*Merops apiaster*) which also includes North Africa and parts of Asia in its wide range. This sharply defined and colorful bird is extremely handsome. The beak and a facial mask, which flares backwards from the lores, are black. This contrasts not only with a reddish eye but also with a broad, flaring, and rather flat swath of dull yellowish-buff on the distinctive throat and lower facial area. This color area is bordered in black. The forehead is rather pale but subtly shades to a rich lilac-purple on the crown. Rust-orange covers the lower nape, back, mantle, and central portion of the wings. The rest of the coloring is a lovely shade of greenish-blue. Sexes are alike. The overall size is nearly eleven inches.

The Blue Throated Bee Eater from Borneo (*Merops viridis*) has a long slender beak and long slender extensions of the two central tail feathers. A rather narrow black mask covers the lores, surrounds the eyes, and widens on the upper cheek area where it terminates abruptly. A bright chestnut-brown covers the entire top of the head and the mantle and ends in a sharp V-shape. Underparts are a soft sky-blue on the lower facial and throat areas gradually adding a pastel greenish shade on the chest that fades appreciably on the abdominal area. The lower back, rump, and uppertail coverts are also a very pale greenish-blue. The tail is slightly more bluish, and the wings are a duller shade tinged with more of a greenish hue. This is a very beautiful bird, and the overall silhouette is characteristic for the average member of this exotic family. The overall size is nearly eleven inches including the tail of five inches.

The Carmine Bee Eater from Africa (*Merops nubicus*) is especially beautiful with its long and graceful tail, the two central extensions of which may extend three inches beyond the normal tail feathers. The general size is approximately the same as the European Bee Eater. Sexes are alike.

The black mask of the preceding species is nearly identical in scope on this bird; and the black beak is long, slender, and noticeably curved. The eye is red and serves as a bright contrast to the dusky bluish-slate head, chin, and throat. The rump and uppertail coverts are a pale sky-blue. Some of the wing feathers also show this shade. The rest of the bird is richly clothed in carmine with a deeper shade on the wings and tail.

This is a beautiful bird, but it rarely is available.

CHAPTER 26

Rollers, Broadbills, Trogons, Mot Mots, and Colies

All the birds in this chapter are extremely rare in aviculture and are not easily managed. Their delicacy mainly extends to a reluctance to accept domesticated diets. All except the colies are highly insectivorous in the wild state and should, like the birds in the previous chapter, have greater amounts of live food and insectivorous food in their diet. Rollers owned by the writers have usually been interested only in horse meat and mealworms. Mynah meal mixed with the horse meat helped to round out the diet.

ROLLERS

Those rollers which are the most abundant in aviculture come from India. The Indian Blue Roller (*Coracias benghalensis*), reaching nearly thirteen inches, is larger than the Greater India Hill Mynah in body size, tail length, and especially in the very extensive wingspread. The head is also very large. Some of the loveliest and softest shadings of mauve, lilac, lavender, purple, and brilliant shades of blue occur on this species. A description is quite impossible.

A large, dark, and rather dusky cap on the head is faintly turquoise-gray shading into a dull grayish-olive-blue color which extends over the neck, back, and scapular area. Brilliant turquoise glows on the wings near the shoulders. Deep and lustrous royal blue in a very broad band cuts across the centers of the outer six flight feathers and is repeated in a lesser degree at the bend of the wing and on the underside of the huge wing.

The tail is banded with a dark hybrid shade of royal blue and turquoise near the base of the tail and at the outer tips. The extensive area between these colors is a lustrous and lovely shade of turquoise-green. The two central tail feathers are the same dull shade found on the back.

Facial areas below the cap on the head are a dark pastel shade of lavender centered mainly on the throat and upper chest areas. Heavy streaks of buff radiate downward and outward from the throat. These colors gradually

281

The broad wingspan of the Indian Blue Roller is brilliant and beautiful with several shades of dazzling blues ranging from pale turquoise to deep cobalt blue. Photographed at Palos Verdes Bird Farm.

fade into a dull and subordinate shade of lavender-brown which continues until the tail feathers brighten up with a glowing shade of greenish-turquoise on the underside.

Rollers are peaceful, docile, and inactive despite their large size. There are several other species which show minor differences. Some have long extensions on their outer tail feathers to give added grace and greater charm.

BROADBILLS

The very unusual birds belonging to the broadbill group are also extremely rare in aviculture and seldom obtainable. The beaks of most species are very broad but rather flat and short and in some cases covered at the base by a dense crest of tiny feathers. Most of the individuals which figure in aviculture have large heads, heavy bodies, and short tails.

The Green Broadbill (*Calyptomena viridis*) is nearly six inches long and comes from Borneo, Malaya, and Sumatra. The male is predominantly a brilliant green with black markings on the wings and cheeks. The large head appears even larger because of a strange small-feathered crest which nearly covers the beak but which fails to decorate the head in any other way. The female is dull green and lacks the black markings.

Hose's Broadbill (*Calyptomena hosei*) of Borneo is about eight inches long and similar in shape. The male has a lovely shade of pale blue starting

on the upper chest and continuing through tne elongated undertail coveri
The female has blue restricted to the abdomen.

The Long Tailed Broadbill (*Psarisomus dalhousiae*) from Borneo is
brilliant bird reaching ten inches in length including the rather long ta:
The head is large, and the beak is very broad. The basic grass-green boc
coloring is highlighted by some soft blue in the wings and a bright bli
crown patch surrounded by a black head. A broad yellow collar surroundir
the eyes separates the black from the green. A vivid yellow spot occurs c
each side of the head behind the ear coverts.

Though there are other broadbills, none, to the writers' knowledg
have been kept generally in aviculture.

TROGONS
The most beautiful and highly coveted member of the trogon family
easily the unbelievably lovely Quetzal or Resplendent Trogon. Covering
nearly worldwide range, trogons not only represent but also seem to epitomiz
the tropics. Their rich, haunting and strange full-bodied calls are frequentl
used on motion picture soundtracks to add a tropical atmosphere. Member
of this family are delightful and beautiful, but they are seldom available an
usually bring high prices. Even so, they are easily worth every penny and wi
give more than equal measure in returned enjoyment.

The diet, though more insectivorous than the average softbill is readil
accepted in captivity. The short thick beaks are usually surrounded by blackisl
bristles. Trogons are actually among the most ideal of the truly exotic bird
in the softbilled kingdom after acclimation. They are very much at home ir
aviaries because of a natural calmness. They greatly prefer shade to sunshine

QUETZAL (*Pharomachrus mocino*)
The Quetzal or Resplendant Trogon is richly ornamented in a very long,
graceful, and filmy tail, a brilliant metallic green, and vivid red on the underparts. Few birds could ever achieve such an exotic appearance, and few are
known by such interesting names.

The name Quetzal was bestowed by Aztec Indians long before this
country was invaded by Europeans. Its extravagent plumes were used in
tribal ornamentation and later on women's hats. Now properly protected
and remarkably idolized, the Quetzal is the stately and revered national bird
of Guatemala. Strictly protected in Guatemala, neighboring countries gladly
export Quetzals of various subspecies and exact high prices for them.

The head of the male is surrounded by a sunburst crest radiating from
the eyes. This crest is most extensive on the top of the head and nearly covers
the bill. Lower radiations are less abundant but are nevertheless physically
prominent. The entire area of the head, neck, throat, and upper chest as
well as the remaining upperparts and tail are brilliantly glossed in metallic
green. Scapulars are greatly and gracefully elongated in a glossy and shiny
green to present one of the major features of this fascinating bird. Remaining

The male Quetzal or Resplendent Trogon in color shimmers in iridescent greens with bright red on most of the underparts. It is an extremely handsome, rare, and expensive bird which is a true aristocrat in the avicultural world. The female is less ornamented, but she is nevertheless very attractive.

underparts are brilliant red. The long tail is present for approximately six months out of the year.

The female shows great moderation by the absence of the long tail, flamboyant crest, and a greatly reduced brilliance in the green. Underparts are grayish-green down to the abdominal areas which show red through the undertail coverts. The underside of the tail is whitish with bold black striations caused not by bars but by overlapping white tips. This feature is very noticeable in both sexes. Though quite beautiful in its own stead, it cannot compare with its far more exotic male counterpart. The basic size is about fourteen inches, but the long tail plumes of the male may reach an additional length of twenty-four inches.

CUBAN TROGON (*Priotelus temnurus*)

Perhaps the most abundant of all trogons in aviculture, at least in the Western Hemisphere, is the strikingly beautiful Cuban Trogon. This is the bird whose exotic and penetrating calls lend character to jungle sets in motion pictures. An accurate description of the sounds from this bird would be impossible, but anyone who loves nature would undoubtedly be delighted upon hearing them and would probably recognize them at once.

The male has upperparts predominantly glossed in rich metallic green. A broad and extensive white area covers the chin, throat, lower cheek area, and chest. Remaining underparts through the undertail coverts are brilliantly glossed in a most intensely rich shade of red. The short and stout beak is mostly reddish except for a dark near-black on the upperpart of the upper mandible. The black wings are gaily and haphazardly accented by prominent white areas. The tail with its blackish central feathers and white outer feathers has each feather ending in a flaring swallow-tailed effect to add a pronounced and exotic accent. Smaller than the Quetzal, the Cuban Trogon is approximately eleven inches in length and is a very desirable bird for advanced aviculturists.

The female, slightly smaller, has a rose pink on the abdominal area and a hint of rose on the grayish-white chest.

None of the other trogons have extensively been kept in captivity. Most are very beautiful and deserve wide avicultural study. The care for any others would be the same as for the Cuban Trogon.

MOTMOTS

Motmots, for the most part, are a distinctive group of birds ranging from Mexico to Brazil in the shady thickness of the tropics ranging from humid to arid zones. All have broad and flat beaks and large flat heads. Most have a fascinating tail which has two quite long central naked shafts with broad spatulated tips. Upperparts are basically green, usually with a soft turquoise shading on the head. Sexes are very similar.

The structure of the tail with its small racket-tipped ends has been the subject of considerable controversy among bird authorities. The general opinion of observers is that the birds carefully trim away the feather parts to bare the naked shafts and to flaunt the exotic tips. The writers cannot verify these ideas; but, if true, the birds must be given credit for extraordinary good sense in developing a very distinctive accent. Not all motmots exhibit these interesting tail appendages, but most do.

Nests in the wild state are situated in rather long tunnels gouged out of earthen cliffs or banks. Some, given similar environments, have bred in captivity.

The Brazilian Motmot (*Momotus momota*) and several subspecies with very slight differences are, on the average, about eighteen inches long, more than half of which is devoted to the long tail. This species is one of the largest of all motmots as well as one of the most frequently available. The forehead and eyebrow are a rich cobalt-blue surrounded by a blackish shade on the upper head area and by brownish-buff covering the chin, throat, chest, and all underparts through the undertail coverts. Upperparts are green. Two black apostrophe-like marks accent the central chest area, and the tail is grayish-black.

The Turquoise Browed Motmot (*Eumomota superciliosa*) is quite similar but ranges merely twelve inches in total length. A black throat is delicately bordered by blue on the sides. There are several different subspecies with quite fanciful names.

COLIES or MOUSEBIRDS

Rarely available, colies or mousebirds from Africa are extremely interesting and rather expensive. Though possessed of a graceful shape with a very long and slender tail and a handsome crest with a slightly straggly and startled appearance when it is erected, colies are nevertheless clownish and awkward in their activities. Huge feet and heavy legs give adequate strength for indulging in gymnastics and for clinging to perches in any position or angle, upside down, sideways, or perching in a normal fashion.

The name of mousebird was bestowed upon them because of their stealthy habits of creeping and running about in underbrush. The long tails remind some people of rats or mice, and the basic mouse-gray coloring undoubtedly contributed to the name. Mousebirds have not only emulated mice and rats in the aforementioned traits but also contribute damage to crops in a similar manner. In their wild state, they are not usually appreciated. One of these despicable traits includes carrying off youngsters from other birds' nests to include them in their omnivorous diets.

In captivity, however, colies are greatly admired. They require more fruit in their basic diet than the other birds in this chapter, but care is otherwise the same. Basically, these birds are very gregarious and love company. They usually stay near the ground in dense shrubbery and are not happy unless kept in planted aviaries. They do not fly as much as most birds.

The Tacazze Sunbird has a handsome shape with a long bill and long tail extensions. It is mostly dark but has a beautiful iridescence. The Blue Naped Coly or Mouse Bird is an acrobatic comic and is rarely available to bird fanciers. It is not a large bird; but it has a long tail and large, sturdy feet and legs. The crest and blue nape highlight the mousy grayish-brown coloring which is subdued but attractively smooth. The Black Tit is an extremely active and vivacious species with a handsome crest. The black head and chest are contrasted by a large white facial patch and another on the nape. The remaining coloring is very subdued. This species is rarely available and difficult to transfer to domestic diets.

STRIATED or SPECKLED COLY (*Colius striatus*)

The body of the Striated Mousebird is approximately four to four and a half inches, and the long tapering tail is variable between seven and eight inches. The upperside is brownish-gray, and the underparts are narrowly barred with gray on a buffish or pale background. The facial area is blackish and the cheek area is a very pale near-white shade. The large feet are bright red, and the short beak is black and white.

Many slight variations occur in the several subspecies. A blue spot occurs, behind the eye in *nigricollis*. The Abyssinian race, *leucotis*, has a brownish throat and whiter cheek patch. Such slight differences as these and a few others not mentioned are unimportant to the aviculturist except for the possible assumption that some of the variations may erroneously be thought to be sex differentiation.

BLUE NAPED COLY (*Colius macrourus*)

The quietly attractive Blue Naped Mousebird has a bright blue patch on the nape and red on the base of the upper mandible extending through the lores and surrounding the eyes. The rest of the coloring is mousy-gray, darker on the upperparts and tinged with buff on the underparts. Though the size is similar to the preceding species, the tail is considerably longer. Males have slightly longer tails than do females.

The Red Faced Coly (*Colius indicus*) is very similar to the Blue Naped except for the absence of the blue on the nape, slightly more red on the lores, and a subtle cast of green added to the gray on the upperparts.

Other species of mousebirds have not, in the knowledge of the writers, been kept in captivity.

CHAPTER 27

Pittas

One of the popular terms for pittas is "Jewel Thrush." Though most characteristics differ considerably from thrushes, the jewelled adjective is appropriate except that no gemstone could possibly match the living brilliance of many vivid hues found on the many different species of pittas.

Pittas in captivity are indeed rare jewels. They are difficult to obtain even at rather costly prices. The subsequent acclimation to a domesticated diet is usually a disheartening task with little cooperation from the birds. Pittas avidly accept live foods but are very slow to discern the values of inanimate insectile mixtures. Live foods should be offered in a variety and, if possible, mixed with standard softbilled fare. Mealworms are, of course, an important source; but a sole reliance on this inadequate item leads to a slow deterioration and death. Nectar food helps immeasurably during the transition period. Once satisfied with domestic diets, pittas become reasonably halfway hardy and have even successfully reared young in aviaries. The ideal aviary is a conservatory aviary because of the need for a warm and humid environment.

Pittas are mainly terrestrial in the perpetually dense twilight reaches of lush overhead foliage. Softly mulched earth has helped to evolve a weakness in the feet which often becomes a primary problem in captivity. Concrete or soil floors are inadequate and dangerous. The writers add a thick layer of peat or decaying leaves to cushion the standard aviary floors and natural logs on the floor to provide some perching variations.

Among themselves pittas are not always peaceful. In the wild state they stake out territorial claims and defend these areas from other pittas. In an aviary they badger and chase each other but seldom cause any damage. One flashing gesture which may be meant for intimidation is a frequent spreading of the wings. This gives the bird fancier a good chance to view brilliant colors. They have a thrush-like gait which consists of short and rapid spurts of running punctuated by abrupt stops and frozen immobility. They fly only when disturbed and usually for short distances while staying close to the ground. At night, they prefer perching in twos in branches close to the ground. The short tails are emotional indicators and frequently waver slowly up and down in precise and stealthy movements while the bird stands motionless.

All pittas have the same basic odd shapes with only slight variations among the different species. The heads are large, the beaks stout, the bodies stocky, the tails extremely short and small, the legs long, and the feet quite large. Sexes in most species are alike.

Pittas are native in Africa, India, Borneo, Ceylon, Burma, Sumatra, China, Australia, and the Philippines and, surprisingly, are migratory. The Western Hemisphere has its near counterpart in similarly shaped Ant-Thrushes ranging in Mexico, Central America, and South America. Ant-Thrushes have very colorless plumage and are almost completely overlooked in aviculture.

HOODED PITTA (*Pitta sordida cucullata*)

Perhaps the most prevalent of the family to be found in aviculture is the Hooded Pitta which usually arrives from India. It is not quite seven inches long. Though very beautiful and fascinating, it usually is considered to be one of the least colorful of the family.

The top of the head is brown to the nape of the neck. The rest of the head is black including the chin, throat, cheeks, lores, and lower nape of the neck. The major coloring is green, soft and dark on the back and wings, paler and slightly tinged with blue on the underparts. Lustrous and brilliant turquoise covers a large patch at the base of the wing. The black flights have an extensive white wing bar. Brilliant turquoise again occurs in a wide somewhat crescent-shaped area covering the rump and uppertail coverts. The very short and expressive tail is black rimmed with turquoise, and the feet and legs are flesh colored.

The most brilliant and glossy red in the world brightly enhances the underparts reaching from the center of the upper abdominal area through the underside of the tail. A narrow black border surrounds the red at its beginning on the abdomen and at the tip of the tail.

The writers once had a dozen of these beauties and could not resist spending a great deal of time with them. Perhaps, because of this large number in one aviary, they were more peaceful than they usually are purported to be. Though secretive in the wild, these became very tame and confiding enough to accept food from the hand. The quiet secretive nature of pittas seems to have replaced a natural flighty tendency to panic found in most wild birds. This trait is possibly caused by an unwillingness to take sudden flight.

There are several slightly differing races of this widespread species. The subspecies *mulleri* from Borneo is slightly smaller and is known as the Green Breasted Pitta.

INDIAN or BENGAL PITTA (*Pitta brachyura*)

The second most widely available pitta is the Bengal or Indian Pitta. Also nearly seven inches long and more diversified in pattern, the writers were equally captivated by this species. It is not any more attractive than the Hooded Pitta because, if anything, the variations are slightly more cluttered.

Red underparts, turquoise on wing patch, rump, and uppertail coverts are the same as for the Hooded Pitta. The tail also has the same pattern but is slightly longer. Flights show less white and an added tinge of blue. Back and wings are also green.

The beak has a slight tinge of reddish at the sides of the base. The top of the head to the nape is brownish-buff with a prominent black stripe running down the center. A long slender white eyebrow borders the lower boundary of brown and separates a broad elliptically shaped black area extending from the lores, encircling the eye and cheeks, and broadening on the nape. White interjects a noticeable accent by underlining the eye. A broad flaring patch of white covers the chin and throat area and serves as a contrasting but diminishing lower border for the black. Underparts from the white throat are pale buff interrupted only by the brilliant red.

There are several subspecies occurring over a widespread area. One race, *moluccensis*, (formerly *cyanoptera*) is more properly known as the Blue Winged Pitta even though this popular name is also often applied to the Indian Pitta. Mostly similar, this bird has a far more extensive brilliant turquoise wing patch and the absence of the white borders above and below the eye.

OTHER PITTAS

None of the remaining pittas are available to aviculturists on a regular scale or at the present time. Shipments are very sporadic and not completely reliable. However, it is hoped that conditions will in time improve so that some of these far more beautiful subjects may be studied by zoos and advanced aviculturists.

The Giant Pitta (*Pitta caerulea*) from Malaya, Sumatra, and Borneo is nearly eleven inches long and is one of the far less attractive species. Sexes differ greatly, and the male is marked with prominent blue on the back and wings and a blackish shade covering the top of the head down to the nape. A sharp accent is a narrow black collar. Lower facial areas and throat are dusky grayish-buff, and underparts are paler shades of buffish-gray. Flights are black. Females have brownish collars, brownish tops of the heads, and reddish-brown on back and wings.

The smaller and very colorful Blue Banded Pitta (*Pitta arcuata*) of Borneo is predominantly brilliant red and slightly less than six inches long. Bright green covers the back and wings balanced by a dazzling shade of red on the top of head and broadening on the sides of the neck while extending to the lower nape. Underparts from chest through undertail coverts are equally brilliant red. The lores, cheeks, chin, and throat are golden and are gradually scaled with reddish on the upper chest. Bright bands of turquoise-blue cross the chest, slash across the wings, and trail behind the eyes.

The Blue Headed or Baud's Pitta (*Pitta baudi*), also from Borneo, is not quite seven inches long. Sexes differ with a brilliant male and dusty-brownish female. The top of the male's head is a rich glossy blue followed by an extensive black mask. A wide flaring throat area is white followed by a black chest. Underparts are deep blue. The black-tipped tail is a paler shade of blue, and the back and rump are dark red shading into brown and black on the wings. A bold white bar crosses the scapulars and a less noticeable white area marks the flights. The female is basically brownish, darker above and paler below. The throat is whitish and the tail blue. The white areas of the wing, similar to those of the male, brighten the dark wings.

The Garnet Pitta (*Pitta granatina*), nearly six inches in length, occurs in Malaya, Sumatra, and Borneo. This is a very dark bird marked with luminous turquoise on the wings and on a long area trailing behind the eyes. Smoldering and glowing purples cover the back and chest and burst into dark glowing red on the underparts. The top of the head is glossy black, and the flights are dull black.

The Banded Pitta (*Pitta guajana*) from Malaya is very differently marked and lacks richly glossed colors. Nearly eight inches long, the sexes differ in that the female is less bright and lacks a blue abdominal patch. The male shows a blackish head dominated by a long golden-yellow eyebrow which extends from the nostrils to the nape of the neck. The upperparts are dull brown except for a prominent white line crossing the scapulars. The tail is dull bluish. The chin is whitish merging into a yellowish throat. From the chest through the undertail coverts, equal but prominent narrow bands alternate with yellow between blackish-brown except for a dark blue central abdominal patch.

Several pittas occur in Burma but are not likely to become available. These include Phayre's Pitta, Blue Naped Pitta, Fulvous Pitta, Greater and Lesser Blue Pitta, Guerney's Pitta, plus a few described above. Australian, New Guinea, or South Pacific pittas are not likely to become available and will be omitted.

Philippine pittas may become available from time to time in sporadic shipments. One of the most important possibilities is the Red Breasted Pitta (*Pitta erythrogaster*) which has a wide range with subspecies reaching to Australia. Though several colors are casually mixed and haphazardly arranged in this slightly less than six-inch species, a brilliant and uniform red extends from the lower chest through the underparts. A narrow black collar extends boldly across the lower throat and extends faintly across the nape to divide the rather dull chestnut head from the adjacent brighter blue on the mantle and chest. Green interferes somewhat on the bend of the wing, but the rest of the upperparts and broad chestband are vivid blue.

Koch's Pitta (*Pitta kochi*) is about two inches larger, but basically similar to the above, and is less well defined in more modest and duller colors. Very rare even in its restricted native Philippine range, it is not a likely addition to the avicultural fancy.

Steere's Pitta (*Pitta steerei*), also from the Philippines and also rare, is characterized by black head and nape, pinkish-white chin and extensive throat area, green upperparts with turquoise on the wings and uppertail coverts, and a lovely shade of soft turquoise on the underparts. Black on the abdomen is matched by vivid red on the vent and undertail coverts.

African pittas include the African Pitta (*Pitta angolensis*) and Green Breasted Pitta (*Pitta reichenowi*). They are far less colorful and far more cluttered in the overall color scheme and not likely to be as avidly coveted.

CHAPTER 28

Thrushes

The huge family of thrushes offers several species from around the world which have become avicultural favorites. Though the size and shape vary considerably, all members are sprightly and active. All are characterized by quick movements and frozen pauses.

Highly insectivorous, thrushes should be given more than average live food and some raw meat in captivity. Otherwise the diet is the same as for standard softbills. The acclimation period is difficult for some species and amazingly easy for others.

Thrushes are noted for their lovely seasonal songs as well as their beauty. Often aggressive towards their own kind, the bird fancier should maintain no more than one pair of each species in an aviary. In some cases, individuals become pugnacious to closely related species. The bird fancier must carefully observe and be a good judge in order to mix many thrushes in one aviary.

Quite a few thrushes are native to the United States and cannot be kept in captivity. Occasionally an injured specimen or abandoned nestling may be found and given sustenance by a bird fancier. Most of these birds thrive very well under such care and usually reward their benefactors with warm and tame friendliness.

The *Hylocichlid* thrushes fall into this category. The Hermit Thrush (*Hylocichla guttata pallasi*) is a charming and rather small thrush which furtively frequents shrubbery in Southern California. The writers have hand-fed many individuals until they were able to fend for themselves. Upon liberation, they all have stayed nearby almost as if they felt they could come again if help were needed. Dull brownish upperparts and pale underparts with large dark brown spots on the chest form a drab color scheme, but the large friendly eyes and shy but confiding personality help to make this a much cherished pet.

Other thrushes of the genus *Hylocichla* occurring in the United States are the Wood Thrush (species *mustelina*), Wilson's or Veery Thrush (species *fuscescens*), Gray Checked Thrush (species *minima*), and two races of the species *ustulata*: Olive Backed and Russet Backed Thrushes.

294

The native Wood Thrush, like all *Hylocichlid* Thrushes, is not a colorful bird; but it is a charming subject easily nursed back to health.

Some thrushes are not presently permitted entry into the United States or into certain states. Both the Mistle Thrush (sometimes called Missel Thrush) and the European Blackbird are prohibited. The Mistle Thrush (*Turdus viscivorous*) is not important in American aviculture, but the European Blackbird is quite often available. This latter species will therefore be covered later in the chapter.

Several fine thrushes occur in Europe. Some are offered annually to American importers, and some species are never offered. Various countries have their own protective laws which reflect many different outlooks. The handsome Ring Ouzel (*Turdus torquatus*) has never been offered on any dealers' lists sent to the writers, but the European Song Thrush is offered annually. Wheatears and Bearded Reedlings from Europe and Forktails from India and many areas in the Orient are among the members of the thrush family which have never occurred on lists sent to the writers.

Many so-called blackbirds are thrushes, but these should be differentiated from American blackbirds which are more closely related to the birds in Chapter 36.

Hylocichlid Thrushes, such as this Olive Backed Thrush, all have spotted chests and dusky brownish upperparts. This species has an olive cast on the back.

SHAMA THRUSH (*Copsychus malabaricus* or *Kittacincla macroura*)

Perhaps the best known and most highly coveted of all thrushes is the wonderful and somewhat expensive Shama Thrush. Several races with slight differences exist in India, Ceylon, Borneo, Burma, Malaya, Indo-China, and the Philippines. The usual species found in aviculture is the one from India. All species frequent forested areas.

The Shama is a charming bird of exquisite proportions and intriguing mannerisms. The color scheme is dark but sharply contrasted and glossy in several areas. As a songbird it is seldom equalled during its singing season if given proper care and diet.

Often aggressive, the Shama has a tyrannic tendency to become the boss in most aviaries. It is best housed in collections of average-sized softbills but should carefully be watched with a cautious eye to allay any extremes of aggressiveness.

Though not easily acclimated, the Shama Thrush eventually takes kindly to captivity and is easily managed after the critical initial period. Hand reared individuals are very tame, always fascinating, and more easily acclimated when exported to various parts of the world.

The male, which has a body length of nearly five inches and a tail of six inches, is dark and glossy. Head, throat, upper chest, back, and wings are glossy black with purplish reflections. The rump, uppertail coverts, and thighs are white. Underparts are a rich chestnut shade. The beak is black, and the feet and legs are flesh colored. The long tail has dull black central feathers with graduated feathers on the sides boldly tipped in white.

The female is similar in shape but has a slightly smaller tail. She is drably colored in a dull earthy brown. Immatures resemble females for some time.

DHYAL THRUSH or MAGPIE ROBIN (*Copsychus saularis*)

The very popular, less expensive, and easily acclimated Dhyal Thrush is very simply colored in black and white. The total size is nearly eight inches including the long thrushlike tail. Several very similar races occur from India to the Philippines, but the most likely prospect for aviculture comes from India.

The Dhyal Thrush or Magpie-Robin from India is readily available and is one of the best softbilled birds for beginners. Dhyals are easily managed. Aggressive and personable, the Dhyal Thrush is recommended for advanced or novice fanciers. Owned by William Lasky.

The Dhyal Thrush is subordinate to the Shama in its love for dominance but probably exceeds most other softbills of its size. The general care is the same as for the Shama.

Male Dhyals are glossy black on the upperparts except for a very predominant white wing bar and some white on the sides of the tail feathers. The black extends to the lower chest and then changes abruptly to white.

The female Dhyal has dull and dark brown replacing the black. A scattered mottling of white occurs on the chest, sides of the face, and the throat. Immatures are the same as females but quickly show patches of black in their coloring.

DAMA or ORANGE HEADED GROUND THRUSH (*Geokichla citrina*)

The charming Dama Thrush, also called the Orange Headed Ground Thrush, is more terrestrial and heavier bodied than the two previous species. The usual avicultural species comes from India and is regularly available, but there are a few other close relatives. Price and availability ordinarily range somewhere between the above two species. The size is nearly nine inches including the rather short tail.

The head down to the shoulders and all underparts are rusty-orange. A tapering line behind the eye is bluish-gray. The beak is blackish, and the feet and legs are flesh colored.

The male has a slate shaded bluish-gray covering the back, wings, rump, and tail. A bar of slight white occurs near the bend of the wings. Females and youngsters show a brownish shade in place of the gray and have a subdued shade of orange.

Dama Thrushes are easily acclimated and very hardy. They are ideal for aviculture and are peaceful with nearly all softbilled birds. The writers have had many Shamas, Dhyals, and Damas in their varied experiences with birds and thoroughly admire all three.

One closely related species is the White Throated Ground Thrush (*Geokichla cyanotus*). Also from India, this species is very rare in aviculture. Lores, face, cheeks, chin, and throat are white; but two dark brown bars perpendicularly traverse the sides of the face. Other characteristics are the same.

BLUE WHISTLING THRUSH (*Myiophoneus coeruleus*)

The handsome and rarely available Blue Whistling Thrush from India is one of the most stately and hardy of all thrushes. It prefers a terrestrial habitat and is aggressive to smaller birds. Overall size is nearly twelve inches long, and sexes are very similar.

The beak is bright orange, and feet and legs are black. The basic color is a dark and dusky blue which is deeper above and only slightly paler on underparts. Pale bluish-white spots dot the back and underparts.

The writers have closely observed this species and have always placed it

298

in a very high category among softbills. Those owned by the writers have always seemed to be aristocrats of the bird world.

Several species are basically similar with variations either slight or only mildly distinct. The Blue Rock Thrush (*Monticola solitarius*) from India is slightly less than nine inches in length. The male is dull and dark blue with white edges to most of the feathers on the underparts. A considerable extent of brown occurs on the upperparts. The female is duller and somewhat paler.

The Blue Headed Rock Thrush (*Monticola cinchloryncha*) is about seven inches long. Underparts, rump, and uppertail coverts are rusty orange. Upperparts and head are mostly bluish with some white in the wing and some black on the facial areas.

CUBAN RED LEGGED THRUSH (*Mimocichla rubripes*)

The Cuban Red Legged Thrush is sometimes available and finds ready buyers as well as many admirers. The writers have never particularly cared for this species. It is not a good singer and is not particularly attractive. The shape is slender and not really well-proportioned. The body coloring is mostly dull gray. The blackish tail is tipped in white, and some brown occurs near the vent. The chin is white. The legs are reddish-orange. This rather large species is quite aggressive to smaller birds.

EUROPEAN SONG THRUSH (*Turdus musicus musicus*)

The large, handsome, and very charming European Song Thrush is perhaps the most typical member of the family. It combines most of the average characteristics of thrushes along with many traits of the bird which Americans call the robin. It readily adapts to aviculture and has often bred in aviaries. The song is excellent, and the disposition is quite peaceful.

The general activity and mannerisms of the European Song Thrush are very similar to the American Robin. The sizes of these two species vary slightly, and appearance differs greatly. Both birds fulfill in their separate habitats identical gifts of song and pleasurable presence in neighborhood gardens. A very important highlight of their presence is a skillful aid in controlling harmful insects.

Upperparts are dark reddish-brown with varying mottled areas of paler and blackish shades. Underparts are mostly pale buff with dark reddish-brown spots sprinkled generously on the throat, chest, sides, and flanks. Sexes are alike. Behavior is the best test for differentiating male from the female.

AMERICAN ROBIN (*Turdus migratorius*)

The well-known American Robin is not a robin at all. It most definitely is a thrush, but common usage is not likely to be changed. The name of robin, probably given as a result of nostalgia for the much smaller and quite different European Robin, will assuredly prevail.

The American Robin is about ten inches in length and is quite heavy-bodied. The male is somewhat variable in color according to the season. The female is similar but much duller in general coloration. Youngsters have characteristics of most thrushes by having large spots on the pale chest. Other colors are greatly reduced.

The male in color is blackish on the head and upperparts and rusty-red on the underparts. The beak is dull orange-horn with some black on the upper mandible. During the out of season phase, colors are less intensified and much duller.

American aviculturists have little chance of adapting this species to aviculture except for injured individuals or abandoned nestlings. The experiences with these birds, if they become available, are nearly always very fascinating. These robins become wonderfully tame with a comic show of aggressiveness, but they really have a tender and soft heart for their bene-factors beneath the bravado.

EUROPEAN BLACKBIRD (*Turdus merula*)

Though prohibited entry, the European Blackbird still remains important in American and European softbilled aviculture. It has often been reared in aviaries in Europe but seldom if ever in the United States. For some indescribable reason, European Blackbirds are often sent as substitutes for other birds and are almost always passed by inspectors of incoming birds.

The male is the most desired individual of the species. The writers have observed the European Blackbird in many parts of Europe. Upon reflection, memories are accompanied with the amusing recollection that this poorly colored bird with its marvelous song was always distracting the authors from famous landmarks such as castles, cathedrals, palaces, or famous architectural masterpieces. The gift of nature's finest and most musical endowments has always seemed far more important to the writers than the cold stonemasonry of talented architects. Even more amusing has been the consistent consternation of tour guides who extoll the virtues of their countrymen while the writers absentmindedly followed an obscure birdsong.

The male European Blackbird is less than ten inches in length. The overall coloring is dull blackish with some glossiness on the crown, mantle, back, and wings. The beak is yellowish. The female has very dull and cluttered shades of brownish which are darker above and paler below.

GRAY WINGED BLACKBIRD (*Turdus boulboul*)

The sometimes available Gray Winged Blackbird from India is larger and better proportioned than the European Blackbird. The general color scheme of the male is the same as for the European Blackbird except for pale gray areas across the wings. The size is nearly ten inches long.

The female has a dull brownish shade replacing the black.

This species is a good singer and readily adapts to captivity.

BLACK ROBIN

Several species of thrushes occur in South America which fit the general description of Black Robins. An accurate classification is difficult since all

The South American Giant Mountain Robin is a thrush and is a large version of the European Blackbird. Seldom kept because of its aggressiveness towards other birds and because of its drab appearance, this bird rarely has a chance to demonstrate its truly endearing qualities. This bird is one of the most cherished pets at the Palos Verdes Bird Farm. Bold and aggressive, Robbie is the undisputed boss over all the birds at the Bird Farm and thoroughly enjoys his semi-liberated existence. He has a beautiful song which must be heard at very close range to be appreciated because it is a "whisper song." Robbie prefers to sing and strut at night in dim lighting.

resemble a large version of the European Blackbird with yellowish legs.

The species pictured in this book is probably *Turdus atrosericeus* from Colombia and Venezuela, but the writers have not verified an exact identity. It is called by various names such as Giant Mountain Robin, South American Black Robin, Black Thrush, and possibly also by other names. Regardless of its ornithological classification, the individual pictured was one of the finest and most frequently rewarding of all pets ever owned by the writers.

The overall size is nine inches including a tail of three and three-eighths inches. The body is much heavier than the above two species. Feet, legs, and beak are yellowish-orange. A very prominent fleshy eye ring is yellow. All feathers are dull black with some faint tinges of brown on several areas of the underparts.

This Black Robin is extremely aggressive and resents all avian intruders. It is completely unsafe with smaller birds. For this reason, it is not very popular with aviculturists; and it is generally not considered attractive enough to rate separate quarters. Few people have ever heard it sing.

The writers have been very fortunate with the Black Robin pictured in this book and have had experiences of very close friendship with this wonderful bird.

When first obtained, this Black Robin already showed signs of age. In addition one foreleg was badly injured, and the other leg had a very painful swelling on the ball of the foot. Plumage was battered and frayed, and the bird was indeed a sorry sight.

For want of a better name, this pathetic creature was called Robbie. His original price was not high, but his incapacitated condition deserved and received the utmost attention and care. He was given liberty on an enclosed patio. He had shrubbery to explore and kingdoms to conquer. Earthworms were planted in all available soil. A carefully balanced diet, clean perches, and regularly tended clean soil helped to restore Robbie's health in a very short time. Plumage reparations took a longer time, but eventually his condition and health were perfect and robust.

As Robbie came out of his deterioration, his personality became more bold and increasingly aggressive. He staked his claim to the entire patio and ruled it constantly. He completely accepted the presence of equally free Macaws, Cockatiels, Halfmoon Conures, and a Trumpeter but never quite reconciled himself to an equal status with Coleto and Greater India Hill Mynahs which also shared the enclosed patio. He harried and successfully bullied these latter individuals to a point of meekness. Robbie had conquered his kingdom and wielded a regal authority for the next seven years.

His ruling power occasionally extended to bullying humans. Fashionable open toed shoes on women became fair game for Robbie, and his aggressive probing caused a considerable loss of composure for many misunderstanding women. He unsuspectingly would dart out of the shrubbery in a rapid manner towards these open toed shoes, and feminine dignity was quickly lost in a fancy side-stepping jig.

Robbie had two very intimate displays to insure endearment of all who witnessed such scenes. His song was always reserved for an afterdark strutting display which rarely was bestowed upon anyone other than the writers. Striding across the tops of cages with puffed out feathers, lowered head, and drooping wings, Robbie would offer the writers one of the sweetest but quietest songs ever heard. The writers call it a "whispering song" because one must lean forward at a close range to capture every note and trill. The song was apparently composed of all the sounds that Robbie considered pleasant. Most of all it sounded like a distant chorus of many canaries. It always seemed impossible that so many voices could be accumulated in one song. The song display was even more charming because it was given with a feeling of gratitude for good care and complete devotion to its benefactors.

The other display was a frequent and swashbuckling affair of bravado to establish a firm reign over his domain. This display always occurred during the daytime and nearly always was directed towards the writers. Anyone who was not familiar with Robbie's personality usually considered the beginning of this display as an outright attack, but a smile of approval always appeared

302

as Robbie ended his performance with a tiny song while standing on an open hand.

The very active display started with a fast brush against the head of one of the writers. Rapid jumps into the air and sharp thrusts against the top of the head were accompanied by flapping wings, open beak, and various sounds. The object of this questionable affection, one of the writers, offered a hand above his head.

Robbie immediately transferred his pouncing tactics to the extended hand and gradually settled down to a strutting song display while standing on the hand.

This fascinating display was given every day. Regardless of other pressing demands, a pause to allow the complete cycle of the performance was always a pleasure. Without a doubt, Robbie was one of the most fascinating and wonderful of all the many pets ever owned by the writers.

CHAPTER 29

Robins, Robin Chats, Redstarts, Blue Birds, Ruby Throats, and Blue Throats

All members of this chapter are offshoots of thrushes but share many characteristics with that family. All are quite rare in aviculture because of unavailability despite the many species spread around the world. Some are more or less regularly offered but not often imported. Most are exquisitely dainty in their habits, and many are beautiful. Sharp and active movements on the ground are punctuated by frequent pauses of frozen inactivity.

The diet must be somewhat more refined than the standard softbilled fare, and acclimation periods are usually difficult. Even though the Ruby Throats owned by the writers quickly adapted to the regular diet given to most softbills, the writers prefer the more intricate diet given to delicate softbills.

Most of these birds are peaceful in mixed collections, but some are aggressive towards their own kind. In the wild state separate areas are claimed, and intruders are driven off. Most members do not require heat during the winter and seem equally at home in hot or reasonably cold weather.

ROBINS

The true robins are much smaller than the thrush that Americans call the "Robin Red Breast." The rapid and precise movements as well as most habits, however, are the same. Most are very rare in aviculture.

The best known of all robins is the small and friendly European Robin (*Erithacus rubecula*). This very charming species is frequently kept as a cage bird in Europe, and it has a tendency to possess its surroundings with an extensive authority. It has no qualms, despite its diminutive size, about asserting its self-assumed leadership.

The male European Robin has a bright and glossy rusty-orange front which includes the forehead, lores, lower facial area, sides of the neck, chin, throat, and chest. His remaining colors are drab and subordinated. Brown covers all the upperparts, and dusty grayish-white covers the remaining underparts. The female lacks the orange highlight but is otherwise the same. The beak is small; the eyes are large; and the feet and legs are strong.

The European Robin is sometimes called the British Robin.

The true Japanese Robin (*Erithacus akahige*) (not *Liothrix lutea*, which is called by this name and by Pekin Nightingale) is very similar to the European Robin and is very highly prized by specializing fanciers even though it is not as good a singer.

The Loo Choo or Temminck's Robin (*Erithacus komadori*) is another Oriental relative similar in many respects to the European Robin. Black occurs on the forehead, chin, throat, chest, and flanks. Remaining underparts are white. Bright rusty-orange occurs on the crown and nape, and brown covers the wings and tail. The female lacks the black and orange. This species is sometimes called the Riu Kiu Robin because it originates in the islands bearing that name.

The Indian Robin (*Saxicoloides fulicata*) is perhaps the most frequently available of all robins to dealers, but it is seldom imported. This is a shy bird which is not often seen if housed in a planted aviary. Even in unplanted aviaries, it seeks the highest and most secluded spot and ventures forth only at feeding times. Yet, whenever live foods are offered, it is one of the first birds to snare its share.

The charm of this piquant bird's active movements and peaceful coexistence is a great joy to any bird lover who pauses to observe his birds. The writers have had several Indian Robins and have enjoyed them immensely. Unfortunately, females always seem to outnumber males both in importations and in aviary bred specimens.

The total length is nearly seven inches, but nearly half of this length is absorbed by a long and highly active tail. The body is slender and quite small. There are several subspecies of this furtive bird extending far beyond India, but the most likely available subspecies is the one described here. Another popular name for this species is the Brown Backed Robin.

The male is dark and glossy, but the female is dull brown all over. A bright white patch on the lesser wing coverts of the male is conspicuous especially in flight. The male has black on its cheek patches, inner flights, rump, and outer tail feathers. All these areas are glossy. Remaining areas are dark brown except for a reddish shade extending from the vent through the undertail coverts. The Ceylon race (*leucoptera*) has a black beak.

ROBIN CHATS

Robin Chats are closely aligned to thrushes and robins. The legs are long; but other characteristics, habits, and diet are the same. Robin Chats are

305

The Black Throated Redstart is not a particularly attractive softbill, but it is robin-like in its alertness and has a fine personality. This species is prohibited to American fanciers because it is native to the United States.

rarely available to aviculture. A colored picture of a Robin Chat is included to give a general idea of the average shape and proportion. There is no need to go into great detail on any of the several species scattered around the world because none are important in aviculture. If they become available, they will become excellent additions to the avicultural fancy.

REDSTARTS

Redstarts also fall mostly outside the scope of aviculture. The diet and most characteristics are the same as for robins, but most Redstarts are larger than the group of birds accurately called robins. If these shy members do become available to aviculture, they should be considered somewhat delicate especially in the beginning.

The European Redstart or Common Redstart (*Phoenicurus phoenicurus*) is very attractive with its reddish-brown underparts and grayish upperparts. The rump and uppertail coverts are the same color as the chest. Tail and flights are blackish. A broad forehead extending onto the sides of the head is frosty in a pale silvery-gray. Chin, throat, and sides of the face are black.

The White Capped Redstart (*Chaimarrhornis leucocephalus*) is from India. A bright white cap offsets a jet black which covers all upperparts through the wings and underparts to the chest. The eyes are reddish-brown, and the beak is black. Remaining underparts, rump, uppertail coverts, and most of the tail are reddish-chestnut. The tail is broadly tipped in black. Sexes are alike, but the male is slightly larger.

BLUE BIRDS

Blue Birds are closely related to robins and are often called Blue Robins. Most are native to the United States and are therefore prohibited to American aviculturists. Once in a while an injured specimen comes into the hands of an American bird fancier, and it is usually given the attention it deserves.

Some Blue Birds are occasionally sent to Europe, but shipments are very infrequent. A few British aviculturists have succeeded in building domesticated strains with aviary bred birds. The writers hope the progress will continue. These aviary bred birds should be placed only in the hands of very sincere and dedicated aviculturists so that the strains may expand.

The diet and care should be the same as given to robins.

The Eastern American or Common Blue Bird (*Sialia sialis*) is about six inches long. It ranges in several subspecies throughout the lowlands of the eastern parts of Canada, the United States, and Mexico. The male is bright blue on the upperparts with a softer shade on the head. Dull chestnut marks the throat, chest, sides, and flanks. Abdominal areas are white. The female is much paler in the same general coloring. Youngsters are mostly brownish with pale spots on the back, throat, chest, and sides. The wings and tail show some blue.

The Western Bluebird (*Sialia mexicana*) is similar in size and shape. The range of the several subspecies is basically the same as the above except

307

that this bird occurs on the western side of the continent and prefers mountainous highlands. The male is similar to the above species but has a throat varying between blue and pale-gray. It also may have some brown on the back. The female is similar but is paler in shading. Youngsters resemble the young of the Eastern Bluebird but have more blue on the wings and tail.

The Mountain Bluebird (*Sialia currucoides*) is slightly larger. This species is migratory, as are all members of this genus. It winters in Mexico and summers in a wide mountainous range extending from Alaska to Arizona and New Mexico. The male varies in blue shades in an overall color scheme. Back, wings, and tail are bright blue. The head, throat, and chest are soft and pale blue. Remaining underparts are bluish-white. The female has considerable areas of soft grayish-brown which are especially prominent on the head and back. Immatures are like the female but are lavishly spotted on the back and chest.

BLUE THROAT (*Luscinia svecica*)

Several subspecies of Blue Throats, averaging six inches in length, exist from Europe to Burma. All are very rare in aviculture. The general shape is robin-like, but the long legs indicate an active terrestrial preference. Upperparts are dull brownish. Some red occurs in the tail. A pale eyebrow is the only relief from the dull upperparts. A large area covering chin and an expansive throat area is brilliant blue with a prominent red swath across the upper chest. A variable color scheme follows. Blue is first followed by a dark brown band. Underparts are white except for a red crescent on the lower chest. The female has a brownish shade across the chest.

RUBY THROAT (*Luscinia calliope*)

The Ruby Throat is the same size as the Blue Throat. Most characteristics are the same. Upperparts are dull brown. A bright and dominant red covers chin and throat area of the male but is lacking in the female. White lines cover the upper area of red and form a prominent eyebrow which also covers a slight forehead area. The chest is dull brownish, and remaining underparts are white. This species occurs throughout most of Asia.

The Indian species, Himalayan Ruby Throat (*Luscinia pectoralis*), lacks the white area lining the red throat. Facial areas and chest are black, and the red is somewhat reduced.

The writers have had Ruby Throats on varying occasions and have never found them difficult. They thrive best in planted aviaries which have soft soil floors. Only a few advanced aviculturists seem interested in Ruby Throats and Blue Throats.

CHAPTER 30

Clarinos, Solitaires, Mockingbirds, and Nightingales

Mockingbirds, Clarinos, and Solitaires known in aviculture occur in the New World; but nightingales of aviculture occur both in Europe and the New World. All are noted for their exquisite songs rather than for appearance. All are reasonably peaceful except with their own kind. Mockingbirds require the simple standard softbilled diet and are easily acclimated. They are alert, very intelligent, active, and somewhat aggressive despite their description above as "reasonably peaceful." They should, of course, be housed with birds their own size.

In the United States, native mockingbirds are illegal except in cases of abandoned babies or injured individuals. Babies are easily hand fed if instructions in Chapter 2 on diet are followed. Injured adult birds quickly become acclimated through the standard procedure given in Chapter 3. Mockingbirds are more insectivorous than the average softbill and should be given some raw meat.

Nightingales are less adaptable than mockingbirds but will follow the same procedure as given for Solitaires except for the addition of some raw meat. Because native birds are illegal and others are difficult to get, American aviculturists will rarely be able to obtain any of these melodious songsters with drab plumage. Their feet are sensitive, and cages or aviaries must be kept clean. Males should be kept separate because in the wild state they claim certain territories and fight other nightingales.

Solitaires, including the closely related Clarino, are occasionally available from Mexico and rarely from Cuba. Native Solitaires, such as Townsend's Solitaire from Western United States, are prohibited. Short and wide beaks with bristles at the corners are generally characteristic.

Exceptionally charming and naturally friendly even in a cage, Solitaires are quite sedentary compared to other members in this chapter. The Clarino

Clarinos are members of the Solitaire family and are among the most charming of all softbilled birds. The quiet gray coloring is enhanced by large friendly eyes and a confiding, friendly personality. Its greatest gift is an entrancingly melodic song which gives everyone the distinct impression that the song is an intimate secret between the bird and its chosen audience. Owned by William Lasky.

is the calmest and tamest of all. Seemingly aware of their drab and unattractive coloring, Clarinos compensate by giving their listeners one of the most varied, quietest, and sweetest of all songs in the bird world.

Unfortunately, Solitaires and Clarinos are rather difficult to acclimate to domesticated diets. They love mealworms and easily bend natural ratios of balanced diets out of proportions if given too many. Also, because of the willingness of this bird to sing directly into the face of anyone who will pause to listen, the silvery richness and melody of the song prompts the listener to reward the bird with a little tidbit which is usually a mealworm. The songs are amazingly frequent, but the listener must curb his impulse to give rewards beyond the normal ratio.

The diet should be very refined such as is offered to most delicate softbills. An unbalanced or harsh diet may suffice for a time, but the end result will always be a sudden and unexpected death. Unless the bird fancier is prepared to give extra attention to the diet, it would be better to bypass Clarinos and Solitaires.

All the birds in this chapter have large eyes to add to their sight in dark forests or during their night songs.

CLARINO or BLUE SOLITAIRE (*Myadestes unicolor*)

The charming Clarino, seven inches in length and sometimes called the Slate Colored or Blue Solitaire, is not pretty. The dull gray coloring with its slight hint of blue is unassuming and not smooth. Variations in shadings give less attractiveness, but no other solitaire has bluish-gray above and on the wings. Large dark eyes surrounded by white rings are friendly and confiding and help to reveal the bird's true disposition and calm personality.

The Clarino quickly endears itself to anyone who even slightly admires birds because of its generous gift of song. The song is quiet and intimate but richly melodious with silvery trills and exquisite notes which are indescribable but completely lovely. It shows no fear of humans and is quite reluctant to retreat even upon the approach of total strangers.

The response to such an exquisite and intimate song is at first a chilling ripple running up the spine followed by a tranquil sense of great peacefulness.

A close relative is the Guatemalan Blue Solitaire (subspecies *veraepacis*).

JILGUERO or BROWN BACKED SOLITAIRE (*Myadestes obscurus*)

In its native Mexico, the Brown Backed Solitaire is called *Jilguero la Selva* which, roughly translated, means Songbird of the Woods. The description is accurate because the song is beautiful and because woodsy habitats are preferred.

The Jilguero is more slender and more active than the Clarino, but the size is similar. The writers much prefer it in an aviary rather than in a cage. Most of the coloring is gray. The eye ring is whitish; the throat and abdomen have a whitish tinge; and the back and wings are olive-brown. A subspecies, *oberholseri*, is called the Guatemalan Brown Backed Solitaire.

311

TOWNSEND'S SOLITAIRE (*Myadestes townsendi*)

Ranging from Oregon to Chihuahua, Townsend's Solitaire is illegal in captivity in the United States. It occurs in heavily wooded areas and may at times be exported to Europe from Mexico.

Slightly larger but even more drab in color, Townsend's Solitaire has the traditional white eye ring surrounding the large eyes. Upperparts are brownish-gray with tail and wings dull reddish-brown edged in a whitish shade. Underparts are gray. The black beak, as in other species, is short.

CUBAN SOLITAIRE (*Myadestes elisabeth*)

The Cuban Solitaire or Clarino is smaller than the Mexican Clarino. A slight brownish cast on the upperparts and a paler shade on the underparts are distinctive. The eye ring is a fainter shade of white.

Usually more frequently available to aviculturists, the Cuban Clarino is also purported to have a louder song than its musical cousins.

MOCKINGBIRDS

The group of birds called mockingbirds also includes the so-called Mocking Thrushes. All are larger, more aggressive, and more active than solitaires. They are also far more easily managed in captivity and are quickly acclimated. The songs are loud and clear and, in some species, often heard deep at night if the moonlight is bright.

MEXICAN BLUE MOCKING THRUSH or BLUE MOCKINGBIRD
(*Melanotis caerulescens*)

Perhaps the most likely and one of the most desirable species of mockingbirds is the Mexican Blue Mocking Thrush, often called the Blue Mockingbird. This dusky blue species, along with several similar subspecies, comes from Mexico. It is occasionally imported but not well known among aviculturists. The writers have had several of these birds and have thoroughly enjoyed their presence regardless of their innate shyness. Even so and despite proper diet and excellent plumage, the writers have seldom heard these birds sing. Perhaps this is because they have never housed them in planted aviaries.

The size ranges between nine and ten inches including the long rounded tail. The basic coloration is dark blue tinged with a dull duskiness. Upperparts are brighter, and underparts are paler. A large elliptical facial area covering the ear coverts and rather more than the lores is dark slate-blue. The beak, feet, and legs are black. Most of the plumage on the underparts shows indeterminate streakiness of paler and darker shades.

NORTHERN or COMMON MOCKINGBIRD (*Mimus polyglotus*)

The standard mockingbird with which most Americans are acquainted is the Common Mockingbird of the United States. This species varies between eight and nine inches in length. The basic color scheme is pleasantly dispersed in black, white, and gray. Upperparts are grayish with white in two wing bars and on the base of the primaries. Central tail feathers are blackish. Underparts are mostly grayish-white.

The Mexican Blue Mocking Thrush is a handsome dusky blue species with a rather long tail. It adapts easily to captivity and thrives on standard softbilled diets. Though rather large, it is nevertheless peaceful and shy. Usually it poses in a more crouched position as if it were about to take flight.

The Mexican races show less white. Several races across the United States and Cuba vary slightly, but the basic pattern is the same. In fact, all species of this genus are very similar.

Mockingbirds prefer to live near human habitations; and, because of their song and their amazingly voracious appetite for harmful insects, most people welcome their presence. Each pair stakes a claim to a certain area and carefully guards it from other mockingbirds. They pay little attention to small birds, but they are very adept in attacking larger predatory birds.

They also annoy cats in a very clever manner. They repeatedly swoop down on the cat and turn upwards with a very narrow margin of safe distance.

The native black, white, and gray Mockingbird is a garden favorite over most of the country because of its voracious appetite for insects and its variable melodies. It is illegal in captivity, but many rescued nestlings and injured specimens are carefully nursed to independence by thoughtful bird lovers each year. The diet is simple, and the birds usually become very tame during this time.

The Brown Thrasher is related to mockingbirds and should be given the same care during recuperation from injuries. Unlike the native Mockingbird, it holds little interest for aviculturists.

Mockingbirds show no fear of cats and are usually successful in turning a constant annoyance into intimidation.

When a mockingbird wishes to sing, he selects the highest and most openly visible perch possible. Usually this is the top of a telephone pole. From this vantage point, he pours forth a loud and clear song which proclaims his presence for a considerable distance. No one ever objects even though the song is at times delivered in the middle of the night if the moon is bright. It is a highly variable repertoire of musical sounds. Melodic trills include many sounds appropriated from other sources. This bird is an amazing mimic, and any copied sounds are more musical if delivered from a mockingbird.

In a few instances, mockingbirds have even been reported to talk. These exceptions, not verified by the writers, have always been rescued nestlings which have been hand reared. In captivity, young mockingbirds soon exhibit a tame sauciness and a swaggering personality if proper training techniques are followed.

Other mockingbirds of the New World include the Graceful Mockingbird (*Mimus gilvus*) which is larger and more silvery than most mockingbirds. The range includes Central America and Northern South America as well as neighboring islands. The most likely available subspecies (*colombianus*) is called The Colombian Mockingbird.

The mockingbird family includes Thrashers which are not important in aviculture.

The American Catbird, with its smoky shadings of grays and slate and dusky red undertail coverts, is closely related to Mockingbirds and Thrashers. It is not important in aviculture. In Australia, Catbirds are more closely allied to the intellectual Bower Birds.

NIGHTINGALES

The European Nightingale (*Luscinia megarhynchos*), which migrates to Africa during September or October and returns to Europe for the breeding season, is softly colored in a pale reddish-brown shade, darker above and lighter below. The throat and abdomen are particularly light. The shape is similar to solitaires, but the size is approximately only six inches in length. The personality is much like that of the Clarino, and the lovely song ranges somewhere between solitaires and mockingbirds.

Just as do mockingbirds, nightingales sing during the night as well as during the day, but individuals vary in their preference and in the quality of their song. The song before the nesting period often becomes a marathon of duration which lasts much longer than the song of any other bird.

Also from Europe, the Thrush-Nightingale (*Luscinia luscinia*) is larger and has a spotted chest. Requiring similar care, this bird is not considered quite the songster as the above.

The Orange Billed Nightingale (*Catharus aurantiirostris*) of Central and Northern South America has rich rufous wings, paler reddish-brown head and tail, grayish underparts, and a bright orange bill. Unfortunately, it is rarely available. The care is the same as for the above species.

CHAPTER 31

Larks and Meadowlarks

Not many members of these two groups can legally be included in aviculture. Skylarks cannot be imported into the United States, and trapping is outlawed in some European countries. Magpie Larks from Australia have been reared in captivity in the San Diego Zoo, but the parents were obtained only through strictly regulated zoo permits. In the main course of aviculture, these birds are not available. Meadowlarks are not available to most aviculturists in America. Native species are strictly protected except in rare instances of permanent injuries which deny any possibility of surviving in the wild state. Cuban Meadowlarks are not likely to be obtainable for some time to come. Meadowlarks are large bodied and short-tailed birds.

Military Starlings from South America are the same in shape and size and are just about the only likely species in both groups attainable by bird fanciers through standard channels.

The diet is the standard softbilled fare, and all species are easily fed and congenial to other aviary inmates.

The Horned Lark is an attractive and unusual bird which requires the same care as given to Meadowlarks. It also is native to the United States and is denied to American aviculture.

This immature Eastern Meadowlark bears the same basic markings as the mature Western Meadowlark, but the yellow on the underparts of the youngsters is greatly subdued for protective coloration.

The writers attest to the lovely and cheerful songs of Skylarks and Meadowlarks. All their lives have been spent in close proximity to Western Meadowlarks, and it is quite impossible to bypass the ringing lyric and joyful trills of this latter species without an admiring pause of gratitude. Western Meadowlarks skillfully reduce mankind's most sophisticated yearnings to a thorough and relaxing appreciation of the finest of nature's endowments. Western Meadowlarks may not be the most beautiful of birds, but their lovely cheerfulness is unmatched at least in Western United States. The writers have had the privilege of rearing two young nestling Western Meadowlarks to juvenile independence before liberating them. Though the efforts were considerable, they could never repay the pleasure given by the cheerfulness of these wonderful birds.

SKYLARK (*Alauda gulgula*)

The Skylark, with similar sexes, is a dull bird of basic tan with carelessly arranged dark markings, darker above and paler below. There is a hint of a crest. Several forms of Skylarks occur, but all are nearly the same in appearance.

EASTERN MEADOWLARK (*Sturnella magna*)

A large V-shaped area of black occurs on the throat and chest of the Eastern Meadowlark. Underparts are a clear golden yellow. Two blackish

319

eyebrow lines extend above the eyes. Upperparts are brownish-tan with black striations probably designed for protective coloration.

The body is very large and stocky and the legs are long and thrushlike indicating a preference for ground dwelling.

WESTERN MEADOWLARK (*Sturnella neglecta*)

The Western Meadowlark is a very similar bird except for its much paler coloring. The basic pattern is much more inclined to a drab protective coloration. The personality is charming and winning, but the species cannot be legally held captive. A few bird fanciers take over the project of caring for immature fledglings or injured birds.

MILITARY STARLING (*Sturnella militaris*)

The Military Starling from South America is not a true starling, but it is closely related to meadowlarks. The shape and size, nearly ten inches, are the same as for the meadowlarks. The beak is also sharp and long with black tips and blackish running the full length of the top on the upper mandible.

The basic coloring is the same except for some bright red coloring. Two red spots occur just above the lores. The chin, throat, and chest are also bright red with irregular borders.

Remaining underparts are buff with darker brown streaks. Upperparts are varying shades of brown with feathers darkly centered and lightly margined. A pale whitish eyebrow extends from the red area above the lores to a tapering point on the nape. Sexes are very similar.

CHAPTER 32

Birds of Paradise and Bower Birds

"They wandered from Paradise." So someone said long ago, and the name Bird of Paradise has clung tightly ever since. Though males are adorned with some of the most unbelievably exotic ornamentations in the world, the most transcending quality is the sometimes almost ethereal and fantastic ability to change shapes in elaborate displays designed for the more earthly passions of courtship and vanity.

Whatever the basic motivations, the Birds of Paradise comprise, outside of the more intellectual Bower Birds, some of the highest and most aristocratic forms of all birds in the world. Unfortunately, the plenitude of these beauteous creatures started a downward trend with the coming of man into their native habitats.

Mankind, whether on the level of primitive savagery or savage sophistication, is seldom contented with his lot. Primitive male savages beautified themselves with the gorgeous plumes of the Birds of Paradise. Centuries later, sophisticated women discovered the beauty of plumage; and the hunt was on for the lucrative markets of sophistry. Populations of these precious creatures dwindled while milady's hats grew more flourishingly abundant.

Protective measures were finally instituted, perhaps too late for the bird lovers who would like to domesticate the various species. Women now resort to peroxide bleaches, henna rinses, and fragile lipstick shades among their various adornments in order to camouflage their natural endowments. Fortunately, man's (or woman's) ingenuity leads to other artificial developments whenever natural sources are depleted. Unfortunately, some of the greatest depletions of natural resources have always been some of nature's greatest treasures.

Birds of Paradise, though now extremely rare and intelligently strictly protected, are not extinct. Preventive slaughter and regulated captivity may help tremendously to restore formerly abundant populations in the wild state. Many countries have laws which prohibit importation of plumage.

321

Overlooking the naturally endowed beauty, coveted and envied by mankind, the various Birds of Paradise efficiently perform a mundane service for mankind and nature by consuming an inordinate quantity of harmful insects in the wild state.

The writers feel a tremendous gratification in the great avicultural rarity and high prices demanded for Birds of Paradise. These factors usually mean that aviculturists will bend every effort to furnish every requirement in order to bring about a satisfactory diet and environment for easy reproduction. The fact that a few of the world's most dedicated aviculturists have succeeded in this precept is a most hopeful sign in the accomplishment of the basic tenets of aviculture.

Most zoos have one basic precept: to show various birds and animals, rare or common, to the public. Commendably, this precept often sparks a desire in many to study ornithology and to participate in aviculture. For the most part, however, the desire merely becomes another of man's vain desires to display rarities. This characteristic all too often holds true in cooperative or civic zoological ventures as well as in those greatly rare ventures of individuals in establishing private zoos.

Those few individuals and zoos which are able to obtain Birds of Paradise should expend every effort to perpetuate and to establish avicultural domestic strains of these fantastic birds. To indulge in the sole luxury of exhibition is hardly more commendable than the vain adornment of plumage on a lady's hat. The true significance or value of these birds is unrealized by the average layman on his rare Sunday outing to the zoo.

The continuation of Birds of Paradise in their natural ranges is due mainly to their preference for dense and impenetrable jungles which preclude entry by most men, including the aforementioned avaricious plumage hunters of the past. Also, many species come into breeding age and reproduce before they develop their full plumage. In some cases, full plumage takes a very long time to develop. In undeveloped stages, the birds are usually bypassed because of their drab feathers. Fortunately, polygamy is often practiced in the wild state, and the ordinary appearance of the female usually escapes the notice of human predators.

Forty-three discovered species of Birds of Paradise under various names are known. Not all of these species are known in aviculture and could not possibly be covered in one chapter. Admittedly there are many omissions and many blank spots of those birds covered. All species, unless otherwise indicated, come from New Guinea or nearby islands.

The displays are often too extravagant and complicated for believable word descriptions. Then too, the writers' experience of Birds of Paradise is far too limited to be considered authoritative.

Measurements cannot be given for these birds except in generalized and sketchy instances. Though carefully observed wherever possible, none of

322

the various Birds of Paradise have ever come into the hands of the writers. The layman's concept from pictures is that these are large birds. The average size range is from about four to ten inches in basic size excluding plumes and other ornamentation.

In captivity, Birds of Paradise are easily managed and long lived in proper accommodations if given the proper diet. Usually they are quarrelsome among themselves and should be given separate aviaries. Because of active natures, the aviaries should be spacious. The writers prefer seeing these birds in planted aviaries because the birds love vegetation. Though some species are very secretive and not easily observed in densely planted aviaries, the birds are obviously much happier in such environments.

Suitable aviaries differ according to climate. Birds of Paradise require humidity and a reasonably warm temperature. They avoid direct sunshine. In cold climates, the most suitable aviary is a conservatory aviary. The writers have observed Birds of Paradise thriving in conservatories in Holland, Northern California, and in the Tropical Bird House at the London Zoo. In the San Diego Zoo, open aviaries with covered shelters seem adequate in the mild climate, but mist sprayers are necessary to provide proper humidity. In the zoo in Honolulu, the accommodations are similar to those in San Diego; but the writers could locate no mist sprayers. Presumably, the warm climate is sufficiently humid.

Birds of Paradise are said to be related to crows and not too distant from the honeysucker families. The diet includes fruits and insects. The main diet is the standard softbilled fare with some raw meat; but the writers would surely offer nectar food and, wherever possible, baby mice as well as a variety of live foods.

The bright colors and exotic ornamentations occur only on the male. A prolonged moult and regrowth period give an eclipse plumage usually lasting from May to September. Since the seasons in the native habitat are reversed from ours, breeding seasons usually occur in our fall and winter months. Females, varying with different species, are usually drab and ordinary in appearance. For the most part, they will not be described in this chapter.

The greatest champion of Birds of Paradise in aviculture is Sir Edward Hallstrom. Among his many other avicultural accomplishments in Sydney, Australia, Sir Edward's name ranks synonymously with Birds of Paradise because he is responsible for the presence of these magnificent birds in many of the world's leading zoos.

LESSER BIRD OF PARADISE (*Paradisaea minor*)

The lavishly plumed Lesser Bird of Paradise is perhaps the most typical of the genus and one which represents the basic picture in the layman's mind of "a Bird of Paradise." It also is one of the most frequently available among these great rarities.

The beak is bluish-gray, and the eye is yellow. A small forehead and chin area are black. The extensive throat area is dark metallic green. Underparts, wings, and tail are dark velvety brown. The head, mantle, shoulders, and back are brilliant yellow. Two long wires extend from the center of the tail, and a great abundance of plumes originates on the sides of the chest and lower back. When the wings are folded, these origins are hidden; but, during the flamboyant display, they are erected in a feathery shower. The head is bent forward and the tail lowered to the perch. The vibrating plumes with yellow centers and white outerparts extend nearly over the head in an ecstatic attempt to draw attention of the drab female or in a social display with many males in a show of vanity.

A subspecies, *finschi*, is called Finsch's Bird of Paradise.

GREATER BIRD OF PARADISE (*Paradisaea apoda apoda*)

The Greater Bird of Paradise of the Aru Islands is similar but a little

The beautiful male Greater Bird of Paradise raises a shower of plumes over his back during his elaborate nuptial display. This is just one phase of his elaborate display. New York Zoological Society photo.

Count Salvadori's Bird of Paradise has a shape similar to several members of the genus *Paradisaea*, but the long filmy plumes are deep and rich red. New York Zoological Society photo.

larger. The basic overall size is about twenty-two inches long, and the back is more brown. The plumes are a little shorter and less full than those of the Lesser and are faintly tipped in brown instead of white.

The subspecies *salvadorii* is called Count Salvadori's Bird of Paradise. This race has a narrow yellow collar separating the throat from the very dark upper chest. The back is brown, and only a small shoulder bar is yellow. The plumes are very rich red and less extravagant.

The subspecies *raggiana* is called the Raggiana or Count Raggi's Bird of Paradise. The plumes are longer, fuller and range from red to orange with pale tips. Abdominal and ventral areas are buffish-brown.

EMPEROR OF GERMANY'S BIRD OF PARADISE (*Paradisaea guilelmi*)

Similar in shape and general appearance, the Emperor of Germany's Bird of Paradise has fewer and less luxurious plumes, but the filaments are more lacy. The plume color is yellow at the more prominent base with white on the remainder. The two black wires seem more bold. The yellow starts at the back of the crown and cuts inward at the lower throat to separate the chest. The yellow shoulder area is more extensive.

In the second part of its display, this species hangs upside down, weaves from side to side so that its raised plumes show a swirling sway.

Sir Edward Hallstrom in Sydney, Australia, succeeded in rearing two youngsters of this species.

GRAY CHESTED BIRD OF PARADISE (*Paradisaea decora*)

The lovely Gray Chested Bird of Paradise from the D'Entrecasteaux Islands is extremely rare in aviculture. Somewhat similar in general shape and pattern to the Lesser Bird of Paradise, there are nevertheless very noticeable differences in coloring. The plumes are red; the chest is purplish-gray; and a narrow collar of yellow separates the chest from the bright green throat area.

RED BIRD OF PARADISE (*Paradisaea rubra*)

The Red Bird of Paradise is one of the more beautiful of the larger species. The male has a yellowish-ivory beak followed by dark metallic green over most of the head, cheeks, and throat. At the top of the crown are two somewhat bulbous swellings of feathers deeply cleft in the center. Soft filmy feathers of golden yellow follow on the upper chest, lower crown, nape, mantle, shoulder, and scapulars. Wings, underparts, and the standard tail are reddish-brown.

Long, filmy, but luxurious plumes grow from the sides of the chest, are covered by the folded wings, and extend far over the tail. Two long, slowly spiralling wires trail from the tail.

PRINCE RUDOLPH'S BIRD OF PARADISE (*Paradisaea rudolphi rudolphi*)

The beautifully and luxuriously plumed Prince Rudolph's Bird of Paradise, whose plumes are not fully developed in the picture, is very different

326

The Emperor of Germany's Bird of Paradise has bright yellow on the back of the neck and shoulders and again on the inner areas of the plumes. The plumes are usually more prevalent than those of the bird in this picture. New York Zoological Society photo.

Prince Rudolph's Blue Bird of Paradise usually has far more plumes than this picture indicates. The blues are both bright and soft, but the general coloring is dusky. During its elaborate display, this bird hangs upside down from its perch. New York Zoological Society photo.

from other members of the genus. The beak is larger and is pale bluish-gray. The general body coloring ranges from velvety-black on the head with purplish iridescence on the neck to dusky-black on the chest. Lower chest and upper abdomen are dusky-blue changing abruptly to a wide black band bordered in red on the abdomen.

The wings are bright blue. The plumes are soft deep blue in the center, paler at the tips, and a pale shade of near-orange on the sides. The eye has whitish crescents above and below. Two very prominent and thick wires extend from the center of the tail.

This bird, also called the Blue Bird of Paradise, displays in an upside down manner with a broad fan-shaped plume spread and a greatly puffed lower chest and abdomen. From this position, the bird sings softly. It truly is one of the most distinctive members of the entire family.

The subspecies *margaritae* is called Margaret's Blue Bird of Paradise.

KING BIRD OF PARADISE (*Cinnurus regius*)

The elegantly styled male King Bird of Paradise is one of the most exotic of the smaller Birds of Paradise, and this species may be the smallest of all. The female is ordinary in appearance. Dr. Sven Bergman of Sweden was successful in a first breeding of this species, and pictures of the pair and two youngsters appear in this book.

The male of this widespread species has a bright yellow beak. The eye is dark reddish-brown with a pale outer ring and topped by a bright green spot above. The entire head down to the chest and all upperparts including the wings and tail are brilliant red. A band of bright green crosses the chest below the lower boundary of red. The remaining underparts are white.

The short, square tail has two glamorous wirelike appendages extending from the center in a curious pattern. The shape taken by these wires could best be described as an inverted and curvy "Y" with a short base and curled feathered tips in green.

Brown side plumes tipped in green, are normally hidden beneath the wing but can be erected in a flamboyant fan-shaped spread.

The plain-colored female is reddish-brown. She is very pale and minutely striated with a darker shade. Dr. Bergman's youngsters, as can be seen in the color plates, are basically colored and patterned like the female except the mellow reddish-brown is duller and has most of the reddish tinge removed.

A very excellent and detailed account of this remarkable achievement occurred in the July, 1959, issue of *Foreign Birds*, the Magazine of the Foreign Bird League. The pictures as well as the following excerpted information were taken from Dr. Bergman's very fine article.

The male's courtship display starts by raising the wires and spreading the wings in a cup-shaped position. After this, facing the female, the wings were fully spread and constantly vibrated. Then he changed his position by hanging upside down for about ten seconds with spread and vibrating wings

329

and a widespread open beak showing a bright greenish-yellow gape. This completed, he released his hold and flew back to the perch to sing to the hen. During the song the tail wires vibrated constantly.

A second display following shortly brought the two birds closer. Side fans were expanded and drawn up towards the head. The tail wires were raised over his back, and the white chest feathers were greatly puffed. The raised head swayed from side to side.

The female became more familiar and active during this second display and occasionally pecked at his feathers. This elaborate display may be enacted several times a day.

Interest in actual nesting grew slowly but seemed definite because the female centered her attention on one nestbox. The actual breeding occurred in our summer season. The eggs were rather large. The male sat nearby but was not seen helping in feeding the hen or in incubating the eggs. He offered encouragement and entertainment by frequent displays in front of the nestbox. He paid attention to progress of both eggs and young when the female left the nest for feeding and bathing.

Dr. Bergman wisely added crushed shells for needed calcium, and the female was observed frequently eating these shells before laying and after hatching.

Incubation time was eighteen days, and the youngsters left the nest on the fourteenth day, short tailed but fully feathered and able to fly. In the wild state, the youngsters may stay longer; but domestic breeding may, as in some other instances, have accelerated the period. Incubation starts with the first egg. From all indications, one egg is laid every day with hatching following the same procedure.

Dr. Bergman's obviously successful diet included the following: raw meat, *fresh* ant eggs (or live pupae), hard boiled chopped egg yolk, finely chopped apple and tomato, soaked raisins, boiled rice, and small mealworms and grasshoppers. Grasshoppers became increasingly important after fledging.

The out of season male coloring, during and after the moult, if the writers glean correctly, seems to be somewhat less than four months.

A subspecies (*similis*) is Stresemann's King Bird of Paradise.

GENUS PAROTIA

Members of the genus *Parotia* are small, very dark, and short tailed. The generally unassuming appearance in natural repose is enhanced only by long wires with spatulated feather tips, bright shiny eyes, and varying metallic accents differing with species and subspecies.

The most amazing transformation occurs in the display. The body feathers spread out in a flaring and almost completely enclosed skirt. Strutting and various movements to enhance the flare of feathers give a marvelous performance.

The Greater Six Plumed Bird of Paradise (*Parotia sefilata*) has a flashing

The Greater Six Plumed Bird of Paradise (genus *Parotia*) is a small bird with an iridescent golden gorget and six long spangle-tipped wires extending from the back of the neck. In repose, its shape is rather ordinary; but its display dance brings about an amazing transformation in appearance. New York Zoological Society photo.

and flaring throat patch of iridescent golds and greens which are sometimes flashed with reds and purples. Some glossed purple occurs on the back, and some white occurs above the beak. Eyes are blue.

The Golden Crowned Six Plumed Bird of Paradise (*Parotia carolae chrysenia*) is similar but has a large forehead patch of metallic copper and gold. Other quite similar members are Wahne's Four Plumed Bird of Paradise (*Parotia wahnesi*) with a longer tail and reddish forehead; Lawe's Six Plumed Bird of Paradise (*Parotia lawesi lawesi*), smaller than the foregoing; and the White Flanked Six Plumed Bird of Paradise (*Parotia carolae carolae*).

GENUS LOPHORINA

Members of this genus are mild in appearance while in a normal stature but flare magnificently in display. Huge fan-shaped feather structures on the nape and throat spread sideways in extraordinary metamorphoses.

The Lesser Superb Bird of Paradise (genus *Lophorina*) is a small bird which, while displaying, shows a broad flare of metallic green across the chest. It lacks the broad collar which flares above the head as found in a larger subspecies. New York Zoological Society photo.

The Superb Bird of Paradise (*Lophorina superba*) is mostly dark brown with metallic turquoise and lavender scales on head and chest. Some purplish scales also appear on the sides of the face. The inside of the mouth is yellow which is effectively used in the display.

In display the brown collar rises in a huge crescent-shaped fan. The throat also flares outward in a similar winglike shape, which, while smaller, is more colorful and more pleasantly balanced.

The Lesser Superb Bird of Paradise (subspecies *minor*) is smaller but is basically the same except for a uniform metallic green on top of the head and the flaring throat feature.

GENUS DIPHYLLODES

Members of the genus *Diphyllodes* are medium in size. The Magnificent Bird of Paradise reaches nearly seven inches in length, and others vary only

The Golden Winged Magnificent Bird of Paradise (genus *Diphyllodes*) always shows the curled wires on the tail; but, when it displays, a large golden neck ruff becomes prominent. New York Zoological Society photo.

slightly. All are heavy bodied with prominent heads, have rather ordinary shapes in repose, and have two long outflaring circular wires extending from the center of the tail. The displays usually consist of dramatic gymnastics while moving up and down on vertical perches and often hanging sideways in a horizontal position to reflect sunlight. Feather puffing usually extends a huge neck ruff and a great vest which struts forward and hangs even below the feet.

The Magnificent Bird of Paradise (*Diphyllodes magnificus magnificus*) shows a huge golden upstanding neck ruff and a brilliant green vest which starts at the throat. A zipperlike pattern of dark and light striations starts at the throat and continues through the lower chest. The back is deep red fading to golden on the wings. The unshapely head is bright reddish-brown fading to blackish-brown on the chin and lower facial areas. The lower abdomen and the remaining underparts are varying shades of brown. The lower back, rump, uppertail coverts, and tail are striated with darker and lighter shades of reddish-brown which become progressively darker on the tail.

Hunstein's Bird of Paradise (*hunsteini*) and Golden Winged Magnificent Bird of Paradise (*chrysopterus*) are very similar subspecies.

Wilson's Bird of Paradise (*Diphyllodes respublica*) shows more green on the body, more prominent and green horns above the eyes, and shorter, more recurved, and slightly feathered tail wires. The size is slightly smaller than the above, and the top of the head is covered in bare blue skin surrounded and traversed down the center of the crown in fine lines of small black feathers. The yellow on the inside of the mouth is more of a noticeable contrast. Some yellow and crimson occur on the neck and back.

TWELVE WIRED BIRD OF PARADISE (*Seleucides ignotus ignotus*)

In repose the long-billed Twelve Wired Bird of Paradise has an egg-shaped body and twelve fine wires for a tail. The head and very extensive chest area is dark brownish-black with greenish scales on the sides. Underparts are yellow, and wings are purplish.

In a display pose, the beak is pointed skyward to make room for a balloon-puffed chest which especially makes use of the highlighting green scales on the sides. Six wires on each side of the tail bend skyward. The overall pose is bizarre and unlike even the most imaginative poses of most birds of paradise.

LONG TAILED BIRD OF PARADISE (*Epimachus meyeri meyeri*)

Chief characteristics of the dark and dusky Long Tailed Bird of Paradise in repose are an extremely long and slender tail of two thick and shaggy, glossy blue-black feathers, a dark head dominated by a bright yellow eye, and a long sickle-shaped bill. The rump is metallic with coppery-green iridescence, and the breast has blue-black iridescence. It sometimes is called the Sickle Billed Bird of Paradise.

During the display, it assumes an extremely weird spoon shape from a head-on view by extending and erecting long feathers to such an extent that it

The Strange Twelve Wired Bird of Paradise (genus *Seleucides*) is odd both in repose and in display. The wires on the bird in this picture seem less prominent and more disarrayed than usual. The yellow underparts add a bright splash of color, and the display pose is weird. New York Zoological Society photo.

The Long Tailed Bird of Paradise, shown here in repose, assumes an odd spoon-shaped appearance during its display. New York Zoological Society photo.

The Ribbon Tailed Bird of Paradise (genus *Astrapia*) is also a slender and graceful member of an extravagantly ornamented family. New York Zoological Society photo.

Princess Stephanie's Bird of Paradise (genus *Astrapia*) is a very colorful species with high glosses and a graceful shape. New York Zoological Society photo.

seems impossible to have concealed them on the moderately slender bird in his normal stance.

A great hood, rimmed at the top in metallic violet and bordered by a narrow pale line, contrasts sharply with the basic dark brown and the small black forehead and the crown with two tiny bright eyes. The beak opens from time to time showing bright yellow on the inside of the mouth. The sides also flare outwards and are flattened to add to the spoon shape. Short, but broad, pointed tail feathers fan outwards to give a bold and coarsely bearded effect to the lower end of the spoon's bowl. The two long ragged tail feathers add the handle to the spoon.

Bizarre, exotic, and unusual, this species is very rare in aviculture.

A subspecies (*bloodi*) is called Blood's Long Tailed Bird of Paradise.

GENUS ASTRAPIA

The species of the genus *Astrapia* usually kept in aviculture, if they can be obtained, are characterized by long slender bodies, sharp beaks, and long tails varying in width from slender to wide. Overall shapes are graceful and beautiful giving a slightly similar silhouette comparable to some of the whydahs.

The writers can offer little information on these species except that they include the following birds. The narrow Ribbon Tailed Bird of Paradise (*Astrapia mayeri*) has a slender but very long white tail and a strange forehead crest nearly covering the beak. Lord Rothschild's Gorgetted Bird of Paradise (*Astrapia rothschildi*) is dark and has a very long tail which is both broad and usually straggly. The basic color scheme is the same as for the following. Princess Stephanie's Bird of Paradise (*Astrapia stephaniae*) is particularly similar to Lord Rothschild's Bird of Paradise insofar as shape is concerned. The coloring is basically olive green, darker and more velvety above. Bright purple iridescence occurs on the wings and tail. The head and extensive throat area show bright green in a high gloss. Ear tufts are glossy blue. Coppery-green feathers tipped in reddish-copper surround the chest.

A subspecies of the latter is Mayr's Gorgetted Bird of Paradise (subspecies *ducalis*).

MAGNIFICENT RIFLE BIRD (*Craspedophora magnifica*)

The Magnificent Rifle Bird of New Guinea is magnificent because of its unbelievably flaring display. With beak turned skyward to bring the brilliant triangular throat patch of metallic green into its most predominant view, the male then waves his head sideways to cast iridescence to all front view observers. The wings and chest fans are spread in an extremely extensive strutting and rounded display.

Most of the coloring, except the throat patch, is velvety black; but iridescent purplish-green or blue areas highlight some parts of the body. The beak is long, slender, and curved.

The bird pictured is the subspecies *intercedens*.

The male Magnificent Rifle Bird can change from an ordinary bird into an awesome flaring sight during his nuptial display. The iridescent throat gorget flashes brightly as the head sways from side to side. The Magnificent Rifle Bird is closely allied to Birds of Paradise. New York Zooiogical Society photo.

In repose, this bird resembles a large and plump honey eater with its curved beak. Grassy plumes hang from the sides like a sparse grass skirt trying to hide the abdomen and tail. The top of the head shows bluish-metallic shades.

The Australian subspecies of the rifle bird is similar except for a shorter plumed grass skirt affair. Other rifle birds occur in Australia, but they are not available to aviculture.

BOWER BIRDS

Many ornithologists attribute the highest degree of evolutionary and intellectual avian development to the bower birds. This status has not been given lightly. Bower birds, from New Guinea and Australia, and closely related to birds of paradise, have some truly remarkable characteristics. Two of the several species figure in aviculture. These are Regent's Bower Bird and the Satin Bower Bird. Regent's Bower Bird is very beautiful, but others in the family are mostly unattractive.

Bower birds, lacking the beauty or specialized exotic adornments and displays of birds of paradise, have evolved a fantastic courtship procedure which is nearly unbelievable. Each species has its own self styled bower which is meant to be a honeymoon cottage for charmed females. Courtship is elaborate and carefully prepared even though the actual consummation of the marriage is short lived. Colorful bower birds build the simplest bowers, and plain birds build the most elaborate ones. The antics of courtship usually attract a considerable excited audience of various species of other birds.

Male bower birds do not pursue females. The female is easily attracted by the male's architectural prowess and by his assembled gifts, and so she comes to him. His architecture may range from elaborately constructed teepees and maypoles to carefully arranged tufts of tall grasses prepared by tamping down adjacent areas.

To these areas he brings his attractive baubles and carefully arranges them to glint in the sunlight. Careful arrangement is frequent to capture the moving sun's reflections. These eye catching baubles may consist of bright and colorful glassy pebbles, shells, or anything bright which provides a fanciful decoration. The most desirable color is blue. Flowers are often used and replaced after wilting. The display or mating area is usually carpeted with soft grasses or ferns.

Strutting, calling, and, in some cases, erotic rolling on the grassy carpets soon result in attentive audiences which usually includes an interested female. After her demure approach and subsequent mating, she disappears to erect her own nest and care for her offspring in solitude. The male continues to rearrange his bower in the possible hope that his mate will return. She, of course, is busy with other matters and will attack any male who happens into the vicinity. One would expect a polygamous nature from a bird with such an elaborate and inviting attraction; but, from all observations, the male is faithful to his mate even though he contributes no subsistence in rearing the young. Hens usually thoroughly dominate the males in captivity and desire no companionship after fertilization. In fact, they frequently kill any male in the same aviary.

The most beautiful of all bower birds is the Regent Bower Bird (*Sericulus chrysocephalus*) from Australia. Rarely available, highly coveted, and high priced, the Regent is one of the most desirable of aviculture's many beautiful idols. It falls short of the beauty of birds of paradise only in effusive ornamentation. The shape is of a birdlike standard; the coloring is outstanding.

The basic coloring of the male after a four year maturation is velvety black and vivid golden yellow with reddish-orange accents on the tips of many feathers. The pattern is trim and intriguing, and the overall appearance is glowing. Most of the coloring is black. The secondary flights are golden yellow. From the forehead to the mantle the same coloration is highlighted by reddish-orange touches. A pattern variation occurs above the eyes by an intruding line of black which extends above the eyes and forms a vertical eyebrow. After this, an inward flare of black surrounds the cheeks and retreats so that the sides of the neck remain golden. From here, a broad semicircle includes the rest of the neck and mantle in the sharp golden pattern. The feet and legs are black, and the beak is a horn color with blackish tips. The golden eyes have black pupils.

The female, slightly larger, is drab brown with cluttered paler spots and a black crown. Youngsters resemble the female.

The male Satin Bower Bird of Australia (*Ptilonorhynchus violaceus*) is an all black bird with satiny-blue glossed reflections, a greenish-horn beak, and a greenish rim around the eye. The female is dull greenish and gray with a black beak rimmed on the edges by greenish-horn. The greenish eye ring is also present. The beak is much thicker than that of the Regent Bower Bird.

CHAPTER 33

Crows, Ravens, Picathartes, and Jackdaws

None of the birds of this chapter are avicultural favorites. Some are too commonly available to receive attention, and others are too rare to be obtainable. Those common species are invariably dull, unattractive, and usually too aggressive for the average collection. Those commonplace individuals which are kept as pets are often handfed specimens which have been given very careful treatment in the hope that they will learn to talk. Crows, ravens, and jackdaws are, in some respects, regarded as the "poor man's mynah." The price is extremely reasonable, and adequate training may induce these birds to talk.

American crows and ravens and European jackdaws and rooks are all extremely hardy. The diet is the standard softbilled fare with certain additions. The writers have never extensively kept these birds and so have relied upon another authority who has. James Doughty, whose experience with these birds is vast, recommends the following additions to the standard softbilled diet for best results: boiled corn or scratch feed and a powdered vitamin-mineral supplement which is easily sprinkled atop other foods. The diet of these birds is omnivorous and scavenging, and the standard softbilled diet is inadequate. Especially lacking in average diets is a satisfactory mineral supplement which can be provided in powdered commercial supplements.

Picathartes, on the other hand, are extremely rare in captivity and are usually treated in a similar manner as given hothouse plants. The standard softbilled diet plus conservatory accommodations are usually considered adequate.

There are many crows spread around the world. Those near at hand are apt to be considered mundane, and those from afar are more likely considered rare and exotic. Some are in fact delicate and are not likely candidates for aviculture. Others in faraway lands are considered too common and inadequate for exportation even though the above characteristics of bird fanciers might lend far greater sales appeal.

Kenneth Eklund and tame crow, hand-fed from fledgling age.

The American Crow (*Corvus brachyrhynchos*) is about sixteen to eighteen inches long. It is an overall black with some purplish and bluish glosses. The black beak is rather thick, and farmers usually despise its all inclusive diet which usually includes their crops. Taken as nestlings and hand reared, these crows become excellent pets and will learn to talk. Usually they are not considered favorably as aviary birds.

The American Raven (*Corvus corax*) is twenty-three to twenty-five inches long. It is the same as the above except for a larger size and recurved bristles over the base of the beak.

American laws regarding birds are changeable. At the moment of writing the native species is protected. The last moment and possibly the next moment may show no protection. Bird dealers and fanciers never quite know how they stand with ravens, but many individuals nevertheless keep ravens as individual pets with the ultimate object of teaching them to talk.

Crows and ravens occur over most of the world in many variations, but few are important in aviculture. In Europe the Choughs and Rooks nearly assume a similar status to American crows and ravens. Many zoos throughout the world covet the black and white Australian Piping Crows.

The Jackdaw (*Corvus monedula*) from Europe to India has silver-gray on the nape and sides of the neck. The sexes are alike, and the size is about twelve inches.

The White Necked Picathartes from Africa is an unusual long legged and bald headed crowlike bird. Both this species and the similar Gray Necked Picathartes are extremely rare in aviculture. New York Zoological Society photo.

The Bald Crows or Picathartes are very unusual, long-legged members of the crow family. Both species are from Africa and are among the proudest offerings of those fortunate zoos able to obtain them. The two species are the White Necked Picathartes (*Picathartes gymnocephalus*) and the Gray Necked Picathartes (*Picathartes oreas*).

The White Necked Picathartes has a black beak with a reddish spot on each side of the upper mandible. The eye is brownish, and the bare skin on most of the head is flesh colored. A large circular area on each side of the back of the head is dull blackish. The upperparts from the mantle are slate. The remaining areas are white. The Gray Necked Picathartes has more black on the face and gray on the neck.

The relative status of these birds is controversial. Tossed back and forth by authorities among crows, starlings, and thrush-babblers, the writers feel they are distinctly different enough to be classed in their own category.

CHAPTER 34

Magpies, Pies, Magpie Jays, and Jays

The birds in this chapter, often flamboyant and amusing, are among the larger softbills. None should ever be kept with small softbills. Even most medium-sized softbills are out of the range of safe inclusion with these birds.

Those birds owned by the writers which are included in this chapter have always been among the hardiest and most easily fed of all softbilled birds. They take very kindly to captivity and, if young enough, become very tame pets.

The diet is very simple. Standard mynah pellets set the pace as the basic food. Additional raw meat is necessary, and some fresh fruits are desirable. The native high-ranking intelligence and natural curiosity make the dietary acclimation an easy and short-lived phase. Peanut butter is helpful for plumage and additional nourishment. If mynah pellets are not available, substitutes in the chapter on diet must be formulated by the bird fancier. In the long run, however, mynah pellets will prove to be the least expensive and best basic food.

Magpies and pies are large and long-tailed birds which are essentially the same except for popular delineations. The names may differ, but the basic precepts of care and generalized descriptions are nearly identical. Magpie jays fall into this same category but have greatly restricted habitats. Jays occur throughout the world and are very similar except for shorter tails and a more noisy friendliness which is not always accepted by mankind.

MAGPIES

Very few magpies have become important in aviculture, but all are interesting. Simple care and great hardiness characterize the average magpie. Handfed nestlings are common in several parts of the world, but many of these birds do not fall within the confines of aviculture. Handfed babies are usually kept as individual pets wherever they may be available. These birds nearly always fulfill everyone's requirements for pets if they are taken at the proper early stage of development.

Two American magpies become important in American aviculture. Legal entanglements and poorly defined laws leave some bird fanciers in a perplexing situation in regards to native magpies. They sometimes are not sure whether their humane efforts are quite within the laws.

The writers are often similarly mystified by the actual letters of many laws regarding native fauna. If a native bird needs care, the writers have attended to its needs first and have wondered afterwards about the legality. The moral requirement is always fulfilled even though man-made laws may occasionally be circumvented. The writers have never meaningfully bypassed any laws regarding native birds, but they may have misinterpreted some of the ambiguous wordings.

The American Magpie (*Pica pica hudsonia*) has many subspecies extending throughout the world. It is known in the United States as the Black Billed Magpie and in Europe and the orient as the European Magpie. The beak is black.

The color scheme is glossy black and bright white. White occurs on the underparts after the large black bib and in the wings. The tail is long and graceful. Anyone passing through this bird's native habitat cannot help but notice its beauty.

Youngsters have a basic coloring of dull gray replacing the black areas and brownish-white replacing the white areas. The overall size is variable according to subspecies, but it averages eighteen inches. The long tail ranges between eight and ten inches in length.

A very attractive relative is the Ivory Billed Magpie (*Pica nuttalli*) from Central California. This magpie has a bright ivory-yellow beak and occurs in a very limited range. It is slightly smaller than the above and has yellowish bare skin behind the eye. Over the last fifteen years, the writers have had a very few hand reared Ivory Billed Magpies as pets and have much preferred them over the less attractive Black Billed Magpie.

Of the several magpies, the Azure Winged Magpie (*Cyanopica cyanus cooki*) seems to be distributed mostly to European aviculturists. This magpie is smaller and has better coloring. Pale blue marks both wings and tail. A partially erectile crest is black.

CISSAS

Cissas also are included in the group of magpies. All cissas are very rare in aviculture and are usually expensive by comparison. Most cissas have a basic green coloration which fades drastically in captivity. The captive coloring is a soft blue which, if anything, is more attractive than the original color.

The Green Cissa (*Kitta chinensis* or *Cissa chinensis*) is the only member of the family which is at all frequently available. The beak, feet, and legs are red. A blackish shade covers the lores, surrounds the eyes, and tapers to a diminishing eyebrow on the sides of the neck. The flights are reddish-brown, and bold white tips occur on the inner flights. The graduated tail has considerable white areas on the tips. The remaining color is green in the wild state, but it fades to a soft blue in captivity unless given a color holding supplement. A recumbent crest, hidden most of the time, is partially erectile. The total length is nearly fifteen inches long including the tail of eight inches.

There are two very distinctive relatives which do not figure prominently in aviculture. One is the Yellow Breasted Cissa which has yellow underparts, and the other is the Ceylon Blue Magpie which is beautifully patterned in rich cobalt blue and chestnut.

PIES

Those birds which belong to the group of pies are usually called magpies. They are very similar in habits, and the dividing line is really quite thin. Only one bird in this group is important in aviculture.

RED BILLED BLUE MAGPIE (*Urocissa erythrorhyncha*)

Easily the best known and most easily obtainable member of pies and magpies is the very beautiful Red Billed Blue Magpie from India, also called the Occipital Blue Pie. This ideal creature is flamboyant in every sense of the word. The brilliant colors and long, graceful tail are not often matched in readily available avicultural subjects. This bird is comparatively inexpensive as well as very hardy and easily acclimated. It also is amazingly considerate in its peaceful demeanor. In groups of large softbills, the Red Billed Blue Magpie is usually the target of bullies; but it is active enough and cautious enough to escape most attacks. In short, it is ideal for both novice and experienced fancier.

The body of the Red Billed Blue Magpie is seven inches long measured from the top of the head to the base of the tail.

The graceful tail is about fourteen inches long in its full splendor. The tail feathers are long and have graduated lengths. The tip is slightly curved. The five pairs of tail feathers are shortest on the outer side of the underside of the tail. Each pair becomes progressively longer and helps to support the two longest feathers lying on top of the others.

Looking at the undersides of the tail feathers, a very pleasant pattern becomes rather dominant. The major shading is grayish, but broad bands of white mark the end of each feather preceded by a narrow black band. The uppersides of the tail feathers have deep royal blue instead of dull gray. The black band and bluish-white tip are present.

The major coloring is a lovely shade of cobalt or royal blue. Some gray subdues the back. The tips of the wing feathers are bluish-white preceded by narrow black borders. The uppertail coverts have blackish tips. The large beak as well as feet and legs are orange. The eyes are golden-orange with black pupils.

Black covers the head, neck, and circular bib extending onto the chest. Remaining underparts through the undertail coverts are an off-white shade.

The crown has a broad swath of very pale bluish-white extending down the center to a tapering point on the lower nape.

Sexes are alike and are very difficult to determine.

MAGPIE JAYS (*Calocitta formosa*)

Magpie Jays, quite rare in aviculture, extend from Mexico to Costa Rica. These large birds have long tails like magpies and an incessant activity. In the wild state these birds are very noisy, but aviary life has a fortunate tendency to quiet them down a bit.

Nomenclature is variable. Often these birds are called Plumed Jays because of the long and loosely gathered crest feathers. Several slightly varying races occur.

The average size of Magpie Jays is twenty-four or twenty-five inches long including the long tail of about nineteen inches. The long tail adds a desirable gracefulness, and the crest adds a curiously startled air of dignity.

Black highlights the crest feathers, forehead, lores, and a broad border separating the dark upperparts from the pale underparts. A very prominent necklace band is also black. Underparts, including most of the face, are white. The tail is a bright but dark blue with white tips on most of the sides. Wings, back, mantle, and nape are gray with some blue and purple highlights. Sexes are alike, but males are slightly larger.

Collie's Magpie Jay (subspecies *colliei*) has a longer tail and more blue on the upperparts. Black occurs on the throat and chest.

JAYS

Those birds called jays occur in most parts of the world. They are noisy and aggressive. Color patterns run rampant, but personalities are always fascinating.

LANCEOLATED JAY (*Garrulus lanceolatus*)

The widely distributed Lanceolated Jay from Europe to Burma in several slightly differing races is seldom offered to aviculturists. The most vivid characteristic is a barred effect on the wings and tail. Pale but bright blue alternates with rich black striations. Some white occurs on the primary coverts and secondary flights preceded by a dull black shade. The tips of the tail show a similar coloration. Black covers most of the head except for the chin and throat. A mild crest is partially erectile. The chin and throat are streaked in black and white. Remaining plumage is a soft shade of quiet grayish-brown softly mixed with a mild shade of lavender.

Sexes are alike, and the overall size is nearly thirteen inches long. The beak is slate with blackish tips.

The Lanceolated Jay is sometimes called the Black Throated Jay, but this incongruous name is totally inappropriate. The most readily obtainable avicultural race comes from India. One species has a blue patch on the sides of the neck instead of a black and white throat. The basic body coloring is reddish-brown, and white is absent on the wings. This bird is called the

The large and handsome White Throated Magpie Jay (top left) is very active and unusually peaceful for its size. The dark areas are dusky purplish-blues, blacks, and grays pleasantly balanced with whites. Collie's Magpie Jay has an eight inch body, a thirteen and a half inch tail, a two and a half inch crest, and a one and one-fourth inch black beak. The head from the back of the crest and through a large chest bib is black, and the eyes are dark brown. Shades of blue ranging from brilliant cobalt to pale turquoise accent a thick, short eyebrow, a tapering mark under the eye, and a large area under the base of the lower mandible extending out to the lower cheek area. The beautiful crest has bluish tips fading to white. The back of the crown and all remaining upperparts are lustrous deep cobalt blue. The outer four pairs of graduated tail feathers (usually folded under the two central tail feathers) have broad white tips on both sides. The underside of the tail is dull black. Underparts from the bib through the undertail coverts are white.

The dark and lustrous Longtailed Glossy Starling (top right) is similar to most Glossy Starlings except for the long tail. It is reasonably rare and somewhat expensive.

Hoopoes (lower left) are handsome and fascinating avicultural subjects, but they are seldom available and difficult to transfer to domestic diets. The basic orange-buff coloring is pleasantly accented by black and white, and the flamboyant erectile crest adds an exciting flair.

Rothschild's Mynah (lower right) is a very rare species from Bali. Mostly white, this handsome species has pleasant black accents on the tail and wings and a bluish bare facial area. The long filmy crest is especially attractive. These sketches are not drawn in any ratio to size.

351

Himalayan Red Crowned Jay (*Garrulus bispecularis*)

Lidth's Jay from Japan is similar in basic coloration except for blue on the head, breast, tail, and wings. This rare species is seldom offered to aviculturists.

BLUE JAYS

Many of the so-called Blue Jays fall outside of the scope of aviculture because they are very seldom available. Those birds in the United States are usually protected by law. A few individuals fall into bird fanciers' hands during fledgling or recuperative stages. In nearly all cases, these hapless victims recover and may become very tame pets.

The Turquoise Jay (*Cyanolyca turcosa*) is one of several handsome and similar but seldom available members of a large family. Attractive and hardy, the Turquoise Jay with its blue shades and black accents is aggressive to smaller birds. New York Zoological Society photo.

The Violaceus Jay (*Cyanocorax violaceus*) is a handsome but rare species from South America. The blue and white are subordinate to the large black area covering throat, face, and tuftlike crest. New York Zoological Society photo.

The silver eyed Talamanca Jay is mostly white and black tinted with purplish. Some bright blue facial markings add vivid accents. This large and aggressive bird cannot be kept with smaller birds.

The Scrub Jay (*Aphelocoma coerulescens*) has a beautiful shade of blue on the upperparts and a shade of grayish-white on the underparts. A white eyebrow is followed by a grayish-brown cheek patch. This boisterous species is usually most appreciated outside of its natural range. The writers have had several individuals of this species during recuperation, but they have always been happy when the day came for liberation. The range of this bird extends throughout the lower United States and Mexico.

The Pinon Jay (*Gymnorhinus cyanocephala*) from Northern United States has blue underparts.

Stellar's Jay (*Cyanocitta stelleri*) is a very handsome blue bird with a stately crest and a mischievous personality. The size is about twelve inches. Black marks the head, neck, and upper chest. The writers have often become so intensely interested in Stellar's Jays that such monumental landmarks as Yosemite Falls and the many awesome natural formations in Yosemite National Park have faded into the background. The witnessing of the amusing contests between Stellar's Jays and local squirrels for tasty delicacies offered by visitors is a never-ending enjoyment.

There are many blue jays which show minor variations. All would become important in aviculture if they were available because of boisterous personalities and raucous individualism.

The San Blas Jay (*Cissilopha san-blasiana*) is beautifully bedecked in black and blue. The total size is eleven inches long including a tail of five inches. The bright yellow eyes have black pupils. Underparts, neck, head, and beak are black. Remaining upperparts, downwards from the shoulders, are bright blue with a richer shade on the tail. The thick neck gives a heavy but streamlined appearance.

The Talamanca Jay (*Cyanocorax affinis*) is also called the Purple Jay. Underparts are white, and upperparts are black along with the head and broad bib extending onto the upper chest. Bright purplish-blue accents occur above the brilliant silvery eyes. Dark purplish highlights occur on the wings.

GREEN JAYS

Green jays, like cissas, fade in captivity. The yellow underparts turn white, and the green upperparts become a soft shade of blue. A proper domestic diet includes a satisfactory color holding agent and plenty of sunshine. Either phase, natural or faded, is quite beautiful; but the writers always feel an anxiety for those birds which fade in captivity. They feel an ineptitude in trying to furnish a satisfactory native diet despite the easily accepted domesticated diet.

The most beautiful of the green jays is the Inca or Peruvian Jay (*Xanthoura yncas*) which ranges in several subspecies from Mexico to Bolivia. The total size is between nine and ten inches long including a tail slightly less than four inches long. Upperparts are green, and underparts are yellow. The eyes are a piercing shade of yellowish-straw punctuated by black pupils.

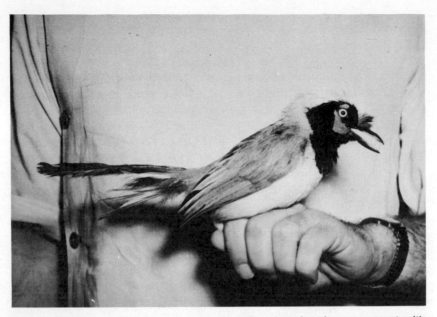

South American Green Jays are attractive and noisy comics, but they are aggressive like all jays and should never be kept with birds smaller than themselves. In many instances, the yellow chest and green back fade to a near blue and white. Brilliant blue marks a bristly crest above the beak and the sides of the face. Photographed at Palos Verdes Bird Farm.

A large black area covers all the facial areas and a bib reaching to the upper part of the chest.

A prominent group of brilliant blue bristles occurs above the forehead in a tuftlike crest extending partly over the beak. This same shade in a velvety texture occurs in a short but broad eyebrow which is wider at the top. A similar triangular patch of blue occurs on the side of the face.

Another green jay, native to Texas and Mexico, is far less attractive because it lacks the blue-bristled tufts on the forehead. The head is also smaller, and the underparts are green instead of yellow. Other races occur in Central and South America, but none attain a high status in aviculture.

CHAPTER 35

Glossy Starlings, Starlings, and Mynahs

The birds in this chapter show tremendous variation in size and color patterns. Perhaps the only common ground is a simplicity in diet and innate hardiness. Mynah pellets can serve these birds an excellent and total nourishment. The condition of robust health and glossy plumage of several birds pictured in this book attests to the efficiency of mynah pellets. Though the writers offer additional fruits and raw meat to most of these birds, these extras have always proved to be superfluous. Of their own accord, several of the birds in this chapter have systematically eliminated every dietary item except mynah pellets; and they have always been healthier as a result.

Brilliance of refracted coloration is not easy to capture with a camera. Those birds pictured from this chapter are usually even more beautiful than the photographs will show. Carefully angled glints of sunlight add to the metallic luster of these birds. Glossy starlings are especially endowed with this heavy overlay of metallic brilliance.

Sexes are alike in nearly all species. Males are bolder in body and stance than females.

Many starlings are called mynahs or grackles. The relationship and nomenclature of the smaller members of the family are interchangeable.

None of the three categories in this chapter is complete. Many of these birds fall outside the realm of aviculture and are therefore omitted. A few individuals have wandered into bird collections, but these exceptions cannot be counted as important. Those members of the genera *Sturnus* and *Acridotheres* are not permitted importation into the United States.

SUPERB SPREO (*Spreo superbus*)

A description of this magnificent African Glossy Starling is totally inadequate. The seven and one-fourth inch size includes a tail of two and one-fourth inches. The broad-chested and squarish build along with the large head seem quite mundane until one tries to describe the coloration. Feet and legs are black, large, and powerful. The beak is also black, and the startling eyes have a rich metallic straw shade with black pupils.

Glossy black covers the entire head and a bib extending onto the upper chest. Upperparts are solid and heavy in their rich and shimmering iridescent greens. The tail is black with lustrous blues and greens.

A whitish band separates the lower boundary of the chest. Most of the remaining underparts are bright chestnut. The vent and undertail coverts are white. Dull black covers the undersides of the tail and flights, and the remaining undersides of the wings are white.

Sexes are alike, but the female is slightly smaller.

Other similar but less attractive members of the genus *Spreo* are unimportant in aviculture.

ROYAL STARLING (*Cosmopsarus regius*)

The long tailed Royal Starling is one of the most beautiful members of African Glossy Starlings. The body size is about equal to the above species, but the more graceful contours and long tapering tail of about thirteen inches present a very elegant appearance. The brilliance of the diversified colors also adds great beauty.

Metallic green covers the head, nape, and back. The wings and uppertail coverts are swathed in rich purplish-blue. The tail dims to a dull brownish shade, but it still retains a rare elegance. The throat and upper chest offer a brilliant purplish bib which glows at every conceivable angle. Bold yellow covers the remaining underparts through the undertail coverts. Metallic iridescence is not needed in this bright yellow. It stands far and above the richness of other coloration.

LONG TAILED GLOSSY STARLING (*Lamprotornis caudatus*)

The popular and comparatively inexpensive Long Tailed Glossy Starling is richly clothed in varying shades of dark iridescence. The tail is long and adds dignity. Several species are very similar. The above mentioned African species is the only important member of the genus in aviculture.

OTHER GLOSSY STARLINGS

The remaining members of the family of African Glossy Starlings are simply patterned and glowingly colored. All are very dark, and several are nearly alike.

The Green Glossy Starling (*Lamprocolius chalybaeus*) is approximately the same size as the Superb Spreo except for the smaller head, longer tail, and more slender shape. The eyes are bright yellowish-orange. Feet, legs, and beak are black.

The plumage is a dazzling mixture of glossy green, blue, and purple. This species is the most easily and inexpensively available member of the family. It sometimes is called the Blue Eared Glossy Starling.

The Purple Headed Glossy Starling (*Lamprocolius purpureiceps*) is similar but has a very definite purplish gloss covering the head. A less dazzling shade of purple occurs on the tail. The Purple Glossy Starling (*Lamprocolius purpureus*) exhibits a less extensive purple on the head.

Many other glossy starlings exist, but the differences in descriptions are usually very difficult. Also, most are rarely available to aviculture.

COMMON STARLING (*Sturnus vulgaris*)

The Common Starling is now widespread in various parts of the world. Its introduction is looked upon as a tiresome nuisance, but in its native habitat this pretty creature devours many harmful insects. In introduced areas, it usurps the natural ranges of other birds and boisterously drives them away. It is vehemently hated wherever it occurs in the United States and is feared by natives of those areas not yet invaded.

The Common Starling is a pretty bird. The basic coloration is glossy purplish-blue. Many white spots deploy the original coloring, but these variations enhance the austere shades instead of detracting from them. The beak is a pale shade of yellowish-ivory.

Handfed nestlings become marvelous pets.

ROSY PASTOR (*Pastor roseus*)

The Rosy Pastor extends from Europe to Ceylon. The basic coloring is a soft shade of rose except for the black on the tail, flights, head, and neck. The beak is reddish-orange. A recumbent crest is occasionally partially erected. Sexes are alike. This species has an out of color season of dull but pale brown. It is always desirable but not often obtainable.

COMMON MYNAH (*Acridotheres tristris*)

The widespread but not very popular Common Mynah is a swaggering individualist. This species takes hold of any area to which it may be introduced. As a result, it is one of the various mynahs which is very strictly prohibited in the United States.

The head, neck, and wings are blackish-brown. Some white occurs in the wings, on the undertail coverts, and on the ventral area. The beak and a bare area behind the eyes show a bright yellow. Remaining areas are brown.

A similar Indian species is called the Bank Mynah, and another is called the Indian Jungle Mynah. The Brahminy or Pagoda Mynah is similar and closely related.

ROTHSCHILD'S MYNAH (*Leucopsar rothschildi*)

Rothschild's Mynah from Bali is very rare in aviculture. Bold black occurs on the tips of the tail and wings. A broad greenish-blue area of bare skin covers the lores, surrounds the eyes, and tapers to the sides of the neck. The beak is a dull horn shade, and the feet and legs are soft gray. All the remaining color, including the huge recumbent crest, is white.

GREATER INDIA HILL MYNAH (*Gracula religiosa*)

One of the most popular of all pet birds in the United States is the Greater India Hill Mynah. Its ability to talk is unexcelled, and its rate of learning is amazingly rapid. Fortunately, nearly all of the mynahs annually imported are hand reared fledglings and are completely tame. Trapped adults are wild and worthless as pets.

The writers are very fond of the Greater India Hill Mynah. They look forward to the late spring and summer seasons of availability just for the privilege of handfeeding the fledgling imports. To walk into an aviary full of baby mynahs is the same as walking into a din of cacophony. Each bird vies for the most advantageous position and loudly screams for food and attention. Huge gaping mouths and discordant pleas for mynah pellets cannot be bypassed.

Although most imports are self-feeding when they arrive, they must be transferred to mynah pellets as a basic diet after arrival. Also, baby mynahs do not like to admit that they are self-feeding because of their great pleasure and satisfaction received by individual attention. The writers wholeheartedly reciprocate. Nothing could be more pleasurable than an affectionate swarm of baby Greater India Hill Mynahs, even though none have become responsibly housebroken.

The gluttonous appetites of baby mynahs will accept any food offered by a human hand. These birds even try to swallow fingers. The advent of mynah pellets is the most welcome innovation to bird fanciers since the cultivation of bird seeds. The writers always feed diced apple, soaked raisins, and raw meat during the changeover period to mynah pellets but gradually limit the proportions until the pellets become the major intake.

Pet mynahs are often subjected to horrifying treatment and impossible diets by uninformed pet fanciers. Scrambled eggs, mashed potatoes, milk, boiled rice, cooked meats, and similarly foolish foodstuffs cause many problems with individual pets.

Many benign pet lovers feel that a day in the sun will be beneficial to their pet mynah. They do not realize that their pet would normally live in the perpetual twilight of dense jungles, and so they place the bird cage in the full glare of the sun with no possibility for the bird to find shade. They do not anticipate the exhaustive convulsions and frequent deaths which result from such treatment. If sunshine is to be offered, the pet mynah should also be given an opportunity to escape into a shaded area when the need arises. The writers have witnessed many agonizing deaths of mynahs caused by overexposure to the sun. This common danger has never been properly touted by experienced bird fanciers, but the omission is long overdue.

The Greater India Hill Mynah occurs in several Oriental subspecies, but the only frequently available races come from India and Thailand. All are very similar in appearance, but the Indian races show greater proficiency in learning to speak.

Adults are ten inches long including a square tail of three inches. The plumage is black with rich glosses shading to blue, purple, and green iridescence. A band of white occurs on the flights. The feet and legs are yellow, and the beak is bright orange fading to yellow on the tip. Fleshy wattles dangle over the nape of the neck. This skin is bright yellow. It starts below the eyes and drops to a point even with the lower mandible. It then extends to the nape where the two sides do not quite meet. A small triangle of black feathers interrupts the fleshy area behind the eyes. Two loose flaps of flesh on the back of the neck are slightly more than a half inch in length. A noticeable central line extends from the crown to the nape; and all the short, broad, and curled velvety feathers seem to reach towards the dividing line.

Fledgling mynahs are not very attractive. They lack the iridescence and velvety texture of the black plumage and the brightness of the beak. The wattles are not only very pale but are also undeveloped. The flaps are absent, and the skin seems to be tautly stretched. The flaps develop slowly, showing slight bulbous swellings at a year of age and slow growth thereafter.

The Lesser India Hill Mynah (subspecies *indica*) is not as adept at learning to talk as the Greater India Hill Mynah. It should be avoided wherever possible since it is a great disappointment as a pet. This subspecies is not frequently offered anymore because most people now recognize its shortcomings. Its low price is not sufficient incentive for substitution.

The Lesser India Hill Mynah is easily distinguishable from the Greater India Hill Mynah. Body size and beak are smaller and more slender, and the bare skinned wattles are very different. They dip down to the nape, but they never pretend to meet. Instead they reach forward to the crown in two bold U-shapes with a wide separation between.

JAVA HILL MYNAH (*Gracula intermedia javana*)

The large and heavy bodied Java Hill Mynah is eleven inches long including the two and a half inch tail. This rare and expensive species has an overall larger size. The beak is very thick, and the wattle flap is about seven-eighths of an inch long. Other characteristics are similar.

The Java Hill Mynah is a superlative talker and is worth its price. Not often available, it usually finds a ready market when it is imported.

COLETO MYNAH (*Sarcops calvus*)

No one would say that the Coleto Mynah from the Philippines is a beautiful bird; but when it is available (which is rare), it is at least significant. Any collection which can boast of a Coleto Mynah is usually a fine group of birds, and the Coleto is a rare but inexpensive addition.

The writers have had several Coleto Mynahs and have always admired the ringing bell-like call note which, if nothing else, is surely different.

The head has a severe bare skin area ranging from chalky white to blushing pink depending upon momentary temperament or temperature. A feathered black line down the center of the head and on a surrounding border add to the bizarre bare skulled shape. The beak, feet, legs, and eyes are black. Underparts and tail are black.

A very unusual shade of true and shining silver marks a partially erectile ruff on the nape of the neck. The same shade is repeated on the lower back, rump, flanks, and uppertail coverts. Remaining plumage is a shiny jet black.

361

Two of the many species of mynah birds. At top, the very popular Greater India Hill Mynah is a favorite pet and excellent talker. At the bottom of the picture is the seldom seen Coleto Mynah from the Philippines. It cannot be called beautiful, but it is interesting. The Coleto can be taught to talk, and it has a pleasant bell ring which is almost ventriloqual. The bare skin on the head is normally chalk white, but it can blush to deep pink The glossy black highlights the shiny silver on back, rump, and nape. Photographed at Palos Verdes Bird Farm.

The overall size is about ten inches in length.

Fledglings are often taught to speak. In fact, this is a great favorite as a cage pet in the Philippine Islands.

Coletos live peaceably with Greater or Lesser India Hill Mynahs, Laughing Jay Thrushes, and other large softbills of similar size. A pair the writers once had selected a Cockatiel nestbox and began nesting operations. Unfortunately, constant disturbances interrupted this activity. However, the writers firmly believe that this species would nest far more readily than the Greater India Hill Mynah if given suitable accommodations.

Sexes are alike. Behavior is the only true test. The diet is the same as for the Greater India Hill Mynah.

CHAPTER 36

Orioles, Hangnests, Troupials, Cassiques, Marsh Birds, Blackbirds, and Cowbirds

Orioles of the old world are quite different from the orioles of the new world despite the basic shade of brilliant yellow on most individuals. New world orioles are also designated as hangnests because of their nestbuilding tendencies. The nests are huge pendulous affairs and are very carefully woven.

The diet is the simple and standard softbilled fare. No variations are necessary, but nectar is appreciated by some. The acclimation period is short, and most members are very hardy as well as long-lived. Pet troupials have been known to live more than twenty years if given proper care. Most of the birds in this chapter are of medium size, and several are quite aggressive. Many are pleasant songbirds. All seem to be very intelligent and thrive in captivity.

Not all of the slightly varying species can be covered in this book. Many are not available to aviculture. Those orioles native to the United States fall under the blanket protection for all songbirds and cannot be kept in American collections.

Very few members in this chapter have been reared in captivity. No breeding successes have been extensively perpetuated.

GOLDEN ORIOLE (*Oriolus oriolus*)

Golden Orioles occur in many areas, but those reaching aviculture usually come from India. At the time of writing, these orioles are seldom available. They have heavy bodies and bulky shapes in the total length of slightly less than nine inches. They are very beautiful, peaceful, and ideal for aviculture.

The male has a large pinkish beak, grayish feet and legs, and a pleasant balance of black and brilliant golden yellow. The black extends past the eyes in a diminishing tapered effect. The flights are mostly black except for yellow

The unpredictable Troupial is sometimes an extremely talented pet. If tamed while young, the Troupial can be taught an amazing range of whistled tunes and even in rare cases can be taught to talk. Brightly attired in golden yellow and black, the Troupial is a showy bird with an aggressive personality. It is not safe with smaller birds. Photographed at Palos Verdes Bird Farm.

365

edges and a bold yellow bar near the base. Black also marks the tail in a broad base tapering inward to the full length of the central feathers. The rest of the coloring is a uniform and vivid golden yellow.

The female has a dull yellowish-green replacing the yellow and a dull shade of brown on the wings. Underparts are paler than the upperparts. Dark but dull olive-gray streaks mark the underparts.

Other Old World orioles are far less available but only slightly less attractive. Only one becomes important in aviculture.

The Indian Black Headed Oriole (*Oriolus xanthornus*) is similar except for a dominant black covering the head and neck and ending in a "V" on the upper chest. The size is about the same, and sexes are alike.

The Maroon Oriole (*Oriolus trailli*) has a dusky shade of maroon replacing the yellow.

TROUPIAL (*Icterus icterus*)

Also called the Bugle Bird and the Common Hangnest, the Troupial is a very handsome South American bird. It is less than ten inches long. Sexes are alike in appearance, but the male is slightly larger.

The Troupial is a very aggressive bird and freely uses its long sharp beak as a formidable weapon against smaller birds. The beak is black with a pale blue-gray patch on the sides of the lower mandible near the base.

A bare bluish-gray skin area slightly surrounds the eyes and tapers to a point behind. The eyes themselves are bright golden-yellow with black pupils. A piercing glare seems to be as sharp as the beak.

Black covers the head, neck, and throat feathers. The lower boundary, extending to the upper chest, ends in irregular and jagged lines. The division of coloring, however, is always sharp and not blended.

The wings and tail are black except for an irregular and broad bar of white slashing across the scapulars into the secondary flights.

Remaining plumage is bright golden-orange in the wild state. In captivity, these areas fade to brilliant yellow. Both shades are equally attractive.

A popular nickname for the Troupial is the Bugle Bird because of a remarkable talent for a shrill whistling mimicry. Much of the reputation is misleading since few adult birds become tame or talented cage birds despite the utmost patience of the owner. Hand reared fledglings are seldom obtainable and are usually much higher in price.

Adults are excellent aviary birds, and their flashing activity exhibits a constant source of beauty. Unfortunately, many adults are imported with clipped wings and are represented as tame birds. In many cases their restricted activity fails to use all of the elements in rich diets. While awaiting the regrowth of clipped wings, the importer may often be faced with the far more difficult problems of bumblefoot.

Several Icterid species from Northern South America are often shipped as Troupials. Differences are often slight.

YELLOW ORIOLE (*Icterus nigrogularis*)

The very attractive and flashy Yellow Oriole from Northern South America may occasionally become available from Colombia. It is smaller and much more peaceful than the Troupial but can be aggressive if it feels it can win. The overall size is seven inches long including a tail of three inches.

The long pointed beak is black except for a silvery shade at the base. The lores, a slight area surrounding the eyes, a narrow border near the base of the lower mandible, and an extensive throat patch are black. The throat patch has an irregular outline.

The wings are mostly black with bold and attractive accents of white on the outer margins of many feathers. The underside of the wings is pale silvery gray. The tail also is black with pale scallops on the undersides of a few feathers.

Bright yellow covers the rest of the bird including a soft filmy texture of armor overlapping the base of the wings out to the shoulders and also including the uppertail and undertail coverts. The yellow is slightly richer on the cheeks and chest. The feet and legs are gray, and sexes are similar.

The Yellow Oriole is a handsome addition to any collection. Besides its great beauty, it has a very alert and vivacious personality. It is easily acclimated and very hardy.

BLACK THROATED ORIOLE (*Icterus gularis*)

The Black Throated Oriole from Mexico and Central America is very similar to the Yellow Oriole. The yellow is more extensive and more conspicuous on the wing covert bars, and the back is black. As in the above species the yellow portions may vary from orange-yellow to golden-orange, but most individuals become bright yellow in captivity. Sexes also are similar, and the basic characteristics are practically identical.

SPOTTED BREASTED ORIOLE (*Icterus pectoralis*)

The Spotted Breasted Oriole from Central America and lower portions of Mexico is apparently becoming naturalized in Florida where it is protected. Incoming shipments to California have been passed by inspectors and presumably are admitted to other ports of entry.

This attractive species is slightly larger and much heavier-bodied than the Yellow Oriole. It is attractive, but proportions are far less streamlined than the shape of the Yellow Oriole described above.

The length from the top of the head to the tip of the tail is eight inches long. The tail is slightly over three inches in length, and the long pointed beak is three-fourths of an inch long.

Further comparisons with the Yellow Oriole show more extensive black around the eyes. The back is black, and very prominent black spots are sprinkled across the chest in an irregular distribution. Feet and legs are also gray. Sexes are similar. The yellow may vary from deep golden-yellow to much paler shades; but these differences are usually attributed to age, length

367

of time in captivity, and differences in diet.

Youngsters are usually more readily available than adults. In the sub-adult phase, most of the black is missing from the face and throat, but the throat does have a black smudge. The shading of black is much duller than the shiny jetness of adults.

The writers have found the Spotted Breasted Oriole very hardy and easily acclimated, but the wings are unfortunately clipped on most incoming shipments. Extraction and regrowth requires a prolonged period of acclimation.

MEXICAN and AMERICAN ORIOLES

None of the following orioles or hangnests are extensively available to aviculture. Some are out of collecting ranges in Mexico. Those native to the United States are illegal in American aviculture, but a few which migrate to Mexico may occasionally be trapped and sent to Europe. Coverage will be brief on these birds.

The Yellow Backed Oriole (*Icterus chrysater*) and its subspecies occur in Mexico. Another popular name is Lesson's Oriole. The size is slightly more than eight inches long. It is similar to the Black Throated Oriole except for the following differences: yellow back, absence of yellow on the wings, and subdued throat patch tinged with brown. Immatures are dulled by a shade of olive on the upperparts.

The Hooded Oriole (*Icterus cucullatus*) of Mexico is very similar in overall pattern to the Black Throated Oriole. It is slightly smaller. The female has duller yellows tinged with olive above and with greenish below. There are several subspecies.

Also found in Mexico, the Streak Backed Oriole (*Icterus pustulatus*) and its many subspecies resembles the Yellow Backed Oriole in many respects. It is, however, smaller and has two distinctive differences: reddish-orange on the chest and head and broad streaks of white and gray on the back and wings. The female is much duller and has gray and olive streaks on the back and wings.

The Black Headed Oriole from Mexico (*Icterus graduacauda*) is also called Audubon's Oriole. The entire head and throat are black with a few black spots marring the precision of the lower throat boundary. The back is yellow, and orange is totally absent. The white wing markings are greatly reduced. There are several subspecies with some extending into the United States. The overall size is about eight inches.

Scott's Oriole (*Icterus parisorum*) is about seven and a half inches long. It is found in both the United States and Mexico. Sexes are different. The male has its entire head, chest, and back in glossy black. A white wing bar is balanced by yellow shoulders. The remaining underparts and rump are yellow, and the tail is mostly black.

The female has grayish-olive replacing most of the black and yellowish-

368

The Orchard Oriole, male above and female below, is a native bird and would not be popular even if it were permissible to American aviculturists. It is perhaps the least colorful of the New World Orioles in its quiet and dusky brownish shadings of orange, red, and black.

olive replacing most of the yellow. The crown and back are streaked and spotted.

Strickland's or Black Cowled Oriole (*Icterus prosthemelas*) from Mexico is similar to Scott's Oriole but has more extensive black on the tail, chest, and wings. The size is about the same. The rump, lower back, remaining underparts, undertail coverts, and a small shoulder patch are bright yellow. The lower chest and upper abdomen exhibit some chestnut. Youngsters show greatly reduced areas of black which are replaced by olive-yellow.

The Black Vented Oriole (*Icterus wagleri*) is also called Wagler's Oriole. It is similar to the Black Cowled Oriole but is larger and has black tail coverts. The yellow areas show a much brighter shade of orange.

Bullock's Oriole (*Icterus bullockii*) is a well-known and handsome species occurring in the United States, Mexico, and Guatemala in its migratory habits. The female is very dull with a basic olive coloring tinged with brown on the upperparts, yellow on the chest, and gray on flanks and abdomen.

The male has black upperparts except for extensive white markings in the wings. Orange covers the forehead and a prominent eyebrow above the eyes. A black line extends through the eyes. Underparts are golden-orange.

The Baltimore Oriole (*Icterus galbula*) is a well-known native American bird. It migrates to southern Mexico in the winter. The basic coloring of the male is vivid golden-orange and jet black. The overall size is about seven inches in length. Black covers the entire head, throat, neck, and back. Most of the tail is black except for outer edges of yellow-orange. The wings are also black except for orange-yellow shoulders, a white scapular bar, and white outer edges of most of the flight feathers. Uppertail coverts and rump are golden-orange like the underparts.

The female is very dull by comparison. The black is superseded by spotted grayish-olive except on the wings. The tail and underparts are pale yellowish, more heavily and brightly concentrated on the chest.

The Orchard Oriole (*Icterus spurius*) occurs in the United States and Mexico. The basic pattern is similar to that of the Baltimore Oriole in both sexes except for an extremely less attractive color scheme. The basic change in the male is a replacement of dull chestnut for all yellow parts. The female has no brightness in any of the coloring. The size also is smaller.

MEXICAN or YELLOW WINGED CASSIQUE (*Cassiculus melanicterus*)

The Cassique, known popularly in aviculture as the Crested Cassique, bears two popular ornithological names: Mexican or Yellow Winged Cassique. It is ten inches long including the broad tail which is four inches long. The long greenish-ivory beak is a sharply pointed length of one and three-eighths inches. Eyes have a pale brown iris and black pupils. The feet and legs are grayish-black.

Several characteristics mark this bird as being unusual and exotic. A strange powery-musk odor is unique but not unpleasant. The flamboyant lateral crest resembling an Aztec headdress is distinctly different. The rich black and bright yellow pattern of the male is extremely attractive. Frequent and often very aggressive displays are fascinating but bullying to many birds even larger than themselves.

The nuptial display is often expounded in lavish affection to females or aggressive warnings and belligerent attacks upon other species. During the display, a ratchety and staccato squeal, totally lacking in musical ability is uttered along with a flaring upraised crest and a challenging erotic lifting of feathers on the back and rump. If this display is spurned by any birds nearby, regardless of genera or species, the immediate response is a direct attack which is sometimes very unpleasant to birds which cannot adequately defend themselves.

The display of the crest is particularly fascinating. The long flexible feathers, limited in number, stem from the forehead and the forepart of the crown. They curve gracefully outwards and downwards in an arc towards the cheeks. A frontal view is necessary to appreciate the exotic flair of the crest. When at rest, the crest feathers lie backwards following the natural curve to the back of the head.

The basic male coloring is deep velvety black. Secondary coverts and scapulars, rump, sides of the back, upper and undertail wing coverts, and broad sides of tail feathers are bright yellow.

The female is similarly patterned except for duller black plumage and smaller size.

OTHER CASSIQUES

The Yellow Billed or Chisel Billed Cassique (*Amblycercus holosericus*) is smaller and totally black except for the greenish-ivory beak and pale whitish-yellow iris. This species is also known as the Prevost Cassique.

The Yellow Rumped Cassique (*Cacicus cela*) from Central America and northern South America has similar markings to the Mexican Cassique except for smaller yellow areas on the wings and the absence of the crest. It is slightly larger except for the smaller female. The hen's plumage is considerably duller. Males have blue eyes.

GIANT CASSIQUES or OROPENDOLAS

The Giant Cassiques are usually called Oropendolas. The beaks are much larger and extend to the upperparts of the crown. Crests, if at all present, are little more than diminished hairs.

The Montezuma Oropendola (*Gymnostinops montezuma*) from Mexico is a very large bird extending to nearly eighteen inches in the male and nearly fifteen inches in the female. The bill is black tipped in orange. A pink area of bare skin occurs at the base of the beak and on the facial area. The head, neck, and chest are black followed by a shade of chestnut. Some yellow occurs on the hindparts.

The Chestnut Headed or Wagler's Oropendola (*Zarhynchus wagleri*), also from Mexico, is smaller but has the same overpowering large beak which is greenish-ivory. Glossy black occurs on wings, back, abdomen, and part of the tail feathers. Chestnut covers the head, throat, chest, and rump. Some bright yellow appears on the rump. The bare cheek areas are conspicuously absent.

Bobolinks (male left and female right) are not given much avicultural consideration. They are protected natives and are not very colorful despite the attractive pattern of the male. The care is the same as for blackbirds and orioles.

MARSH BIRDS

Closely related to icterids and seldom available, marsh birds are usually not as attractive. Though easily adaptable to aviculture and quite hardy, marsh birds have nevertheless seldom become popular in aviculture. There are not very many members, and some emulate other more frequently available birds.

The Yellow Headed Marsh Bird (*Agelaius icterocephalus*) has occasionally been imported in considerable numbers from South America. It is about seven inches long. The color pattern is very simple but very attractive. The beak and lores are black. The head is bright yellow, and all remaining coloring, including feet and legs, is black. Wings and tail are glossy, and remaining black areas are like soft velvet.

Females are dull brownish with some yellowish shading on the head and chest. Since they are not colorful, they are rarely imported.

The writers have had many Yellow Headed Marsh Birds. Though hardy, easily acclimated, peaceful, and inexpensive, they present a few problems. Toenails grow very long and need frequent clipping to prevent entanglement in aviary mesh. The accepted diet has also been far too limited.

Despite the offerings of a complete softbilled and seed fare and the inclusion of other birds which accepted both diets, these birds steadfastly refused to follow the examples set by the other birds. Only two items were ever accepted: plenty of mealworms and prodigious amounts of canary seed. Though these limitations caused some consternation to the writers, they must admit that the birds fared very well and never showed any dietary deficiencies. If it is at all possible, however, the writers would suggest every effort in order to extend the variety of food intake.

The writers have never had any other marsh birds and cannot say whether or not the same problems arise with other species.

The Yellow Shouldered Marsh Bird (*Agelaius thilius*), also from South America, is less attractive and usually is not given avicultural consideration. The male is all black except for a bright patch of yellow on the shoulders and wing coverts. The female is mostly dull brownish.

The remaining marsh birds show variations of pattern but are clothed in black and red. None are adequately represented in American aviculture and therefore need not be considered in this book. They include the Scarlet Headed Marsh Bird, Flame Shouldered Marsh Bird, Argentine Red Breasted Marsh Bird, and Guiana or Cayenne Red Breasted Marsh Bird.

BLACKBIRDS

American blackbirds are a singularly uninteresting lot and not very desirable avicultural subjects. The diet is omnivorous and includes softbilled fare as well as seeds.

The Red Winged Blackbird (*Agelaius phoeniceus*), which can also be called a marsh bird since it belongs to the same genus, abounds in Southern California. It boldly swaggers across lawns and gardens like starlings and nearly crowds sparrows from wild bird feeding stations. This species is interesting to watch, but it is aggressive to the other birds. Its main value is in the consumption of harmful insects. On farms, its consumption of important crops assumes an entirely different aspect; and it is often considered an extreme nuisance.

The writers have nursed many individuals back to health. They take kindly to captivity and recuperate rapidly. Because they are larger and nearly as abundant and as bold as sparrows, these birds become the most frequent

The male Red Winged Blackbird during its in color season is rather attractive. His major coloring of black is mostly glossy, and a broad wing bar is bright red. In captivity, this color fades. The male out of season and the female are both dusky blackish-brown, and the red all but disappears.

target of undisciplined children who are given air rifles by irresponsible parents. Surprisingly enough, most of these robust birds recover from such wounds, but their absence of temerity puts them right back in the same target range after they are liberated.

The total length is about eight inches. A seasonal color change occurs. During the in color phase, the male is very attractive and is frequently coveted by zoos and collectors outside of its natural range. While in color, the male is rich glossy black with bright red shoulders followed by a yellowish-buff bar across the scapulars. Unfortunately, the red fades drastically in captivity.

Females and out of color males are clothed in a soft shade of dull soot with a reasonable extent of blackish spots.

The Yellow Headed Blackbird (*Xanthocephalus xanthocephalus*) is less than ten inches in length. It occurs in the United States and ranges southward to Mexico and northward to Canada.

The male is similar to the Yellow Headed Marsh Bird in color pattern, but the distribution of the duller yellow is more extensive. Black covers the beak, lores, and a tapering extension surrounding and trailing behind the eyes. The yellow head extends down into the chest and accents the shoulders. Some white occurs in an irregular wing patch. The remaining plumage is black. The female is grayish-brown with a dusky dullness over most of the plumage except for a yellowish chest streaked with white.

The Yellow Headed Blackbird is similar to the Red Winged Blackbird in its swaggering and pompous habits. Its diet is applauded by some and cursed by others depending upon productive or non-productive environments. Both insects and grain seeds are consumed.

Though its dark coloring is pleasantly glossed with shiny highlights, the Purple Grackle, male and young shown here, is not admired by many aviculturists.

Both the Purple Grackle (above) and the Cowbird (below) are uninteresting and largely unsatisfactory avicultural subjects despite great ease in caring for them. They are very aggressive towards smaller birds and too colorless for the enthusiasm of bird fanciers.

COWBIRDS (Genus *molothrus*)

The writers cannot commend any cowbirds to aviculturists despite some of the attractively designated popular ornithological names. Personal experience has always been considerably less than ideal with these very aggressive and unattractive birds. The writers much prefer to leave them to one of their natural and more beneficial habits of picking ticks off the backs of cattle.

The writers once ordered a South American shipment of birds which bore the intriguing name of "Purple Tanagers." When the birds arrived, they readily accepted all forms of domesticated diets including seed-eating and softbilled fare, and their acclimation was extremely successful. They then quickly bullied their way into a complete command of their aviaries. Beautiful and costly rarities were cowed away from very necessary foods and sought refuge in every secluded spot to escape the aggressive onslaughts. Instead of "Purple Tanagers," they were Shiny Cowbirds (*Molothrus bonariensis*).

The bright and attractive descriptive names applied to cowbirds now leave the writers unmoved. Glossy Cowbirds, Shiny Cowbirds, Silky Cowbirds, Chilean Cowbirds, and Screaming Cowbirds are still cowbirds with the same basic personalities. The writers steadfastly avoid them.

CHAPTER 37

Tits and Nuthatches

Tits and nuthatches are small, stocky birds with large heads, thick necks, short blunt beaks, and, usually, short tails. All are very active birds and are blessed with a great agility and strong feet for climbing and clinging. Their flight is precise and acrobatic. Gymnastics include great poise while hanging upside down, sideways, or perching upright in a normal manner. Beaks are designed for probing into crevices of rough bark for insects and for opening thickly covered seeds or thinly shelled nuts.

Only one species is readily available in both groups. This highly popular pet, quickly adaptable in cage or aviary, is the Japanese Tumbler. Part of the popularity and availability stems from the careful acclimation to domesticity before Japanese exporters ship them. None of those other species of either group are usually acclimated to domestic diets before shipments. The importer is faced with the doubly difficult task of acclimation to domestic diet and new climates. For this reason, as well as for rare availability, few of these birds are offered by most importers. Most are therefore omitted from this chapter.

Japanese Tumblers are offered an omnivorous diet by the writers. This includes standard softbilled fare as well as parrakeet mix, sunflower seeds, health grit, and cuttlebone. Since they thrive on this diet, the same foods have been offered to all members in this chapter; but the writers have seen no acceptance of any but the items in the softbilled fare for these other members.

Nuthatches accept and cherish nutmeats from walnuts, pecans, and peanuts; but the acceptance often means hiding and storing away for a future consumption when other foods become scarce.

This chapter includes selected individuals out of both groups rather than the unnecessary complete coverage of both groups. Two nuthatches have assumed roles in aviculture. Both are rarely available and not highly coveted by fanciers.

JAPANESE TUMBLER (*Parus varius*)

Easily the best known member in this chapter is the Japanese Tumbler or Bucket Bird which also is occasionally and more properly called the

378

Nuthatches and Creepers have quiet and furtive habits while they are busily engaged in seeking hidden insects in the rough bark of forest trees. Though shy by nature and constantly active, it is quite possible for bird watchers to approach reasonably closely while the birds are concentrating on their work. Native Nuthatches, such as this White Breasted Nuthatch, though fascinating, are not available to American aviculturists; nor are they as colorful as their counterparts from India.

None of the Creepers, such as this Brown Creeper (right), are important in aviculture. They are not particularly attractive, and they are difficult to keep alive.

Variegated or Varied Tit. This very intelligent bird is easily fed and becomes a most fascinating pet. Its gymnastic gyrations are more than adequately entertaining.

A keen intellect and alert eyes coupled with this acrobatic skill have combined to make this bird one of the most popular and unusual of individual pet birds. Pet shops often have Japanese Tumblers in unique cages. Visitors are always amazed upon seeing for the first time the animated backward somersaults, the adept pulling up of a tiny bucket dangling on a long string to snatch a delectable morsel, or the efficient emulation of a woodpecker in hammering open sunflower seeds.

The cage for the Japanese Tumbler may be metal or bamboo, but the basic characteristics are always the same. The cage is tall and a little enclosed balcony extends from the uppermost area of one side. A little bucket drops about fifteen inches from a string hung from the middle of the balcony.

The bird quickly learns to pull up the bucket by hanging it just a short distance from the small opening in the bottom of the balcony. A mealworm is then placed in the bucket. Unable to overcome the temptation but intelligent enough to overcome the obstacle, the Tumbler grasps the string and pulls the bucket up. Gradually the string is lengthened until the bird achieves a remarkably deft retrieve even though the bucket dangles fifteen inches below the balcony. The beak is used in pulling the string up, and the grasping toes hold the string fast during the next tug.

The balcony also serves as a springboard for deft aerial somersaults to the perch below. This particular and unusual talent has given this bird the name of Tumbler.

Japanese Tumblers also are cleverly used as selectors for fortune cards by Japanese fortune tellers whose trades are greatly enhanced from a tourist standpoint by the employment of these birds.

As aviary birds, Japanese Tumblers are companionable to most softbills ranging in size from Pekin Nightingales to orioles. They are alert and active

Bright eyed with interest and curiosity, the Japanese Tumbler possesses an amazing intellect. Though it has a somber color scheme, it is a popular pet because of its amusing habits and tricks. Photographed at Palos Verdes Bird Farm.

This unique cage was designed exclusively to accommodate the special talents of the Japanese Tumbler. A member of the Tit family, the Tumbler is one of the most unusually intelligent of all pet birds.

enough to escape the aggressive forays of some of the larger birds. However, they are not suitable companions for the average small finch because of a deadly unsportsmanlike aggressiveness. In an aviary, Japanese Tumblers easily demand rapt attention of astonished viewers because of a tireless and seemingly endless number of perfect and precise perpendicular or looping circular flights interrupted only by occasional digressions to hawk any insect which may wander into the aviary. The aviary must have a safety door because of the silent and slippery ability to sneak out of the door when anyone enters the aviary.

The diet of Japanese Tumblers is omnivorous and easily administered. All of the innumerable individuals ever received by the writers have already been acclimated to domestic diets. In large shipments numbering over a hundred Tumblers, some murderous tendencies become manifest; and any specimen down in energy and stamina is attacked, murdered, and eaten by his companions. The addition of raw meat and separation of individuals with lowered stamina help to alleviate such attacks.

Mynah pellets, sunflower seed, parrakeet mix, health grit, fruits, greenfood, and live food are the dietary ingredients. A little raw meat is also important, but it should be given sparingly to caged pets.

The main charm of the relatively inexpensive Tumbler is in the aforementioned talents and not in its coloring. It has an interesting pattern but no bright colors. The size is four and a half inches long including a mildly forked tail of one and three-fourths inches. A sturdy and bluntly pointed blackish beak is three-eighths of an inch long. The beak is a powerful hammer useful in opening sunflower seeds and peanuts.

A pale tan encircles the crown, covers the lores but excludes eyes, and flares backwards to include the cheeks. Behind the cheeks this shade tapers off at the lower end of the neck. An irregular darker tan stripe down the center starts at the back of the crown and widens till the lower end of the neck is reached before it stops abruptly. The remaining area of the head is black including a broadly flaring throat patch which also covers the forepart of the chest. A narrow black cap goes as far as the nape of the neck. The eyes are big and black with a mischievous glint.

The mantle is brown; the rest of the upperparts are gray and slightly blended with brown. The rest of the underparts, except for the gray underside of the tail, are basically dusty-tan; but a darker and richer brown marks the sides and almost meets in the center of the chest. Feet and legs are gray.

GREAT TIT and GRAY TIT (*Parus major* and subspecies)

The pleasant but rarely available Great Tit ranges in many subspecies over a tremendous area from Europe, through parts of Africa, and many parts of Asia. An average size is about five inches.

The head is glossy black contrasted by a very large facial patch of white covering an area from the lores to the hind part of the sides of the neck. A smaller white patch occurs on the nape. The beak is black, and the eyes are orange. Upperparts are dark gray, and underparts are grayish-white. The flights and tail feathers are blackish edged in white. The black throat extends into a slender V-shaped area covering the center of the underparts. Females are purported to have a narrower black on the underparts. Variations occur because of the many different subspecies.

The Gray Tit from India is a smaller subspecies and is the one most likely to become available. Those which the writers have had in the past were always rather expensive compared to the Tumbler.

382

GREEN BACKED TIT (*Parus monticolus*)

The more attractive Green Backed Tit from India is quite a rarity in aviculture. It has the same basic pattern as the Great Tit, but the back is green bordered with yellow on the nape, and the underparts are bright yellow.

BLUE TIT (*Parus caeruleus*)

The pretty Blue Tit from Europe and parts of Asia is seldom found in aviculture, but it is a charming species and worthy of consideration. A bright blue cap is surrounded on the forehead and facial areas by a very subdued shade of bluish-white. Black covers a narrow chin, and a sharply flaring black throat patch reaches out to embrace the lower boundaries of the cheeks. Black also narrowly surrounds the beak, covers the lores, and continues in a fine band to the nape of the neck where it broadens considerably.

The back and mantle are soft green, and the wings and tail are blue fading in some areas to the pale facial coloring. Underparts are a dull pastel shade which resembles yellow tinged softly and faintly with green.

CRESTED BLACK TIT and INDIAN BLACK TIT (genus *Lophophanes*)

Two similar species from India are the Indian Black Tit (species *rufonuchalis*) and the Crested Black Tit (species *melanolophus*). Both are very rare in aviculture but have handsome crests.

The Indian Black Tit has a white patch on the nape and large white cheek patches. The rest of the head, throat, and chest are black. The back and mantle are olive-gray. Wings and tail are slate-gray. Remaining underparts are soft gray. Some reddish-brown occurs at the lower base of the white patch on the nape. Traces of orange mark the undertail coverts and the sides.

The Crested Black Tit is smaller and has rusty-orange spots on the wings. The overall shading is paler.

Another similar Indian species is the Brown Crested Tit (*dichrous*). Brown replaces the black areas, and grayish-brown covers the remaining upperparts.

YELLOW CHEEKED TIT (*Machlolophus xanthogenys*)

The Yellow Cheeked Tit from India is the prettiest species of this family the writers have ever owned, but it is also very difficult to get.

Black covers the top of the head and shapely crest, chin, and throat; and a narrow black line extends through the chest to the abdomen. A long trailing eyebrow of bright yellow extends behind and slightly above the eyes. A large cheek area is bright yellow. The upper chest is also bright yellow changing slowly to a quieter shade tinged with green on the lower chest and abdomen.

Upperparts are attractively varied. The back, mantle, and shoulders are soft green with black centers on many feathers. The wings are mostly black with soft shadings of blue in some areas. White tips and margins add bright contrasts.

383

SULTAN TIT (*Melanochlora sultanea*)

The possession of the brilliant and beautiful Sultan Tit from India, Malaysia, Burma, and Sumatra is a goal not yet realized by the writers. This is a rather large bird nearly eight inches long. Sexes are different. It is practically nonexistent in aviculture because of unavailability.

The male has a large and flamboyant yellow crest and rich golden-yellow underparts from the chest through the undertail coverts. The rest of the coloring is glossy-black except for paler undertail coverts.

The female has a paler shade of yellow and greenish-brown in place of the black areas.

CHESTNUT BELLIED NUTHATCH (*Sitta castanea*)

The unusual Chestnut Bellied or Chestnut Breasted Nuthatch from India and Burma is not very colorful, but its odd and active mannerisms make it quite distinctive. This species averages slightly less than six inches in length. Most bird fanciers bypass nuthatches and therefore miss many pleasurable experiences. Seldom available and rather expensive, nuthatches also show difficulty in becoming accustomed to domestic diets.

Nuthatches for the most part resemble kingfishers in miniature with heads usually tilted upwards and with bodies usually in other than upright

The Chestnut Breasted Nuthatch is rare, but it is the most readily available member of a curious family. His strong claws enable him to climb trees searching for insects hidden in crevices of the bark. He hangs upside down almost as much as he perches right side up. Hardy and easy to keep, this nuthatch is very entertaining in a shy, secluded manner. Photographed at Palos Verdes Bird Farm.

statures. They like to hang upside down or sideways on tree trunks or branches.

Sexes in Chestnut Breasted Nuthatches are easily distinguished. The male is deep chestnut on the underparts and grayish above. The slightly upturned beak is followed by a black line from the lores to the side of the nape of the neck. The female is paler on the underparts.

There are several Indian species with slight variations. Most have much paler underparts.

VELVET FRONTED NUTHATCH (*Sitta frontalis*)

The most beautiful of all nuthatches is the very colorful Velvet Fronted Nuthatch which ranges from India to Burma and Ceylon. The size is slightly less than five inches long.

The beak is red-orange with a blackish tip. Black in the male covers a large forehead area, lores, and a long trailing eyebrow ending in a slightly expanded and blunt end on the side of the nape. The eye is yellowish-straw with a highly noticeable black pupil. Upperparts are bright and glossy cobalt-blue. Underparts are lavender.

The female lacks the black eyebrow.

This species is very difficult to get, and the writers have seldom been able to obtain it. It is just as charming as the foregoing species and far more colorful; but it is less hardy.

CHAPTER 38

Warblers and Wrens

The very small and delicate birds in this chapter are difficult to get and difficult to keep. Only the most advanced aviculturists attempt these fragile creatures, and the diet must be the most refined of standard softbilled diets.

Fortunately the bird market now offers an all-purpose food which may be substituted for heavy and oily mockingbird food. The standard mockingbird food is quite wrong as a basic diet for these birds because of its indigestibility. Fruits, fruitflies, and various types of small live foods should also be offered. Grated cheese and nectar food are fine additives. Mealworms, if

Two small and delicate native birds deserving care of bird lovers after injuries are the colorful Yellow Warbler (left) and the pert little Chickadee which belongs to the Tit family.

offered at all, should be very small or should be soaked for a few minutes in scalding water to soften the indigestible outer coverings.

Since warblers and wrens are so very seldom available to even the most experienced of aviculturists, there seems little point in going into any detail on any of the various individuals. Those rare exceptions usually are locally injured specimens or trapped birds depending upon natural range. Except in cases of injury where the birds deserve treatment and careful feeding, the writers prefer to bypass these birds. They should not, and probably never will, become favorites in aviculture.

Many are very attractive birds in these two groups. Perhaps most notable are the lovely Fairy Wrens of Australia. Though coveted by several specializing fanciers, actual attainment is a great rarity.

Vireos and Kinglets also fall generally into these groups of birds.

Two native warblers with which American aviculturists may become familiar if they work at nursing injured birds back to health are the pretty little Black and White Warbler (left) and the Myrtle Warbler (right).

Wrens are difficult to maintain in captivity and even more difficult to nurse back to health if they are injured, but the bird lover may succeed in such an attempt if proper directions for a refined diet are followed. These wrens are the House Wren (above) and the Long Billed Marsh Wren (right).

389

All Kinglets, such as this Golden Crowned Kinglet (above), are small and delicate and should be given very refined diets. The basic pattern is the same in most species, but the center of the head varies brightly with different species.

The native Hermit Thrush (below) is another *Hylocichlid* Thrush which is smaller than most in the group. It appreciates any care it is given and readily responds to treatment and handfeeding if injured.

CHAPTER 39

Tanagers, Chlorophonias, and Euphonias

All the birds in this chapter are from the New World. The species available to aviculture are from Mexico, Central America, and South America. Those from the United States are protected and cannot legally be admitted to American aviculture. Some of these protected species extend into Mexico and are occasionally shipped to Europe.

Tanagers encompass several genera including the brilliant Calliste Tanagers, the colorful Euphonias, and the green Chlorophonias. Some tanagers comprise the most popular and colorful of the inexpensive, hardy, and easily acclimated softbills. Some are too colorless to be included in aviculture, and many do not occur in collecting areas. A few show an extremely close relationship to honeycreepers. For the most part, none can be considered as singers.

Most large tanagers are very easily acclimated and very hardy. The smaller chlorophonias, euphonias, and callistes are delicate. These more tender species must be given carefully refined diets balanced between standard softbilled fare and nectarine diets. Greenfood is quite important for tanagers. The larger and hardier species thrive upon standard softbilled diets but usually appreciate the non-essential nectar. Many tanagers are hardy, but the more delicate species must be given heat in cold climates. Temperatures should not drop below 40 or 45° F. Humidity is important for most because of their tropical habitats.

Sizes of tanagers vary considerably. None are large birds, but a few are aggressive to other tanagers and must be carefully watched. The beaks of most are far more blunt on the tip than the conical beaks of finches, but the body shape is otherwise very similar.

Successful breeding is not often accomplished except in the case of Blue Tanagers. Nests of most are rather small and cup-shaped. The incubation period is about twelve days for some and up to twenty-three days for others. Youngsters leave the nest in a surprisingly short time averaging about ten to twelve days. A sufficient weaning period may extend two to three weeks beyond the fledging period. Curiously, those youngsters of species nesting close to the ground leave the nest earlier than those species which nest in high trees.

Chlorophonias build dome-shaped nests with side entrances. Nesting periods for these birds extend slightly beyond three weeks.

BLUE TANAGER (*Thraupis episcopus*)

The most commonly available as well as the least costly tanager is the lovely Blue Tanager from Mexico, Central and South America. This bird is very hardy and easily acclimated. It takes kindly to captivity and is long lived on a standard softbilled diet.

Both sexes are alike in general appearance. Behavior is the true differential test. Blue Tanagers are the most easily bred of all tanagers in captivity.

The total length is six inches long including the tail of slightly more than two inches. The stout half inch beak is black on the upper mandible and silvery-gray on the lower mandible. The eyes are brownish, tinged with a purplish-wine shade. Feet and legs are bluish-gray.

Three shades of blue, all very attractive, cover the entire plumage. Very bright and lustrous cobalt blue occurs on the shoulder patches. The wings and tail are glossy but pale in an odd shade of blue mixed with turquoise. The remaining plumage is a pale and soft blue, rather dull in a way and not far from pale gray. A hint of green softly blends with the blue on the back and the rump.

The Blue Tanager is peaceful and quiet. Its calm blues enhance the brighter and flashier colors found on many other avicultural softbills. It is a fine addition to any collection and is an especially good subject for beginners.

Since the Blue Tanager has a widespread range, some slight variations occur. Most of those birds shipped to commercial aviculture are probably the typical race described above. The scientific name of *Thraupis verescens cana* frequently crops up in avicultural and ornithological literature and is also called the Blue Tanager. The writers have never verified any differences, but this latter species is purported to be the one with the cobalt or violet shoulders. A Mexican species, called Blue-Gray Tanager (*Thraupis virens*), also fits this generalized description.

One quite different race is occasionally imported. The White Winged Blue Tanager (subspecies *coelestis*) has white shoulders and a white wing bar.

The Palm Tanager (*Thraupis palmarum*) is a closely related but separate species. Flights are black, and the rest of the coloring is a hazy mixture of many dull shades, none of which are attractive. The general appearance is a drab gray, but closer observations reveal smoky hints of purple, blue, and green haphazardly distributed and not at all assertive.

The Palm Tanager, often called the Gray Tanager among aviculturists, is a very hardy bird slightly larger than the Blue Tanager. It is not at all popular because of its extremely dull coloration.

STRIATED TANAGER (*Thraupis bonariensis*)

Seldom available to American aviculturists, the Striated Tanager ranges southward from Brazil. It is a very attractive and quite hardy species.

Sexes differ in coloring. The female is dull grayish-brown. Upperparts are darker, and underparts are paler. The throat and rump show a tinge of yellow.

The male is extremely attractive. The beak is silvery-gray with some black on the upper mandible. The feet and legs are grayish-black. Brown eyes are surrounded by black which also covers the lores, chin, and a thin forehead band. The rest of the head is blue down to the lower nape and throat. A narrow black band borders the lower extent of the blue near the upper chest. The mantle, shoulders, and back are solid black. The black wings show pale blue edges on all except the primary flights. Bright yellow covers the rump and all underparts with a touch of orange on rump and upper chest. The uppertail coverts are dark bluish-gray, and the tail feathers are black with blue edges.

A very similar subspecies (*darwinii*) is Darwin's Tanager. It is smaller and has a greenish back.

Some of the remaining species of the genus *Thraupis* are very attractive but not as yet available to aviculturists in the United States. They are from South America out of the reach of normal collecting ranges.

The Archbishop Tanager (*Thraupis ornata*) has a purplish shade on the head, chest, and sides; dark green on the upperparts; yellowish shoulders; and a dull but contrasting grayish-black on remaining areas.

The Blue Capped Tanager (*Thraupis cyanocephala*) and the Olive and Blue Tanager (*Thraupis olivicyanea*) are rather similar but occur in different ranges. The two dominant features are bright blue on the head and underparts and a yellowish-green on the upperparts.

The Yellow Winged Tanager (*Thraupis abbas*) has a purplish shade on the head, black wings with bright yellow patches, black tail, and olive tinges added to the grayish-blue upperparts. Except for the yellow, none of the plumage is bright.

MOUNTAIN TANAGERS (*Compsocoma flavinucha*)

Sharply marked with dazzling brilliance and remarkable contrasts, the Mountain Tanagers from South America easily rank highly among the most beautiful birds in the world. They are highly coveted, reasonably expensive, quite hardy, not often available, and just about the most aggressive members in this chapter. They are also among the largest of all tanagers with a length of nearly eight inches. Sexes are very similar.

No one could pass by this great beauty without an admiring pause or a lingering awesomeness. Black in a jet velvet softness covers the beak, forehead, face, sides of the neck, back, rump, and uppertail coverts cutting a deep V-shaped area on the flanks behind the legs. Parts of the wings are also black.

Brilliant and lustrous cobalt blue emblazons the shoulders followed by a slightly paler shade on the tail and the outer rims of the flight feathers.

A perfect contrast is the vivid yellow on an extensive cap and all the underparts. The feet and legs are grayish-black. The marvelous balances of symmetry of pattern and color brilliance are unbelievable.

The Blue Winged (subspecies *cyanoptera*) and the Blue Shouldered Mountain Tanagers (subspecies *sumptuosa*) are quite similar. The name of the Green Backed Mountain Tanager (subspecies *victorini*) is self-explaining in its only appreciable difference.

The Hooded Mountain Tanager (*Buthraupis montana*) is larger but lacks the yellow cap. The blues and blacks on the upperparts are more subtly blended and include a purplish cast.

CRIMSON COLLARED TANAGER (*Phlogothraupis sanguinolenta*)

The brightly colored Crimson Collared Tanager has a rather restricted range in Mexico and is very seldom available to bird fanciers. It is about seven inches long and is mostly glossy black. The beak is bluish-gray. Bright but deep red covers tail coverts on both sides and covers a broad area from most of the crown to the lower throat and upperchest. The forehead, chin, and facial areas remain black.

RED EARED TANAGER (*Poecilothraupis igniventris*)

The very rare and brilliant Red Eared Tanager is mostly black with some colorful accents nearly as bright as those found on the Mountain Tanagers. Sexes differ in that the red is less vivid and paler, and the ear patches and wing patches are smaller on the female. Bright red forms a crescent-shaped ear patch and brightens the rump and underparts starting with the chest. Very bright blue shoulder patches add a further variation.

SCARLET TANAGERS

Two very similar Scarlet Tanagers are *Ramphocelus brasilius* from South America and *Piranga olivacea* from North America. The latter migrates to northern South America during the winter. The former species is slightly more brilliant and far more likely to be available to aviculture since the other species is prohibited in the United States. Since both are so very similar, the writers have found it a difficult task to prove admissibility of incoming shipments. In most cases, they have found a terse prohibition of all Scarlet Tanagers which just might be an easy way for inspectors who do not completely know the finer details of their jobs.

Scarlet Tanagers, about six and a half inches long, are mostly colored in brilliant red. Black covers the wings and tail. The South American species has a black beak with a silvery-gray base on the lower mandible. The female is dull reddish-brown, darker above and paler below. The North American race has a less intense shade of red and an orange-horn beak with some black atop the upper mandible. Black wing feathers are less extensive. The female is dull greenish above and pale greenish-yellow below.

Youngsters resemble the females.

Both species fade drastically in captivity. A strong color-holding agent is necessary to retain the richness of red. Carotene in oil is the best source for color retention, but soya powder is often used with success.

Scarlet Tanagers are hardy and easily acclimated. They are large and robust and are ideal for aviculture. They occasionally have been bred in captivity but most successes have been in planted aviaries.

The White Winged Tanager (*Piranga leucoptera leucoptera*) is similar except for two white wing bars and a black facial area including the forehead, lores, and eye areas. The size is about five inches long. The female is dulled by yellowish-olive above and golden-yellow below. The wing pattern is present.

SILVER BEAKED TANAGER (*Ramphocelus carbo*)

The darkly glowing Silver Beaked Tanager is one of the more readily available tanagers. It ranges from Trinidad to Peru but usually is available to aviculturists from Colombia. This bird is often erroneously called the Maroon Tanager which is similar but much brighter.

The size is about seven inches long including the tail of two and a half inches. The beak is dark gray with a prominent pearl-gray base on the lower mandible. The wings and tail are dark brown, and the abdomen is blackish. Flanks, rump, and chest are deep maroon-brown. Remaining upperparts are dark reddish-brown.

The Maroon Tanager has the same general size and pattern. However, it is much richer in color and more sharply contrasted. The maroon coloring is especially bright and glowing. The texture is like velvet, and color changes are gradual blends.

ORANGE RUMPED TANAGER (*Ramphocelus flammigrus*)

Also known as the Variable Tanager, the Orange Rumped Tanager from Colombia is slightly over seven inches long with a tail of two and a half inches. The stout beak of a half inch is silvery-gray with black tips. Eyes have a deep shade of burgundy. Feet and legs are gray.

The male is very decidedly colored in two intense shades. A soft velvety black covers the entire plumage except for a vivid and glossy deep red-orange covering the lower half of the back, rump, and uppertail coverts. A few orange feathers occasionally surround the vent.

The female is a dull mixture of brownish-gray, olivaceous-orange, and grayish-black. Females are seldom imported because they are not attractive.

This species is beautifully proportioned, active, and very showy. The tail fans outward whenever the bird so desires. It can be and sometimes is aggressive with smaller birds or other tanagers in the breeding season but is otherwise very peaceful.

The Yellow Rumped Tanager (*Ramphocelus icteronotus*) is exactly the same in every respect except that yellow replaces the orange coloring. This species ranges from Panama to western Ecuador.

The Scarlet Rumped Tanager (*Ramphocelus passerini*) is the same as the above except that bright scarlet replaces the orange or yellow on the above two species.

Another somewhat similar but more variable species is the Crimson or Scarlet Backed Tanager (*Ramphocelus dimidiatus*) which ranges from Panama to Venezuela. Bright blood-red covers the lower chest, lower back, rump, and uppertail coverts. The head, neck, upper back, and upper chest are crimson-maroon. Wings and tail are black, and the abdomen is brownish-black. The black beak has some silver on the lower mandible. This species is more insectivorous than many tanagers and especially requires more meal-worms during the touchy acclimation. The native name is *Sangre de Toro*.

WESTERN TANAGER (*Piranga ludoviciana*)

The attractive and prohibited Western Tanager from the United States and Mexico is about six and a half inches long. The male has a bright red head blending softly and slowly with a yellow which covers all the underparts, rump, and an area down to the mantle. The tail, wings, back, and mantle are black except for two pale yellowish-white wing bars which are quite irregular in design.

Winter plumage of males is somewhat less attractive since the red on the head is greatly reduced and is replaced mostly by a dull olive shade. The beak is brownish.

The female is far less colorful with yellowish-olive upperparts except for very dusky wings and dull yellowish underparts. The wing bars are present but greatly reduced in intensity. The beak is brownish.

The writers have had a few of these wonderful birds brought to them injured or exhausted from migration. They recuperate rapidly and can be liberated in a very short time. They happily become domesticated and are ideal aviary birds, but they are illegal in the United States.

SUMMER TANAGER (*Piranga rubra rubra*)

Another tanager native to the United States and not ever likely to be available to aviculturists is the Summer Tanager. This bird ranges from New Jersey to Florida with migrations extending to Cuba, Mexico, Central and South America. It is well worth mentioning because it is not a shy bird and may frequently become the target of juvenile marksmen. Injured specimens may be brought to those people who love birds and will take the time required for nursing them back to health.

The length is about seven inches, and coloring differs between the sexes. The male is in full color only after several years. Adult male plumage shows an overall red in varying shades. The crown and rump are brightest, and the wings and tail are shaded with brown. Underparts are clearer but have a darker shade of red.

The female is basically a pale olive-green with yellowish accents on the crown, rump, and underparts. The wings are dulled by gray. Immature males are basically like females but show blotches of red in varying degrees according to age.

Cooper's Summer Tanager (*Piranga rubra cooperi*) is the subspecies counterpart in western United States and western Mexico. The red coloring is paler, and the size is slightly larger. The beak is yellowish-brown.

HEPATIC TANAGER (*Piranga flava hepatica*)

The Hepatic Tanager may become available to European aviculture from Mexico, but it is illegal in the United States. It is very similar to Cooper's Summer Tanager described above, but the male is darker red and both sexes have a black beak. The male also has a cheek patch of brown.

BLACK TANAGER (*Tachyphonus rufus*)

The handsome and velvety Black Tanager from South America is a great contrast in the family of tanagers. The length is about eight inches. The male is entirely jet black except for a little white bar on the wings which is partially hidden while the wings are folded. The female is reddish-brown and because of this very dull coloration is very seldom imported. The male has a more pleasant song than found in most tanagers.

This Black Tanager is a very hardy and a most pleasant addition to any aviary. Its main beauty is the softness and velvety texture of the black plumage. The coloring and peaceful demeanor enhance the more colorful birds in most collections.

Another Black Tanager, the larger Red Crowned Black Tanager (*Tachyphonus coronatus*), from South America, has a red stripe down the crown. This handsome bird is quite aware of its added attractiveness and frequently expands the bright stripe conspicuously during the nuptial display. The white wing bar is less noticeable.

Both species are hardy.

MAGPIE TANAGER (*Cissopsis leveriana*)

From the north of South America comes the large Magpie Tanager. Both sexes are alike in their black and white plumage. Upperparts are black, and underparts from the lower chest are white. Eyes are yellow. The Lesser Magpie Tanager (subspecies *leveriana*) comes from Ecuador and is very similar.

SWALLOW TANAGER (*Tersina viridis*)

The short but broad-beaked Swallow Tanager from Central and Northern South America is a great rarity in aviculture. It is not hardy. This bird is about six inches in length. The male is particularly lovely. Most of his plumage is an exquisite shade of turquoise. Blackish shading occurs on the flights and on abdominal striations. A prominent mask of black covers the beak, forehead, face, chin, and throat. Eyes are golden-orange with black pupils, and lower underparts are whitish.

The female lacks the black facial area and is mainly greenish with turquoise wing patches. Sides, lower chest, and remaining underparts are pale yellow with greenish striations. The beak is blackish but is less intense than that of the male.

This species is delicate and should be housed in a conservatory aviary in most areas.

PRETRE'S or SPINDALIS TANAGER (*Spindalis zena*)

The Spindalis or Stripe Headed Tanager available to aviculturists comes from Mexico. Pretre's Tanager is a subspecies from Cuba but is otherwise much the same. The size is about six inches in length, and sexes are different in coloring.

The male shows black with two alternate stripes of white on the head. A neck collar of brownish-orange is followed by an olive mantle. The chest is dull orange. Tail and wings are black with white wing bars.

GRAY HEADED TANAGER (*Eucometes penicillata*)

The sweet singing Gray Headed Tanager with several fairly large-sized subspecies, some lightly crested, occurs from Mexico through Costa Rica, Panama, and Nicaragua. This is an exceptionally rare form in captivity. Both sexes are alike.

A black beak and dark eyes contrast pleasantly with the gray of the head and neck. Olive-green occurs on the remaining upperparts, and yellow brightens the underparts.

RED ANT TANAGER (*Habia rubica*)

Another pleasant songster, the Red Ant Tanager has mostly been omitted from aviculture. With a size of about seven inches in length, this bird shows a dull coloration and a difference in sexes. The male is darkly and dully clothed in subdued red. A scarlet, occasionally erectile crest concentrates down the center of the head and is flanked on the sides by fine black lines. The female is mostly dull olive with a quiet shade of yellow on the throat. The crest is less conspicuous and is dull orange in color.

CALLISTE TANAGERS

The really fantastic beauty of most tanagers occurs in the extensive and variable group of Calliste Tanagers. Sexes are usually alike. The richness of colors and minutely defined pattern variations provide some of the world's most beautiful birds. They are not good singers, but the dazzling colors and patterns are completely adequate beyond expectations. No one could sensibly also ask for a song after seeing such visions of loveliness.

Callistes are smaller than the aforementioned tanagers and considerably more delicate, but they are excellent aviary birds if given proper diet and accommodations.

MRS. WILSON'S or GOLDEN MASKED TANAGER (*Tangara nigrocincta*)

There are several subspecies of the Golden Masked Tanager, but all are aviculturally called by the names of Golden Masked or Mrs. Wilson's Tanager.

398

The minor variations seem to be in size rather than in color.

This is a very beautiful bird with unusual color features. The beak and a small facial area covering the lores, forehead, and surrounding the eyes are black. These areas are followed by a metallic turquoise which is particularly noticeable on the forehead and cheeks.

The remaining parts of the head, neck, and throat show a very strange and elusive coloring which is unique in the bird world. A rich golden-buff with a honeyed mellowness and a metallic shading show variations of brilliance according to light and the viewing angle. This area is especially difficult to photograph effectively.

Most of the remaining plumage is black except for brilliant turquoise on the rump, undertail coverts, and sides. A bright wing patch is also metallic turquoise. Outer webs of the flight feathers are emblazoned with a greenish shade of turquoise. Underparts below the black chestband are dull white. Feet and legs are blackish.

The entire pattern is deftly arranged in slightly varying and almost indescribable shades and hues. Youngsters are mainly cloaked in dull green shades with gray on the chest, buffish-white on the abdomen, and blackish on the wings and tail.

SILVER THROATED TANAGER (*Tangara icterocephala*)

Most importations containing Mrs. Wilson's Tanager will also have some Silver Throated Tanagers. Though less attractive, or at least less dramatic in coloring, the Silver Throated Tanager is slightly larger and is a bird of strong fascination and pleasant disposition for any collection. It is usually less expensive and hardier than the above.

Sexes are alike, but males are often slightly brighter. The forehead, crown, and face are bright yellow bordered on the lower areas by a black line which also covers part of the lores. The beak is silver-gray, and the eyes are reddish-brown. The chin, throat, and a tapering band through the nape are silvery-white. Remaining underparts and rump are bright yellow. The mantle, back, and shoulders are basically yellow with black markings nearly equalling the yellow areas. Primary and secondary flights and tail feathers are blackish with greenish edges.

BLACK EARED GOLDEN TANAGER (*Tangara arthus*)

The extremely handsome Black Eared Tanager occurs in mountainous areas from Venezuela to Bolivia. Sexes are alike. The picture in this book hardly does justice to this bird's great beauty because it does not convey the smoothness of the golden-yellow beauty of most of the plumage. The black beak is slightly surrounded by black plumage followed by black eyes, a small black triangle behind the eyes, and a large black cheek or ear patch following the eyes. The wings and tail are mainly black with golden yellow and white edges on most of the feathers. All remaining plumage is a smooth and sunny golden-yellow. The Venezuelan subspecies *arthus* has brown underparts.

FLAME CROWNED TANAGER (*Tangara parzudakii*)

Also called the Black Eared and Orange Faced Tanager, the rather large Flame Crowned Tanager from South America is a very rare beauty. Sexes are alike. Avicultural specimens are very seldom available and are delicate at first. The species name is sometimes spelled *pardusakii*.

The predominant coloring is a flaming red covering the forehead, crown, and part of the cheeks. The black beak follows with adjacent velvety-black plumage which covers the chin and lores and surrounds the dark eyes. The red blends into a yellowish shade on the lower facial area. A huge hind cheek area is black separated from black upperparts by yellowish-orange on the top and dull whitish on the sides of the neck. Underparts are very dull brownish-buff with dark undertail coverts. Most of the upperparts are black. White on the lower back and rump fades into a pale bluish-white on the uppertail coverts. A dull grayish-white wing bar is followed by some turquoise markings on the wing.

The Flame Crowned Tanager is an excellent addition to aviculture and is reasonably hardy after a touchy acclimation period.

The Spangle Cheeked Tanager from high up in the mountains of Costa Rica and Panama is scientifically called *Tangara dowi*. This dark and large species has black on its head, throat, cheeks, and neck. Some green spangles occur on the cheeks and neck. The mantle is blackish, and the rump is greenish. A touch of red occurs in the middle of the crown. Blue borders occur on the black feathers of the tail and wings. A buffish-brown occurs on the underparts except for black and green on the chest.

CHESTNUT HEADED or BLUE RUMPED GREEN TANAGER
(*Tangara gyrola*)

The Blue Rumped Green Tanager is one of eight similar races of Chestnut Headed Tanagers which follow the same basic and simple pattern. The head is chestnut or brownish-bronze; the beak is black or grayish; the feet and legs are blackish-gray; and the remaining plumage is basically green with variable shades of blue according to differing races. The species is about four and a half inches long and has a build which is slight for a tanager and heavy for a honeycreeper. Eyes are deep reddish-brown. Sexes are alike, but in some races the female is paler.

The species described thus far ranges from Costa Rica to Bolivia and the Guianas. The Green Shouldered Tanager from Colombia (subspecies *deleticia*) has a more slender shape and more of a blue shade on the underparts. The subspecies *desmaresti*, called Desmarest's Tanager from Venezuela, has more of a reddish tint on the head and a more uniform green covering the remaining plumage except for a brownish tinge on the wings. The Ecuadorian Red Headed Calliste Tanager is the subspecies *nupera* which hails from Ecuador and southwestern Colombia. The Bay Headed Tanager (subspecies *bangsi*) has a yellow nuchal collar, a yellowish wing patch, blue underparts, brown thighs, and green vent.

SPOTTED or YELLOW BROWED TANAGER (*Tangara chrysophrys*)
Another appropriate name for the Yellow Browed or Spotted Emerald Tanager is the occasional popular name of Speckled Tanager. The body is rather plump, and the beak is short and thick. The tail is also rather short. In a uniform coloration, many people might feel that the proportions are too stout to be attractive, but the black spangled effect and finely etched pattern are so unusual and interesting that no one notices the shape.

Most of the plumage is bright but soft green. Yellow on the facial area, most prominent on the eyebrow, shades quietly into the green. The throat, chest, and most underparts are whitish with a gradual change to dull grayish-green with a hint of yellow on the flanks, abdomen, and undertail coverts. The beak, lores, feet, and legs are blackish. The eyes are also dark.

Upperparts from the crown to back and underparts on the chest and sides are beautifully spangled with black spots. Some turquoise surrounds many of the small black spots and is particularly noticeable around the larger black areas found in the wings. The tail is green with some black areas.

This is a very unusually patterned bird. Most spotted patterns are of little consequence as far as beauty is concerned, but this is a most magnificent exception.

There are several races and similar species. The one described above is the most usually available species. It ranges from Costa Rica down to Venezuela and Ecuador and is also present on Trinidad.

BLACK AND GREEN or SCALY BREASTED TANAGER (*Tangara nigroviridis*)
Delicate and seldom available, the beautiful Black and Green Tanager from Ecuador is also called the Scaly Breasted Tanager. The beak, forehead, chin, and much of the face are velvety black. The crown, lower facial area, sides of the neck, back, and rump are bright turquoise in an indefinable mixture of blue and green. Some of the wing and tail feathers are bordered in blue. The chest also is clad in scaly turquoise markings. The eyes show a bright reddish-brown surrounding black pupils.

This species is difficult to keep and rarely arrives in good condition. Once acclimated, it becomes half hardy in proper surroundings; but it is often the target of closely related bullies.

BLUE NECKED TANAGER (*Tangara cyanicollis coeruleucephala*)
The very rare and quite small Blue Necked Tanager from Eucador has a brilliant blue on the head and neck. A pale turquoise-green with a silvery tinge covers the shoulders, lower back, and rump. Wing and tail feathers are mostly black but have turquoise borders. Velvety black covers the lores, chin, mantle, and underparts.

401

YELLOW CROWNED TANAGER (*Tangara xanthocephala*)

The small Yellow Crowned Tanager along with similarly named sub-species is a small and rarely available bird ranging from Colombia to Bolivia. Black covers the forehead, chin, throat, lores and a ring around the eyes. Black also covers the mantle, wings, tail, and a nuchal collar with some green bordering the feathers on the wings, tail, and mantle. Golden-yellow covers the cheeks and crown. Turquoise-green covers the back, rump, chest, and sides. A buffish-brown shade covers the abdomen and ventral areas.

A subspecies called the Golden Headed Tanager has a brighter shade of yellow.

RUFOUS CROWNED TANAGER (*Tangara cayana*)

The main challenge in the domestication of the Rufous Crowned Tanager is in its touchy acclimation period. It is not a particularly beautiful species despite its delicacy. After acclimation, however, it proves itself as being very hardy. It ranges from Colombia to Brazil.

A reddish-brown marks the crown after a black facial patch. A dull turquoise-green covers the mantle, back, and most of the underparts. Wings and tail are bordered with bluish-green.

BLUE WINGED TANAGER (*Tangara cyanoptera*)

The nondescript Blue Winged Tanager from Venezuela is one of the few Calliste Tanagers which is not lovely although it does well in captivity. The head, neck, and throat are black. The wings are mostly blackish, but blue highlights provide prominent edges. The tail is blackish. Remaining plumage is very dull and is washed with a tinge of green. Black occurs on some of the outer tips of the feathers. The female is even less colorful.

PLAIN COLORED TANAGER (*Tangara inornata*)

The Plain Colored Tanager which ranges from Mexico to the middle of Colombia fully lives up to its name. It is not a favorite in avicultural circles. The only bright coloring is a dash of blue on the wings. Remaining plumage is gray. Upperparts are more slaty, and underparts range from light gray on the chest to a whitish shade on the abdomen. Sexes are alike.

SUPERB TANAGER (*Tangara fastuosa*)

The rare, fairly hardy, and superlative Superb Tanager from eastern Brazil is one of the most excellent examples of Calliste Tanagers. Its great beauty would be difficult to surpass in the bird world. The size is about five inches long, and sexes are alike. The head, chin, and nape are green. The broad back of black connects in a narrow line to a black throat patch. The beak, a small loreal area, and very small forehead are also black. Orange-red occurs on the lower back, rump, and uppertail coverts; and some yellow occurs in the wings. Blue covers the remaining areas with some shades of black on the wings and tail. Underparts are considerably paler but are nevertheless bright blue.

A closely related species is the Tricolored Tanager (*Tangara tricolor*) from southeastern Brazil. In this slightly smaller species, the red-orange is replaced by yellow on the rump. Underparts have some green next to the blue. Bluish-green also occurs in the wings.

The Paradise Tanager (*Tangara paradisea*) from South America is similar. The green of the head is paler and far less extensive with a black replacement above and a deep blue replacement below. Some yellow replaces the orange-red on the lower rump and uppertail coverts. The wings show an absence of yellow. A large throat patch is very dark blue, and the remaining underparts are of a much paler shade of blue.

BLUE AND BLACK TANAGER (*Tanagrella cyanomelaena*)

The handsome and small Blue and Black Tanager has yellow on the crown and rump and pale chestnut on the underparts starting with the abdomen and continuing through the undertail coverts. Black covers most of the remaining upperparts except for a blue shoulder patch and bluish edges on the wing and tail feathers. A bold collar crosses the underside of the neck. The remaining underparts are blue down to the upper chest and sides.

Sexes are distinguishable by the duller and more greenish shade on the head of the female.

CHLOROPHONIAS

The basic characteristics of chlorophonias are the major green coloring, large heads, thick necks, and short but blunt black beaks of one-fourth of an inch in length. None of these birds are quite as hardy as most of the tanagers, and none are easily acclimated to domestic diets. Most chlorophonias are about three and three-fourths inches long including the tail of one and one-fourth inches, but there are some variations in size. Most tanagers and euphonias are far more attractive than most chlorophonias. Therefore, most fanciers do not offer suitable consideration to this group despite their low prices.

Chlorophonias are, as a rule, delicate birds which must be given the more refined softbilled diets and nectar food.

As a rule, most of the chlorophonias in importations are immature birds. Adult coloration comes from one to two years of age, and youngsters are likely to be dismissed as unworthy of avicultural consideration during this time. Sexes usually differ considerably with males carrying the more colorful banners. Immatures and females are usually colored about the same in a dull greenish shade with variations according to species.

The Blue Crowned or Turquoise Naped Chlorophonia (*Chlorophonia occipitalis*), shown in this book in an immature stage, is a species ranging from southeastern Mexico to northern Nicaragua. It is also called the Mexican Green Tanager. The male, in addition to his main color of green, has turquoise on the crown and on the nape. Yellow occurs on the forehead and on a stripe above the eyes and on most of the underparts below the upperchest. A black

403

or brown band separates the green from the yellow on the chest. The sides and flanks are green. The female and immature males have more green, less blue, and less yellow and are much less colorful.

The Green Chlorophonia (*Chlorophonia chlorocapilla*) has blue above the eyes, on the nape, and on the rump. This is a slightly smaller and more delicate Brazilian species which is seldom available.

The male Golden Browed Chlorophonia (*Chlorophonia callophrys*) is very similar in pattern to the Blue Crowned Tanager, but it is much larger.

EUPHONIAS

The euphonias present a slightly more extensive and more popular selection of varieties to aviculturists than chlorophonias, and they are more colorful. The general shape of the body and beak is very similar. The size of most species is slightly less than four inches. Males are colorful, and females are usually dull green.

The diet for euphonias is the same as for chlorophonias. It should be of a refined nature and should include nectar. The writers have always found both chlorophonias and euphonias to be extremely peaceful to closely related birds as well as to finches. Because most are small, they have never included these birds with any larger softbills who might be aggressive.

Some euphonias can be considered as quite pleasant songsters.

The Scrub Euphonia (*Tanagra affinis*) is named because of its preference for dry and scrubby districts in Mexico. The approximate size is about three and a half inches. The female is grayish-olive, brighter on the upperparts with highlights on the forehead and rump and paler and duller on the underparts. The male shows bright yellow on a head patch which includes the forehead and forepart of the crown. Bright yellow again starts between the lower throat and upper chest and continues through the remaining underparts. The remaining upperparts, chin, and throat are black with a high purple gloss.

The Scrub Euphonia is also called Lesson's Euphonia. A subspecies (*godmani*) has white on the undertail coverts and is called the Pale Vented Euphonia.

Bonaparte's Euphonia (*Tanagra lauta*) from southern Mexico to western Panama is very similar. The male, however, has the golden-yellow extending on the underparts through the chin and throat. A small amount of white occurs in the wing. The female is similar to the above species.

The Violet Tanager (*Tanagra violacea*) is very similar but with perhaps more violet glossiness in the black areas. This species occurs from the Guianas to southeastern Brazil and is more likely to be available in Europe than in the United States.

The Yellow Crowned Euphonia (*Tanagra luteicapilla*) from Central America is also similar to the Scrub Euphonia. The black throat of the male

404

is present, but the yellow is far more extensive on the crown and reaches nearly to the nape.

The Blue Hooded Euphonia (*Tanagra musica*) from Mexico is an extreme rarity in aviculture. It is about four inches in length. Bright blue glosses the crown, nape, and sides of the neck. Remaining upperparts, sides of the head, and throat are black with glossy purples and blues. Remaining underparts and forehead are reddish-brown. The female is like most hen euphonias except for a pale shade of chestnut on the forehead and bright blue on the crown and nape. Several subspecies occur, but none differ appreciably from the above described pattern.

Gould's or Olive Backed Euphonia (*Tanagra gouldi*), also from Mexico, is about three and a half inches long. Upperparts of the male are glossy in a brownish shade of olive. The throat and chest are dull olive. The forehead is bright yellow, but remaining underparts are dull brownish with some flecks of olive on the sides. The female is like most female Euphonias except for a dull chestnut shade on the forehead and a dull brownish on the undertail coverts.

CHAPTER 40

Honeycreepers

If this book were a worldwide bird watchers' manual or a book slanted towards ornithology, bananaquits and honeyeaters would come within the scope of this chapter. Since it is mainly an avicultural treatise, the above varieties must be omitted since they are not available to modern aviculture despite their desirability in many instances. This chapter is therefore narrowed down to the fascinating and lovely honeycreepers.

Honeycreepers, often called Sugar Birds, are closely related to tanagers; but they have long, slender nectar-feeding beaks. There are two basic groups. One group is typified by the Yellow Winged Sugar Bird. The other is typified by the Black Headed Sugar Bird which has a less sharp beak and closely resembles many calliste tanagers in appearance and habits. Ornithologists, interested in anatomy sometimes more than general habits, have placed them in a closer relationship than would most aviculturists who look mostly to appearance and general care to determine categories. The opinions of ornithologists must not be discredited or overlooked. Indeed, they have given aviculturists a greater insight in the proper care of most members of the tanager family. Tanagers, especially the more delicate callistes, should be fed with a close attention to the needs of most honeycreepers. Adaptations and inclusions of the basic diet of honeycreepers are most important for many tanagers.

The honeycreepers of Mexico, Central America, and South America are very important to aviculture. Reasonably easy to maintain with certain special dietary requirements, honeycreepers are the most easily obtainable of nectar feeders to aviculturists in the United States. They are less available to European fanciers but are more highly coveted in most countries of Europe.

The diet of different honeycreepers is variable during the touchy acclimation period. The hardiest and most readily available is the Blue Honeycreeper or Yellow Winged Sugar Bird. Other forms are very rare in aviculture. The basic diet for the Blue Honeycreeper is simple. Nectar, as described in Chapter 2, is the basis. Sponge cake, fresh fruits, and mynah meal rather than heavy and oily mockingbird food should be offered. Small live insects or very small mealworms should also be offered.

Other honeycreepers do well on the same diet, but the acclimation period is more difficult. The inclusion of a well established and domesticated Yellow Winged Sugar Bird helps to wean others onto the domesticated diet.

Honeycreepers are small, peaceful, and very tame birds. They often are housed with finches in average aviaries. Perches quickly become soiled and must be cleaned often. Some of the more rare and more delicate species fare better if given accommodations in conservatory aviaries. In such environments, honeycreepers, with a lush background of tropical foliage, were once beautifully described as "flying flowers" because of their vivid and flashing colors. Whoever originally bestowed this term on these or other birds deserves commendation for such an accurate and appropriate description.

Honeycreepers are among the world's loveliest birds. The shapes may be ordinary, but the colors of most species are magnificent during the "in color" phase.

Males out of color and females are similarly undistinguished by soft and drab colors.

Yellow Winged Sugar Birds have been bred in captivity. The female incubates in the delicately constructed nest for twelve or thirteen days. Both sexes feed the youngsters for about fourteen days.

The domestication of honeycreepers to the fullest degree will still require much effort on the part of bird fanciers. The most serious and dedicated aviculturists have sometimes succeeded but have often been remiss in reporting adequate details to avicultural periodicals. Adequate maintenance is very often achieved, but the true test is in the willingness of the birds to breed. In addition to acclimation, a difficult period for male honeycreepers occurs during the changeover to nuptial plumage. This phase requires extra live foods and very close attention to diet.

YELLOW WINGED SUGAR BIRD (*Cyanerpes cyaneus*)

The beautiful Yellow Winged Sugar Bird, often called the Blue Honeycreeper and sometimes called the Red Legged Honeycreeper, is only four inches long including a tail of one and one-fourth inches. The black beak is five-eighths of an inch long.

The male in color is a dazzling jewel; but out of color he resembles the drably colored female in soft, plain green. While he is in the eclipse plumage phase, his legs remain bright red while the female's legs are very dark with only a slight tinge of red. Sexual distinction is therefore always obvious.

While in nuptial plumage, the male glows in black and royal-blue. Vivid accents are a heavy metallic cap of turquoise and bright flashes of yellow covering the major portions of the underside of the wing. Noticeable only while in flight, this accent gives the bird its name. While out of color, the yellow remains in a greatly reduced shade.

Deep royal-blue surrounds the turquoise patch and covers the chest, sides, and part of the abdomen. On the upperparts, the same shade occurs on a broad area in a V-shaped pattern emanating from the tip of the forewings to the back. The rump is of the same shade. An elliptical black marking covers the lores and extends behind the black eye. Remaining coloration is velvet-black.

PURPLE SUGAR BIRD or YELLOW LEGGED HONEYCREEPER
(Cyanerpes caeruleus)

The brilliant Purple Sugar Bird, usually called the Yellow Legged Honeycreeper in the United States, is smaller than the Yellow Winged Sugar Bird. The basic size is three and a half inches long including the tail which is slightly less than an inch long. The black beak is approximately a half inch long.

The male glows in a slightly darker shade of deep, nearly violet, royal-blue than found on the Yellow Winged Sugar Bird. This shade is, however, not really purple. The turquoise cap is missing, but a black throat bib has been added. A black eye patch covers lores and extends slightly behind the eyes. The wings, tail, and vent are black. The remaining color is the lustrous blue described above. The legs are outstanding in bright yellow and are contrastingly tipped in black toenails.

The female has rusty-orange patches on the sides of the face and on the throat. Undersides are slightly blotched with yellow, and the remaining areas are green. Her beak is blackish, and her feet and legs are grayish.

The Purple Sugar Bird from South America is perhaps second in availability among this group, but it still is a great rarity in the United States. It is not as hardy, and the acclimation period is quite difficult.

A similar subspecies, *isthmicus*, is called the Isthmian Sugar Bird. This race occurs in a more northerly range, mainly in the vicinity of Panama. The Shining Sugar Bird *(Cyanerpes lucidus)* of Mexico and Central America is slightly larger and brighter. Otherwise it is the same as the Purple Sugar Bird. Both of the above are seldom available to aviculturists.

BLACK HEADED SUGAR BIRD *(Chlorophanes spiza)*

Third in availability in the family of honeycreepers is the Black Headed Sugar Bird from South America. This species is larger than most other honeycreepers and more closely resembles a few of the intermediate calliste tanagers. It reaches nearly five inches in length and has a rather heavy body. It is an extremely handsome bird with a thicker and less curved beak than found on any of the above species. It also is more easily acclimated.

Color divisions are smooth, sharp, and nicely contrasted. The upper mandible is black, and the lower mandible is a creamy yellow. The eyes are reddish-brown. The jet black head forms a curious pattern which uniquely enhances the beauty of this vivid bird. The boundary of the black starts at the rear of the crown and curves down around the cheeks dropping to a point on the sides of the lower end of the throat. It then cuts sharply up to the lower beak.

The rest of the coloring is lustrous turquoise-bluish-green. Some areas lean towards greenish shades, and others lean towards bluish shades. Feet and legs are grayish.

The female has the same coloring on the beak and body but lacks the black on the head.

This species is inclined to be less peaceful than the honeycreepers listed above.

One subspecies (*guatemalensis*) is called the Guatemalan Green Sugar Bird. This is a Central American race with a smaller and less distinctive pattern of black on the head. Another subspecies (*subtropicalis*) occurs in Colombia. Green Sugar Birds are usually very aggressive and should not be kept with other honeycreepers.

BLUE SUGAR BIRD (*Dacnis cyana* or *Dacnis cayana*)

The Blue Sugar Bird, ranging from southern Mexico to Brazil, is much like the foregoing in shape although it is slightly smaller. Black masks the large throat area, back, the mantle, wings, and tail. Except for the black eye patch covering the lores and a tapering strip behind the eyes, the remaining color is turquoise-blue. The beak is like that of the above species but is slightly less distinctive.

The female is basically green but has a tinge of yellow on the underparts. It has a grayish throat.

The Red Thighed Sugar Bird (*Dacnis venusta*) of South America is similar to the above except for more extensive blue and red thighs. The female is also similar to the above species except for a bluish rump and buff abdomen.

CHAPTER 41

Zosterops and Sunbirds

All the members of this chapter are mainly nectar feeders. White Eyes, or Zosterops, are the lowest in cost, most readily available, hardiest, and easiest to maintain.

Only two species of sunbirds are regularly offered. These are from India, but they are very rarely imported. Sunbirds are very delicate in captivity until the initial acclimation phase and transfer to domestic diets have been completed. Even then, they are not easily maintained in standard accommodations.

Spider hunters are closely related to sunbirds and are widely spread over India, Borneo, Burma, Malaysia, and the Philippines. They are shaped like sunbirds but have dull greenish colors. Since they are as difficult to maintain as sunbirds and far less attractive, they are not important in aviculture. The diet should be the same as for sunbirds except for additional live food.

Flower peckers are in some ways related to sunbirds. Though many are very pretty and are sometimes offered from India at low prices, American importers nearly always bypass them. They are difficult to acclimate, and the slight demand is hardly worth the efforts. The beaks on these birds are far more blunt and short and the bodies stockier than those of sunbirds. The writers would therefore offer them a basic sunbird diet plus extra quantities of fruits.

WHITE EYES (genus *Zosterops*)

White Eyes or Zosterops of the family *Zosteropidae* are sometimes called Spectacle Birds, and in Australia they are called Silver Eyes. The eighty-five species and many subspecies are distributed over a huge area from Africa and India to Australia. Of the twelve genera, only twenty-two species fall outside the genus Zosterops; and they are not important in aviculture.

Most of the differences in the varying species are extremely slight. Size, extent of eye ring, and slight variations in coloring do not change the basic aspects. Most of the Zosterops reaching aviculture arrive from India, Japan, or Hong Kong. All are essentially the same, and the Indian or Oriental White

410

The White Eye or *Zosterops* is a somberly colored little softbill with a very prominent white eye ring. Abundant and inexpensive, it is one of the easiest to keep of all small softbills and is surely one of the most charming. Photographed at Palos Verdes Bird Farm.

Eye (*Zosterops palpebrosa*) adequately deserves a description. Others need not be mentioned because of unavailability.

The overall coloring is dull olive-green, darker above and somewhat yellowish on the throat and central chest area. The abdomen is grayish. This coloring fades slightly in captivity on a standard diet. A bright and prominent ring of small white feathers surrounds the eyes and gives the popular name of White Eye. The small blackish beak is slender, sharp, and curved in the tradition of nectar feeders. The size is small, about two and a half inches long. Sexes are very difficult to distinguish, but the male usually has a more prominent yellow on the throat and chest.

In general appearance, Zosterops look more like warblers, but they are more closely related to sunbirds. They are excellent subjects for the novice aviculturist to gain experience with some of the smaller and more delicate softbills.

White Eyes are very hardy and are easy to feed. They seem to love aviculture. They use the standard nectar food plus fruit, sponge cake, peanut butter, live food, and mynah meal. The writers have offered mynah pellets on most occasions in place of meal with utmost success. The birds seem to prefer them over the meal. The writers always give soya powder instead of milk in the nectar food. The soya powder is fed dry in a separate dish. White Eyes are always the first to take to it and quickly teach others to do the same.

Highly insectivorous by nature, White Eyes are very adept at catching small insects in flight. Flies, small moths, and fruitflies are quickly snapped up. Keen attention and watchful waiting are the keynotes when any insect ventures into an aviary containing White Eyes. Good judgment and swift action always result in speedy capture.

White Eyes do not require conservatory aviaries as do hummingbirds and sunbirds, but they greatly appreciate planted aviaries. Small flowering shrubs which attract insects are particularly valuable in supplying the live food requirements of these birds.

Zosterops are peaceful and are good companions for even the smallest of finches. They are active and evasive enough to be housed with most softbills ranging up to the size of the Red Eared Bulbul.

In every way, the lovable White Eye is an excellent addition to any bird fancier's collection. The writers have had up to a hundred at a time and have found them to be among the most easily maintained of all softbills. Moreover, their great charm and beguiling activity easily steal the spotlight of attention from such colorful birds as the Lady Gould Finch. The writers happily include them among their prime favorites in aviculture.

White Eyes have been reared in captivity, but such an accomplishment is a very noteworthy success reflecting great skill of the aviculturist in supplying every requirement. The fibrous and suspended nests are small with fine grasses and spider webs included in the construction. Incubation usually takes eleven or twelve days, and fledging ordinarily occurs between nine and thirteen days. Youngsters are weaned between two and three weeks after leaving the nest. Both parents assist in rearing the young and in incubation.

SUNBIRDS

The vast and colorful family of beautiful sunbirds is the Old World's component and nearest similarity to the hummingbirds of the New World. Actually, they are not related. They have far less flying skill, but they have far greater use of their legs. The colors of most males are brilliant and heavily iridescent. Sizes range from three to eight inches long including the elongated tail streamers found on some species. Females are usually very dull in coloring and lacking in extra ornamentations. Several species show particularly dull coloration and will never be popular in aviculture.

The diet is the same formula as given to hummingbirds. Sugar requirements are not as high because of the reduced energy output. Some sunbirds enjoy a little soft fruit and may take other small insects, but the mainstay is the special nectar food and fruitflies. Sponge cake is also appreciated.

Housing, for most species, is best in humid conservatory aviaries or temperature controlled bird rooms. European fanciers often keep sunbirds in large cages about three feet long. Perches must be replaced or cleaned often in such housing.

Sunbirds are found most frequently in better zoos or in the collections

412

of advanced aviculturists in Europe. British bird fanciers almost annually bench several fine specimens at their major bird shows. In America, sunbirds are nearly nonexistent; but the writers hope to add a little interest by spotlighting a few selected individuals which have successfully been maintained in aviculture.

Sunbirds do not travel easily and must be given utmost care after reaching their destination.

Of the one hundred and four species and many subspecies in existence ranging through Africa and India and extending to Australia, New Guinea, and the Philippines, relatively few will ever become available to aviculture. But those that do will be among the brightest and glowing stars of aristocratic aviculture.

One short chapter cannot hope to be a full representation of this great family. Nothing less than a full book would do justice to these vivid birds. Instead, this chapter is meant as an introduction to sunbirds with a suggestion that this is a highly specialized branch of aviculture. Successful fanciers should contribute frequently to avicultural periodicals to expand present knowledge. Availability usually comes only after a sufficient demand.

PURPLE RUMPED SUNBIRD (*Nectarinia zeylonica*)
One of the two most readily available sunbirds is the Purple Rumped Sunbird ranging from India to Ceylon. The colors are brilliant; but the short tail and stocky body of this species lend a rather ordinary appearance to an extraordinary family.

The male has the entire head and upperparts glossed in purplish-bronze with extra purplish highlights on the rump. Chest and underparts are bright yellow fading slightly on the abdomen, flanks, and undertail coverts. Some subspecies have noticeable green glosses on the top of the head.

The female is similar in shape and has a faded shade of yellow on the chest. Upperparts are dull brownish with no iridescent brilliance or purplish shading. The size of both sexes is small and approximates the overall silhouette and general size of the White Eye.

The generic name of this species is often in dispute among aviculturists. In addition to the above genus name, *Cinnyris*, *Cyrtostomus*, and *Leptocoma* are interchangeably used by ornithologists. Most of these names have doubtlessly been relegated to a former status, but the writers will not presume to say which generic name will supersede the others.

PURPLE SUNBIRD (*Nectarinia asiatica*)
The Indian Purple Sunbird is the second most likely available in the family of sunbirds. It too is saddled with disagreements in generic names. Besides *Nectarinia*, the Purple Sunbird is known by such other generic names as *Cinnyris*, *Cyrtostomus*, and *Leptocoma*. Several subspecies give slight variations.

The main difference of the male from the male Purple Rumped Sunbird is the glossy purplish-black underparts. Tufts of yellow and red occur on the undersides of the shoulders.

Eclipse plumage of the male resembles the female with brownish upperparts and head of varying shades and pale yellow on the chest and underparts. The male in out of season coloring has shades of black on the wings and tail and a black streak down the middle of the throat and chest.

MALACHITE SUNBIRD (*Nectarinia famosa*)

The Malachite Sunbird from Africa is beautifully shaped but not brilliantly colored. Moreover, the male undergoes an eclipse plumage phase. The main charm lies in two long and graceful central tail feather extensions which balance the very long curved beak.

The main coloring is dark glossy green burnished with coppery highlights. The beak, feet and legs, flights, and tail feathers are blackish. Abdominal areas are dark blue, and some yellow occurs on the flanks. The chest has scaly striations of dark iridescence.

The female has dull brown replacing the green and buffish-brown on the underparts. The flights and tail feathers are duller and paler because of a brownish tinge.

Two races occur.

TACAZZE SUNBIRD (*Nectarinia tacazze*)

The beautiful Tacazze Sunbird, also from Africa, is a bird of colder climates. In its graceful shape, it is similar to the Malachite Sunbird. The two central tail feathers, however, are not as long. The tail still has a beautiful shape.

Rich purplish iridescence covers the mantle, shoulders, back, and rump. Flights and tail feathers are glossy black with some purplish highlights on the central tail feathers. The head is rich and glossy pale brown. The chest is brownish-purple in a glossy shade, and remaining underparts are purplish-black. Beak, feet, and legs are black.

The female is brown in varying shades. Underparts are paler, and flight and tail feathers are very dark.

Two races occur.

SCARLET BREASTED SUNBIRD (*Chalcomitra senegalensis*)

Several slightly varying races of the Scarlet Breasted Sunbird occur in Africa. The tail is short, and the beak is shorter than the beaks of the two species above. Most of the bird is black, but two bright and glowing iridescent features give brilliant highlights. The first is a lustrous green covering the forehead, upper crown, face, chin, and throat. The second is a vivid scarlet on the upper throat and chest.

The female is olive-brown on the upperparts. Underparts have dark streaks on a dull yellow background. A mild bronze iridescence occurs on flight and tail feathers.

YELLOW BACKED SUNBIRD (*Aethopyga schetioe*)

The genus *Aethopyga* contains many of the most brilliant sunbirds, and most of them are denoted by the name Yellow Backed Sunbird. In nearly all species and most subspecies, an additional name is added before the basic name to connote geographical location or to commemorate some individual. These additional names help to distinguish the nomenclature and to show that there are differences among the various species and subspecies called Yellow Backed Sunbirds.

In most cases, the names are deceiving because the extent and brilliance of the red far exceeds the yellow which usually is confined more to the rump than to the back.

The shape of *Aethopyga schetioe* is very pleasing. The two central tail feathers of this Indian species are elongated, and the side feathers are sharply graduated to meet them. The overall effect of the bright green tail gives a crisp outward V-shape.

Iridescent green occurs on a large cap covering the forehead and crown and again in a trailing line from the corner of the lower mandible to the sides of the throat. Brilliant red occurs on the forepart of the body including the face, throat, chest, nape, mantle, and shoulders. Most of the wings are brown with pale edges on each feather. The rump is yellow. A blackish band on the lower chest separates the brilliant red from dull grayish-white covering the remaining underparts.

The female is dull greenish above and grayish-white below.

LA TOUCHE'S SUNBIRD (*Aethopyga christinae latouchii*)

The less colorful and very rare La Touche's Sunbird of the same genus as the above is from China and Indo-China. The red of the male is reduced to the facial, throat, and upper chest areas. The trailing mustache is broader, brighter, and longer. Upperparts are green, and flights are blackish. Underparts start with a greenish shade on the lower chest and fade to white.

The female has greenish-yellow underparts and olive upperparts with some black on the head.

CHAPTER 42

Hummingbirds

The New World's finest and most astonishing contribution to the world of birds is the tremendous family of hummingbirds of the suborder Trochili. Peters' **CHECKLIST OF BIRDS OF THE WORLD** lists 121 genera, 319 species, and a total of 656 races. A few species occur in the United States. These have many brilliant colors but lack flamboyance in shape. As the climate approaches the tropics through Mexico, Central America, and northern South America, the shapes unfold into the most exotic of appendages, ruffs, and other seemingly extraneous decorative feathers. These are among the most beautiful and vivid birds in the world. They are also among the most unobtainable and most difficult to maintain in captivity. Fortunate zoos and dedicated aviculturists are the most likely recipients of hummingbirds in captivity. The average fancier and even most of the advanced fanciers will cautiously bypass hummingbirds.

The diet is amazingly simple but not always easy to supply. Hummingbirds require a preponderance of carbohydrates to satisfy the requirements of tremendous activity, which reach the highest metabolic rate of all warm blooded animals in ratio to body size. Other requirements such as animal proteins fall into a more standard and comparable ratio to size. There are variations according to different species. Those with the most rapid wingbeats require far more carbohydrates. Hummingbirds must replenish depleted energy by eating many times a day.

The diet in captivity consists simply of nectar food and approximately fifteen fruitflies per day. Directions for both items are given in Chapter 2. The maintenance of a constant supply of fruitflies cannot be overstressed. Inadequate diets result in a torpidity which is similar to the condition of the body during the night. When constant torpidity is reached, the bird will not live.

The proper mixture for nectar is often a matter of controversy. The writers use honey because of its purity and digestibility. Some authorities prefer to use sugar instead of honey. Proportions are also controversial.

In Southern California experiments with hummingbirds in the wild, several mixtures were offered in identical feeders. Some mixtures contained honey in varying proportions; some contained sugar in varying proportions. Still others used commercial syrups, and one used saccharine which was completely ignored. The greatest preference of the birds in this experiment showed that the birds in this area preferred a mixture of cane sugar and water in EQUAL proportions. The amount consumed was an average of one-eighth of an ounce per day.

Of course, this experiment cannot be considered conclusive for hummingbirds in captivity because these birds doubtlessly found live foods and other supplements. Neither can it be considered conclusive for all hummingbirds in the wild state because only a few species of the vast family participated. Nevertheless, the experiment is helpful to many people who hang hummingbird feeders to entice these brilliant gems into their gardens.

Hummingbirds are attracted by red. Of the many styles of especially designed feeders many have red near the openings. If red is absent on clear glass or plastic feeders, the liquid must be colored red with food coloring and must be visible before any initial attraction is possible.

The commercial market now offers prepared foods and concentrates for hummingbirds for the convenience of wild bird watchers and bird lovers. These red colored foods, available in liquid or concentrated pill form, fulfill the carbohydrate needs of the birds but do not furnish the animal protein factors. In this way, the hummingbirds perform a helpful service by consuming harmful insects in the gardens they frequent.

Hummingbirds have forsaken the standard use of their feet and prefer the amazingly powerful use of their wings. As the evolution of development progressed, the feet grew smaller and weaker while the wings grew stronger. Now, hummingbirds use their fragile feet and legs for perching only. There is no mobility without the use of wings. Perches should be immaculate and flight areas ample in aviaries.

Most of those hummingbirds kept in captivity are from South America and are best maintained in well planted conservatory aviaries in temperate climates. These aviaries offer much needed humidity as well as natural surroundings. Overcrowding must be avoided because of a natural pugnacity and an ability to carry out severe battles.

Hummingbirds observed in the wild by the writers frequently indulge in sadistic and playful mock battles. The most important weapons in this strange game are swift and precise wings and sharp swordplaying beaks. The whirring wings and squeaky voices add excitement. The flights usually take the form of a swinging pendulum. The adversaries fly to and fro and indulge in well-aimed thrusts at their opponents in flight. In wide open wild environments, these battles are usually harmless. In more confining captivity, however, a serious consideration must be given to extra feeding stations and spacious flights to avoid an insidiously slow exhaustion of the oppressed by the domineering individuals who cannily prevent the weaker ones from gaining access to food supplies.

The writers once witnessed a huge flock of migrating hummingbirds. The quiet little foothill glen with its enshrouding oaks was alive with whirring sounds and buzzing activity of the birds at twilight before settling down for the night's repose. The mock battles seemed far more harmless than usual. The general object seemed to be the dispersal of restlessness rather than aggressiveness. This was one of the most fascinating and spellbinding of all the bird watching experiences of the writers.

Ruby Throated Hummingbirds in migration have achieved the awesome non-stop flight from Florida across the vast Gulf of Mexico to Central America. In order to perform this amazing feat, these migrants store carbo-hydrates in their bodies for energy. The extra weight from this storage may total half again their total body weight.

Hummingbirds love to bathe. The usual routine involves diving into sprays or shallow pools. They do not bathe like most birds because of the especially adapted wings and feet.

The greatest beauty of hummingbirds occurs in the metallic brilliance of their various colorings. These metallic shades are caused by refractions depending upon the angle of lighting for maximum appreciation. Photo-graphy is extremely difficult because average lighting shows these refractions as dull blackish shades. The properly lighted areas are usually minimal, but even small areas captured by photographers are always dazzling.

Iridescence is structural rather than pigmentary. Another photographic problem in capturing hummingbirds is the nearly impossible technical diffi-culty in picturing the birds without blurring wings. To catch a hummingbird stopped in clear and concise flight requires the utmost in technique and advanced equipment.

The coverage in this chapter of the astounding number of hummingbirds involves a difficult problem in selection. All are admirable, but not all are available. The selections of the writers are those individuals which have been proven to be successful in captivity and those with the most fanciful decora-tions. Many must unfortunately be omitted in a chapter of this size and scope.

Hummingbirds native to the United States find their way into aviculture by default. Usually these individuals are injured or unreared nestlings. Immature birds are easily reared by the diet previously mentioned and be-come enchantingly tame. Injured adults usually have irreparable wing damage which cannot be repaired to a satisfactory extent to be efficient in the wild state. These infrequent specimens usually assume a calm and mild poise in captivity which reflects utmost confidence in their benefactors. Anyone who has brought a hummingbird through a crucial injury deserves the admiration of bird fanciers everywhere.

The vivacious and plentiful Ruby Throated Hummingbird is not available to American fanciers who specialize in nectar feeding birds because it is a native of the United States. However, it is among the easiest to keep in captivity of all this specialized family and does not require the humidity of its more exotic South American cousins. The male shimmers in green iridescence on the upperparts and dazzles a brilliant ruby gorget.

A few statistics may be interesting. Hummingbirds weigh from two to twenty grams. The wingbeat ranges from eight or ten times to eighty times per second. Smaller species usually have more rapid wingbeats. Propulsion power occurs in both upbeat and downbeat of wings as opposed to the lifting power obtained only from the downbeat of wings of other birds. The basic color is green, but variations are great. Females are usually dull in color. Males usually carry the colorful iridescence and extra decorations. The beaks are variable. Some curve downwards in a decided arc, and others curve slightly upwards. On most species, except those embellished with extra long tail feathers, the tail is less than one-third the total body length. Some tails are longer or broader or swallow-tailed. Variations beyond this point are myriad. Other variations include beards, crests, ruffs, and extensile collars.

Polygamy is a frequent practice. The brighter and more decorated males are the more likely species for polygamy. Nests are carefully woven. Incubation ranges from twelve to sixteen days. Males usually do not help during this period. Fledging time, variable depending on food supplies, may range from ten to thirty days. Variations seem related to metabolic rate and degree of torpidity. Youngsters resemble adult females until the first moult which usually occurs at the age of a year.

RUBY THROATED HUMMINGBIRD (*Archilochus colubris*)

Most Americans' experience with hummingbirds will be with the Ruby Throated Hummingbird which has a traditionally small size and standard shape. The male has a bright red metallic gorget and a vivid green cap. The dull female has some green iridescence on the head, back, and rump. Underparts are a dull gray.

A close relative occurring in Southern California is the Black Chinned Hummingbird (*Archilochus alexandri*). The throat gorget becomes a vivid purplish hue in the right light. The back is iridescent green, and the chest is white. The female is dull except for a hint of iridescence on the back. Underparts are grayish-white.

FORK TAILED EMERALD HUMMINGBIRD (*Chlorostilbon canivetii auriceps*)

The beautiful Fork Tailed Emerald Hummingbird from Mexico is a great rarity even in the finest zoos.

The accompanying plate is taken from John Gould's great works. In this plate, the technique especially developed by Gould for hummingbirds' iridescence is not quite clearly displayed on the head and chest of the males.

A cap on the head and most of the underparts are iridescent in coppery-yellow tinged with green. The tail is distinctly swallow-tail in shape. Mostly black, some of the tail feathers have large white tips. The back is dark and burnished in copper.

The female is mostly dull in coloring. Iridescence is greatly reduced in extent and intensity.

ECUADORIAN SWORD BILLED HUMMINGBIRD (*Ensifera ensifera ensifera*)

The Andes of Venezuela, Colombia, Ecuador, Peru, and northern Bolivia have one of the most unusual of hummingbirds. Though not colorful, the Ecuadorian Sword Billed Hummingbird has a most distinctive feature in its greatly extended beak which is out of all proportion to size. In an aviary, other hummingbirds frequently assume the long beak is a perch and settle down on it much to the annoyance of this unusual bird. The beak is given a basic strength by the extended head which tapers out to meet it.

The tail is broad and squarish with slight swallow-tail proportions on the sides. Iridescence occurs on a coppery-bronze head, on the sides of the greenish throat, and on a bronzed-green chest.

420

STREAMER TAILED HUMMINGBIRD (*Trochilus polytmus*)

The Streamer Tailed Hummingbird from Jamaica is one of the more desirable of hummingbirds in captivity. Two races occur. The subspecies *polytmus* has a bright red beak with a black tip. The subspecies *scitulus* has a black beak and is found in a much smaller range in Jamaica.

Two very long black tail feathers are slender but have heavy undulations on the tips of the barbules. A black cap has some iridescence on the crown. Underparts are iridescent green. Remaining upperparts are grayish-green.

GREEN TAILED SYLPH (*Aglaiocercus kingi mocoa*)

The lovely and dainty Green Tailed Sylph also has two long tail feathers. The tail feathers are vivid green with a slight tinge of blue. Upperparts are green with a brilliant green crown. A purplish gorget is elusive for photographers. The female has a shorter tail and less iridescence.

This subspecies comes from the mountains of Venezuela and Bolivia. Several races exist. The main variations are in length of tail feathers.

FRILLED COQUETTE (*Lophornis magnifica*)

The Frilled Coquette from central and southern Brazil is a short tailed species which is distinctive because of a bright red cap terminating in a crest and an unusual ruff extending from the sides of the neck. The beak is red but is tipped in black. The red on the top of the head is not iridescent; but the green covering the forehead, forward facial area, chin, and throat is vividly iridescent. The erectile ruff on the sides is mostly white with prominent bands of green iridescence on the tips. Most of the upperparts and underparts are bronzed in a brownish shade. The broad and short tail is reddish-brown.

The female has a reddish gorget and iridescent bronzy-green on the head and back. A white band across the back separates the copper rump from the uppertail coverts.

CRIMSON TOPAZ HUMMINGBIRD (*Topaza pella*)

The Crimson or Beautiful Topaz Hummingbird is perhaps the most beautiful of all hummingbirds. Its South American range includes Surinam, British Guiana, and southern Venezuela. Seldom seen in its own range, this flashing gem usually stays in the upperparts of very tall trees.

Brilliant and extensive iridescence occurs in several colors on the male. A long streamer tail is unique in its crossover effect near the base of the remaining standard-sized tail feathers. The dark head accents a very heavy metallic brassy-gold gorget outlined in black velvet. The chest is a deep orchid pink. Undertail coverts are brassy. Undersides of wing and tail are rufous. Uppersides are bronzed in brown.

The female lacks the streamer tail and is much duller. A pale rose gorget is much diminished in size. Underparts are greenish-bronze, and the thighs are whitish.

421

The extremely exotic White Footed Racket Tailed Hummingbird has a very handsome
tail and large white balls of fluff on the legs. Another species is very similar but lacks the
white fluff on the legs. The Crimson Topaz Hummingbird is one of the most brilliant
of all hummingbirds with far more extensive and colorful iridescence than most hummingbirds. The long central tail feathers add a further exotic flair.

WHITE FOOTED RACKET TAILED HUMMINGBIRD (*Ocreatus underwoodi*)

The White Footed Racket Tailed Hummingbird, which ranges from Venezuela to Bolivia in the lower slopes of the Andes, is one of the most delightful of all hummingbirds. Long tapering tail feathers give way to two central shafts with broad blue rackets on the ends. Large and fluffy balls of white feathers occur on the legs. A small white spot follows the eye, and the body coloring all over is iridescent green.

CHAPTER 43

Manakins

The rare and exotic Manakins of Mexico, Central and South America are best fed on a similar standard fare for delicate softbills. Usually two meals per day are offered. One successful formula includes grated hard boiled egg and carrot mixed with banana and mynah meal. Grapes and diced bananas are added to this mixture. If they can be enticed onto mynah pellets, they will derive most of their basic nutrition. Nectar food is given during acclimation and sometimes afterwards.

In a way, these birds are related to the birds in the following chapter and have huge gapes, but they show many basic characteristics of some tanagers. Sometimes they are described as midgets of the Cotinga clan. Few are available to aviculture, and the ones which are imported become avicultural prizes if they can be successfully acclimated. In nearly all cases, manakins should not be housed together because of a basic aggressiveness towards their own kind. In cold climates, manakins should be housed in warm aviaries with controlled temperatures. Conservatory aviaries are ideal.

Some manakins have impressive, noisy, and complicated displays resembling those of the birds of paradise in their deep and almost impenetrable habitats. They emit crackling or popping sounds from their beaks and rustling sounds from their wings which sometimes are used for intimidation. Displays vary but are usually centered around a small area on the ground. This area is completely free from litter. Perches in the form of sticks or branches become an integral part of the setting for the displays.

Some display areas of certain manakins occur high up in trees instead of ground areas. Other manakin displays consist of lowered beaks and outspread wings with elaborate stances and frequent turnings. Unfortunately, the displays are not frequent in captivity.

Most manakins seem to be polygamous. Females apparently build their own nests, incubate, and rear young by themselves while males are busy elsewhere.

SUPERB MANAKIN (*Chiroxiphia pareola*)

One of the prettiest and most coveted of manakins is the Superb Manakin or Blue Backed Manakin from Venezuela to Brazil. Approximately four inches long, rather heavy-bodied and short tailed, the Superb Manakin lives up to its name.

The male is predominantly black, sometimes glossy, with dull brownish tinges on the flights. Two brilliant accents occur in a flattened red crest and in a lustrous turquoise area covering the mantle, shoulders, and back. The legs are yellow.

The female is the same size and shape. The bill is black as in the male, but the remaining coloring is dull and dusty green, dark on upperparts and pale on underparts.

LONG TAILED MANAKIN (*Chiroxiphia linearis*)

The graceful Long Tailed Manakin is about the same size as the above species and is similar in many respects except for two very long and slender central tail feathers of black on the male. This species occurs from Mexico to Costa Rica and is very rare in aviculture, but it is one of the most outstanding members of the family.

The female is similar to the above species but has longer tail feathers of a greenish shade and bright orange legs.

The male has the flattened red crest and the blue back patch ranging from turquoise to azure. The legs are bright orange.

YELLOW THIGHED or RED HEADED MANAKIN (*Pipra mentalis*)

The similarly shaped Yellow Thighed Manakin, sometimes called the Red Capped or Red Headed Manakin, is less than four inches including a tail of nearly one inch. The head and neck of the male are flame colored. A slight chin, underside of wings, and thighs are pale yellow. The eyes are whitish, and the legs are yellow. Remaining areas are blackish. The female has a shade of yellow mixed on the throat and abdomen, but the major coloring is dull and dark green on the upperparts and paler on the underparts.

Other manakins of the genus *Pipra* are even more rare in aviculture. The male White Headed Manakin (*Pipra leucocilla*) is all black with a white cap. The Velvety Manakin (*Pipra velutina*) is a small and delicate bird about three and a half inches long including a one inch tail. The male is mostly black with a cobalt blue crown. The female has the dull greenish pattern of most manakins with darker upperparts and paler underparts.

EDWARD'S MANAKIN (*Manacus manacus*)

Starkly colored in contrasting black and white, Edward's Manakin from South America is sometimes called the Black and White Manakin. The size and shape are about the same as for the Superb Manakin.

The male has a trim black beak and cap tapering to the nape. Black covers the area below the shoulders on the wings and lower back. Brownish tinges mark the flights. The rump and uppertail coverts are grayish shading to black on the tail. Remaining parts on the broad neck, mantle, and underparts are white except for a shade of gray on the flanks and undertail coverts. Legs are orange-yellow.

The female is like most female manakins except for a very pale yellowish shade mixed with green on the underparts.

A subspecies, *leucochlamys*, from Ecuador, is called the Ecuadorian Manakin. Grayish-white covers the chest. The powerful feet are of a dark reddish shade.

WHITE COLLARED or CANDE'S MANAKIN (*Manacus candei*)

The White Collared or Cande's Manakin, quite similar to the above species, is from southern Mexico to Costa Rica. The basic pattern of the male is the same; but a shade of green occurs on the lower back, rump, and uppertail coverts. Bright yellow occurs on the abdomen. The legs are orange.

The female is the same as the above except for a brighter shade of yellow mixed with the green underparts. The legs are the same as in the male.

GOLDEN MANAKIN (*Manacus aurantiaca*)

The rare Golden Manakin of South America is golden-yellow and black in the male. The pattern is similar except for yellow replacing the white in the above species.

GOULD'S MANAKIN (*Manacus vitellinus*)

The best example of Panama's manakins is the noisy Gould's Manakin. Slightly less than four inches long, the male of this species is also dark-capped and white-breasted. A blackish shade covers a head cap, shoulders, back, and tail. The throat, upper chest, and nuchal collar are bright orange-yellow. Some yellowish occurs on the wings, and the remaining upperparts are olive-green. The legs are orange. The female is very similar to the above species.

There are several remaining members of the manakin family, but they are not at all important in aviculture. The male Yellow Crowned Manakin (*Heterocercus flavivertex*) from Venezuela to Brazil is dark with a yellow crown and whitish throat. The Club Winged Manakin (*Allocotopterus deliciosus*) from a limited range in Colombia and Ecuador has a red crown backed by a cinnamon shade covering most of the remaining feathers. The inner wing feathers show a noticeable thickening on the quills. The Cirrhate Manakin (*Teleonema filicauda*) of South America has blackish upperparts, yellowish underparts, bright red on the head and throat, and yellow on the forehead. The outertail feathers are elongated.

A dull species is the Thrush-like Manakin (*Schiffornis turdinus*) which, with subspecies, is spread from Mexico to Brazil. Also called the Brown Manakin, the basic coloring is olive-brown, darker on the upperparts and paler below. A reddish-brown shade occurs in the wings and tail. The size is much larger and reaches nearly six inches in length.

CHAPTER 44

Cocks-of-the-Rock, Cotingas, Umbrella Birds, and Bell Birds

Members of this chapter all come from southern parts of the New World including Mexico, Central America, and South America. Nearly all are exotic, and most are beautiful. All are rather closely related but show many variations. Some are particularly unusual with strange ornamentations. All members belong to the family Cotingidae. The cocks-of-the-rock are so different that some ornithologists have placed them in a separate family, but the majority still retain them in this basic classification.

COCKS-OF-THE-ROCK (genus *Rupicola*)

Highly coveted and almost revered by advanced bird fanciers, the bizarre cocks-of-the-rock of South America hold a lofty position in the ranks of avicultural rarities. They are brightly colored, strangely shaped, and seldom available. The acclimation period is difficult, not only from the standpoint of climate but also in acceptance of domesticated diets.

Once acclimatized, cocks-of-the-rock are long lived if given proper diet and housing. The Orange Cock-of-the-Rock pictured in this book was nearly twelve years old when the photograph was taken.

Housing must vary according to climate. Those pictured in the Jerome Buteyn collection live outdoors around the year in the mild climate of Southern California. The Scarlet Cock-of-the-Rock pictured at the Dieren-park Wassenaar in Holland lived in an aviary included in a huge tropical conservatory. As can be seen from the pictures, all show the benefits of excellent care and adequate housing. These birds love to bathe and should be given proper facilities.

The items of diet are somewhat controversial and variable. Basically, the diet must include fruits and animal protein or live foods. Usually, the cock-of-the-rock is an expensive bird whose requirements are given careful consideration. Unfortunately, variations must occur because preferences of the birds vary and because available supplies differ. Two feedings daily are customary.

During the touchy acclimation period, most experienced importers make a thick paste of a mixture including avocado, bananas, cooked sweet potatoes, and raw meat. This pasty material is then carefully rolled into small balls about a half inch in diameter. These birds have huge gapes and can easily swallow these balls of food.

Gradually other foods are added and original ingredients sometimes changed. Care must be taken to be sure that the birds are accepting the new foods.

Jack Throp, Curator of the Jerome Buteyn Bird Ranch, feeds fully acclimated birds on the following diet: diced fruits as available including apple, avocado (available nearly the entire year), pear, and banana; soaked raisins or grapes; boiled rice and cooked sweet potato; grated hard boiled egg every other day; and ground horse meat carefully mixed with bone meal.

Mynah pellets are desirable for those individuals which will accept them. Grated carrots mixed with ground insectivorous foods are offered by other fanciers along with most of the above ingredients. Unclothed baby mice, often called "pinkies", are given instead of horse meat twice a week by some fanciers. Mealworms are also avidly accepted. Large snails, a natural food in the wild state, can be offered in captivity but are not always accepted. Shells are smashed against rocks before eating. Cocks-of-the-rock usually fade in captivity and should be given carotene to hold color.

In an aviary, cocks-of-the-rock are peaceful with most medium or large softbills. Of course, very aggressive companions should be avoided. Some aggressiveness on their part occurs during nesting periods, and they have been known to eat other birds' nestlings. For the most part, however, they are well-behaved except to their own kind. In the wild state they claim certain territories and become gregarious only during their unusual courting rites.

Cocks-of-the-rock were so named because of their preference for rocky areas. Their bulky and square, short tailed fowl-like appearance doubtlessly contributed to the popular name. The feet and legs are very strong, and the nearly hidden beak is fowl-like. They originate in mountainous areas in tropical South America. The nesting areas are usually ledges in shallow caves in rocky areas. The nest is roughly constructed and usually has two eggs.

Males during the courting period gather in groups on the ground to go through odd dances of wing-spreading and tail-fanning for a noisy audience of females as well as males awaiting their own turn at performing.

Both species have very odd and perpetually raised rounded crests of very fine feathers. The flaring crest nearly covers the beak and gives a very unusual appearance. The piercing bright eye locates the actual center of the head.

Males are brightly colored, but females and immature birds are very dull brownish in coloring. The Scarlet Cock-of-the-Rock is highly active in an aviary, is larger, and has longer legs in comparison to the Orange Cock-of-the-Rock. The orange species, about a foot long, is far more readily available and considerably less expensive than the scarlet species because some of its native ranges, particularly Colombia, have no restrictions on the export of birds.

ORANGE COCK-OF-THE-ROCK (*Rupicola rupicola*)

The Orange Cock-of-the-Rock, with its wide range from Colombia through Venezuela and the Guianas to Brazil, is sometimes called the Amazonian, Apricot, or Golden Cock-of-the-Rock. About half of the upper-parts and all the underparts are bright and glowing orange. A very dark narrow band borders near the outer rim of the crest. The blackish wing feathers have orange-white markings in the central portion of the outer flights. The inner coverts cascade down the back in broad blackish feathers with prominent pale grayish bands and squarely flared sides. Many of the elongated furry feathers of the lower back and shoulder area stream out to the sides. In advanced age, these filaments may cover the distinctive inner coverts. Tail coverts are deep orange. The brownish tail is tipped in reddish-orange.

The highly individual characteristics of the bird pictured in this book may not be generally indicative of the species. He is, for the most part, very sedentary and perfectly finger tame. When he sits on a human hand, he puffs out his chest, brings the forward part of his crest down to the chest, and closes his eyes. One does not quite know where plumage ends and flesh begins. This strong willed character apparently dislikes movement. He strikes at any individual with whom he is not acquainted in the aviary and hits the wire with an alarming blow to startle any stranger outside the aviary. The savage-ness of his performance seems to be directed towards intimidation.

SCARLET COCK-OF-THE-ROCK (*Rupicola peruviana*)

The brilliant Scarlet Cock-of-the-Rock occurs in several slightly varying subspecies. The subspecies *peruviana* is known as the Andean form. The sub-species *aequatorialis* from Ecuador is referred to as the Equatorial Scarlet Cock-of-the-Rock. Another subspecies, *sanguinolenta,* from the western slopes of the Andes, is merely called the Scarlet or Red Cock-of-the-Rock.

Slightly larger, perhaps because of the longer tail, and far more active in flight, the Scarlet Cock-of-the-Rock is more colorful than the orange species. The crest is softer and more full but lacks any border around the edges.

The beak is yellowish-orange when it is visible, and the prominent eye is nearly the same shade. Bright scarlet, variable in captivity because of degrees of fading, covers the head and upperparts through the mantle, shoulders, and back and underparts through the undertail coverts. The tail and most of the wings are black. Gray inner wing coverts are very broad but less flamboyant and more rounded than those flaring outwards on the orange species. These long flimsy feathers are nevertheless usually separated along the barbules during flight to give a shaggy and lacy effect.

COTINGAS

Of all the highly coveted birds in very advanced aviculturists' or zoological collections, few are quite as elusive or as delicate as those found among the cotingas. Many fanciers have felt a great triumph in securing some of the various rare species only to be sadly disappointed in quick losses because of inadequate acclimation. Importers with any experience usually bypass cotingas. Only foolishly rash amateurs or the most wisely experienced advanced aviculturists will attempt the importation of cotingas.

Though the dietary requirements are basically simple, the acceptance of domesticated foods is quite another matter; and the acclimation period is very difficult. Basically, the dietary requirements are the same as for the cock-of-the-rock and for tanagers, but the formation of the balls of food must be smaller. Heat and humidity in most cases should be provided during acclimation. Some species can forego these requirements after a suitable acclimation period.

Only a few of the many species ranging from the lower boundaries of the United States to Argentina have ever been represented in aviculture, and the successful establishment in captivity has been even more rare. The writers cannot stress too strongly the necessities of adequate facilities and the willingness to give extra care before recommending the importation of cotingas. Unless one is willing to supply these needs, the birds are much happier in their native habitats and should not be subjected to an unwanted or inadequate captive life. There are far too many readily adaptable birds of great beauty for the average or novice fancier.

Once acclimated, cotingas are not difficult to manage. The average cotinga is probably best described as thickset but thrush-like in shape with varying sizes. As in the cocks-of-the-rocks, the beak can open into a huge gape. Tityras and becards fall within the cotinga category, but neither group is important in aviculture. An obvious and rather close relationship is easily surmised by the similarity of beaks and surrounding bristles of some of the many members.

The beautiful male Purple Throated Cotinga (*Cotinga cayana*) shows much iridescence on an extensive turquoise-blue covering the head, underparts, mantle, and rump. A bright and glossy purplish area covers the chin and a flaring throat area. A greenish shade covers the back and parts of the wings, but the wings are nearly enshrouded in black. The tail is definitely blackish. Small and dark striations and scaly effects mark the crown and back. The size is medium, and the South American range extends from the Guianas to the Amazon.

The female is dull with a basic brownish shade heavily marked with darker and lighter areas on each crescent-edged feather.

430

The Long or Large Wattled Umbrella Bird is one of the most bizarre of all members of an unusual and exotic family. Very rare and expensive, it is seldom found except in fortunate zoos. New York Zoological Society photo.

The huge gaping mouth of this young male Three Wattled Bell Bird is getting set for a loud ringing call which subdues the sounds of most birds. New York Zoological Society photo.

The Lovely Cotinga (*Cotinga amabilis*) of Mexico is similar and is about seven inches long. The abdominal area is rich purple. Wing coverts and secondaries, as in the above species, are edged in blue. The female is similar to the above species.

The Blue Chatterer (*Cotinga cincta*) from Brazil is similar, but a broad blue area crosses the chest. The wing feathers and a small forehead area are nearly totally blackish.

Rieffer's Cotinga (*Pipreola riefferii*) of Colombia is smaller with a brilliant green as the predominant coloring with yellow underparts.

The Orange Breasted Green Cotinga or Chatterer (*Pipreola jucunda*) is also smaller. It has an orange breast which is edged with black and a yellow abdomen. The black head and throat are contrasted by green on the remaining upperparts.

UMBRELLA BIRDS (genus *Cephalopterus*)

The strange umbrella birds of South America are usually unavailable to aviculturists and only rarely found even in the better zoos. The diet is the same as for cotingas and cocks-of-the-rock.

The Ornate Umbrella Bird (*Cephalopterus ornatus*) and its subspecies *penduliger*, called the Long Wattled Umbrella Bird, are about ten inches long. Both have an umbrella or mushroom crest which reaches forward above the beak whenever the bird desires. A greatly elongated feathered appendage drops from the forepart of the chest to a point below the tail. It usually hangs in front of the perch. The latter subspecies from the Western Andes has the longest wattle reaching eleven or twelve inches. Females lack the appendages and have only a slight hint of a crest.

Some umbrella birds have a swelling throat pouch for displays, but this is variable in different races.

BELL BIRDS (genus *Procnias*)

The fabled bell birds of South America emit ringing bell sounds which carry in amazing clarity and volume for great distances. Even if they were not so rare, they could never be considered suitable for aviaries in neighborhood residential areas without comparable tirades even from neighbors three blocks away. Bell birds, however, are very rare in aviculture and are regarded as prize acquisitions for zoos and large collections of advanced fanciers.

The diet is the same as for the cocks-of-the-rock. The huge gape of the mouth is astounding. Equally difficult to acclimate, the bell bird's ultimate price is necessarily far more than the original purchase price. Youngsters acclimate more easily than do adults, but all ages and species must be considered expensive after acclimation.

Bell birds are comparable in size and shape to the Greater India Hill Mynah. This would make their overall length about ten inches long including a tail of three inches. The neck is somewhat more slender than that of the popular mynah.

The usage of the term "exotic" is often thought to refer to beauty, but it equally applies to rarity, strangeness, and distance. Bell birds are exotic because of the latter definitions. They are not beautiful, but they are striking in appearance. The shape is not only ordinary but also ungainly and a shade on the ugly side. No one would deny that they are unusual.

NAKED THROATED or BARE THROATED BELL BIRD (*Procnias nudicollis*)

The most frequently available of bell birds is the Naked Throated Bell Bird. It is snow white with some brown streaks heavily laced on the nape, shoulder, and scapular areas. The bare forehead, throat, and facial areas, excluding cheeks and barely surrounding the eyes, are an unusual shade of bright blue-green during the breeding season. These areas are not only bare skin but they also show heavy wrinkles on the throat. The large eyes, the wide and flat beak, and the feet and legs are black.

THREE WATTLED BELL BIRD (*Procnias tricarunculata*)

The Three Wattled Bell Bird has been displayed in only a few zoos. The body is chestnut with some white spots. The head and throat are white with some chestnut on the boundary areas. Three long and fleshy strings droop more than an inch. One projects from the forehead, and one emanates from each corner of the mouth.

This is a very odd bird with a huge gape and a loud ringing call.

The strange and rare Bell Bird has white plumage and brilliant turquoise-green facial skin. Though not a beautifully proportioned bird, its appearance is striking; and its loud bell-like voice commands attention from a wide radius. Owned by Jerome Buteyn.

434

CHAPTER 45

Barbets and Woodpeckers

Barbets are all stocky birds with rather large heads, thick necks, standard sized tails, and very thick beaks. Bristles surround the beak. Many are very interesting, and some are very colorful. The size, ranges and temperaments vary considerably. As a rule, barbets are too aggressive to be housed with average birds of their own size. Individual exceptions do occur, but the writers prefer to include most barbets with birds robust in size and an ability to defend themselves. In several instances known to the writers certain barbets have been known to murder thrushes and chloropsis.

Barbets take readily, though sometimes noisily, to aviary life and thrive on standard softbilled fare. The writers offer extra fruit and raw meat to satisfy their requirements.

Barbets nest in holes and trees, pounding out the sites in much the same manner as a woodpecker. With this talent, they sometimes have been known to cause damage to wooden aviary walls.

None of the various barbets are low in price. They are not always available and the acclimation period is a difficult one for importers. Not all can be covered in this book, but those known in aviculture will be explained. Those most commonly available come from India, but one with perhaps the most distinctive character and charm is from South America.

Diminutive versions of barbets are the Tinker Birds of Africa. These are interesting little birds, but they are not available to the field of aviculture.

Woodpeckers pose many enigmatic contradictions to aviculturists. Zoos and bird fanciers usually consider them very delicate in captivity. The writers have had little experience with woodpeckers, but their experience leads to the same conclusion of delicacy. Those available to aviculture usually originate in India, but the acclimation period is extremely difficult for these birds because of their reluctance to accept domesticated foods.

Bird watchers who assume the project of caring for injured birds or routed nestlings report completely opposite experiences with native American birds. The writers have frequently heard from these bird lovers that woodpeckers are the easiest of wild birds to rescue and to feed in captivity.

The bright and smoothly colored Red Headed Woodpecker (left) has a brilliant red covering the entire head and neck. The black upperparts are attractively broken by bright white accents, and most of the underparts are white. In its mountainous and foothill ranges, this native bird pecks holes in most of the fence posts to store acorns which in turn attract certain insects which form the major part of the diet. It is highly beneficial but sometimes noisy in its energetic hammering.

The Downy Woodpecker (right) is smaller and more variable in pattern. It is more delicate in captivity than the Red Headed Woodpecker.

The opposite poles of experience may possibly be explained by differences in native environments. Those species from India seem to be the delicate ones, and native American species are the ones which enjoy captive lives. In fact, rescued nestlings usually become remarkably tame.

The diet of woodpeckers in captivity is a matter of controversy, but the writers strongly urge the use of nectar food and peanut butter as the two most important items in addition to the standard softbilled fare and plenty of live food.

For the most part, woodpeckers at the present time must remain outside the realm of aviculture. This verdict also extends to closely related wood-hewers, wrynecks, tree creepers, and piculets.

Native woodpeckers with their bright colors and the more quietly colored flickers are among the most interesting subjects for bird watchers. They are large enough for easy observation and active enough to hold attention. Flickers are brownish and have comparatively dull colors, but their personalities are similar.

The Yellow Shafted Flicker, also native to the United States and easily kept in captivity, shows a broad collar across the upper chest and very prominent spots. The undersides of the wing and tail have extensive areas of a yellowish shade. The stiff and spiny tail feathers give support to the bird when it clings to the sides of trees in this fashion. This one is eyeing the cameraman with a protective, yet cautious glare because of a close approach to the nesting hole in the side of the tree.

Pileated Woodpeckers, of which there are several different species around the world, all have similar tapering crests. They usually are colorful but are not extensive in aviculture.

TOUCAN BARBET (*Semnornis ramphastinus*)

The writers' favorite barbet is the Toucan Barbet of South America which is sometimes called the Toucan Billed Barbet. This unusual thick billed barbet is more colorful, more exotic, and more interesting than any other barbet to come into the possession of the writers. Unfortunately it cannot stand some of the very hot summer days found in southwestern United States and must be given protection from such weather. It is rare both in captivity and in the wild state.

The personality is also unusual and for the most part relatively peaceful except with smaller birds. The writers have had up to two dozen of these birds at one time and have been captivated by the amusing personalities. Two loud call notes never fail to attract attention. One is a short popping sound usually uttered in a group and quickly picked up by the rest of the Toucan Barbets. When all are participating, one is reminded of the popping sounds of popcorn over a fire. The other call note is a long braying sound not unlike the heckling bray of a donkey. In fact the bird even assumes the

438

The curious and amusing Toucan Barbet from South America is one of the most attractive members of an unusual family. It has two sounds, both incongruous and amusing. One sound is like a braying donkey and the other like popping popcorn. Photographed at Palos Verdes Bird Farm.

This large Himalayan Barbet just arrived from Thailand and is minus a tail. It is a very dark colored bird and not particularly attractive. It nevertheless is quite interesting. In certain environments it is extremely noisy and is always aggressive to other birds. Owned by Ed Parks.

position of a braying donkey with head tipped up and neck outstretched to give maximum volume to the vocal chords.

No one could object to the noise if they could view the preposterous clownishness during the performance. The pleasant comic buffoonery of the Toucan Barbet lifts it into a position unique among birds.

The large and thick yellowish beak has a black spot on the sides spilling onto both mandibles. The eyes are reddish with black pupils. A triangular area of black starts at the lower corner of the lower mandible and covers lores and eyes and forms a curved eyebrow above the eyes. The forehead and crown are black, and a narrow black area extends down the center of the head to the lower nape where it widens into a half collar. Remaining facial, chin, and throat areas are soft and pale gray except for the near white line slicing through the eyebrow and bordering the black on the crown.

The back is brown, and the wings and tail are slate gray. The chest is dark red spilling brightly through the center of the abdomen. Sides, lower abdominal areas, undertail coverts, back, and rump are dark golden-yellow.

Feather texture, except for wings and tail, is soft and furry. Sexes are alike, and size is rather large. Two similar races occur: *ramphastinus* from the subtropical zone of the Ecuadorian Andes and *caucae* from the subtropical zone of the Colombian Western Andes. The small Costa Rican or Prong Billed Barbet (*Semnornis frantzii*) similar in many respects, completes the genus. Fortunately Toucan Barbets in a colored plate and a black and white picture are included in the illustrations.

BLUE THROATED or BLUE CHEEKED BARBET (*Megalaima asiatica*)

The most frequently available and perhaps the most popular of barbets is the Blue Throated or Blue Cheeked Barbet. Five similar races extend from India to Borneo and Thailand. The size is close to eight inches, varying somewhat with different races; and sexes are alike.

The basic coloring is green. Some blue appears on the tail; and bright blue covers all of the facial area, chin, and throat. Red, sided with black, covers the forehead and crown. A black band intersects the red across the crown. Some red also occurs on the sides of the throat at the dividing line between the blue and the green. The eye is red, and the beak is mostly pale horn with black irregularly marked along the top of the upper mandible. In some cases, black also occurs on the lower mandible near the tip.

GREEN BARBET (*Megalaima zeylanica*)

Six races of the Green Barbet, one called Hodgson's Barbet and another called the Lineated Barbet occur in India, Ceylon, the Malay Peninsula, Thailand, Java, and Bali. Though naturally some variations exist, the total coloring is far less attractive than the Blue Throated Barbet. The head, neck, and chest are pale brown with many whitish streaks. The beak is a pale horn color and is long and comparatively slender for a barbet. The rest of the bird

441

is bright green, darker above and paler below. The eye is surrounded by a pale ring of bare skin.

Though the Green Barbet is imported nearly as often as the Blue Throated Barbet, only a few fanciers show any interest in it. The size is larger than the above, and the coloring uninteresting by comparison. It is quite hardy and easily acclimated, but the writers usually try to avoid it.

The Small Green Barbet (*Megalaima viridis*) from India is smaller, has a darker brown head, whitish above and below the eyes, and a paler shade on the chin and throat. The chest is pale buff streaked with darker brown.

GREAT BARBET or GREAT HIMALAYAN BARBET (*Megalaima virens*)

The Great Barbet has four races extending from India through Burma and Thailand to China. The subspecies pictured is the nominate race (*virens*) from Thailand. The race from India (*marshallorum*) is frequently called the Yellow Naped Great Barbet and is slightly more colorful.

The size of about twelve inches is larger and the body stockier than any of the foregoing. The beak is very large and powerful. The disposition is far more aggressive than characteristic of most barbets.

The head is black with blue-green highlights. Olive-brown marks the back and chest. Green covers the wings, tail, and rump. Underparts are pale yellow streaked with bluish-green markings. Sexes are alike.

The subspecies *marshallorum* is lighter in shading and more diversified in color. Streaks of yellow occur on the nape.

COPPERSMITH BARBET (*Megalaima haemacephala*)

The very pretty Coppersmith Barbet, sometimes called Crimson Breasted Barbet, has five races ranging over extensive areas from India to the Philippines. This is a smaller species and one which gives some problems during acclimation. The size is slightly less than six inches. It is a very worthwhile addition to any collection, but it is not often available. The various races may differ slightly.

The forehead and forepart of the crown are bright red. The eye and bare eye ring are also red. A large crescent of red covers the upper chest. The beak is dull blackish. Yellow matches the brightness of the red by boldly marking areas above and below the eye and by covering the chin and throat. In a duller and darker shade, yellow borders the lower side of the crescent of red on the chest. Dull black covers the lores and continues in a separating line surrounding the eyes and trailing back to the sides of the neck. The black serves as a highly effective and contrasting setting for the bright yellows and reds. It surrounds the red and yellow of head and facial areas and covers the lower cheek areas. It then fades slightly to brown on outer extremities.

Remaining upperparts are green with some brown and blue on the wings. The underside of the tail is also green. Remaining underparts are pale greenish-white with prominent streaks of dark olive-green.

FIRE TUFTED BARBET (*Psilopogon pyrolophus*)

The very rare Fire Tufted Barbet from Malaya and Sumatra is about ten inches long. This is a very pretty bird mostly green in color with color diversification most noticeable on the head and upper chest. Upperparts are darker than the underparts. The flights show some dull orange and brown, and the underside of the tail is tinged in blue.

A reddish tuft of fine bristly feathers extends forward above the greenish-horn colored beak. A dark smudge crosses the center of both mandibles of the beak. The forehead, crown, and nape are blackish-brown extending in a collar which encircles the upper chest. The female is purported to be more blackish on the lower part of the crown. A whitish band crosses the center of the crown and trails in an extended eyebrow. The cheeks are grayish. The throat is bright green shading into a broad orange-shaded crescent extending from the sides of the neck across the lower throat area.

GROOVE BILLED BARBET (*Lybius dubius*)

A strange but colorful barbet is the Groove Billed Barbet from West Africa. The horn-colored beak is particularly broad and grooved on the upper mandible. The edges, because of this grooving, are irregular and jagged. Most of the upperparts are black except for a straw-colored rump. The major coloring of the underparts is bright red. A large yellowish-flesh area surrounds the eyes followed by a patch of red on the lower cheek area which is divided from the red of the lower parts by a bold black line. An irregular black band crosses the lower chest. The flanks and the underside of the tail are black. Feet and legs are flesh colored.

A close relative is the Double Toothed Barbet (*Lybius bidentatus*). Also from Africa, this species is similarly colored in black and red but is less distinctive. The beak is less broad and grayish, but the grooves give a jagged double tooth appearance. The red from the cheek area is unbroken by the absence of bands of black. The flanks are whitish, and the upperparts are heavily mixed with brown as well as some dull red on the top of the forehead and crown.

BLACK COLLARED BARBET (*Lybius torquatus*)

The Black Collared Barbet of Africa, with similar sexes in its six slightly varying races, is strikingly colored. The beak is blackish; the lores are blackish; and a large area including the head, chin, throat, and chest are bright red. A broad black border extending onto the mantle surrounds the red. Upperparts are grayish-black with some yellow on the wings. Underparts are pale yellowish-white. Youngsters lack the red and have dull black instead.

ORANGE BREASTED or PLAINTIVE BARBET (*Capito aurovirens*)

The Orange Breasted Barbet from South America is a colorful but rare bird. So many varieties of the genus are so very similar that the writers are not positive that the species in the colored plate is correctly identified. All species in this genus and in the genus *Eubucco* are rare in captivity.

The male pictured is dull in coloration except for a bright red cap covering the entire head and nape and an extensive golden-yellow area stretching from chin through chest. The olive-brownish body coloring extends forward to include eyes and facial areas. Pale whitish areas give a slight eyebrow effect and a chin marking. The beak is bluish-gray with blackish tips.

The female has gray on the head with only traces of red and yellow.

The specimen pictured and its mate live peaceably with a collection of thrushes, bulbuls, and birds of similar temperament.

CHAPTER 46

Toucans and Toucanettes

Of the many excesses in the bird world, none seem quite so illogical as the large, colorful, and flamboyant beaks of toucans and toucanettes which comprise the family Ramphastoidea and the family Ramphastidae. These very lightweight beaks add a comic and exotic flair which matches bright and alert personalities. Tame toucans are really a great joy and become very affectionate companions.

Untame toucans and toucanettes are best kept in large aviaries because of their incessant activity and clumsy panic. Their flight is awkward and damaging during fright. Most toucans and toucanettes in good plumage have feathers which, except for flight and tail feathers, resemble finely combed fur. They remain very well groomed if given frequent and adequate bathing facilities. The fascinating tongue is a long splintery affair.

While poised, these birds exhibit an amazing innate sense of precision and alertness. Many tame toucans are quickly taught to catch grapes tossed from considerable distances. If the grape falls anywhere in the vicinity of the toucan, it will be snapped up before it reaches the ground.

In the wild state this talent undoubtedly helps to catch insects in flight. In captivity, toucans should never be kept near finches because they can also catch these tiny birds in flight. Though they seldom eat finches, their rapid shaking and strong clamping quickly kill the hapless victim. In all fairness to the toucans, this characteristic does not seem to indicate a viciousness nearly so much as it seems to be a game, but the bird fancier must be on his guard.

Toucans live peacefully with many large softbills. Selection of companions should be carefully made and cautiously introduced. Many birds smaller than themselves may bully toucans unmercifully. Nearly any bird in these size groups may become bullies and may gradually wear down the resistance of other birds by chasing them from food supplies. Once a toucan is weakened from malnutrition, it rarely can be saved. It refuses to cooperate and will go off food completely. Forced feeding is useless because it will expend every effort to regurgitate the food.

A collection of various toucans is an awesome sight, but toucans and toucanettes are their own worst enemies until they become fully acquainted.

Toucans, if tamed while young, are delightful pets. This young Cuvier's Toucan is still in straggly immature plumage and is still quite small. Photographed at Palos Verdes Bird Farm.

After the cautious introductory period during which wars may rage at any time, close observation and quick action on the part of the aviculturist is necessary. Familiarity encourages peace amidst toucans, and after awhile the newly introduced individual is usually allowed to enter the group in peaceful co-existence. The larger the group, the more chances for peace. If all members are introduced into a large planted aviary at the same time (naturally the trees and plants should be strong enough and resilient enough to withstand the weight of the birds), the chances for peace are even greater from the very beginning.

The writers have kept up to a dozen toucans and a dozen various aracaries at a time in one medium-sized aviary with no problems of pugnacity because all were introduced into the aviary at the same time. However, any attempt to introduce a newcomer would immediately mean an all-out gang war to defeat the intruder. The bird fancier must develop a sixth sense and keen judgment to try to predict the many possible responses of birds, and day to day observations must be given to evaluate the extent of harmony in such collections.

Youngsters are usually smaller than adults. They lack body bulk and beak length. Growth into adulthood is rather slow in most cases, and youngsters must be protected from dominating adults. Females are usually distinguishable by shorter beaks if they have full adult coloring.

The diet is extremely important. If anything, toucans should be overfed to encourage adequate intake. If bullies are present, extra feeding stations are necessary. The writers have found the most important single item for a well rounded diet is mynah pellets. A frugal amount of diced apple, soaked raisins, and some raw meat are also offered; but overuse may lead to exclusion of the mynah pellets and therefore result in an unbalanced diet.

In the wild state, these birds use small, dry, and rather hard fruits as a dietary basis; but, in captivity, the usual tendency is to give too many soft fruits which are quite different from the natural fare. Dry mynah pellets help appreciably to bring the natural texture into balance. The simple diet can easily be verified in its efficiency by the many toucans which the writers have frequently kept in excellent health for many years.

If proper diet and environment are given, toucans and toucanettes are quite hardy. In Southern California's mild climate, which still becomes reasonably cold at many times and which often lacks humidity, toucans show complete comfort. In really cold climates, these birds must be given heat if temperatures frequently drop below forty-five degrees and if hearty good condition is to be maintained. Colds, induced by drafts and lower temperatures, show extreme difficulty in treatment.

Toucans to be tamed should be young birds. At early ages, these birds are thoroughly adaptable to domesticity and become inordinately affectionate

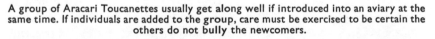

A group of Aracari Toucanettes usually get along well if introduced into an aviary at the same time. If individuals are added to the group, care must be exercised to be certain the others do not bully the newcomers.

447

and completely finger tamed. Adults of most species defy taming and can inflict severe injuries with their fast moving and adeptly grasping beaks. A well aimed punch, for instance, may destroy an eye; and a rapid grasp and subsequent sideways shaking may result in a painful and well-tweaked nose if an untame bird is brought into close proximity to one's face. Though the "bite" of an untame bird lacks sufficient leverage to be harmful, it can be painful; and the rapid sideways shaking gives a foothold which enables a greater infliction of pain. On the other hand, a tame bird likes nothing more than a gentle caress and an expression of affection. His soft and harmless reciprocation is a tremendous compensation for time spent in taming. His playfulness and gentleness offer far greater rewards than one might usually expect.

At night, most toucans roost in a similar manner. Their huge beaks are tucked into their wings, and their tails are amusingly held in a perpendicular stance.

Toucans neither sing nor talk. Their voices are not often raised except as calls for hunger or attention. If these basic needs are neglected, toucans may emit harsh, grating, and monotonous calls which may bring protests from nearby neighbors. The only other sounds are soft rattlings which curiously resemble chuckles of contentment usually emitted while pet birds are receiving the attention they fully deserve.

The writers are often asked if toucans talk. The answer is always no. Usually the uninformed questioner is disappointed, and the writers often feel exasperatingly tempted to ask "What more could anyone ask than the charming affection given by such an exotic beauty?" Instead, a discreet silence and a gentle steering towards a mynah bird usually results in all-around satisfaction.

Toucans are for bird fanciers who can appreciate unusual personalities and unusual beauty and not for the average person who demands additional performances. Throughout this book and *Parrots and Related Birds* the writers have mentioned many birds which are their great favorites. It is true the writers have great regard and love for most birds, but their wide range of favorites always is evidenced by some unusual characteristic. In most cases, returned affection may be the prime source of admiration. Tame toucans completely fulfill this requisite, and a collection of untame toucans easily fulfills an appreciation for the unusual and exotic. By all means, this fascinating family fills every requisite for inclusion among the finest of the favorites of the writers.

Often, those toucans and toucanettes available in the United States are seldom available in Europe. The reverse of this is also applicable.

SULPHUR BREASTED TOUCAN (*Ramphastos sulfuratus sulfuratus*)

The very beautiful Sulphur Breasted Toucan from Mexico is the most prevalent member of the clan available in the United States. It is relatively inexpensive in a medium price range.

The variable sizes average sixteen inches including the long squared tail of five to six inches. The broad beak, not included in the overall measurement, is five inches more or less according to age and sex.

The beak is basically pale green with varying shades of blue and some yellow and orange. Nearly one-third of the end is maroon preceded by blue on the rims of the mandibles. Some dark bars are prominent in this area. A large bar of orange starts near the base of the upper mandible at its lower part and tapers to an end just before the maroon begins. A deep black margin on the beak denotes the point of connection where the beak joins the head.

The eye is emerald green with a pale grass-green surrounding the bare facial area. A bright sulphur covers the large area of stiff and filmy feathers on the lower facial, throat, and chest areas. A narrow band of red frames the lower area. The ventral area and undertail coverts are scarlet in a rosette of long curly feathers.

The rest of the bird is black except for a large white patch on the rump. The strong, heavy feet and legs are silvery-blue in color.

A similar subspecies (*brevicarinatus*) is called the Short Billed Toucan from Central America and northern South America. The bill is shorter in this race, but other characteristics are the same.

CUVIER'S TOUCAN (*Ramphastos cuvieri*)

Cuvier's Toucan from northern South America is second in availability of toucans in the United States. It usually is a much more tameable subject than the Sulphur Breasted Toucan but is usually higher in price.

Slightly less variable in color, the size is usually somewhat larger in adulthood. Since the average tame specimen to come into the hands of bird fanciers is young, the size may be considerably smaller both in body and beak than the adult.

The large beak is variably six to seven inches long. The body length is approximately sixteen inches long including the tail of five and a half inches. Very long and wide, the beak is mostly black with a narrow yellow band running the full length of the upper ridge and spilling across the tip. A wide band of yellow at the base changes into a faint sky blue on the lower mandible. A prominent black band separates the yellow and blue from the head.

A bare facial area of blue surrounds the dark eyes and is replaced by thin and stiff furlike white feathers which extend downwards over a large and broad area curving around the lower chest area. Red borders the lower boundaries of the white chest.

The rest of the plumage is black except for yellow uppertail coverts and a vent surrounded by a chrysanthemum-like rosette of red feathers. Feet and legs are bluish-gray. One subspecies, *oblitus*, occurs in parts of Brazil.

RED BILLED TOUCAN (*Ramphastos tucanus*)

The rare Red Billed Toucan from southeastern South America is quite similar to Cuvier's Toucan except for a reddish-maroon area in the centers of

449

both upper and lower mandibles. Variations occur greatly according to sex and to age. The voice is usually noisier, and it is therefore less commendable. This species is far more rare in the United States than Cuvier's Toucan.

SWAINSON'S TOUCAN (*Ramphastos swainsonii*)

The somewhat rare Swainson's Toucan from southern Central America to northern South America is exceeded in demand by pet loving aviculturists only by the more rare but equally desirable Toco Toucan which, in itself, is the epitome of desirable pets in the family of toucans.

Swainson's is a large toucan with a huge and flamboyant beak reaching from six to eight inches in length. Variations in size usually occur according to age and sex.

The beak's coloring is a relatively simple scheme. A narrow band of deep yellow starts at the base of the upper mandible and widens as it approaches the tip. This coloring is followed by a blackish border which gradually pales to include a reddish-maroon over the remainder of the upper mandible and nearly all of the lower mandible except the blackish tip.

The bare area surrounding the greenish eyes is bright green. The large patch covering chin, throat, and upper chest is yellow at the top shading into white at the base. A narrow red band borders the lower area. The rest of the coloring is black except for white uppertail coverts and scarlet undertail coverts similar to Cuvier's Toucan.

Similar species and subspecies of *ambiguus* known as Wagler's Toucan from northern South America may wrongly be identified as Swainson's Toucan since there is little difference.

TOCO TOUCAN (*Ramphastos toco toco*)

The aristocrat of the toucan family and one of the most completely charming pets is the large Toco Toucan. Now rarely available from its usual Brazilian center of importation, the asking price is rather high; but it usually is acceptable to bird fanciers who are familiar with the natural talents and traits of this bird. All those individuals which have come within the writers' experience have been naturally tame comics.

Toco Toucans are very large, perhaps the largest of the family. The huge beak is bright orange with irregular darker striations. An extensive area on the tip of the upper mandible is black. The base is broadly rimmed in black, and a large bare facial area is bright orange. The orange or hazel brown eye is broadly rimmed in rich cobalt blue flesh. The huge white bib covering the chin, throat, and chest is shaded in yellow at the lower boundaries.

The rest of the coloring is black except for the white rump and red undertail coverts.

Toco Toucans, easily trained and quite naturally friendly, are the favored and most coveted of the toucan family. There is one subspecies, *albogularis*, from southern Brazil.

450

Swainson's Toucan has a very large and distinctively colored beak with its deep reddish-maroon and yellow. Highly coveted, Swainson's Toucans are not readily available. The beak on this adult male is only slightly larger than that of the female. New York Zoological Society photo.

The brightly colored Ariel Toucan is quite rare in American aviculture. The chest is bright golden orange-yellow, and the beak is shiny black except for a band of yellow near the base. Sexes are alike, but this bird is an adult male. New York Zoological Society photo.

GREEN BILLED TOUCAN (*Ramphastos dicolorus*)

Quite rare in the United States but more prevalent than most toucans in Europe, the Green Billed Toucan is a very colorful species. Unfortunately it seldom is available in young tameable stages. It is extremely pugnacious to most toucans but is a good companion to other large toucans after careful introduction.

The total size, exclusive of beak, is fifteen inches including a tail of six inches. The beak is three and a half inches long and one and a half inches broad.

The beak is mainly a pale and dull olive-green with a concentration of bright and light grass-green on the top of the base of the upper mandible. Some deep red on the sides of the jagged rims are joined irregularly by dark streaks. A broad but irregular black band margins the base of the beak.

The eyes are pale sky-blue with black pupils. A bare triangular facial area starting at the base of the beak and surrounding the eyes is orange-red.

Upperparts are black starting on the forehead and extending to the tip of the tail. The only interruption is red on the rump. The undersides of tail and wings are dull black.

The abdomen is black, but the remaining underparts are very colorful. Cheeks, throat, and upper chest are yellow with an overlying deeper shade almost reaching orange in the broad central area between throat, cheek, and lower boundary of yellow on the chest. The usual effect is one of a yellow background overlaid by deeper area in all but the outer margins. The lower chest and upper abdomen are bright red.

ARIEL TOUCAN (*Ramphastos vitellinus ariel*)

The Ariel Toucan from Brazil is rare in the United States and is usually known only by advanced fanciers. It is a particularly attractive species with glowing colors of many contrasts.

The long beak is more slender and more curved than that of most members of the genus. The body is also more slender. The beak is a shiny jet black with a band of yellow near the connecting point divided by a fine black line at the connection of beak to head.

An emerald eye is surrounded by a triangular area of bare skin of a bright red-orange color. Golden orange-yellow covers the large bib which extends into the chest. The rest of the bird is jet black.

SULPHUR and WHITE BREASTED TOUCAN (*Ramphastos vitellinus vitellinus*)

The Sulphur and White Breasted Toucan from Venezuela, the Guianas, northern Brazil, and Trinidad is even more rare in the United States. The color differences from the above subspecies are quite remarkable. Though the beak is black and has a similar bar near the base, the coloring is grayish. The bare area surrounding the eye is blue. The huge bib is white with sulphurous yellow in the center and a band of red bordering the lower base.

The closely related Keel Billed Toucan (subspecies *culminatus*) is very similar to the Sulphur and White Breasted Toucan except that it lacks the yellow in the center of the chest.

Two subspecies (*pinto* and *theresae*) are not covered in this book because they are never available.

TOUCANETTES and ARACARIS

Though there are three genera and many physical variations in the group of toucanettes, a few basic characteristics are common. All have bodies which are smaller and more slender than toucans. Bills are also more slender but often of a similar length found in many toucans. The tails are all rather long, but are more rounded on the ends. Most are lower in price and not greatly coveted compared to the average toucan except those rarities in which specialized bird fanciers are particularly interested. Also, most are quite hardy and require the same diet as toucans. Aracaris of the genus *Pteroglossus* all have a very toothy jaggedness on the hooked beak and a power to inflict bites which rival a few of the parrots. Most aracaris, ranging from fourteen to sixteen inches, are trapped adult specimens which cannot be tamed. Therefore, the demand for these birds is greatly minimized in proportion to other members of the group.

COLLARED or BANDED ARACARI (*Pteroglossus torquatus*)

The most commonly available of this genus is the Collared Aracari with its six similar races from Mexico to northern South America. This bird with its slender body, long narrow beak, and long pointed tail has many variable and sometimes muddled colors. Because most individuals available to the bird fancier are adults, this species is rarely considered tameable.

The long slender beak is mostly blackish except for a bold yellowish-horn rim around the base and a horn color covering most of the upper area of the upper mandible. The jagged sawtoothed edges of both mandibles are horn colored.

The bare triangular flesh area surrounding the eyes is at first blue lapsing to red in the sharply angled area behind the eyes.

Upperparts, head, throat, and upper chest are black. The lower chest and underparts have a basic yellow ground coloring, but these areas are smudged with streaks of red particularly surrounding a blackish spot in the central chest area. A broad black band separates the chest from the abdomen. The underside of the tail is dull black.

Subspecies may show variations in length of beak, size, extent of black on the chest and variations of red on the yellow underparts. All will satisfactorily fulfill the name of Collared Aracari for the aviculturist but may provide some confusion if sex differentiation is desired.

SCARLET RUMPED ARACARI (*Pteroglossus erythropygius*)

The very similar Scarlet Rumped Aracari from Ecuador has a large red area covering lower back, rump, and upper tail coverts. The bare skin surrounding the eye is dull red, and the beak is mostly a pale horn color with a broad area of black on the lower part of the upper mandible and on an extensive tip of the lower mandible. A second band of brownish-black occurs at the lower part of the body near the ventral area.

CHESTNUT CHEEKED ARACARI (*Pteroglossus castanotis*)

The Chestnut Cheeked Aracari from northern South America is rarely available, but its size, basic pattern, and habits are similar. The beak has more black on the upper mandible and some red near the base. The bare skin area surrounding the eye is blue. The black upperparts give way to a chestnut area on the cheeks. The dark central area on the chest is absent, and the band separating chest from abdomen is red.

This species is sometimes called the Chestnut Eared Aracari.

MOUNT RORAIMA ARACARI (*Pteroglossus aracari roraimae*)

The very rare Mount Roraima Aracari from southeastern Venezuela, British Guiana, and Surinam is similar to the above except for the lack of a chestnut shade on the cheeks, a darker blue surrounding the eyes, and a broad horn colored band covering the lower part of the upper mandible.

Maximilian's Aracari (*Pteroglossus aracari aracari*) of Brazil is very similar but has traces of red at the upper boundary of yellow on the chest. Another similar subspecies is the Cayenne Aracari (subspecies *atricollis*).

DOUBLE COLLARED ARACARI (*Pteroglossus bitorquatus bitorquatus*)

The Double Collared Aracari is perhaps the most attractive of all aracaris because of its uniformity and sharpness of coloring.

The upper mandible is yellowish, and the lower mandible is white at the base with a slender angular line of black broadening to include rather more than the tip. A blue eye ring is surrounded by bare red flesh. An extensive cheek area shows a slight shading of blue on the black head. A tinge of red occurs on the lower part of the nape, and a shade of green on the wings varies the black upperparts.

A broad yellow band borders the black on the lower throat boundary. A broad swath of very bright and uniform red crosses the chest followed by golden-yellow through the undertail coverts. A dark indeterminate shade crosses the ventral area. The underside of the tail is blackish.

The Double Collared or Double Banded Aracari comes from South America along with two similar subspecies. Reichenow's Aracari (subspecies *reichenowi*) lacks the yellow band separating the lower throat of black and upper chest of red.

There are several species of very rare aracaris which seldom reach American aviculturists. These species come from South America and include the Many Banded Aracari (*Pteroglossus pluricinctus*), the Black Headed or Green Aracari (*Pteroglossus viridis viridis*), Lettered Aracari (*Pteroglossus viridis inscriptus*), Yellow Billed Aracari (*Pteroglossus flavirostris flavirostris*),

Azara's Aracari (*Pteroglossus flavirostris azara*), and the Duchess of Leuchtenberg's Aracari (*Pteroglossus mariae*).

GENUS AULACORHYNCHUS

Most of the members of this genus lack imaginative color schemes and are far less desirable than toucans for the average fancier. Still a few receive attention because they are usually far lower in price. Most range between twelve to fourteen inches.

EMERALD TOUCANETTE (*Aulacorhynchus prasinus*)

The attractive Emerald Toucanette with its fifteen slightly variable sub-species is the most readily available member of the genus. In many ways, it is also characteristic of the genus with its slender shape and long slim bill. One subspecies, *caeruleogularis*, is called the Blue Emerald Toucanette.

The long bill is rough and ragged on the rims but far less jagged than members of *Pteroglossus*. Mostly blackish, the beak has a broad yellow swath covering most of the sides of the upper mandible. A triangular area of almost bare flesh is grayish-green surrounding a large brownish-red eye.

The rest of the bird is a soft and furry pastel green, darker and richer on the upperparts. The tail is very dark, and some red occurs on the undertail coverts.

RED BILLED GREEN TOUCANETTE (*Aulacorhynchus sulcatus erythrognathus*)

The rare Red Billed Green Toucanette and its similar subspecies *sulcatus* from Venezuela are also mostly bright but soft green. Some pale blue surrounds the eye. The bill is dark red. ·

RED RUMPED GREEN TOUCANETTE (*Aulacorhynchus haematopygus*)

The very pretty Red Rumped Green Toucanette with its two subspecies *sexnotatus* and *haematopygus* comes from South America. The dark beak is mainly blackish-maroon with a whitish band around the base. The eyes are surrounded by bare skin of red. The basic bright green plumage is varied with soft but vivid blue on the chin, throat, upper chest, and tail feathers. Broad red tips on the tail feathers are somewhat softer and more attractive than the hard and bright red found on the rump.

SPOT BILLED TOUCANETTES (Genus *Selenidera*)

Six species, one with three subspecies, comprise the genus *Selenidera* and are called Spot Billed Toucanettes. All are from South America except one species from Central America. All are very rare in aviculture.

The writers have never owned any of these unusual birds but have been fortunate in observing a few different species.

A picture taken at Dierenpark Wassenaar in Holland is included in this book. Though this species is not the most colorful, it gives a good pictorial representation of the·dominant and most representative characteristic: the broad but rather shortened beak with unusual dark bars on the sides.

Spot Billed Toucanettes, from all indications, show sexual differences in coloring around the bare eye area: green for females and blue for males. The writers, unable to verify this as a fact, feel they can offer it quite reliably through other aviculturists who have forwarded information from personal experiences. Nesting is extremely rare for any toucan or toucanette in captivity, and so these color differences may possibly even be differences in species. At any rate, the writers will try to gain personal experience with members of this genus before the next edition of this book comes out.

The best known member, simply called Spot Billed Toucanette, is the species *maculirostris*. The wings, back, and rump are green. Head, except for the bare facial area, and underparts are brown. The tail on the underside is dull blackish flanked by red undertail coverts and tips on the tail. A subspecies, *gouldii*, is known as Gould's Toucanette. It is similar but has a broad dark band on the upper mandible. The male purportedly has a black head and yellow bands on the nape and behind the eyes. Lower parts are reported to be black with traces of orange, red, and brown. The female reputedly has both head and chest colored in reddish-brown.

CURLY HEADED TOUCANETTE (*Pteroglossus beauharnaesii*)

The extremely rare and unusual Curly Headed or Curl Crested Toucanette is set apart in a subgenus of *Pteroglossus*. This subgenus is named *Beauharnaisius* and has just the one species mentioned above.

The glossy black feathers on the top of the head are remarkably curled to give a very bizarre and rather artificial appearance as if it had just returned from a beauty parlor. Facial and throat areas are pale buff with several black-tipped feathers and a paler area on the ear coverts. The remaining upper plumage, except for red on rump and mantle, is dark green. A basic yellow on the underparts is haphazardly mixed with red.

SECTION IV
CHAPTER 47

Touracos and Plantain Eaters

Though not traditional avicultural subjects, many of the more advanced aviculturists are very successful in housing and caring for the unusual birds in the following chapters. Many of the birds in this section require specialized diets and careful handling. Most of the larger species should be given aviaries to themselves or should be housed with companions of similar dispositions. Even then, hazards of varying temperaments may be asserted.

The wonderful birds in this section are mostly available to zoos and wealthy aviculturists because of the financial aspects of acquisition and upkeep. Perhaps the only exception is the Stone Plover which, though rarely imported, is inexpensive but lacking in glamour. The remaining birds in this section are often flamboyant in coloring, size, or shape, or are highly coveted because of their rarity. They invariably are great display birds.

In ornithology, touracos are sometimes called Go Away Birds.

Touracos and plantain eaters are all very active forest birds of solitary demeanor from Africa. Sexes are alike. Rather large, within an average size totalling seventeen inches including the tail, they all have long squarish tails and somewhat resemble arboreal fowls. Very adept and precise in flight, these birds are able to disappear quickly from bird watchers though their ringing calls belie their presence. In aviaries, there are not many places to hide. This domestic shortcoming does not preclude an amazing activity; but it does help to instill a reasonable calmness and, in a few cases, even tameness with proper handling.

The standard softbilled diet is acceptable and offers adequate nourishment, but considerable encouragement must be added during the dietary acclimation phase. Live foods placed upon inert domestic foods help, and a previously domesticated bird quickly leads the newcomers onto satisfactory domestic foods.

Breeding successes are unfortunately extremely seldom. Nests are usually loosely constructed of rude sticks on the tops of low trees and usually contain two eggs.

There is no clear-cut division between the popular names of plaintain eater and touracos. Many fanciers use the names interchangeably.

HARTLAUB'S TOURACO (*Tauraco hartlaubi*)

The best known species of touracos in aviculture is Hartlaub's Touraco. Well proportioned, tailor shaped, and average sized, this lovely creature is sleekly groomed, well glossed, and very beautiful. The beak is short and blunt with a recurved tip on the upper mandible. The overall demeanor is one of elegant poise, great activity, and precise, self-confident movements.

The large body is balanced by a long tail and a shapely but not tall crest of innumerable small feathers. The crest is glossy bluish-black. The dark eye is fronted by an elliptical patch covering lores and extending to an area just over the forward part of the eye. A bright red surrounds the eye, and a fine line of white extends from the lower boundary of red tapering to the nape of the neck. All underparts, back, and neck are glowing olive. Wings are glossed in dark greenish-blue with red around the lower rim. The tail is blackish.

The generic name is disputed. Some list it as *Tauraco*, and others call it *Turacus*.

Several touracos are very similar to Hartlaub's Touraco but all are very rare in aviculture.

The Black Billed Touraco (*Tauraco schutti*) has a smaller crest of green instead of black. The forward patch of white above and before the eye dwindles to a fine line of white which also extends behind the eye. The red surrounding the eye is greatly reduced. On the whole, this is a less attractive species than the above.

The Violet Crested Touraco (*Gallirex porphyreolophus*) has a strong sheen of violet overcasting the blackish crest, wings, and tail. The red around the eye is present, but the white markings are absent.

A very short and well tailored greenish crest adorns the White Cheeked Touraco (*Tauraco leucotis*). A bold band of white, slightly off center to the perpendicular, highlights a space from the upper eye area to the lower neck. Though behind the ear, the white line nearly touches it. Both red and white areas surrounding the eyes are greatly reduced. A well-known subspecies is Donaldson's Touraco (*Tauraco leucotis donaldsoni*).

The White Crested Touraco (*Tauraco leucolophus*) is similar in every way except for loreal and eye areas and the vivid white which covers the entire head and neck. A prominent triangular area of black glossed in blue and purple covers the lores, the forehead, an extensive eyebrow area, and an area surrounding the eye which is very narrow around the lower eyelid. The beak is yellowish with a shade of slate near the base.

SCHALOW'S TOURACO (*Tauraco schalowi*)

The very shy and elusive Schalow's Touraco is a very beautiful species if its nervous disposition would allow it to be seen. The crest is very long, pointed, and greatly recurved. The basic coloring is a bright, glossy green darkening to dull black on the lower chest and further underparts. Some red occurs in the flights, and the tail is dark blue. Red boldly surrounds the eyes with a white line above becoming broader on the lores. Another faint white line is extensive from the lower part of the lores to the nape of the neck. Black fills the remaining loreal area. Tips of the crest are whitish.

Livingston's Touraco (*Touraco livingstonii*) is very similar except for more prominent white on the facial areas and the tips of the crest.

WHITE BELLIED or WHITE BREASTED TOURACO (*Corythaixoides leucogaster*)

The very different White Bellied Touraco is basically slate-gray and white. The tall upstanding crest is balanced by the long tail. All parts are slate-gray except for the white underparts surrounding the curved, slaty bib and extending through the undertail coverts. Some white also occurs on the tail and at the base of the primary flights.

BLUE TOURACO or GIANT PLANTAIN EATER (*Corythaeola cristata*)

The very rare Blue Touraco, ranging between twenty-eight to thirty inches, is also very different in color scheme and crest. The yellow beak is tipped in bright orange. The head, neck, back, wings, and upperside of tail are bluish-black. Underparts start with a dull greenish chest and a dull reddish abdomen fading to a reddish-black on the undertail coverts. The underside of the tail is black at first shading to yellowish in the broad center and abruptly ending in a broad black band. The crest is very full and shaped somewhat like a cockscomb.

VIOLET PLANTAIN EATER (*Musophaga violacea*)

The handsome and closely related Violet Plantain Eater is covered mostly in dull violet-black coloring except for red in the wings and a very brightly marked head with a waxy gloss. The lower mandible and central part of the upper mandible are bright red-orange. The upperpart of the broad beak which extends to the top of the crown is bright yellow. The eyes are rimmed in red, and a bright white accent mark extends broadly beyond the lower rim of the eye. The top of the head is a shade of very dull red.

CHAPTER 48

Kingfishers, Hornbills, and Hoopoes

GENERAL CARE

None of the members in this chapter are greatly favored by private aviculturists, but hornbills are favorites in many zoos because of their bizarre appearance and great size. Hornbills are excellent for zoos because of these reasons, and they acclimate easily. Hoopoes are very difficult to acclimate to domestic diets, and most kingfishers are bypassed because they are presumed to be too difficult to feed especially during the acclimation to domestic diets.

Kingfishers with their large beaks are basically divided into two groups. One group stays near water and depends almost entirely upon fish and aquatic insects for a diet. The other group inhabits dense forests and jungles and depends on a more standard softbilled fare with a decided insectivorous preference.

The family of kingfishers has some of the most beautifully colored and best patterned members to be found in aviculture. As aviculture progresses many species will doubtlessly be in high demand. All have large heads, thick necks, and thick beaks which are also usually long. The tails are short. The dull and unattractive Kookaburra adapts easily to domestication and is a prideful offering in several fortunate zoos which the writers have visited. Other far more beautiful species should be forthcoming when importers learn the acclimation period can be no less trying than for many of the popular favorites. Of course, they must become available to importers before this hurdle can be jumped.

Like hawks and owls, kingfishers regurgitate pellets of undigested food and fats and should have considerable roughage in the diet.

Hornbills vary tremendously in size and coloring. Usually the smallest ones are less interesting and far less attractive, but the price is adjusted downwards in a proper ratio. Hornbills are noted for their huge beaks which have extraordinary casques on the tops of the upper mandibles. Ordinarily the large size results in clumsy ungainliness. The tail is long in a traditional

461

The Belted Kingfisher from the Americas is mostly grayish and white with some chestnut on the sides and lower chest. The spiny and rangy crest adds distinction. This kingfisher lives mostly on fish and is difficult to transfer to a domestic diet.

ratio to body size. The diet is the standard softbilled fare, but the consumed quantity is much greater and varies according to size.

The most readily available hornbills come from India, but the natural range of the many species extends from Africa to the Philippines.

Baby hornbills become enchanting pets. Their awkward clumsiness and almost hideous appearance lent to an endearing and sweet personality blend in an absurd caricature which no bird lover could resist. These hand fed nestlings quickly form an attachment for humans which rivals the loyalty given by most dogs. The writers once had such a pet which had been a hand fed nestling. It was a rare Rufous Hornbill from the Philippines; and it dogged every footstep seeking recognition, assurance, and usually a bit of food. A picture of this much cherished creature appears in this book. This picture shows the clumsy and grotesque silhouette and gives an idea of the uninteresting and plain color pattern of the immature, but it could never convey the ludicrous delicacy emanating from the long and languid over-hanging eyelashes which give an appearance of aloofness tinged with boredom.

In all species, immatures have dull coloration and slowly developing casques. The larger the casque in adulthood, the slower it develops during the long process of maturation.

Hoopoes are very seldom seen though often offered by exporters in Europe and India. The offers are not frequently accepted by importers because of the great difficulty in transferring these birds to domesticated diets. Hoopoes offered by European exporters usually have been transferred to domestic diets; but those from India, though less costly, are usually risky because they lack this very important acclimation.

If not accustomed to domestic diets, hoopoes should be given a loose soil floor generously planted with earthworms and mealworms. The long probing beaks help in finding an adequate food supply under these conditions. The change to domesticated diets is very slow and frustrating to the bird fancier.

KINGFISHERS

The Kookaburra (*Dacelo novaeguineae*) from Australia is the most coveted and best known of all kingfishers in captivity. It also is one of the largest. Frequently called the Laughing Jackass, the Kookaburra is a bird of dull coloring ranging from dusty buff to brownish-black.

The thick beak is brownish-black above and buff below. A broad and long trailing patch following the eye covers the ear covert and tapers sharply on the lower side of the neck. A dark crescent on the lower nape fills the area between. The chin and throat are particularly whitish. Upperparts from the back and including the wings are dull brownish-black, but many of the feathers have whitish tips. The dusty buff underparts show some subordinate darker striations.

The Kookaburra is protected and has a very beneficial reputation in its wild state as a destroyer of rodents and reptiles, including snakes. In some cases, they also rob other birds' nests. (The writers know of only one other bird which will attack snakes: the California Road Runner.)

The Kookaburra's reptilian diet of snakes has not been confirmed by the writers. In captivity, the diet is the standard softbilled fare with extra raw meat and, if possible, a young mouse daily.

The White Throated Kingfisher (*Halcyon smyrnensis*) from the Philippine Islands is a colorful and easily managed species with a broad white bib starting

463

at the chin, broadening on the upper chest and tapering to a point on the lower chest. Remaining underparts are dark brown through the undertail coverts. The underside of the tail is bluish-gray. The head is very dark brown and the beak is only slightly lighter. The lovely blue upperparts starting on the mantle are broadly marked with black on the wings.

A subspecies (*gularis*), also from the Philippine Islands, has paler brown with a reddish tint and a far less extensive white which is restricted to the chin and upper throat. The beak is reddish.

The Sacred Kingfisher of Australia (*Halcyon sancta*) has a pale blackish beak with black continuing a line through the lores, under the eyes, and broadening on the nape of the neck. Upperparts are turquoise, and underparts are buffish-white.

There are many other kingfishers from many parts of the world which deserve mention but which cannot be covered in this book. Many are exceptional in their beauty, and many would be very desirable avicultural subjects if they were available.

HORNBILLS

One of the most colorful of all hornbills is the rare Rufous Hornbill (*Buceros hydrocorax*) from the Philippine Islands. The writers have been privileged to own Rufous Hornbills both in adulthood and immaturity. The clownishness of the immature bird is described above, but the adult assumes a stately air in trying to overcome its great and awkward size. Sexes are the same, but the female is slightly smaller than the male.

The forepart of the beak is a horn color blending into a bright rose-red on the base and on the huge concaved casque. A broad band of black surrounds the beak and covers the eyes. A small patch of white follows on the chin and extends to the lower sides of the neck. Remaining parts of head and neck are a rufous shade. Dark and dull brown covers the remaining parts except for the abdomen and tail which are very pale rufous-buff.

Immatures are a dull brown speckled with dusty buff. The blackish beak lacks the huge casque but has a slight overgrowth on the upper mandible which very slowly assumes an adult shape.

The Great or Concave Casqued Hornbill (*Buceros bicornis*) is from India and many neighboring areas extending even to Burma and Sumatra. This is not an attractive bird. It has a very startling appearance and a large size averaging forty inches including the tail but excluding the beak.

The plumage is a dull black marked with white across the wings in three places. In a color reversal of white on the underside of the long, broad, and squarish tail, it has a broad black band about two-thirds of the way down. The neck and top of the head are flesh colored. A narrow black area on the crown and chin enlarges to include most of the facial area and is dominated by a reddish eye. The huge casque and beak are yellow with a dull reddish tip on the beak.

An immature Rufous Hornbill gives little indication of the beautiful plumage and huge rose-colored casque above the beak, both of which develop very slowly. Its dull plumage and awkward, clumsy shape and large size are delightfully offset by long, langorous eyelashes and soft confiding eyes. They become extremely tame pets during the immature stage.

The Rufous Hornbill from the Philippine Islands is one of the more attractive members in the Hornbill family. Hornbills are usually overlooked by aviculturists because of their large size, but they are highly coveted zoo attractions. Owned by Jerome Buteyn.

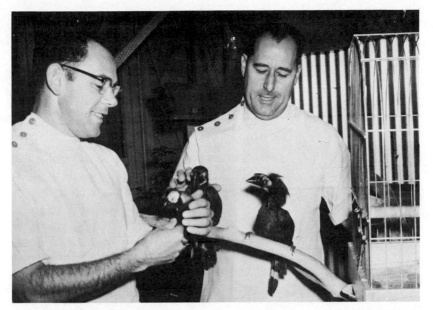

The authors, Henry J. Bates and Robert L. Busenbark, inspect unusual new arrivals from the Philippine Islands: immature Tarictic Hornbills and a Coleto Mynah.

The Pied Hornbill (*Anthracoceros coronatus*) is much smaller and much blacker. White occurs on the wing, tail tips, underparts, and lower cheek area. The eyes are surrounded by white with a fine black line cutting through to the corners of the beak. The huge beak and casque on the upper mandible are yellowish-horn with some black on the forward end of the casque.

The Rhinoceros Hornbill (*Buceros rhinoceros*) is like the Great Hornbill in overall appearance, but the casque is slender with an unconnected horn projecting forward. This rare form comes from Borneo, Java, and the Malay Peninsula.

The Wreathed Hornbill (*Aceros undulatus*) from India, Burma, Borneo, Java, the Malay Peninsula, and neighboring areas is another huge and very ugly bird. The casque is greatly reduced in size, but it is distinctively lined with many deep cleaves. There are several quite similar races of this bird.

Tarictic Hornbills of the genus *Penelopides* are much smaller. These variably colored birds all come from the Philippines. There are two species with a total of ten races native to the Philippines. The writers have had Tarictic Hornbills during immature phases. The basic coloring ranges from dull black to slate with a whitish band across the tail.

The casque atop the upper mandible is a narrow ridge which varies considerably in length and coloring between immaturity and adulthood.

467

The Pied Hornbill from India is one of the most prevalent of all hornbills to be found in captivity. Availability over other hornbills, rather than greater attractiveness, makes this large bird a frequent exhibit in many zoos. New York Zoological Society photo.

Variations in size of different species are limited, but coloring varies. Immature specimens are much like many of the dull Ground Hornbills.

There are many other hornbills which do not reach aviculture. Therefore, they are not covered in this chapter. All require the same care and feeding, and nearly all have unusual features characteristic of the family. A few may become available from time to time to various zoos, but most bird fanciers will bypass them.

HOOPOE (*Upupa epops*)

Hoopoes with their many slightly varying subspecies range from southern Sweden in the north to Sumatra and the Malay Peninsula in the south. All are very similar in coloring and form. Description is difficult for the most part, but the overall size is approximately twelve inches long. Proportions are shapely, and the body size is balanced with a long tail, a long and slender curved beak, and a flamboyant fanlike crest.

The basic ground color is orange-brown with many blackish and whitish accents on the tips of the crest feathers and on the tail feathers. The wings have broad black markings flanked by smaller white areas.

CHAPTER 49

Trumpeters

No birds are quite so happy to be domesticated as are trumpeters. They adore mankind and lavish affection upon anyone who will even half-heartedly return it, and no human who loves birds could resist the affectionate overtures. They bow with outspread wings, utter strange chuckling sounds of joy, dance with a comic happiness, and race imaginary rivals to amuse their fortunate owners. No one can help but take these delightful creatures to heart.

The unofficial greeter at the Palos Verdes Bird Farm is a White-Winged Trumpeter who delights in entertaining visitors. Those skeptics who believe that birds should not be maintained as captives of men soon change their minds when they see the obvious happiness of this amusing creature.

Though he often possesses an undisguised air of dignity, which at times borders on hauteur, this trumpeter rarely passes up the chance to rush up to visitors with an elaborate and strutting wingspread bow accompanied by tiny chortling sounds. Such an elaborate display frequently puts the puzzled and timorous visitor on the defensive. Fearing an attack, the uninitiated visitor may retreat hastily. When the greeting is explained, the timid visitor invariably becomes a devoted admirer of this avian charmer.

Many children try to pet the trumpeter, but they always must be taught the proper procedure. The pet of the Palos Verdes Bird Farm goes into a hypnotic ecstasy when he is gently stroked on the head, chin, or sides of his face; but he dislikes being petted on his back and will shrink from such attempts. If the stroking stops before the trumpeter feels it should, he stands fixed in the same position hoping it will resume. He always shows his appreciation by bowing and spreading his wings while uttering his little chortling sounds.

If visitors are slow to recognize his presence, the trumpeter may go into an elaborate dance which shows his fine sense of comedy. Usually he selects a small discarded object, such as a wad of paper or anything at hand, and tries to give it animation. He tosses the object with a sideways twist of the head and chases after it to retrieve it. In this activity and the race which follows it, the trumpeter gives the distinct impression that he is confident he has all the grace of a ballerina despite being built like a miniature ostrich.

The trumpeter is ever curious. No activity escapes his attention. The writers, more than once, have had to wash his beak and face because of his fascinated probings into paint buckets. Fortunately, the writers always use paints which are completely safe for birds and have had no complications. Furthermore, the trumpeter enjoys the attention while receiving the face-washing.

Trumpeters enjoy their spotlight of attention and are loath to share it with other birds once they have been so spoiled. If any newly introduced bird shows a threat to his domain, the trumpeter races up to the bird with a dominating wingspread which cannot help but intimidate the intruder. Should such an action not be effective, the trumpeter will strike at the intruder with flailing legs and an occasional well-aimed blow from his hard, fowl-like beak.

This attack is not directed upon other pet birds which ordinarily remain upon perches; but, if they happen to fly off and threaten the floored domain which the trumpeter has claimed, the trumpeter will attack even though the offender may be infinitely better able to defend itself. Macaws and cockatoos, though adequately armed with powerful beaks, pale at the onrushing trumpeter's awesome display and hurriedly climb out of his reach. It is because of this protective characteristic that many people in South America use the trumpeter as a watchdog in their poultry flocks. Trumpeters are quick to determine their station in life and have an unusually acute devotion to duty.

The trumpeter utters curious sounds. As mentioned before, the sounds of joy are short chuckling chortles. Those sounds which are meant to be intimidating are deep bass drum sounds which come from deep within the body and sound as if they are muffled at the time of utterance. There is an indescribable ventriloqual quality about these sounds which is probably because the bird shows no visible muscular exertion in their utterance. If there is any further sound, the writers have never heard it. The only sounds uttered in the presence of the writers have been rather quiet. One would have to be accustomed to the danger herald before the sound could be an effective warning.

Trumpeters come from South America and are restricted to a single genus consisting of three species and several subspecies or races. All are similarly shaped, and the size varies only slightly. The White Winged Trumpeter is the most readily available species in aviculture, but all species have similar ungainly and gangling proportions coupled with an exotic appearance.

WHITE WINGED TRUMPETER (*Psophia leucoptera*)

The total height in a natural stance is twenty-one inches, but this includes legs of seven and a half inches and a long neck which is at the very least six inches long. Descriptions are really inadequate, but the good picture in this book will help bring into focus the various aspects of the overall

The White-winged Trumpeter has an unusual and gangling appearance, but it is without a doubt one of the most affectionate and endearing pets in the entire bird kingdom. This one is a special pet at Palos Verdes Bird Farm.

appearance. There is a very intent and serious expression about the face which neither camera nor language can capture.

The oval pheasant-sized body tilts upwards and slopes backwards to the point of the tail and then falls abruptly downwards. A fowl-like head is perched atop the long neck. The beak in adults is a bright yellowish-horn shade and dull grayish-black in immature birds. The changeover is very slow and starts at the base of the beak.

Feet and legs are grayish with a hint of silver blue.

A large oval of white covers the lower half of the back when the wings are folded. When the wings are outstretched, this white area is shown on the lower areas of the inner flight feathers.

The rest of the bird is black, but variations in feather structure provide several differences. The short head feathers are very soft and have a velvet texture while the wing covert feathers are long and hairy. The scaly neck feathers have a high gloss of metallic purples, blues, and greens. When the wings are outspread, the scapulars show these same glossy shades.

Both sexes are very much alike, but authorities say the female has a slightly shorter beak and a less bold head than the male.

The enthusiasm for living among people does not extend to breeding in captivity. Very little is known about the breeding habits of the trumpeter, and reports differ considerably.

Trumpeters are poor flyers and reach their high roosting places by leaping to graduated levels. To escape enemies they prefer to run rather than fly.

The Yellow Winged Trumpeter (*Psophia ochroptera*) is similar to the above except for a pale shade of yellow in place of the white wing area. As yet, it is not known aviculturally.

The Gray Winged Trumpeter (*Psophia crepitans*), as the name indicates, shows gray where the White Winged Trumpeter shows white. A soft, irregular band across the back is dull reddish-brown.

The Green Backed Trumpeter (*Psophia viridis*) is brightly colored with metallic green wing coverts. Though the wings are mostly grayish, there is a faint shading of rusty-brown which is more heavily concentrated on the back.

The trumpeter's diet is indeed simple if we can judge satisfactorily from the one long-time pet pictured in this book which is a favorite of the writers as well as of many visitors. When first obtained, this trumpeter ate any type of live food offered as well as chicken scratch food, diced fruit, and an occasional pellet of mynah food. As time passed, he gained a marked preference for mynah pellets and gradually came to ignore scratch feed, mealworms, and diced fruit.

For a long period, this delightful and comic bird has thrived on just mynah pellets which really constitute a basic and balanced diet for many birds.

With some regret, the writers must admit that the diet of mynah pellets has not shown the same effect on droppings which it shows with mynah birds and several other softbills. In most cases, the loose droppings of softbilled birds become more firm and less copious when they are fed on the basic mynah pellets. Not so with the trumpeter. The frequent and incredibly voluminous droppings seem almost to exceed the amount of food intake. If the reader has ever owned a pet duck or goose, he will readily understand the unexpressed thoughts of the writers. A concrete patio becomes a slippery hazard if not washed down with a monotonous frequency. A garden, which these birds love, quickly becomes well-fertilized.

In the beginning, the feeding of mealworms was quickly termed a waste because as soon as the bird consumed them there seemed to be a very hurried attempt to expel them with the effect of the gastric juices serving only to deaden the worms. The shell of the mealworm was not in the least affected by the bird's digestive system. Although there never was an actual comparison between the number of mealworms consumed and those expelled, the writers feel that they would be quite safe in stating that none was actually digested.

Another trait of the trumpeter, which the writers have never been able to discourage, is bathing at dusk. Most birds sensibly bathe in the early morning and have all day to dry so that there will be no danger of dampness to cause chills and illness at night. Again, not so with the trumpeter. This one never considers a bath until an hour before sunset. The lavish bath consists of a complete soaking; and, with frequent wing lifting and splashing, an area of nearly a four-foot radius is so completely dampened that there is hardly any water left in the rather large and deep bird bath. After this labored effort, the trumpeter climbs, jump by jump, to the highest and most secluded spot possible and appears very well satisfied with another happy day. There have been no ill effects from this late daily bath and no indication that a change is at all likely.

Notwithstanding the above very slight worries and disadvantages, the White Backed Trumpeter is a great joy and is different from any other pet. The companionship and devotion to its master is unparalleled in the bird world, and the comic expression of this affection is a continual delight.

CHAPTER 50

Plovers, Bitterns, Cranes, and Flamingos

Among other unusual groups of fascinating birds are these extraordinary subjects sought by a few of the most advanced and admiring aviculturists. The main reason these birds fall into the same chapter is their basically rare inclusion in aviculture plus their long legs. All other characteristics are unrelated, but the writers feel they should be included even though the coverage is brief.

PLOVERS

Stone Plovers, also called Thick Knees or Stone Curlews, occur in several parts of the world. Though they appear to be shorebirds, they are occasionally imported into the United States from the interiors of South America. In these instances, the various races must have abandoned salt water haunts for fresh water streams and rivers.

All forms around the world are nearly the same in appearance. The large head, bold eyes, long neck, heavy body, and stilt-like legs are characteristic. Another main characteristic is a basically cluttered and ordinary color scheme which relies mainly upon drabness and protective coloration for safety from predators. Pale and uninteresting buff is finely streaked with dark brown to provide a protective color scheme. Upperparts are more boldly streaked with dark brown than the less significant underparts. A very large golden eye is also a basic characteristic.

Those individuals which the writers have owned have had certain basic characteristics in common. They are difficult to change over to domesticated diets, but they always have endearing ways despite their clumsy appearance which is totally lacking in glamour. They have a charming habit of quickly bowing their large heads when anything to their liking is proffered.

In the beginning, all domesticated diets are refused except live food which must be moving before it is accepted. Mealworms are the most easily obtainable source of live food and are always accepted. The writers, acknowledging the inadequacy of mealworms as the sole diet, showed considerable perturbance about this inadequate acceptance. Searching for an acceptable food, the writers were nonplussed and astonished to find that the only relished food was live, swimming goldfish. Though quite an expensive diet, the writers gladly offered it as a reprise against their own inexperience. The Stone Plovers suddenly came to life with a great interest and bowed considerably before and after partaking of this aristocratic repast.

In a short time, the Stone Plovers were quite willing to accept anything offered by the writers, but they gradually leaned their preferences towards mynah pellets and thus became thoroughly domesticated, tame, and always entertaining.

The writers feel the popular name of Thick Knee is even less deserving than the modest appearance would indicate. Though the general appearance is quite ordinary and especially lacking in delicacy, the charming personality easily can demand a reappraisal. Highly insectivorous, the Stone Plover easily adapts to aviculture after the trying acclimation period and is thereafter very hardy. All belong to the genus *Burhinus* whether they come from the usual exportation center of South America or from Europe or Africa.

The total height is about sixteen to eighteen inches. The body size is not quite as large as that of the trumpeter, but the head is much larger. It resembles a Bustard in miniature.

The species generally described above is the South American Thick Knee (*Burhinus superciliaris*). The Mexican species (*bistratus*), called the Double Striped Thick Knee, is slightly larger and has greenish legs. The Australian species (*magnirostris*) is even larger. The three African species, a European species, a South American species, and another inhabiting India, Burma, and Ceylon complete the picture of similarity with only slight variations in characteristics and size.

The Egyptian Plover (not a true plover) or Crocodile Bird (*Pluvianus aegyptius*) is usually found in conservatory aviaries in collections of very rare birds. It has an unusually charming and rather shy demeanor, added to a stately and demure color scheme.

The blackish head and back with its greenish cast are interrupted by a white line starting at the upper margin of the lores extending over the eyes and down to the nape of the neck where both sides meet. The whitish chin fades into a buffish shade divided by a greenish-black U-shaped band dropping from the shoulders to the lower chest. Below this is a whitish area gradually fading to a buffish on the abdomen and the undertail coverts. A broad and irregular blackish band crosses the wings flanked on both sides by very pale shades.

The short beak, large head, stout body, and long legs contrast sharply with the very long grayish flights which nearly cover the medium sized square tail.

Egyptian Plovers like pools for wading. In the wild state, they feed upon aquatic parasites found on the backs of crocodiles. In captivity, they follow a standard softbill diet after acclimation.

SUN BITTERN (*Eurypyga helias*)

The rare and unusual Sun Bittern, from Central to South America, is another extraordinary bird which sometimes fits into specialized aviculturists' collections. This is another small headed, long necked, long legged, and heavy bodied bird which faintly resembles a terrestrial crane. The body is slightly larger than the size of a domestic pigeon.

Two outstanding characteristics occur in captivity: a near turkey-like display depending upon outspread wings and bittern-like stealthy snakiness in capturing flies and other insects. The total size stretches nearly twenty inches from feet to top of head.

The Sun Bittern is always a pleasant addition to advanced aviculturists' collections. It has great charm and a readily adaptable personality to avian life but it is rarely obtainable. It inhabits dense jungle floors in a secretive manner and stays close to the ground with a preference for semi-aquatic conditions.

The long pointed beak is dark on the upper mandible and pale horn on the lower mandible. The bluish-gray head has an added snaky appearance given by two long white lines: one over and behind the eyes and the other curving from the lower mandible under the lower cheek area and dipping for a short distance down the neck.

The pattern on the body, wings, and tail is one of complicated and cluttered beauty. Most of the colors are blue-gray, earthy browns, and warm reddish-browns. These shades are irregularly arranged in alternating lighter and darker bands with camouflaging striations. There are some white spots appearing irregularly on the wings. A broad blackish band occurs on the tail rather near the tips. In some ways this bird emulates the pattern of the peacock, but the coloring is much more modest.

The large wingspread, used in the ebullient display, shows greater variation in both pattern and color. Bright reddish-browns are extensively revealed with black tips on the long flights.

Displays are directed at females, sunlight, or anything which arouses a thinly veiled interest in intimidation. The Sun Bittern loves to display and usually needs little excuse. The usual display includes broadly fanned tail and outspread wings with lowered body.

This is a lovely bird with enchanting tameness. Wherever possible, bird fanciers with proper accommodations will enjoy including it in their collections. It likes a pool and a planted aviary even though it is perfectly hardy without these desirable luxuries in moderate climates.

Rarely bred, the incubation period is nearly twenty-seven days with downy young emerging in an advanced stage of development.

CRANES

The writers have had no experience with cranes except for a short interval with African Crowned Cranes. Jack Throp, Curator of the Jerome Buteyn Foreign Bird Farm in San Luis Rey, California, offers the information which follows.

Cranes are split into two avicultural groups according to diet. Most aviculturists are interested in Short Beaked Cranes which live chiefly on game bird pellets or mynah pellets, grains such as chicken scratch, and green foods. The two most lovely members of this group are the Demoiselle Crane from a very widespread area including Europe and the African Crowned Crane. Usually, these birds do not dig for food.

Long Billed Cranes, such as Lilford's, Saurus, and Sandhill Cranes, all dig for worms, tender roots, and grubs. In captivity, these may be fed raw meat, fish, mynah pellets, game bird pellets, chicken scratch, and green food.

All cranes should be given room in a large aviary so they can successfully forage for their foods.

The various cranes need not be described here because they form a very specialized fancy which, in itself, deserves a separate book. The African Crowned Crane pictured in this book gives a quite graphic idea of the exotic appearance of the most beautiful member of the family.

FLAMINGOS

There are four species and several subspecies of flamingos which vary chiefly in coloration. The deepest pink flamingos, called the American Flamingo, usually arrive from Florida where they are often imported from South America. South American, African and Eurasian Flamingos vary greatly from pink to white. Size also is variable.

Flamingos have extremely long slender necks and spindly stiltlike legs which become a hazard in an aviary if they panic. They frighten easily and any entangling branches could result in broken legs. Because of this danger, their aviaries should be rather barren with smooth terrain. Planted aviaries are desirable and should be landscaped with a tropical motif to give an appropriate background to these exotic creatures.

The body is a graceful oval tilting downwards at the tail and is no larger than those of some of the smaller geese. The shortly trailing tail feathers are unlike most birds' tails but resemble elongated and limp uppertail coverts.

The head, small in proportion to overall size, has a huge and strange beak designed for straining small crustaceans and plant life from the water. The very wide beak extends forward and then drops abruptly. The lower edge of the upper mandible after the blunt tip basically angles diagonally upwards to form a rounded triangle. The lower mandible, though large, is shaped to fit the upper more dominant part of the beak. The long neck is extremely flexible and gives a very graceful and unique appearance with its marvelous curvatures.

Nearly all flamingos have black in their flights and some rosy crimson in bright plumage flashes.

In captivity, flamingos are easily fed after learning to accept domesticated diets. Their wading pools and feeding dishes should be kept scrupulously clean. The only real problem in feeding is holding or restoring the quickly fading color.

The diet given by Jack Throp to the flamingos pictured in this book is as follows: boiled brown rice, corn meal, shrimp meal, small pellets of dog food, salt, and a color agent which will be covered in the next paragraph. Some people use pheasant mash and boiled horsemeat in place of the dog food, and others use soaked wheat instead of corn meal.

Color holding and restoration in flamingos have always been the uppermost problems with these beauties. Varied and often expensive additives have been used in experimentation with variable success. The pink coloring depends upon the amount of carotenoids consumed while new feathers are growing. Apparently carotenoids stored in glands, fat, skin, and feathers give no help during this process but must be recently ingested. Both plant and animal carotenoids serve as parts of the natural diet, and both are probably metabolized in nature.

There are many sources of carotenoids both in animal and vegetable dietary substances. Good but very expensive sources in the animal substances are fresh or ground dried shrimp, ground lobster shell, and canned salmon. In vegetable sources, these are carrots, carrot juice, paprika, and fresh ground red pepper. Some of these foodstuffs to be fully effective must be fed in such great quantities that the diet would be thrown out of balance. It would, for instance, be extremely difficult for a flamingo to eat enough carrots to produce a natural color; and if it did, other vital elements would be ignored because of the volume of intake.

Perhaps the safest and purest method of adding carotenoids is by a commercially available concentrate of carotene in oil. There are several brand names of this product, but the one to be used should, of course, be a concentrate. All are vegetable derivatives and are superior sources of natural vitamin A.

Unfortunately, domestically induced coloring, however bright, is always somewhat artificial and never quite approaches the natural shade which has appropriately been named flamingo. Most of the artificially induced color feeding tends slightly to more of an orange tint. This may be possibly affected by an imbalance of animal and vegetable carotenoids normally consumed in the wild state. Also quite possible, but never verified by the writers, is that variations in coloring of species and subspecies in different natural ranges may have different ratios and amounts of carotenoids in available food supplies. This theory has been partially disproved, however, by the fact that several different races have been housed together in zoos. Though given the same

479

diet, the white flamingos for the most part remain white. The variation, even though it does occur, is very slight.

Shipment of flamingos, cranes, or any large and long legged birds poses some difficult problems. Many easily panic during crate movements. If not properly packed, severe injuries to fragile legs or to wings can easily result. The best method of shipment is always by air, and the best packing method experienced by the writers may at first seem somewhat inhumane.

The bird is placed in a sitting position and gently enclosed in a wrapper of fabric to insure immobility of wings, legs, and every part of the body except the head and neck. To be sure, the bird suffers some discomfiture from such shipments; but air shipments insure rapid delivery; and, after arrival, a stretching of legs and wings removes all traces of the immobility. Most important of all is the fact that the bird arrives intact and uninjured.

Those ungainly crates which offer full height so that the bird may remain standing during shipment may, at the outset, seem more kind. However, the percentage of injuries sustained by panic during awkward handling proves that forced immobility and smaller crates are far more humane in the ultimate result.

Flamingos nest in friendly colonies on barren beachlike areas. The nests are large mounds carefully built up with mud and hollowed out in a miniature volcano shaped for the comfort of the setting bird as well as for a holding receptacle for the one or two eggs. The boredom of setting during the thirty to thirty-two days is relieved by neighborly chats or mild arguments with nearby nests and by casually repairing or adding to the nesting mounds. Both sexes share the nesting ordeal. With their long necks they casually and slowly reach out to select pebbles or other materials to add to the sides of the nesting mounds. This is a most fascinating procedure to observe and the bird fancier cannot quell excitement during his observations. After hatching, the boredom ceases because the proud parents are busy stuffing their downy and gangling offspring with regurgitated food.

The display includes raising many plumes on the back in a fountain of gracefulness. In flight, the birds must begin by a long striding and awkward running gait before the wings are spread in a satisfactory take-off. In heavy breeding areas in the wild, man has consistently annoyed these birds by low-flying airplanes so that they might witness the elaborate ascension and graceful flight. As a result, the birds sensibly sought other breeding grounds in South America. The writers hope that inquisitive and thrill-seeking pilots will not continue their search in South America and will allow these birds to nest in peace. Many untended eggs and chicks have died during such forays.

Four handsome but rare Kingfishers which have been successfully kept in captivity are the Sacred Kingfisher of Australia (top left), the White Breasted Kingfisher of certain parts of the orient (top right), the Blue Breasted Kingfisher of Borneo (lower left), and the Kookaburra from Australia (lower right). Sexes are similar in all species.

The White Throated Kingfisher from the Philippines is one of the most attractive members of a fascinating family which are seldom kept in aviculture.

The cluttered mosaic pattern of the Sun Bittern serves as protective coloration in the wild. Close observation reveals beautiful shadings and handsome contrasts. The Sun Bittern is adept at capturing insects and is flamboyant in his strutting displays.

The Giant Oriole (*Gymnomystax mexicanus*), from Guiana to Peru in South America, is large, aggressive, and very handsome in its sharply defined and vivid pattern. Though easily managed in captivity, it should only be housed with large softbills such as Jay Thrushes, Magpies, Magpie Jays, and other birds of similar size and disposition.

An assembly of beauty from some of Australia's finest finches. Lady Gould Finches in black headed and red headed varieties and the handsomely patterned Masked Grassfinch. Photographed at Palos Verdes Bird Farm.

Australia's Parson Finch is a handsome species which breeds well in captivity. It has similar characteristics found in the Shafttail Finch but is not quite as attractive. The chest is browner and upperparts are grayer than the photograph indicates. Also, the large black bib is mostly hidden in this picture.

Shafttail Finches from Australia are among the best of all aviary subjects. The sleek shape and soft colors are brightened by bold black accents. The beak is orange in one race and coral-red in another. Shafttails are good breeders and are among the hardier finches.

The exquisite Lady Gould is available in three different varieties according to facial coloring. Black faces and red faces are found both in the wild and in captivity, but yellow faces are found only in captivity. The female is less colorful especially in the chest than this Black Headed male.

The lovely Star Finch is one of the favorites of Australia's Grassfinches. It is a good breeder and companionable in mixed collections of small birds. The male has a very pretty song. The female has less red on the face. This color plate somehow shows an olive chest. Actually, the chest is bright yellow. The white spots on the red areas are small, but they are far more prominent than this picture indicates.

The Sydney Waxbill, top, is Australia's only waxbill. It is a little heavier bodied than most waxbills, but it is shapely in its dusky attractiveness.

The male Australian Fire Finch, lower, has a vibrant deep red with a lustrous glow, not fully apparent in this plate. Its long tail adds gracefulness, but Its character is one of bloodthirstiness among other birds of similar size.

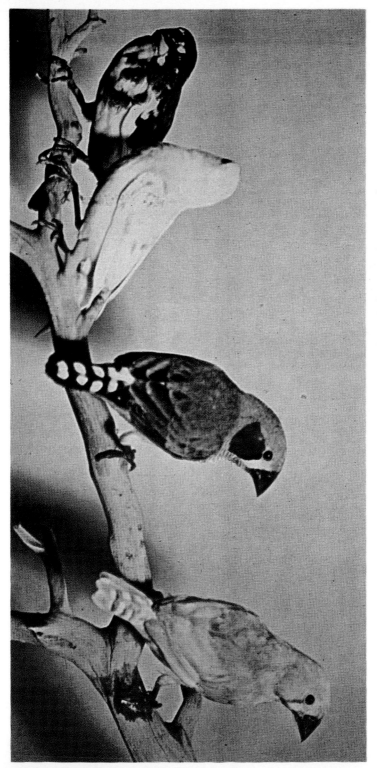

From left to right: Society Finch, a camera shy White Zebra Finch, male Gray Zebra Finch, and female pale Silver Zebra Finch. These birds are among the least expensive and best breeders of all finches. Though very peaceful, they are overly friendly and helpful, thereby discouraging many other birds from continuing nesting operations.

Rare Zebra Finches include a male Normal Penguin (top), male Fawn (center), and Recessive Silver female (lower). Rare mutations of Zebra Finches are being standardized by students of genetics and are bred in increasing numbers.

Diamond Sparrows from Australia are not true sparrows. Very beautiful and highly coveted, they have become rather high priced since the recent Australian ban on livestock exports. The white spots on the black sides and flanks give the bird its name, but the most prominent feature is a brilliant and glossy red extensively covering rump and uppertail coverts.

Two of Australia's popular grassfinches are the Owl or Bicheno Finch, top, and the Cherry or Plumhead Finch, bottom. Neither of these birds has a bright array of colors, but they are nevertheless very popular. The Owl Finch has a very excellent and beautiful pattern. The Cherry Finch has mostly a dull coloration except for a deep shade of plum on the forehead and crown.

The Painted Finch of Australia is a handsome but seldom available species. The male, top, is the more distinctive of the sexes. It is a fairly reliable breeder in captivity.

The Australian Fire Tailed Finch is an extremely rare and highly coveted finch which is not always reliable in captivity. It often shows a mysteriously high mortality rate. A closely related species shows a red patch on the ears.

Society or Bengalese Finches occur in three color varieties: pure white, cinnamon and white, and chocolate-brown and white. No two are alike, and none have ever occurred in the wild state. Societies are excellent breeders and foster parents in cage or aviary. They are also readily available, inexpensive, and very popular.

Pintailed Nonpareil Parrot Finches are shapely and beautifully colored, but the bright red underparts fade drastically in captivity.

Red Headed Parrot Finches are very rare and expensive. An almost legendary avicultural reputation has been built up over the years during their unavailability which would be difficult for any bird to fulfill. The Red Headed Parrot Finch is therefore a disappointment to some people when finally it is acquired. This bird is owned by Carl Papp.

Tri Colored Parrot Finches are also very rare and expensive but at present are more obtainable and less costly than the Red Headed variety. This species is extremely wild and very difficult to photograph. The picture above was finally achieved after many tries, and denotes a characteristic constantly active nature. Owned by Gordon Hayes.

The Pintailed Nonpareil is rather difficult to change over to domestic diets. Mealworms are helpful but should be rationed. Paddy rice is often necessary in the slow process of dietary acclimation.

Australia's Chestnut Breasted Mannikin, top, and the widespread Tri Colored Nun, bottom, are two of the most handsome members of a large family. The Tri Colored is very inexpensive and readily available, but the Chestnut Breasted has always been a little higher in price even before the Australian ban which curtailed all exports.

Society or Bengalese Finches occur in several forms with no two individuals alike. Solid colors such as the chocolate form at upper left and the cinnamon at the lower left are called "selfs." Another solid color is the pure white. The remaining individuals use both shades of brown with varying amounts of white. A few individuals show a blend between the two shades of brown.

Tri Colored Nuns are crisply tailored in uniform shades of black, brown, and white. Peaceful, hardy, and inexpensive, the Tri Colored Nun is usually available and excellent for beginners; but it rarely breeds in captivity.

Indian Spice Finches are hardy, very inexpensive, nearly always available, and peaceful. They are excellent for beginners.

Silverbill Finches are quite lacking in imaginative coloring or pattern; but they are popular, inexpensive, and good breeders. There are two species: the Indian Silverbill on the left and the African Silverbill on the right.

The rarely available Magpie Mannikin from Africa is a rather large and seldom available species. The female at the top is only slightly less colorful than the male below. The dusty buff on the underparts of the female is particularly noticeable.

Two mannikins from Africa are the popular Bronze Winged Mannikin (above) and the rarely available Blue Billed or Two Colored Mannikin (below). The latter species has more glossy areas than the bronzed crown and green areas of shoulders and sides of chest found on the Bronze Winged Mannikin.

Cutthroat Finches are always popular with finch fanciers. Cutthroats are nearly always available in season and are inexpensive. The Cutthroat is a good breeder and usually entertaining. The male frequently does an amusing little courting jig and expends considerable effort in trying to sing. Except for the broad red gash across the throat of the male, the color pattern is a complicated mosaic of earthy tones giving a protective coloration. Hardy and adaptable, the Cutthroat is ideal for beginners.

The rather large and somewhat rare Red Headed Finch is a cousin of that standard favorite, the Cutthroat Finch. This is a very pretty bird and is inordinately hardy. The female lacks the red on the head. It is aggressive to small birds but is companionable to weavers and other large finches.

Strawberry Finches are available in two distinct varieties. The one pictured here is the Oriental or Chinese Strawberry which is brighter red and more prominently spotted than the more easily obtainable Indian race. Note the extra long and curved toenails which need clipping. This species as well as several other finches need regular clipping. Properly sized perches help prevent this condition in Strawberries. The perch in this picture is much too large for such tiny feet.

The Green Strawberry or Green Avadavat from India is not often available and frequently becomes addicted to feather plucking in captivity. Sexes are similar, but the female (above) has less yellow and less prominent black barred flanks.

Male African Fire Finches are brightly colored and thoroughly delightful favorites in the waxbill family. Females are mostly dull brown. These birds are reasonably good breeders and spend a considerable time on or near the ground. Though delicate at first, African Fire Finches are hardy after acclimation.

African Fire Finches. The South African subspecies (male on left and female center) is hardy right from the beginning but it is more rare and more costly. Both sexes are more prominently spotted than the regularly imported Senegal race, but the male in this picture does not show it. Jameson's Fire Finch on right is seldom available and more expensive than the Senegal race. The female is softly shaded with dull rose on underparts.

The Gold Breasted Waxbill is another of aviculture's most popular finches. The male pictured at left is still young. During the second year sunset shades of bright orange-red mingle with the yellow on the underparts. The female, pictured at right, lacks the red eyebrow, the bright chest, and the bars on the flanks and sides.

Two small African Waxbills, which unfortunately did not show their best poses to the camera, are the popular Orange Cheeked on the left and the Red Rumped on the right. The Red Rumped Waxbill is a cousin of the low priced and very popular Red Eared Waxbill, but it is less attractive, rarer, and more costly. It is not a favorite with very many people.

Three favorite waxbills: top left, male Blue Waxbill; right, male Cordon Bleu; lower center, Lavender Finch. The male Blue Waxbill has brighter and more extensive blue on the underparts than the females of the two similar species. The Lavender in this picture is much darker on the tail and upperparts than the normal coloring. This condition is "melanism." This is an odd disorder which causes no harm to those affected, but it detracts from their beauty. Plumage becomes very dark. Strawberries, Lavenders, Gold Beasted Waxbills, and Cutthroats are usually the ones affected. Sunshine, plenty of greenfood, and corrected diet usually help correct the condition.

A trio of closely related, popular, and inexpensive waxbills. In the center is the Red Eared Waxbill. At left is the Greater St. Helena Waxbill, and on the right is the Lesser St. Helena Waxbill.

Two very popular African Waxbills: Orange Cheeked Waxbill (female above and male center) and male Gold Breasted Waxbill (below). These tiny birds are active, vivacious, inexpensive, and readily available.

Lavender Finches are among the most popular and attractive of African Waxbills. They are also quite inexpensive and hardy after an initial acclimation period.

Australia's only waxbill is the pretty Sydney Waxbill. Unfortunately this individual does not clearly show the extent of the long and broad squarish eyebrow above the eyes, and the camera did not catch the rich dark green of the upperparts. Owned by William Lasky.

The somewhat rare Black Cheeked Waxbill is very beautiful in a sedate and somber duskiness. The wings are crisply striated, and the lower chest and abdomen are a deep shade of rich burgundy. Reasonably expensive and only recently available in any quantity, the Black Cheeked Waxbill is peaceful and admirable in any collection of small finches.

Dufresne's Waxbills, from South Africa, are rare and rather expensive. The color pattern is trim, attractive, smooth, and quiet. The bright red on the rump and uppertail coverts provides a brilliant accent. Females lack the black patch covering the throat and face.

Grenadier Waxbills are rare and unbelievably beautiful. The Purple Grenadier at the top is only slightly less vivid and less attractive than the Violet Eared Waxbills below. The males are on the left, and females are on the right.

Both sexes of the very rare Violet Eared Waxbill are really much more beautiful than this or any picture could depict. This plate, taken from Butler's *Foreign Finches in Captivity*, shows the female at the top. The male has a rich glow over all the plumage and a vivid, deeper shade of purplish-violet in a large facial area.

Black Capped Waxbills, left and right, are rare and rather expensive. Quietly but sharply shaded in grays and blacks for the most part, a bright red contrast occurs on flanks, rump, and uppertail coverts. The little Scaly Crowned Weaver (center) has a dour expression from the front with its large walrus mustache. The pale pink beak, feet, and legs contrast with darker and duller colors. The very attractive scaly patterns of crown and wings will be shown in a black and white photograph.

Melba Finches (female left and male right) are very beautiful, quite rare, and expensive. The male has a very pretty song. The Melba occurs in the genus *Pytilia*; and, though it is related to waxbills, it is much larger. Owned by Palos Verdes Bird Farm.

The Red Faced Waxbill, also a *Pytilia*, is far less exciting than the Melba; but It Is still unusual and rather rare. The red in the face is very dark, and most of the body coloring is very dark olive. This is an excellent picture showing in very fine detail the subtle shadings and small variable markings.

The Red Faced Waxbill, above, is not a good representation in this plate from Butler's *Foreign Birds in Captivity*. A very good color photograph, also in this book, shows the more accurate color scheme.

The plate of the male Crimson Winged or Aurora Waxbill, lower, also a Pytilia, is a better representation of a seldom available species. The Aurora Waxbill is a better breeder than any of the other Pytilias.

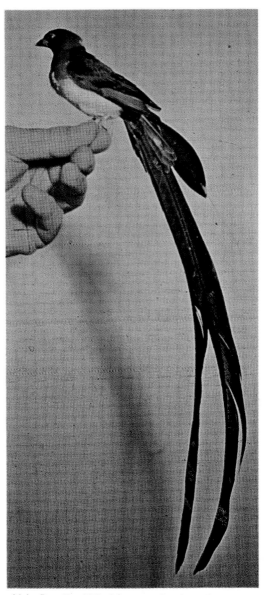

Male Paradise Whydahs in color have lavish tail feathers which never fail to attract attention. Moreover, they are peaceful with even the smallest finches and are inexpensive. Therefore, they are ideal for beginners and always popular with advanced fanciers. Despite the sparrowlike drabness of females and of males in eclipse plumage, the Paradise Whydah is one of the most popular finches in aviculture.

Very seldom available, the Red Collared Whydah is slightly larger and more costly than any of the standard favorites in the group of Whydahs. It is a handsome species but is aggressive towards small finches.

The comparatively rare and somewhat more expensive Broad Tailed Paradise Whydah is a close cousin of the standard Paradise Whydah and has a peaceful disposition. It is slightly larger and exhibits a more extensive and richer shade of brown. The two long tail feathers are usually shorter but much broader than those of the Paradise Whydah.

The Yellow Backed Whydah is not often available and is far less attractive than any of the popular whydahs because its tail is only slightly elongated during the color phase. The basic color pattern is quite similar to that of the Yellow Backed Weaver.

The Giant Whydah is a highly coveted but rarely available member of the whydah family. The male In color is an amazing sight, but out of color males and females are drab and sparrowlike.

The Orange Weaver while in color in the wild state has brilliant red instead of bright orange. A few birds bearing this native coloration are imported, but the next season the red fades to vivid orange.

Pintail Whydahs are second in popularity and availability in the Whydah family. Though inexpensive, males in color are very beautiful. Despite their small size, males while in color are spiteful to small finches and should be housed with weavers and other large finches. The two males in this classic photograph by Mr. McIsaac are in their first season of plumage. In succeeding years, the ribbonlike tail feathers grow progressively longer. Photographed at Palos Verdes Bird Farm.

Two closely related male weavers, one rare and one common, clearly indicate in this picture the slight differences which often may lead to confusion. The popular male Orange Weaver on the left is smaller and has orange extending down into the chest. The rare Crimson Crowned Weaver has orange extending upwards to the back of the crown and a black throat.

Three readily available weavers from Africa are the Orange (top), Napoleon (center), and the Red Billed (bottom). All these birds are males in color. Females and males out of color are drab and sparrowlike.

The brilliant Grenadier Weaver has a fiery red in the wild state but fades to bright orange in captivity. Not often available, it is similar to the Orange Weaver; but it is slightly larger and has the orange extending to the top of the crown instead of the back of the crown.

Napoleon Weavers are second only to Orange Weavers in popularity and availability of all weavers. The male in color (left) is bright yellow and velvety black with the typical weaver pattern on the wings. However, the neck feathers do not form as prominent a ruff as indicated by this colored plate taken from Butler's *Foreign Finches in Captivity*.

The Yellow Backed Weaver is seldom available and not very popular. Females (left) and males out of color are drab and sparrowlike. The male in color has a basic color pattern similar to the Yellow Backed Whydah, but the body is less slender and the tail not as long.

The Red Billed Weaver (male in color at top) is frequently available and low in price, but it is very aggressive to small birds. Russ' Weaver (male in color) below is very similar, but the black facial area is missing. In its place, contrary to this plate from Butler's book, is a dull rose shade with a slight cast of slate.

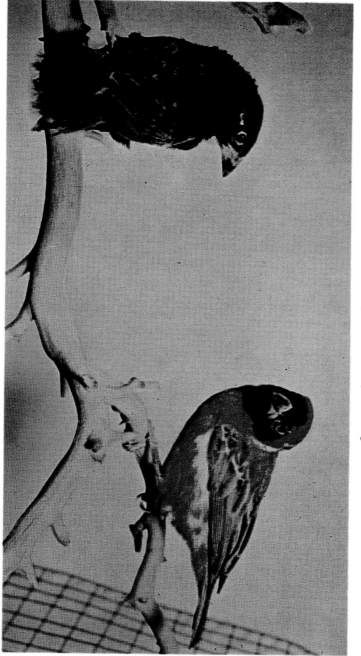

The male Orange Weaver in full nuptial plumage (left) is a fiery sight in native plumage. It is not as hardy upon importation, however, as the previously acclimated orange males which have already faded. The Little Masked Weaver (male in color on right) is a very pleasant weaver and is much more peaceful with smaller birds. Not a commonly available bird, it has recently been imported in steadily increasing numbers.

The Baya Weaver usually comes to bird fanciers from India, but the male in color is far less attractive than this plate from Butler's book indicates. The male (lower right) has a bright yellow cap, but the chest is subdued to golden buff, and the masked facial area is merely dark instead of black. It is not a popular species and is usually included in shipments as a substitute.

Three African weavers which are not always available are the medium sized Half Masked Weaver (top), the large and aggressive Rufous Necked Weaver (center), and the small and charming Little Masked or Atlas Weaver (lower). These birds are all males in breeding dress.

Madagascar Weavers (male in color at top and female at lower right) are rare and quarrelsome, but they have a superb shade of red coupled with subordinate black accents. The closely allied Comoro Weaver (male in color at lower left) has far less extensive areas of red and a larger beak. It is even more rare and more quarrelsome than the Madagascar Weaver.

The Golden Sparrow from Africa is the only sparrow which figures prominently in aviculture. Smaller than most sparrows, it nevertheless is most pugnacious to small finches. It is best housed with larger aggressive finches.

Java Rice Birds, both in the white and gray varieties, are among the hardiest and most popular of the larger finches. These birds can be mixed with parrakeets with no fear of aggressiveness on either side.

Scarlet Rose Finches are sparrowlike in shape and size. The deep rose-red shadings in the males of all species fade to a dull straw shade in captivity.

The male Cuban Melodious has a sprightly and very engaging personality, but he must be watched for aggressive tendencies towards small birds. Most of the coloring is dark and dusky, but the black face and throat have a pansy-like bright yellow from the eyebrow to the chest. The female is very dull.

The glowing Saffron Finch in graceful flight snapped at just the right moment by Mr. McIsaac at Palos Verdes Bird Farm. This South American finch is rather large and aggressive and should not be kept with small finches.

Pileated Finches are not often available; but they are handsome and peaceful, though shy, additions to any group of small birds. Both species, the Pileated (male above) and the Crimson Pileated (female left and male right), are from South America. The basic coloring of the male Crimson Pileated is much softer and more subdued than this print indicates.

Painted or Nonpareil Buntings are favorites in Europe but are prohibited in the United States because they are native to certain southern states. The coloring is beautiful, but the bright red underparts fade to a pale rose in captivity unless given a color holding agent.

The peaceful and shy Crimson Pileated Finch is not often available. It is companionable to small finches even though it is larger than most. The dull brown on the upperparts and quiet rose-brown on the underparts are very soft. The streak down the center of the head is a bright red partially erectile crest. Owned by William Lasky.

The male Indigo Bunting is deep and dusky blue, but the dusty female has only slight traces of bluish-gray in the flights. Popular with European aviculturists, the Indigo Bunting is unfortunately illegal for fanciers in the United States because of its native status.

The male Rainbow Bunting is a quiet but brightly colored species. Though larger than the average finch, it is peaceful with even the smallest bird. The green forehead, though bright, is outclassed by the vivid and glossy blue. Females are softly and quietly shaded.

The European Goldfinch is the most attractive and popular avicultural subject from all of Europe. It has a good song and is frequently hybridized with canaries to produce young-sters which, while not attractive, have superb songs.

The male Painted or Nonpareil Bunting in its wild coloring is brilliant and beautiful and even this picture cannot completely convey its elusive vividness. The mantle is especially glossy and paler in a chartreuse shade. The red coloring needs a holding agent in captivity. The female is very drab by comparison.

Another of Mr. McIsaac's excellent high speed photographs stops a White Headed Nun (above) and a male Green Singing Finch (below) in graceful flight. Photographed at Palos Verdes Bird Farm.

Most people will call this bird a male Green Singing Finch, but it actually is a seldom available close relative with several popular names. It is called the Yellow Eyed Finch, St. Helena Seedeater, or Yellow Crowned Canary.

Though not particularly attractive, the Black Throated Canary on the left and the Cape Canary on the right are very seldom available and usually find a ready market. The Black Throated Canary is a close relative of the Gray Singing Finch but is more diversified in color with its dark throat and yellow rump.

Though European Bullfinches are not permitted entry Into the United States, there are a few occaslonally available. The male pictured here has a far more attractive rose pink on the underparts than this colored plate suggests.

The Gray Singing Finch (above right) is colorless, but it has an exquisite song and is therefore popular. The Alario Finch of South Africa (female at left and male on lower right) is much more difficult to get, but it is much more attractive.

One of the most attractive siskins is the male Colombian Black Headed Siskin on the right. The drab female is on the left. Unfortunately this small and beautiful species is very seldom available. Owned by Palos Verdes Bird Farm.

Two species of Seedeaters from South America are the White Throated (above) and the Bluish Finch (below). Females of both species and of most other Seedeaters resemble the female at the upper left.

The stately and ideal Virginian Cardinal is one of the favorite avicultural subjects of the world, but it is not legal in the United States because it is a native and is protected by law. The female is much less colorful than the male, and the male needs a color holding agent in captivity.

The handsome male Venezuelan Scarlet Cardinal is the only all red cardinal permitted in American aviculture. It has a much larger beak than the Virginian Cardinal and the color is different. The crest is longer and recurved.

(right)

Male Mexican Cardinal showing extensive fading of red from life in captivity. This in no way affects health. Color restoration for cardinals is described in Chapter 18. Also helpful is carotene in oil.

The beautiful Brazilian Crested Cardinal is one of the most popular and frequently available members of the Cardinal group. The female has only a slightly less vivid shade of red.

The male Green Cardinal from South America is vastly different in coloring from most cardinals. At the time of this writing it is seldom available and rather costly. Owned by William Lasky.

The Yellow Billed Cardinal has a less vivid color scheme than the Black Throated Cardinal, and the bill is yellowish. Otherwise, both species are very similar.

This is an excellent representation of the beautiful Black Throated Cardinal from South America. This species is hardy and very active. It is an excellent companion for Pekin Nightingales, Bulbuls, certain thrushes, and other Cardinals.

Hawfinches are frequently offered from Europe and Japan but not often imported. In American aviculture, at least, it is not greatly admired by very many people. This Black Tailed Hawfinch is owned by William Lasky.

Diamond Doves, female left and male right, are excellent and delightful additions to a finch collection. Excellent breeders and inexpensive, these little miniatures are very peaceful if no more than one pair is included in each aviary.

The male Button Quail is far more colorful than the female, but both are charming and fascinating additions to any finch collection.

The Pekin Nightingale is one of the most popular and inexpensive of all softbills. Its cheerful song and perky liveliness are just as important as its hardiness and attractive coloring. The yellow areas on the chin, throat, and upper chest and the chestnut-orange lower boundary on the chest is usually brighter than this picture shows. The upperparts are more olive than this picture indicates.

The strikingly beautiful Silver Eared Mesia is a rather rare relative of the well-known Pekin Nightingale; but it is slightly larger, more expensive, and far more colorful. Owned by William Lasky.

Ideal for beginners, the handsome and hardy Black Headed Sibia is usually inexpensive.
Though the colors are quiet and the shadings are subtle, this is a remarkably beautiful
bird with an aristocratic manner.

The Spectacled Jay Thrush or Melodious Jay Thrush is predominantly a warm brown with paler underparts. A noticeable feature is a bright eye ring of bluish-white which trails behind the eye more than this picture indicates giving the appearance of spectacles. This bird is also a good songbird.

Big saucy eyes and a lively curiosity enable Pekin Nightingales to be first in line at feeding time. Sexes are very similar in these active and colorful extroverts.

White Crested Laughing Jay Thrush from India. This is a very handsome and amusing bird with a raucous laugh and a highly active nature. It is excellent in collections of large aggressive softbills. The fullness of the crest is not readily apparent in this picture.

The White Throated Laughing Jay Thrush from India is less flamboyant and less popular than the White Crested Laughing Jay Thrush, but it usually is slightly lower in price.

The beautiful Gold Fronted Chloropsis is mainly a handsome shade of bright green and is therefore often called a Leaf Bird. The curved beak indicates a need for nectar. Owned by Carl Papp.

Black bulbuls occur in several slightly different races in India. This species is large and aggressive with other bulbuls. It is a pleasant songbird and is usually very calm. This bird in the picture was so poised in a cage for the first time that he won the Kellogg Trophy as best Foreign Cage Bird in the National Cage Bird Show.

One of the most pleasant and least expensive of all bulbuls is the Red Eared Bulbul, a standard import from India. The body coloring is brown and has no greenish cast as shown in the picture. Owned by William Lasky.

The Gold Fronted Chloropsis is an easily trained pet if attempts are made to offer choice foods by hand. Note the intense concentration of this bird as mealworms are brought close to the aviary. Owned by Carl Papp.

The beautiful, expensive, and very rare male Fairy Blue Bird has a richly glossed turquoise-blue plumage in a fascinating outline extending from the forehead through undertail coverts. It also has very tiny feet for a bird of its size. The female is dull and dusky blue all over with just a hint of green shading. Owned by William Lasky.

Gold Fronted Chloropsis snagging a mealworm from a feeding tray at Palos Verdes Bird Farm. Note the rich cobalt-blue beard.

GEORGE W. NOREEN

The two most readily available Fruitsuckers are the Gold Fronted Chloropsis (above) and Hardwicke's Chloropsis (bottom). Hardwicke's is the more colorful of the two, but it is by far the rarer of the two.

Upper: Paradise Flycatchers, female left and male right. This is one of two color phases
of the flamboyant males.
Lower: Celestial Blue Monarch, an example of Monarch Flycatchers from the Philippine
Islands.
These exquisite birds are very difficult to transfer to domesticated diets.

Right: Male Paradise Flycatcher in the other color phase. Left: Derbian
Kiskadee Flycatcher, an ordinary and cumbersome bird which occurs in
a wide range of the Americas and Mexico. The Derbian Kiskadee is very
hardy and easily acclimated but not very popular.

The Hooded Pitta from India is one of the two most prevalent members of a difficult family. The reds and blues are particularly brilliant.

The bright Scarlet Minivet is an excellent avicultural subject; but, unless given a color holding agent, the red fades in captivity.

The Blue Throated Bee Eater is a trimly shaped and attractive member of an extensive and colorful family. Bee Eaters are extremely rare in aviculture and are not easily transferred to domestic diets.

The Indian Blue Roller is really far more attractive than this picture indicates. Except for the missing lavenders and pale violets on the throat, nape, and sides of the neck, the basic colors are all as pictured; but the reproduction left them very flat. The varying shades of blues especially should show a richly glowing luster. The blue cap is pale but should be brighter in this picture. The folded wings hide the richest colors. When outstretched, the huge wingspread shows a dazzling array of subtle and pale shades and vivid deep colors which almost seem as if washed in a luminous glow. This is a very handsome species but it is difficult to transfer to domesticated diets.

Cedar Waxwings sometimes become avicultural subjects within the United States when they fall from migration and are nursed back to health. They are usually much more smoothly groomed than this picture indicates.

The Superb Manakin (upper right) is an exquisite member of an unusual and rarely
available family.

The Cuban Trogon (upper left) is an extremely beautiful and personable bird. Next to its
resplendent cousin, the Quetzal, the Cuban Trogon is the most prevalent and popular
member of the family in the United States.

The brilliant Regent Bower Bird is one of the most beautiful of the extremely intelligent
and highly developed Bower Birds of New Guinea and Australia.

The British or European Robin is a vivacious little bird with a bold personality, but it is
seldom available to American fanciers.

The Quetzal or Resplendent Trogon is another of the aristocrats of aviculture. The brilliance of the metallic green cannot effectively be captured by the camera. Photographed by Hank Bates at the Jerome Buteyn Foreign Bird Farm.

Pittas are rarely imported and are rather high in price. The Hooded Pitta from India, pictured here, is brought in probably more than any of the other species.

The Blue Winged Pitta from Borneo closely resembles the Indian or Bengal Pitta except for the lack of white lines around the eyes and larger blue wing patches. Pittas are rare and difficult to acclimate to captivity, but they are aptly called Jewel Thrushes because of their glowing and b.rilliant colors.

Different species of Rollers vary considerably in size, and a few have slender extensions on the tail feathers. For the most part, however, the soft and delicate patterns and bright flashes of color are similar throughout the family. This Indian Blue Roller has much warmer and glowing shades than this picture indicates.

Male Dama or Orange Headed Ground Thrushes from India are frequently imported and are very pleasant birds. Underparts of the male are the same shade as the head. Females are far less colorful with dull brownish shades on the back and brownish orange on the head and underparts.

Glossy and aristocratic, the shapely male Shama Thrush, left, quickly becomes undisputed master of his aviary and celebrates by frequent outpourings of his melodious songs. The quietly beautiful Black Headed Sibia, right, though strong and sizeable, has a peaceful, almost shy, personality where other birds are concerned.

Male Dhyal Thrushes are patterned after magpies in glossy black and white while females are nondescript in dark, dull shades. Often called Magpie Robins, these birds have a melodious song and are usually sold at a low price.

The American Robin is a large thrush which is very greatly appreciated in its wild state. It, in turn, prefers to frequent human habitations. Though it is legally denied to American aviculturists, a few injured or hand-reared individuals are nursed by bird fanciers until they can be released. They become ideal avicultural subjects during these periods.

Three species of Blue Birds occur in the United States. The Western Bluebird is similar to this Eastern Blue Bird in that both have reddish-brown on the underparts. The Mountain Blue Bird has blue on the chest. Females are very drab.

Meadowlarks are stocky birds with an enchanting song. This Eastern Meadowlark has much more colorful underparts than the Western Meadowlark.

The Red Bird of Paradise is an extremely handsome species with vivid red filmy plumes emanating from the sides and extending over the tail. During the courting display, the plumes are raised over the back in a vibrating shower. The facial and throat areas show a lustrous metallic green.

The Greater Bird of Paradise in full plumage is one of the best members of a fascinating family of very rare exotics. This beauty was photographed by the authors in one of the most beautiful aviaries in the world: Louise Hall at Dierenpark Wassenaar in Holland.

The small and vivid male King Bird of Paradise with its brilliant red upperparts has two attractive wirelike tail feathers with curled feathering on the tips. This species was reared in captivity for the first time by Dr. Sven Bergman in Sweden, and the four pictures in this series show the parents and the two offspring at three weeks of age. The female is dull in a reddish-brown, and the young are similar but have shorter tails and the absence of a shade of red in the brown.

The San Blas Jay from Mexico is unusually attractive in its simple color scheme of black and blue dominated by a bright golden eye. It is not as noisy as many jays and lives peacefully among birds of similar sizes. It should never be mixed with smaller birds.

Two Blue Jays occurring in the United States are crested. Stellar's Jay with a much darker color scheme is the other. Both species enjoy a domestic life but are not often given the chance since the law prohibits bird fanciers from keeping them in captivity.

Red Billed Blue Magpie or Occipital Blue Pie. This lovely Indian species with its long graduated tail is one of the best additions to any collection of large softbills. It is usually comparatively reasonable in price, readily available, very active, and unusually peaceful.

The Superb or Spreo Glossy Starling is one of the most beautiful members of the richly iridescent African family of Glossy Starlings. This picture shows the basic color pattern and the bold eye, but the camera cannot capture more than fleeting glints of the extensive iridescence.

Two of the more distinctively handsome Glossy Starlings are the richly iridescent but dark Longtailed Glossy Starling and the Superb Spreo with its chestnut underparts. Both are extremely hardy and easily maintained in captivity on a simple softbilled diet.

The lovely and long tailed Royal Starling above is very rarely available and is usually expensive. The heavy lustrous iridescence of the dark areas is matched by the sparkling yellow underparts. The Purple Headed Glossy Starling is often available and inexpensive. It is richly glossed in dark greens and purples but the purple is less obvious than this painting shows.

Of the several species of talking mynahs, the Greater India Hill Mynah is the most appropriate for pet fanciers because of availability, reasonable price, and good performance.

The Green Glossy Starling from Africa is all dark except for brilliant orange eyes. A very heavy metallic overlay of gloss reflects blue on the head and ventral area and green on the wings and tail. Other areas are blends between the two and may even include purple. The refracted richness is visible at its best in bright sunlight. Feet, legs, and beak are black.

The Yellow Oriole from northern South America is a very bright and active aviary subject. Alert, intelligent, and reasonably aggressive, the Yellow Oriole should not be kept with smaller birds.

In a flurry of feathers, this Yellow Headed Marsh Bird was caught in an amazing midair photograph by camera artist R. Glenn McIsaac. The Yellow Headed Marsh Bird has a bright yellow head and neck. All other areas are uniform black. Photographed at Palos Verdes Bird Farm.

The Yellow Headed Blackbird has a color scheme similar to the Yellow Headed Marsh Bird except the less bright yellow extends down into the chest. The dark facial area is really black instead of blue as this picture indicates. The female has a drab and uninteresting color scheme.

The most famous Hangnest in the United States is the beautiful Baltimore Oriole which is available to American aviculturists only because of injured specimens or abandoned nestlings. The female has a drab color scheme.

The Spotted Chested Oriole is a handsome, heavy-bodied bird seldom available. The golden-yellow areas are really much brighter than indicated in this picture.

The Velvet Fronted Nuthatch is a vivid and lustrous beauty which is far more colorful than this painting indicates. The upperparts are brighter lavender-blue; the underparts are a warmer shade of lavender; and the beak is a brighter coral shade. Rather difficult to acclimate and seldom available, it is nevertheless a fascinating addition to any collection of small softbills.

(upper right)
The Indian Golden Oriole is the most beautiful and most ideal of the Old World Orioles. The male is brilliant black and yellow. The female is dull and drab in a dusky greenish shade.

(lower right)
The Shama Thrush from India is one of the finest of all softbilled songbirds. The male has glossy black and deep chestnut as its most dominant colors. The female is dull brown.

The most prevalent of all tanagers in aviculture is the lovely Blue Tanager. It is also peaceful, inexpensive, and very hardy. There are three shades of blue on this bird. Soft, almost sky-blue covers most of the body. The flights are glossy greenish-blue. A shoulder patch, not quite captured here, is a glossy, near cobalt-blue.

The handsome Crested Cassique is clothed in velvet black and brilliant golden yellow which is brighter than this picture shows. A long, loose Aztec crest can be raised high above the eyes and casually draped towards the sides of the face. The feathers are not crowded, but they are long and flexible, and they constitute a very unusual headdress during the frequent displays. The long sharp beak is ivory with a slight tinge of green. The body has a peculiar musky odor.

The male Scarlet Tanager of South America has a deeper shade of red than the North American Scarlet Tanager. The dark beak has a silver patch near the base of the lower mandible. The female is duskier and less well patterned.

The male Scarlet Tanager native to the United States is a brilliant bird, but it fades in captivity. The female is dull greenish above and paler greenish-yellow below. The beak is pale in the North American form and mostly black in the South American form.

Red Rumped Tanagers are beautiful in their bright and simple color schemes. The pale silvery-blue beak and a bright red patch covering the rump and uppertail coverts offset a uniform black velvet covering the rest of the body. This species is equally as hardy as the Blue Tanager but is not as frequently available.

The finely contrasting and brilliant Blue Shouldered Mountain Tanager, as this picture adequately shows, is one of the most beautiful of all tanagers. It is reasonably large and, unfortunately, quite aggressive.

The Chestnut Headed Calliste Tanager occurs in several slightly differing races. Some have less blue and varying shades of brown on the head. Desmarest's Tanager particularly has a brighter reddish-brown head. At first, these birds are delicate until the acclimation to a domestic diet is complete. Afterwards, they are reasonably hardy. This picture does not convey the smoothness of the plumage.

Mrs. Wilson's Tanager has several races with slight variations, mostly in size. This race is smaller and has less blue on the shoulders, rump, and uppertail coverts.

Not often available and reasonably expensive, Mountain Tanagers with yellow caps are available in three slightly differing subspecies. The Hooded Mountain Tanager is larger and lacks the yellow on the head.

The very beautiful Spotted Emerald or Yellow Browed Tanager lacks flamboyant colors, but the finely drawn pattern of minute details presents a very distinctive appearance. This species, hardier than most callistes, is not often available but is an excellent addition to any collection of similar-sized birds.

The Black Eared Golden Tanager is a glowing member of the more delicate Calliste Tanagers. The rich, warm, and smooth glowing gold is perfectly balanced by a dark brownish-black ear patch, dark eyes, and a black beak. The back, wings, and tail are mostly dark brownish; but a prominent and lacy network of the golden body color shows through. This species is reasonably delicate until after acclimation and is only half hardy thereafter. The disposition is considerate and peaceful.

The Buff Naped Calliste (*Tangara ruficervix*) is another rare species seldom available to aviculturists in the United States. Its lustrous and smooth plumage is not readily noticeable in this picture of a highly active individual. Owned by Carl Papp.

Mrs. Wilson's or Golden Masked Tanager is one of the more frequently available of the lovely Calliste Tanagers. Acclimation to domestic diets is somewhat difficult in the beginning, but this beautiful species becomes quite hardy afterwards. The velvet black is attractively counterbalanced by lustrous shades of bright blue. The main feature is a brassy metallic shade around the neck. This heavy layer of refracted coloring is highly changeable according to angle of light. Photographs usually show the brassy shade but rarely capture the mellow honey shade which is more attractive.

Two exquisite Calliste Tanagers from South America: Superb Tanager (above) and Paradise Tanager (below). These two tanagers are very rare in American aviculture.

The Violet Euphonia of South America has a basic pattern closely resembling that of Bonaparte's Euphonia of Mexico and Central America. Differences are slight. This is a hardy and very attractive member of the group of Euphonias, but females are dull and dusky.

Left, the female Yellow Winged Sugar Bird is a soft green which is much smoother and more attractive than the bird in this picture. Males out of color are similar but retain a brighter shade of red on the legs. The male Bonaparte Euphonia, center, is a very pleasant and reasonably hardy Euphonia. It is bright, glossy, and peaceful. An immature Chloro-phonia is on the right.

628

An immature Chlorophonia on the left now in dull plumage. Center is a male Yellow Winged Sugar Bird. The brilliant turquoise cap is not shown to best advantage; and the rich, lustrous cobalt blue is usually more smooth. The back has much velvety black; and, in flight, the undersides of the wings show a broad band of yellow. The Purple Sugar Bird on the right is much more rare and rather more delicate. The blue has a purplish tint. The cap lacks the turquoise flair but adds a black bib. The feet and legs are bright yellow.

The beautifully shaped Yellow Backed Sunbird (*Aethopyga schetioe*) from India (above) has, despite its name, only small amounts of yellow. The brilliant and lustrous red and green command far more attention than its yellow.

The Green Shouldered Tanager of South America (below) is one of several races of Chestnut Headed Tanagers, all of which are handsome and easily maintained in captivity.

Sharply and beautifully patterned, the smooth and brilliant Black Headed Sugar Bird is one of the most coveted members of an extraordinary family.

The Red Thighed Sugar Bird (*Dacnis venusta*) is a rarely available South American species which is easily adaptable to aviculture. Owned by Carl Papp.

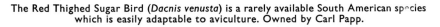

The Scarlet Breasted Sunbird (top) of Africa has dark plumage brightened by brilliant greenish and red iridescence. The beautifully shaped but darkly colored Malachite Sunbird from Africa has an eclipse plumage.

Two beautiful but rare sunbirds are the small La Touche's Sunbird of China (top) and the Tacazze Sunbird from the colder climates of the Kenya highlands in Africa.

The Frilled Coquette Hummingbird is a small species with an exotic erectile ruff on the sides of the neck and a slender tapering crest. The colors of flame-red and green are much brighter than this print indicates. The very bright green around the facial area and throat, or gorget, is especially iridescent.

Baby hummingbirds, especially in the nestling stage, are rarely photographed. Mrs. Van der Meid's painstaking search was rewarded when she discovered this tiny nest of the Ruby Throated Hummingbird with its two thriving babies.

The Fork Tailed Emerald Hummingbird from Mexico is rich in burnished metallic iridescence. The forked tail gives a shapely appearance. This photograph of one of John Gould's plates fails to show the richness of the iridescence perfected by Gould in his original works, but it gives a good likeness of the bird.

The hummingbird family is crowded with excesses or unique distinctions, most of them exotic and beautiful. One very strange excess is found in the exceptionally long beak of this tiny female Ecuadorian Sword Billed Hummingbird.

The glittering male Green Tailed Sylph (*Aglaiocercus kingi macoa*) is another handsome long tailed hummingbird of the tropics which has successfully been kept in captivity.

The Jamaican Streamer Tailed Hummingbird (*Trochilus polytmus*) is another fine example of the beauty of variable hummingbirds. This species has been bred in captivity.

There are several similar subspecies of the Scarlet Cock of the Rock, but all are very expensive and rarely available. Most of the specimens in captivity are to be found in better zoos.

Tame Orange Cock-of-the-Rock in a strutting display while on the hand of one of the authors. This bird, nearly twelve years old at the time of the photograph, has grown extra long filmy orange plumes covering most of the tail and hiding the pattern of the back. Owned by Jerome Buteyn.

Scarlet Cock-of-the-Rock showing the back pattern. This male shows the extent of fading in captivity if color holding agents are not sufficient in the diet.

The Naked Throated Bell Bird is a close relative of the Cocks-of-the-Rock. Unusual and rare, this bizarre creature emits loud and clear bell-like sounds which can be heard from great distances. Owned by Jerome Buteyn.

The Flicker is a medium-large relative of woodpeckers which rarely becomes an avicultural subject. Injured specimens take to captivity readily on a standard softbilled diet but should be given extra live foods, raw meat, peanut butter, and nectar food.

The quite rare Toucan Barbet of South America is easily one of the most attractive and fascinating of all barbets. It is a colorful comic and easy to manage in captivity; but, because its native Ecuadorian range is high up in subtropical mountains, it does not easily withstand hot weather. Sexes are very similar.

The strangely shaped but colorful Groove-Billed Barbet from the western part of Africa is very rare in aviculture, but it is one of the more interesting members of a strange family.

The rarely available Orange Breasted or Plaintive Barbet from South America is quite attractive with its red cap and extensive golden throat. The female is much plainer. The male pictured and its mate, contrary to the disposition of most barbets, live peacefully in a large mixed collection of various thrushes, cardinals, and several medium sized softbills in the aviaries of William Lasky.

The Gold Fronted Chloropsis at the top is a very easily tamed pet. The Blue Throated or Blue Cheeked Barbet is a little smaller than the average barbet, but it is the most readily available member of the group. The blue and red highlights are particularly attractive.

Cuvier's Toucan is a delightful pet and an impish clown. Thoroughly affectionate and ever curious, Cuvier's Toucan vies with the Toco in tameable personalities. The writers have never had one which did not quickly respond to taming.

In the United States at least, the Toucan most prevalent and usually lowest priced is the colorful Sulphur Breasted Toucan.

A very rare Spot Billed Toucanette with characteristic short broad beak and barlike spots on the sides. Photographed by the authors in Louise Hall at Dierenpark Wassenaar in Holland.

The Green Billed Toucan from South America is far more prevalent in European aviculture than in American aviculture. Not easily tamed, it is nevertheless one of the more colorful species. Photographed at the Palos Verdes Bird Farm.

The Collared or Banded Aracari is the most readily available species of the many Aracaris. Very interesting in an aviary, they usually are too adult when imported to become tame pets. Owned by Jerome Buteyn.

Toco Toucans are very large and usually quite expensive. Alert and ever curious, the Toco is the most easily tamed member of the family.

Emerald Toucanettes are small versions of toucans. As with most toucans, they are adept at catching grapes tossed to them from quite a distance. Photographed by the authors at Palos Verdes Bird Farm.

This is a very excellent picture of the very fine Hartlaub's Touraco. Though the dark and glossy back does not show too well, all other details reproduced perfectly. Owned by Jerome Buteyn.

Violaceous Plantain Eater, a handsome relative of Touracos, has an active nature and brightly colored beak of waxlike smoothness. Photographed by the authors at the magnificent Louise Hall in the Dierenpark Wassenaar in Holland.

Two expensive avian aristocrats for advanced aviculturists: Scarlet Cock-of-the-Rock (left) and Hartlaub's Touraco (right). Both of these exotics are very active and should be given large aviaries. Owned by Jerome Buteyn.

The Redpoll (*Carduelis flammea*) is a native of Europe as well as North America and cannot be kept in captivity by American fanciers. It resembles European Linnets in many respects. The red marking on the forehead and crown and the black chin are distinguishing features. There are slight seasonal differences in color, mainly the addition of a pinkish shade on the chest of the males which fades in captivity. Sexes are similar, but the female has diminished areas of red on the head and lacks the pinkish shades on the rump and chest. The general care and feeding are the same as for European Linnets, siskins, and serins. Redpolls are often hybridized with other closely related birds. Despite their drabness, Redpolls are good aviary birds because of their activity and amusing antics. Their song is not spectacular. There are several species of Redpolls which differ very slightly in coloring and size. This species is about five inches long. Photo by Dr. Jesse.

The Black Throated Wattle Eye (*Platysteira peltata*) from Africa is one of those great rarities which is seldom available even to zoos. The female on the left has the black covering nearly all the throat and chest whereas the male has a rather narrow black band across the chest. All other underparts on the male are white. Wattle Eyes are Flycatchers which are extremely difficult to maintain in captivity without great quantities of live foods in as wide a variety as possible. Its care is similar to that required by the Paradise Flycatcher.

The four and a half inch Blue Tit or Titmouse *(Parus caeruleus)* of Europe is a vivacious and acrobatic personality which is rarely kept in captivity. In many European countries it is protected by laws and can neither be kept in captivity nor exported. The Blue Tit is one of the most attractive of all the Tits, with its lovely rich shades of blue and frosty bluish-white around the facial areas. The Blue Tit is delicate during acclimation stages until it learns to accept domestic diets. As with Japanese Tumblers, the diet is omnivorous. Sexes are alike, but the female is less vivid in coloring than the male.

The Cordon Bleu, an African Waxbill, is one of the most popular and attractive of all the birds which fanciers call finches. The female lacks the maroon patch on the side of the head and has less extensive blue in a quieter shade.

The rare Red Crested Touraco from Angola (*Tauraco erythrolophus*) is a very attractive member of an unusual family. This individual has damaged plumage, but most Touracos usually have excellent plumage and are very well groomed. Moreover, their long tails add grace to a well-shaped body. Touracos are extremely active birds, and the brilliant red in the flight feathers of most species can be seen to best advantage while the bird is flying. Photo by Horst Mueller.

The Bicheno or Owl Finch from Australia has in the past few years become exceptionally rare in aviculture in the Western Hemisphere. The failure of aviculturists to establish this species firmly as a domesticated and free breeding bird before or just after the Australian export ban went into effect is deplorable. Formerly quite moderate in cost, it is now one of the more expensive of the Australian finches. Though a number of fanciers are breeding this species, those few who have been successful have been unable to supply the demand for this lively and beautifully patterned charmer. Photo by Horst Mueller.

The Pearl Headed Amadine (Odontospiza caniceps) from Eastern Africa is also known as the Pearl Headed Silverbill. It has only recently become available to bird fanciers. It is more closely related to Silverbills which it resembles in most characteristics except for the far more attractive pattern and coloring. Sexes are alike, but the male is slightly richer in coloring and has larger white spots. The courting dance of the male is, as in the Society Finch, a more reliable indication of sex.

The beautiful Gold Fronted Chloropsis is an extraordinary songbird in spacious, well planted aviaries; but the brilliant green often blends with the leaves of the plants. However it is easily tamed and becomes completely confiding even in aviaries.

In the group of Buntings, the Rainbow Bunting is the most popular member for American aviculturists. There are more beautiful species in the group, but they are either quite rare or are denied to American aviculturists because of their native status. Males, such as the one pictured, greatly outnumber females in importations. This is unfortunate because fanciers usually want pairs. Exporters apparently send more males because they feel the females are so uninteresting in color that they will not find a waiting market. Photo by Harry V. Lacey.

The male African Fire Finch is a favorite member of the Waxbill family and is inexpensive. It ranks alongside the Cordon Bleu in popularity, but it usually is a better breeder. There are several subspecies and closely related Fire Finches.

Zebra Finches are among the most productive of all breeding birds in captivity. The male is very attractive with the bright cheek patch, chestnut flanks with white spots, and zebra lines on the chest. The female lacks these features and usually does not even have the indistinct dark markings on the chest shown in this picture. Photo by Harry V. Lacey.

The beautiful Blue Tit of Europe *(Parus caeruleus)* in a less alert pose. This is the puffed pose usually assumed during rainstorms when it shelters itself in crevices or huddles in fissures in tree trunks.

Gouldian Finches are considered by most people to be the most beautiful of all finches. The male in this photo is hiding most of his brilliant chest. Since the Australian export ban went into effect, avicultural sources for Gouldians have mostly been through bird fanciers who specialize in this species or from Japanese imports. Recently some of the problems regarding Japanese imports have been solved; and by special and prolonged acclimation periods, which mostly involve food processing and gradual changes in diet, several importers are having great success with Japanese bred Gouldians. Prior to this advance, most of the imports from Japan would not change to foods available in other countries. It is interesting to note that there are more Red Headed Gouldians than Black Headed Gouldians now available in this country. Photo by Harry V. Lacey.

The male Scarlet Chested Sunbird (*Chalcomitra senegalensis*) from Africa has brilliant red as its main color feature with iridescent green in a subordinate degree on the head and chin. The female is dusky olive-brown with bronzy highlights on the upperparts and paler shades of yellowish-brown on underparts. Photo by Harry V. Lacey.

In the past few years Red Headed Finches from South Africa have frequently become available. Females lack the red on the head and the well-defined spots on the chest. This species
is larger and more dominant than its relative, the Cutthroat or Ribbon Finch. It should not, in
most instances, be kept with smaller finches. Photo by Horst Mueller.

African Glossy Starlings, of which there are several species, are richly iridescent and are very attractive. Moreover, they are extremely hardy and easily maintained on a standard softbilled diet. Mynah pellets are an excellent single unit food for them if the bird fancier wishes to simplify diet to the ultimate. These Green or Blue Eared Glossy Starlings, now called *Lamprotornis chalybaeus,* may, because of their heavy iridescence, show color variations due to angle of lighting; and the several similar species and subspecies can easily cause confusion in avicultural identification. Photo by Horst Mueller.

Many hybrids are not very attractive; but this specimen, which resulted by a mating of a European Goldfinch to a European Bullfinch, is a beautiful bird. It is
also a difficult achievement. Photo by Horst Mueller.

The Pied factor in Zebra Finches, as in nearly all birds which have the pied mutation, is very
irregular in pattern and often not as attactive as these pictured, particularly when the amount
of natural coloring greatly exceeds the white areas. Photo by Horst Mueller.

Pekin Nightingales are lovely birds with bright personalities and extremely active natures. They are ideal subjects for beginners of softbilled birds. Their songs can be beautiful especially in uncrowded planted aviaries. The writers do not consider them good cage birds because they are too active. Close quarters cramp their style and remove much of the joy which they otherwise convey quite freely in proper aviaries.

The Ruddy Ground Dove (Columbigallina talpacoti) ranges from Mexico to Argentina and is about six and a half inches long. The female has less brown and more gray on the upper-parts and is also more gray on the underparts. This is one of a group of several small doves which can mix with finches in an aviary. Photo by Horst Mueller.

Many different species of the group of Mannikins successfully hybridize with Society Finches, and the appearance of the offspring usually cannot be predicted. Even nestmates often vary considerably. These hybrids are nearly identical to Philippine Spice Finches except for the richer shade of brown. The writers, however, do not know the actual parentage.

Yellow Winged or Red Legged Honeycreepers are excellent aviary birds and are among the easiest of all nectar feeders. The brilliant colors of the male during the nuptial season never fail to attract admirers. The dazzling turquoise cap does not show in this picture, and the legs of the male are usually a brighter reddish shade. The female is actually soft green and not nearly as drab as this picture indicates.

The Virginian Cardinal, such as the male pictured, available to European fanciers is the Mexican race. Birds of the United States cannot be exported to other countries, nor can they be kept in captivity by American fanciers. Photo by Harry V. Lacey.

The Greater India Hill Mynah is one of several very similar subspecies which are very talented talkers. In recent years, nearly as many of the subspecies *intermedia* have been exported from Thailand as from India. Youngsters are usually hand reared in their countries of origin, and when they reach the marketable export age they are delightfully tame birds. The subspecies from Thailand, if anything, now receives better hand rearing than the same race in India and is equally adept at learning to talk. This is an adult male with long wattle flaps and highly lustrous iridescence. Photo by Horst Mueller.

Green Cardinals are excellent aviary birds and are the best breeders of the Cardinals. The female, not pictured, is much duller in color than the male especially in the dominant black and yellow shadings. Photo by Horst Mueller.

There are two races of Strawberry Finches (*Amandava amandava*). The Indian subspecies is the most common and the least costly. It is usually called Tiger Finch in India. The Oriental or Chinese Strawberry Finch is a brighter red and slightly smaller. This member of the Wax-bill family undergoes a seasonal change of color. During the eclipse period the bright male resembles the female which is also pictured here. Photo by Harry V. Lacey.

The Shama Thrush (Copsychus malabaricus) is one of the finest of all softbilled birds, and if properly fed is a superb songster. There are seventeen subspecies ranging from Ceylon and India throughout Southeast Asia. Those available to aviculturists are from India and Thailand. The race from Thailand has a longer tail and is perhaps a little more handsome. The female, in contrast to the male pictured here, has a drab and soft brown instead of the lustrous shades of black and chestnut. Photo by Harry V. Lacey.

Cutthroat or Ribbon Finches are among the most ideal of finches for beginners in aviculture, and they usually retain their popularity among the advanced students of aviculture. The female lacks the ribbon of red and has less boldness in other color patterns. Photo by Harry V. Lacey.

The Pagoda Mynah (*Sturnus pagodarum*) from India and Ceylon is an attractive and very hardy aviary bird. The black cap is actually a recumbent crest not always raised. This species and all members of the genus *Sturnus* cannot be imported into the United States, but many species are popular in Europe because of their bold personalities, maintenance ease, and low cost. They should not be mixed with small softbills. The diet is the simple fare accorded to all mynahs. Photo by Horst Mueller.

Brazilian Crested Cardinals are too large to be included with most small finches; but they do well with large, strong finches and a great variety of small and medium softbills. In a spacious planted aviary they sing quite freely and melodiously, but in average aviaries they are seldom inclined to sing.

Button Quails are excellent additions to an aviary and are delightful birds. The female, center, is less colorful than the male.

There are several species and subspecies of African Orange Weavers. The male on the left
is the standard avicultural subject which bird fanciers call Orange Weavers and which ornithologists more frequently call Red Bishops (*Euplectes orix* or sometimes *Pyromelana orix*).
Perhaps one of the most attractive of the Red Bishops is the Crimson Crowned Weaver
(*Euplectes hordacea*) in the upper right side of this picture. This species and its subspecies
are widely distributed in Africa but are not frequently available to bird fanciers. Females
of all three species are very drably colored. Males when not in color as shown here resemble
females during the non-breeding season.

The Black Crowned Waxbill from Central Africa is a very handsome species, but its two most attractive features do not appear in this photograph. The rump and uppertail coverts are brilliant red. The scapulars and shoulders are finely barred with alternating paler and darker shades of gray and dusky black.

The Southern White Breasted Rail (*Laterallus leucopyrrhus*) occurs in Brazilian and more southerly areas in South America. It is a charming, attractive, and very peaceful addition to aviaries containing finches or small softbills. Omnivorous in diet, small rails such as this species require insectile mixtures as well as mealworms. The writers also feed some raw meat. Rails, often called Crakes, belong to a large family of birds which vary greatly in size, characteristics, and food requirements. Related genera and species are native to most areas of the world.

The Dusky Twinspot *(Euschistospiza cinereovinacea)* from Angola is very rare in aviculture and is not as attractive as most Twinspots. Upper parts not shown in this picture are slate-black. Sexes are very much alike. Twinspots are difficult when first imported because they will usually not accept a well rounded diet which includes insectile or softbilled foods as well as live foods and seeds. This species is closely related to Dybowski's Twinspot.

The Black Backed or Golden Bellied Grosbeak (Pheucticus aureoventris) ranges from Colombia to Argentina. Most Grosbeaks which are available to aviculturists are not very popular. Though pleasant in many ways and easily maintained, few are as attractive as the majority of birds which bird fanciers favor even though some are very pleasant songsters.

690

694

695

696

698

701

703

714

717

719

720

728

729